Entrepreneurship and Religion

This volume is dedicated to Naomï Josephine Dana

Entrepreneurship and Religion

Edited by

Léo-Paul Dana

Adjunct Professor, GSCM – Montpellier Business School, France, on study leave from the University of Canterbury, New Zealand and Founding Editor, Journal of International Entrepreneurship *and* Journal of Enterprising Communities

Edward Elgar

Cheltenham, UK • Northampton, MA, USA

Published by
Edward Elgar Publishing Limited
The Lypiatts
15 Lansdown Road
Cheltenham
Glos GL50 2JA
UK

Edward Elgar Publishing, Inc.
William Pratt House
9 Dewey Court
Northampton
Massachusetts 01060
USA

A catalogue record for this book
is available from the British Library

Library of Congress Control Number: 2009937897

Mixed Sources
Product group from well-managed
forests and other controlled sources
www.fsc.org Cert no. SA-COC-1565
© 1996 Forest Stewardship Council
FSC

ISBN 978 1 84720 572 8

Printed and bound by MPG Books Group, UK

Contents

Contributors

Khaled Abu Asbeh, Beit Berl College, Israel

Alistair R. Anderson, Aberdeen Business School, United Kingdom

Robert Brent Anderson, University of Regina, Canada

Godfrey Baldacchino, University of Prince Edward Island, Canada

Jacqueline Benitez-Galbraith, University of North Carolina Wilmington, USA

Shiv Chaudhry, Birmingham City University, United Kingdom

Dave Crick, Birmingham City University, United Kingdom

Léo-Paul Dana, GSCM Graduate School of Management, Montpellier, France and University of Canterbury, New Zealand

Teresa E. Dana, University of Canterbury, New Zealand

Alain Fayolle, EM Lyon Business School, France

Craig S. Galbraith, University of North Carolina Wilmington, USA

Wafica Ali Ghoul, Lebanese International University, Beirut, Lebanon

Sibylle Heilbrunn, Academic Center Ruppin, Israel

Ivan Light, University of California, Los Angeles, USA

Robert L. Malach, University of Calgary, Canada

Sandra Malach, University of Calgary, Canada

Hadj Nekka, Université d'Anger, France

Edwina Pio, AUT University, New Zealand and Boston College, USA

Neil Robinson, University of Salford, United Kingdom

Carel Roessingh, VU University Amsterdam, The Netherlands

Karen Smits, VU University Amsterdam, The Netherlands

Curt H. Stiles, University of North Carolina Wilmington, USA

Dimitri Tassiopoulos, Walter Sisulu University, Buffalo City, South Africa

Claudio Vignali, Leeds Metropolitan University, United Kingdom

Gianpaolo Vignali, Leeds Metropolitan University, United Kingdom

Morton Weinfeld, McGill University, Canada

Anne White, University of Calgary, Canada

Foreword

This book is a very timely contribution to extending our understanding of entrepreneurship in its social context. For too long the entrepreneur has been characterized as a lonely, isolated economically driven individual, thus ignoring how enterprise and entrepreneurs are products of their society, their culture and, as we learn from this book, their religions. This volume shows how the values developed in religious beliefs and practices shape entrepreneurship. It thus adds considerably to the newer enlightening strand of entrepreneurial literature about the social context, the social process and the social configurations of entrepreneurship. It adds richness, detail and examples that show how the values, beliefs and behaviours that are religiously formed are an integral part of the phenomena of being enterprising. The book contributes to understanding both entrepreneurship and religion, but its greatest contribution is in demonstrating how the synthesis of beliefs and practices combine in entrepreneurial endeavours. In this way, the book provides us with a new and conceptually useful way of framing the individualistic entrepreneur in his and her social and cultural context; enabling us to see how entrepreneurial agency operates within and through a variety of religious contexts.

It seems clear that the intellectual driving force behind this remarkable book has been the recognition that we cannot explain entrepreneurship simply by resorting to individual-level accounts or theories. Although the weakness in these theories has been noted for two decades, it is only recently that we have begun to see informed and convincing counter-arguments such as this volume. As Dana explains, the extraordinary differences in entrepreneurial propensity between some social groups, even those working in similar circumstances, demands an explanation at the same sort of level; that of society or culture. Because religion operates socially and culturally by the development of values that inform attitudes and behaviour, this book provides such explanatory accounts. This is the entrepreneurial application of Durkheim's decisive point that there exists a level beyond and outside the individual, one independent of, and prior to, the individual. This level, *sui generis*, is a 'social fact' and one that shapes what people do and how they think about what they do. The pioneering sociologists recognized the critical importance and explanatory power of these social facts. Indeed, Weber's classic, *The Protestant Work*

Ethic, explained how one religion, Calvinism, shaped both the processes and outcomes of entrepreneurship. This book echoes Weber's ambitions of the explanatory power of elective affinity, in that it charts the role of religions in shaping the practices and processes of entrepreneurship in many contexts.

Dana has brought together a diverse range of scholars to produce a remarkable epistle of entrepreneurial scholarship. One cannot but be impressed by the diversity and range of the material which shares this common focus on the relationships between religion and enterprise and the combining of the sacred and secular. We see explanatory examples of how religion creates market niches; we see how entrepreneurial attitudes are formed or discouraged; we see how values are formed, propagated and reproduced. Importantly, we see how entrepreneurial practices are created in a religious milieu. The authors work from the knowledge of economics, sociology and anthropology to produce insight into how patterns of enterprise are formed and reworked by religious influences. A key focus is values, how these are moulded and how they shape enterprise. The descriptions and explanatory accounts of religious values enable us to recognize how entrepreneurial legitimacy is created and, moreover, how families, networks and society in general, produce and reproduce enterprise. We can, after reading these works, begin to comprehend the immense impact of religion on entrepreneurial activities. We begin to discern the fabric of entrepreneurship through the wefting and weaving of these religious threads.

The material included in these essays is rich; rich in descriptive content; rich in historical context and rich in international contrasts. But each one of the essays brings particular insights into the group studied. For example, Ivan Light's careful consideration of the Protestant work ethic (PWE) is rich in intellectual rigor. He explores far beyond the original thesis and shows how it can be applied to contemporary ideas and current practices. His analysis is profound and theoretically informed to show both the strengths and weaknesses of debates surrounding the PWE. In rich contrast, Wafica Ali Ghoul's review of Islam and entrepreneurship is rich in the detail that explains how Islam impacts on entrepreneurship. By explaining the workings of Islamic scholarship, she is able to show how Islamic doctrine works to support enterprise, albeit in unique formations. In this way we begin to understand the shape of Islamic entrepreneurship. This depth of engagement with the topics is typical of all the essays, each brings informed insights into the role of religion for enterprise.

This book is not just for religious or entrepreneurial scholars, all those intrigued in the power of values and how they shape our society will find much to interest them here. An additional benefit from reading this book is that scholars are likely to be inspired to look at new avenues of entrepreneurial research. I wish this book had been around when I tried to teach about entrepreneurship in its social context; life would have been much easier with these informed sources.

Alistair R. Anderson
Federation of Small Business Professor,
Aberdeen Business School, UK

Introduction: religion as an explanatory variable for entrepreneurship*

Léo-Paul Dana[1]

People with unlike cultural beliefs and religious values have looked at entrepreneurship with varying degrees of legitimacy. The Greek philosopher Aristotle (384–322 BC), a student of Plato and teacher of Alexander the Great, viewed entrepreneurship as unnatural and therefore illegitimate (Aristotle, 1924). Becker (1956) explained that some cultures consider business an unholy occupation. Woodrum (1985) found participation in religious activities to be a predictor of entrepreneurial success among Americans of Japanese origin. Dana (1995a), and Lumpkin and Dess (1996), advocated that a small firm's orientation is grounded in the values of its entrepreneur.

Values and culture shape the environment for entrepreneurship as well as the entrepreneurial event. Aldrich (1979) noted that the environment could provide or withhold resources. From an anthropological perspective, Stewart (1991) suggested that the legitimization of enterprise was a function of culture. From a sociological perspective, Reynolds (1991) confirmed the importance of non-economic factors, such as the legitimacy of entrepreneurship, on entrepreneurial activity. Specht (1993) emphasized the importance of cultural acceptance. Cultural acceptance of entrepreneurship varies among people with different cultural values. Likewise, people from different religious backgrounds have unlike propensities to become entrepreneurs.

Farmer and Richman wrote,

> There is a close correlation of countries in terms of how deeply the Calvinist spirit has penetrated their economic and social behavior with real per capita income and level of economic development. Thus, in 1958, all fifteen countries of the world with per capita incomes of over $700 per year were those which had followed the Calvinist ethic extensively; and, with the possible exceptions of France and Belgium, all were quite extensively Protestant in religion. No country where the Calvinist ethic had deeply penetrated was not included in this list of most wealthy countries, while none of the extensively non-Calvinist nations had yet achieved such economic success. (1965, p. 157)

More recently, Enz et al. (1990) identified different value orientations among various communities and concluded that value orientation may be an important component in entrepreneurs. Some cultures simply value entrepreneurial activity more than do others and empirical evidence suggests that some religions are less conducive to entrepreneurship than are others.

The Government of Canada found that per 1000 Filipino workers in Canada, 18 were self-employed; the same reported that per 1000 Greek workers in Canada, 124 were self-employed (Dana, 1991). How can such differences be explained? Could it be that the Greek Orthodox religion inculcated certain values among members of one group? Indeed, the worldview of Greek Orthodoxy fosters a work ethic and leadership style that may facilitate successful entrepreneurship.

Galbraith et al. (1997) examined differences and similarities in attitudes and cultural norms between two groups in the United States: Catholic Hispanic entrepreneurs and non-Hispanic entrepreneurs; this study hypothesized that the first group consisted of hybrid persona, combining aspects of the traditional notion of the entrepreneur while retaining important cultural characteristics of the Hispanic community. The authors found that successful Hispanic entrepreneurs were also leaders in their Hispanic community; business leaders were often leaders in the religious realm.

Studies that investigate entrepreneurship as if it were an isolated phenomenon – derived from the self and based on psychological traits of the entrepreneur – risk ignoring important causal variables arising from the environment, including the religious milieu. As suggested by Drakopoulou-Dodd and Anderson (2007) the dynamics of embeddedness and social conditioning should be attributed equal weight to the entrepreneur's individual agency.

Religions are depositories of wisdom and of values; furthermore, religious beliefs are intertwined with cultural values. Are prevailing religious beliefs explanatory variables for a propensity for, or indifference about, entrepreneurship? Empirical findings suggest a causal relationship.

Drakopoulou-Dodd and Gotsis (2007) provided a literature review addressing implications of religious convictions in business settings. Religious beliefs – and cultural values deriving therefrom – influence the social desirability of entrepreneurship and its nature as well. Drakopoulou-Dodd and Gotsis (2007) categorised individual outcomes of religious belief.

A religion does not necessarily directly promote or prohibit entrepreneurship. Rather, religions teach, promote and propagate cultural value systems within a given society. Value orientations in turn affect propensity toward entrepreneurial activity. For instance, Methodism accepts disparity between the rich and poor. The wealthy may be charitable, and it can be argued that acquisition of wealth is good in that it allows one to be philanthropic. Asa Chandler, the pharmacist who incorporated *The Coca-Cola Company*, was a devout Methodist and Sunday school teacher who believed that making money was a form of worship. During the following century, Prime Minister Margaret Thatcher (raised with strict Methodist values[2]) stated 'I believe in "Judaeo-Christian" values: indeed my whole political philosophy is based on them' (Thatcher, 1993. p. 509). She emphasized that her political party originated as a Christian party, concerned with the Church and the State in that order, and she stated that religion was the source of a nation's values.

Candland (2000) viewed faith as social capital and Brammer et al. (2007) found that religious individuals tend to hold broader conceptions concerning the social responsibility of businesses than non-religious individuals. Anderson et al. (2000) suggested that a reduction in church attendances cannot be taken as a direct consequence of a reduction in religiosity.

Regardless of whether a person is religious, it can be argued that one is influenced by cultural values propagated by religions. As suggested by Anderson et al. (2000), it seems reasonable to assume that religion has an impact upon the legitimization of enterprise, despite secularization.

In this article, the author combines three decades of personal studies and a review of the literature to discuss ways in which religion shapes entrepreneurship. Blending a sociological understanding of values, with an anthropological interpretation of culture, it will be suggested that religion is a vehicle to perpetuate both values and culture, thus shaping various forms of entrepreneurship. It will be shown that: (i) various religions value entrepreneurship to different degrees; (ii) different religions yield unlike patterns of entrepreneurship, possibly due to value differences (such as asceticism, frugality and thrift) but also due to specialization (sometimes resulting in a monopoly) and networks; (iii) specialization along religious lines shapes entrepreneurship; (iv) credit networks, employment networks, information networks, and supply networks of co-religionists affect entrepreneurship; (v) religions provide opportunities for entrepreneurship; (vi) religious beliefs may hamper entrepreneurial spirit; and (vii) religions have built-in mechanisms for the perpetuation of values.

VALUES AND CULTURE

Feuerbach (1855) argued that religion included values produced by people in the course of their cultural development. Durkheim (1912) and Thomas and Znaniecki (1918) were among the pioneers who studied the concept of values. David Emile Durkheim, son of Rabbi Moise and Melanie Durkheim of Epinal, is well known for his work *The Elementary Forms of Religious Life* (Durkheim, 1912). In this, he identified a pattern of organization consistent within all human societies; for this pattern, he used the term *Structural Functionalism.* In essence, his theory described society as being built upon order that incorporates interrelationship and balance among various parts of its constitution; he argued that construction and identity of any given society is based on shared norms and values as the basis of existence.

One of two major macro-sociological perspectives, functionalism conceives society as a system of interrelated parts in which no part can be understood in isolation from the whole. A change in any part is seen as leading to a degree of imbalance that changes other parts of the system and at times the system as a whole. Functionalism places a great emphasis on values in terms of the functions they perform in a socio-cultural system. As such, it contrasts directly with the other major macro-sociological perspective, conflict theory.

Sociology as well as anthropology provided early definitions. From a sociological perspective, Thomas and Znaniecki interpreted a value as having an acquired social meaning and, consequently, 'is or may be an object of activity' (1918, p. 21). Clyde Kluckhohn provided an anthropological definition of culture as the total life way of a society; he emphasized each culture is formed by values that the people from that culture consider as being normal. He defined a value as, 'A conception, explicit or implicit, distinctive of an individual or characteristic of a group, of the desirable which influences the selection from available modes, means and ends of action' (1951, p. 395). Kluckhohn's theoretical development was published in two famous books, *Mirror for Man* (Kluckhohn, 1949) and *Culture: A Critical Review of Concepts and Definitions* (Kroeber and Kluckhohn, 1952).

Trying to put Clyde's theory into practice, Clyde's wife, Florence, studied Indigenous Americans and co-authored with Fred L. Strodtbeck (Kluckhohn and Strodtbeck, 1961). These authors defined value orientations as

> complex but definitely patterned (rank-ordered) principles, resulting from the transactional interplay of three analytically distinguishable elements of the evaluative process – the cognitive, the affective, and the directive elements

> – which give order and direction to the ever-flowing stream of human acts and thoughts as these relate to the solution of 'common human' problems. (Kluckhohn and Strodtbeck, 1961, p. 4)

They suggested that cultures can be classified according to five value orientations: time; humanity and the natural environment; relating to other people; motive for behaving; and the nature of human nature. During the same decade, Farmer and Richman suggested that religious beliefs 'usually have a direct and very significant bearing on the dominant view toward work and achievement' (1965. p. 157).

Shortly thereafter, Rokeach (1968) defined a value as 'a type of belief, centrally located within one's total belief system, about how one ought or ought not to behave, or about some end-state of existence worth or not worth attaining' (1968, p. 124). Rokeach (1968) considered two sets of values: terminal values and instrumental values. Terminal values are cultural goals to be attained and developed, while instrumental values are the means of achieving the desired goals. Rokeach (1973) provided a new rendition of values and value systems:

> A *value* is an enduring belief that a specific mode of conduct or end-state of existence is personally or socially preferable to an opposite or converse mode of conduct or end-state of existence. A *value system* is an enduring organization of beliefs concerning preferable modes of conduct or end-states of existence along a continuum of relative importance. (1973, p. 5; original emphasis)

Hiebert defined culture as 'the integrated system of learned behaviour patterns, ideas and products characteristic of a society (1976, p. 25)'. Hofstede defined a value as: 'a broad tendency to prefer certain states of affairs over others' (2001, p. 5). Relying heavily on culture and values as key constructs, he stated, 'Values are held by individuals as well as by collectivities; culture presupposes a collectivity' (Hofstede, 2001, p. 5). Schwartz (1992) focused on a variety of values including: achievement; benevolence; conformity; hedonism; power; security; self-direction; and tradition. Some of these values may be influential in determining the social desirability of entrepreneurship and the nature of entrepreneurial activity.

FINDINGS

1. Various Religions Value Entrepreneurship to Different Degrees

Over the years, numerous empirical studies have reported on the influence of religion on the economy or, more specifically, that some religions are more represented than others in entrepreneurship and/or the small business sector. Classical social theorist Max Weber compared taxation figures in Baden, and reported an average of 589 marks per Catholic, 954 marks per Protestant, and 4000 marks per Jew (Weber, 1904); he argued that while Protestantism stressed the development of economic security, Catholics believed that it was easier for a camel to fit through the eye of a needle than for a wealthy man to go to heaven.[3] Weber also studied how religion affected the emergence of entrepreneurship in India; he explained that the Jains, an ascetic religious sect, became a trading sect for purely ritualistic reasons, as only in trading could one practice *ahimsa*, the absolute prohibition of the killing of live things. In contrast, Theravadism, as practised in Laos, discourages entrepreneurial behaviour and noted that the result is a relative absence of Lao men in entrepreneurial activity (Dana, 1995b).

Shapero wrote, 'Some cultures that value entrepreneurship are the . . . Jains . . . Jews . . . Mennonites and Mormons . . .' (1984, p. 26). Writing about Estonia after its independence from the Russian Empire, Liuhto noted, 'Another interesting detail from the statistics is the considerable share of the companies classified as Jewish' (Liuhto, 1996, pp. 319). Analysing the Middle East, after the Second World War, Sayigh (1952) found Christians and Jews to be the prominent entrepreneurs of Lebanon. Gadgil (1959) noted that Muslims, Christians, and Jews were the chief traders of Kerala, in South India. Lasry (1982) noted the percentage of entrepreneurs among Sephardic Jewish immigrants in Montreal as being significantly higher (38 per cent) than among immigrants to Canada, in general. Jenkins (1984) showed that Protestants in Northern Ireland manipulated ethnicity in the realm of economic transactions, and thus dominated the economy in Northern Ireland. In Germany, Klandt found that a Protestant upbringing 'is more likely to lead to independent business activity than a Catholic upbringing' (1987, p. 31). In Britain, Quakers have been (Corley, 1998) and continue to be (Ackrill and Hannah, 2001) overrepresented in the realm of enterprise. In the United States, Kraybill and Bowman (2001) and Kraybill and Nolt (1995) identified a causal relationship between religion and self-employment among the Amish.

In a study of attitudes, Guiso et al. noted that 'with the exception of Buddhists, religious people of all denominations are more inclined to believe that poor people are lazy and lack will power' (2003, p. 228). Zingales suggested, 'Buddhism and Christianity seem most conducive to capitalism, and Islam the least' (2006, p. 228). He elaborated,

> Comparing the average response of different religious denominations we find that, other things being equal, Buddhism seems to promote the best attitudes

> towards the market system. Christian religions follow . . . Islam appears as the religion least conducive to capitalism. Muslims are very much against competition, against private property and less willing to trade off equality for incentives. (Zingales, 2006, p. 228–9)

In contrast, Badawi suggested,

> Islam preaches a holistic and comprehensive notion of development in this world and for the hereafter. It does not negate the pursuit of material development in this world . . . The teachings of Islam are also eminently suited to development in the modern, knowledge-based economy . . . Besides its emphasis on knowledge, Islam also enjoins a work ethic that equips the individual to excel in economic pursuits. (Badawi, 2006, p. 208)

Arslan (2008) tested whether Muslims exhibited some values that corresponded to those encouraged by the Protestant work ethic; using multivariate and univariate analysis of variance, the study found high Protestant work ethic scores among Turkish Sufis.

In a study of Mennonite entrepreneurs in Paraguay, it was found that the Mennonite religion

> values asceticism, frugality and thrift, but not private property. Entrepreneurship takes a collective form and cooperatives are important economic vehicles, providing jobs for indigenous workers and markets for the produce of self-employed farmers. While Mennonite cooperatives thrive here, Indian cooperatives modelled after them have not had the same levels of success. (Dana and Dana, 2007, p. 82)

In the words of Lewis, 'If a religion lays stress upon material values, upon thrift and productive investment, upon honesty in commercial relations, upon experimentation and risk-bearing . . . it will be helpful to growth, whereas in so far as it is hostile to these things, it tends to inhibit growth' (1955, p. 105)

2. Different Religions Yield Unlike Patterns of Entrepreneurship

A contemporary of Weber, Sombart (1911) observed that the economic centre of Europe shifted with the migration of Jews; he linked economic development in Europe to Jewish entrepreneurs.[4] Across the Atlantic, William Howard Taft, former president of the United States, suggested that Jews 'developed trade, poetry, philosophy, science and literature' (Taft, 1919, p. 7). Taft also gave examples of how Europeans prospered by means of Jews, who 'were forbidden to hold land. The nobility manufactured the liquor, and they were willing and anxious to have the Jews sell it, who thus, for lack of other occupation, became the innkeepers, the purveyors in the demoralizing liquor business' (Taft, 1919, p. 10)

In a landmark study comparing different religious groups in New York City, Glazer and Moynihan noted,

> Jews already constitute a majority of those engaged in many businesses . . . In the great banks, insurance companies, public utilities, railroads, and corporate head offices that are located in New York, and in the Wall Street law firms, few Jews are to be found . . . Obviously, in addition to discrimination, one must also reckon with taste and tradition among Jews, which may have had their origin in discrimination, but which may now lead a good number of Jews voluntarily to avoid huge bureaucratic organizations in favour of greater freedom in small companies, as independent entrepreneurs . . . (1963, pp. 147–8)

Iyer noted,

> The case of Indian business communities is slightly different from the generalized pattern observed for the rest of Asia, especially in that such business communities have traditionally evolved within specific religions and castes. Moreover, the religion of the Indian merchant community, in contrast to the general strictures on wealth and profits as in other religions (including Asian religions, such as Confucianism), treats money as neutral and does not condemn wealth generation itself. This has important implications in the ways the Indian merchant community assimilates the contradictory objectives of wealth creation and frugality with religious piety that serves to enhance market reputation. (1999, p. 103)

Circumstance led Jews to become merchants in Alsace:

> Their religion prevented them from working on Saturday, and the Church forbade them labouring in their fields on Sundays. The Church also banned them from giving employment to Christians. In addition, experience taught the Jews that, in times of religious persecutions, it was more convenient to have moveable assets, such as gold, cattle and later diamonds, than to own immovables . . . By the fourteenth century, Jews no longer had a choice; under the Saxon civil code, *Meißener Rechtsbuch*, Jews were banned from owning land. Yet, in Alsace, this did not lead to urbanisation, because Jews were not allowed to live in the cities. Alsace remained part of the Holy German Empire until being acquired in 1648, by the Kingdom of France. At the time, the French army was facing a shortage of horses, and a lack of animal feed for the horses it had. The Jews of Alsace, with their experience in commerce, efficiently supplied the French with horses and with animal feed. The French offered protection to these people who supplied their army and this led to a mass immigration of Jews from central Europe, to Alsace. (Dana, 2006, p. 589)

Controlling for climate, geographic position and other factors, Baldacchino and Dana (2006) compared entrepreneurship in French St Martin with that in Dutch Sint Maarten, the latter more influenced by a Protestant work ethic. While two cultures share a little island, colonial influences have been different, and the entrepreneurship sector reflects this. While Dutch St Martin is home to prosperous traders, French St Martin is home to self-employed farmers.

3. Specialization along Religious Lines Shapes Entrepreneurship

In some cases, certain religious groups specialized in specific economic sectors. For two centuries, Quaker entrepreneurs including John Cadbury, Joseph Fry and the Rowntree family, dominated the chocolate industry across England. Cadbury flourished in Birmingham, Fry blossomed in Bristol, and the Rowntrees prospered in York. John Cadbury expanded his business when he invited his brother Benjamin to join him, in 1847; employees were well cared for, in accordance with religious values.

During the mid-nineteenth century, Seventh-day Adventists in the United States – preaching vegetarian values – established the Western Health Reform Institute, later renamed the Battle Creek Sanitarium, in Battle Creek, Michigan. Aligned with the beliefs of Sylvester Graham (the minister who invented the Graham cracker[5]) patients were required to adhere to strict diets. The superintendent was a fervent Seventh-day Adventist, Dr John Harvey Kellogg, who with his brother William Keith Kellogg invented the modern breakfast cereal, in line with their religious beliefs. Kellogg's thus began with 44 employees in Battle Creek, Michigan. A patient, Charles William Post, founded a competing manufacturer and launched the first nation-wide advertising campaign in the United States. In Australia and New Zealand, the Seventh-day Adventist Church also had connections to the cereal sector; important players included Grain Products and Sanitarium.

In Canada, meanwhile, Methodist entrepreneurs established large department stores. In 1869, Timothy Eaton opened a store introducing fixed prices and cash sales (as opposed to negotiated prices and credit sales) soon expanding into the Eaton's chain; he introduced the mail order catalogue to Canadians in 1884. Robert Simpson opened his first department store in 1872, and this also developed into a national chain of department stores. Norcliffe (2001) noted that Toronto's principal bicycle manufacturers, during the late nineteenth century, were owned by Methodists, including the Flavelle, Harris and Massey families.

Fishberg (1911) observed that Jews were concentrated in precarious occupations such as commerce; he suggested that Jews were 'ambitious and persevering, possessing an enormous amount of "push", which he cannot always bring into play while struggling against adverse circumstances' (1911, p. 531). Raphaël (1980) noted the clustering of Jews in the livestock trade in Alsace. Dana wrote,

> Still forbidden to own land, deprived of entry into universities, excluded from the guilds and not allowed to reside in cities, these people tended to be travelling merchants, linking the urban and rural economies. In September 1791, Jews were permitted to reside in the cities of Alsace, and this helped them expand their commercial networks . . . The fathers and elder brothers would carry their loads on backs. This included utensils, candles and soap, as well as animal hides, laces, string and used clothing. Wealthier merchants used man-powered pushcarts. The exceptions were those known as *Esselje'de* (donkey-Jews), as they would travel from one village to another with a donkey drawn cart; they traded kitchenware and other household items, accepting rags and beehives as payment. Livestock merchants constituted a class of their own. Some had a horse-drawn wagon on which two calves could be transported. At the end of the nineteenth century, Jews had a monopoly in cattle dealing in areas of Baden, Bavaria, Hanover, Rhineland and Westphalia. Until the First World War, most independent cattle dealers in Germany (including Alsace) were Jewish. (2006, p. 590)

Based on oral testimonies of retired entrepreneurs and verified by means of triangulation, Dana (2006) provided an account of the livestock distribution system, which prevailed in Alsace, until the Second World War. In this region of traditional rivalry between French and Germans, the sector was dominated by Jewish entrepreneurs speaking *Jédich-Daitch*, serving as a middleman minority, and dealing between French speakers and German speakers, who did not trade with one another.

In their study of New York City, Glazer and Moynihan found more evidence of clustering:

> Merchandising, garment manufacturing, and entertainment maintain their importance, but to them has been added a sizable range of light manufacturing, and real estate and building. In the latter, especially, Jews play a prominent role . . . In the great office-building boom that has transformed Manhattan, most of the big builders have been Jews: Uris Brothers, Tishman, Erwin Wolfson, Rudin, Webb and Knapp (Zeckendorf) . . . The finest of the postwar office buildings, Seagram's, which is perhaps the most lavish and expensive in use of space and detail, was erected by a company headed by a Canadian Jewish communal leader, Samuel Bronfman . . . (Glazer and Moynihan, 1963, p. 151)

Hawley wrote, 'Amish entrepreneurs tend to cluster heavily in certain small business ventures. This phenomenon can best be described by order of the *Ordnung*, which requires that the Amish establish only those stores and small businesses that meet the product and service needs of the Amish community' (1995, p. 320). Dana explained,

> In order to maintain their values, the Amish try to avoid close contact with people who do not hold the same traditions. Furthermore, due to religious discrimination in the past, the Amish often exhibit a mistrust of outsiders. The

> primary motive of self-employment among the Amish is neither profit nor prestige, but rather the maintenance of cultural values, separately from mainstream society such as to emphasize humility over pride. (2007b, p. 142)

Such segregation, from mainstream society, helps the Amish retain social capital, and this supports Borjas (1992), who analysed ethnic capital and the value of isolation.

An ethnographic study of Morocco noted that some goods

> were sold only by Jews while others were sold only by Muslims. Silversmiths were invariably Muslim, while goldsmiths were Jewish. Jews were also very active in the spice trade, and they specialised in the socio-economic function of distribution . . . Many Jews were peddlers, or suppliers to other vendors, inland. They served as Barthian middlemen. (Dana and Dana, 2008, p. 215)

4. Credit Networks, Employment Networks, Information Networks and Supply Networks of Co-religionists Affect Entrepreneurship

4.1 Credit networks

Credit is at times linked to marriage within the Jain community. Dundas (1992) discussed carefully regulated marriage alliances among Jains, and Laidlaw further explained that when a Jain 'family contracts a good marriage, its credit increases' (1995, p. 355). Iyer and Shapiro (1999) refer to credit networks among Korean and Chinese in the United States.

Juteau and Paré (1996) refer to credit networks of Jewish entrepreneurs in Canada. Likewise, Dana (2006) noted that Jewish cattle dealers relied heavily on other Jews for financing. Co-religionists provided finance when needed. 'A network of livestock merchants, across the region, facilitated the dissemination of knowledge and availability of finance among co-religionists. In the event of bankruptcy, an individual was given assistance by other merchants' (Dana, 2006, p. 594).

Discussing Jewish and Muslim entrepreneurs in Morocco, Dana and Dana noted that 'Merchandise was often purchased on credit, thereby requiring a relationship of trust between supplier and peddler' (2008, p. 215). Again, there was often dependence on co-religionists for finance.

In a study of Catholic Hispanics, Galbraith et al. (2004) suggested that a co-ethnic capital market appears to be the last dimension developed within an ethnic community.

4.2 Employment networks

Porter (1937) noted that entrepreneurs were giving preference to members of their immediate circle rather than giving equal opportunity to outsiders. Raistrick (1950) found Quakers to be clannish and nepotistic.

Kraybill and Nolt (1995) observed that Amish entrepreneurs gave preference in business to co-religionists. Dana's ethnographic study explained the reason behind this: 'While the Amish people believe that a community of voluntary believers is the context for life, the fundamental unit of Amish society and of their economy is the family . . . home-based enterprises allow family members to work together, reinforcing the Amish family unit' (2007b, p. 146).

Galbraith et al. (1997) found that successful Hispanic entrepreneurs, often holding important leadership roles in the local Catholic church, were actively finding employment for other recent immigrants.

Galbraith et al. (2003) and Stiles et al. (2007) suggested that Catholic Hispanic and Muslim Arab entrepreneurs are both dependent on co-ethnic business in their respective enclave, relying upon co-religionists for labour, especially at the start-up phase.

In Malaysia, Abdullah (1992) found that Muslim Malays expressed strong preference for employing Muslim candidates over non-Muslims. In a study of Turkish entrepreneurs, Altinay (2008) likewise found a strong relationship between the religion of an entrepreneur and recruitment.

4.3 Information networks

Apart from co-religionist networks that provide credit or preferential treatment for employees, information networks also appear in the literature and these are sometimes comprised of co-religionists. Boissevain and Grotenbreg observed, 'Hindustanis appear to have a larger network of relatives than do Chinese and Creole businessmen. Given the value they attach to family loyalty, this seems to indicate that Hindustanis have access to a wider information and support network' (1987, p. 117).

A co-religionist information network existed in Alsace: 'They managed the link between the rural and urban economies, providing cash for farmers and a source of meat for consumers. In addition, they spread information as required. If one farmer needed a bull, temporarily, for breeding purposes, a livestock merchant could source this need' (Dana, 2006, p. 590).

There were also individuals who specialised in information:

> Some Jews did not themselves deal with livestock, but served as brokers, or informers who simply sold information which would lead to transactions. These entrepreneurs were called *Schmüsser*, and their commission was referred to as *Sassergeld.* Operating informally, these individuals mingled with the villagers, identified needs and opportunities and then waited by the side of a road, knowing that livestock merchants would be passing by eventually. The *Schmüsser* then sold their information to livestock merchants. (The word they used for this activity was *vermassere*, literally meaning 'to inform.') In order

> to reduce time spent away from their own villages, the transient merchants preferred to pay for this market research, rather than to conduct this time-consuming task themselves. The *Schmüsser* thus formed an integral part of the business network. (Dana, 2006, pp. 592–593)

Likewise in his study of 1200 Muslim entrepreneurs in London, Altinay (2008) found a strong relationship between religion and advice-seeking practices. One interviewee stated, 'If people from the same religion and the background do not help and support each other, who else would do so' (Altinay, 2008, p. 120). Altinay (2008) found that Muslims who practise[6] their religion rely more on advice from co-ethnics.

4.4 Supply networks

Juteau and Paré (1996) and Lee (1999) found co-ethnic suppliers were prevalent among Jewish entrepreneurs in Canada and in the United States, respectively. Lee (1999) noted that this provided access to lower wholesale costs, which could translate to lower retail costs and enhanced competitiveness.

Galbraith (2007) examined buyers and sellers among two groups: Catholic Hispanics and Muslim Arabs, within a US metropolitan area; he suggested that the perceived advantage of intra-enclave buying and selling lies in a sense of ethnic identification that comes primarily from a religion, either Catholic or Muslim, common to each enclave.

5. Religions Provide Opportunities for Entrepreneurship

Religious values may create needs, and these can sometimes be translated into opportunities for entrepreneurship. When Toronto observed a day of rest and streetcars were prohibited on Sundays while bicycles were permitted, bicycle manufacturers – mostly Methodists – made unprecedented sales (Armstrong and Nelles, 1977). In this case, the observation of religion helped entrepreneurs in the bicycle sector.

The production of religious products also provides opportunities for entrepreneurship. Orthodox icons, for instance, bring profits to dealers as well as to those who make the icons. Likewise, religious dietary requirements can yield profits to entrepreneurs catering to specific needs. Buddhism, Hinduism, Islam, Jainism, and Judaism are among religions that have dietary restrictions, providing opportunities for entrepreneurs and even for airlines catering to such religious needs of observers; this is what Aldrich and Weidenmayer (1993) have referred to as 'demand side' entrepreneurship.

In Islam, some food is *halal* (meaning 'permissible' in Arabic), while some is prohibited. All fish with scales (that the Bible approves of as kosher) are *halal*. The Qur'an specifically disallows the consumption of: all blood; the carcass of an animal that died on its own or that was killed by another animal; donkey meat; fanged predators; and pork. Furthermore, the Hanafi School of Islam does not approve of the eating of shellfish, including clams, crabs, lobster and shrimp; observers also refrain from eating frogs. According to Minkus-McKenna (2007), 70 per cent of Muslims worldwide follow *halal* food standards, translating into an opportunity worth an annual US$580 billion. Many McDonald's outlets are serving *halal* food, in Australia, India, Indonesia, Malaysia, Pakistan, Singapore, South Africa and the United Kingdom. Others to serve *halal* food, at selected locations, include A&W, Burger King, Dunkin' Donuts, KFC and Pizza Hut.

The Judaeo-Christian Bible has even more sophisticated guidelines with regards to what may be eaten, and these are outlined in Genesis, and Leviticus and Deuteronomy. The King James Bible states, 'Ye shall therefore put difference between clean beasts and unclean, and between unclean fowls and clean: and ye shall not make your souls abominable by beast, or by fowl, or by any manner of living thing that creepeth on the ground, which I have separated from you as unclean' (Leviticus 20:25). Leviticus 3:17 prohibits observers from eating blood or fat. Leviticus 22:8 elaborates, 'That which dieth of itself, or is torn with beasts, he shall not eat to defile himself therewith: I am the LORD (King James Bible)'. This is understood to mean that it is not kosher to eat food from animals that die themselves or that are killed by another animal. Leviticus also provides details as to what species the Bible allows observers to eat or not. It is not permitted to eat camel, 'he is unclean onto you' (Leviticus 11:4). The hare (Leviticus 11:6); pork (Leviticus 11:7); eagles (Leviticus 11:13); vultures (Leviticus 11:14); ravens (Leviticus 11:15); owls (Leviticus 11:16); cormorants (Leviticus 11:17); swans, pelican and eagles (Leviticus 11:18) are specified as not allowed. The same is true of the stork, the heron and the bat (Leviticus 11:19). Leviticus 11:29 states, 'These also shall be unclean unto you among the creeping things that creep upon the earth; the weasel, and the mouse, and the tortoise after his kind'. Leviticus 11:30 adds, 'And the ferret, and the chameleon, and the lizard, and the snail, and the mole'. It is not allowed to eat scavengers and predators; for this reason, observers refrain from eating catfish, clams, lobsters, oysters and shrimp.

The result of Biblical commandments specifying food laws is a lucrative niche market providing kosher products. Rosen (2008) noted that in North America alone kosher products are a US$14 billion a year business; she quoted Chaim Goldberg saying, 'There's no question that kosher is growing . . . As the world is getting more global, manufacturers . . . see kosher as a very easy way to market their product' (Rosen, 2008, p. 105).

Based in Fair Haven, Newfoundland, Neptune Sea Products is a kosher-sanctioned secondary fish-processing plant; it produces 200 different products, including Cajun cod and wasabi salmon. According to Rosen (2008), sales for the first year of this new venture were estimated to top $2 million. Rosen interviewed the entrepreneur behind Neptune Sea Products and he explained, 'We only use fish that have fins and scales . . . The other main thing is, my employees can't bring in ham sandwiches for lunch' (Rosen, 2008, p. 106).

Fifteen minutes down the road from Neptune Sea Products is the Rodrigues Winery, a family business in Markland. This is the first winery in Newfoundland and the first kosher and sulphite-free winery in Canada, producing wines from local blueberries, cloudberries, cranberries, raspberries and strawberries. Exports are shipped as far away as Japan.

6. Religious Beliefs May Hamper Entrepreneurial Spirit

Buddhism emphasizes the afterlife, and it has been suggested that Buddhists are not focused on entrepreneurial activity (Cousins, 1996). This is especially so among Theravada Buddhists. Lewis wrote, 'Where Theravada Buddhism is the backbone of social and cultural values . . . it may have a restraining effect on the accumulation of wealth and the rise of an entrepreneurial class' (1955, p. 105). Over half a century later, Theravada monks are still highly influential in Lao society.

As discussed by Dana (1995b), Theravada monks have traditionally had a great impact on the educational system in Laos; in former times, the only schools were in wats, and they are still consulted on virtually all matters, thereby playing an important role in a diversity of spheres, ranging from private life to government policy. This is elaborated upon in detail in Dana (2007a). Central to Theravada beliefs is the ultimate goal to extinguish unsatisfied desires. Its doctrine focuses on aspects of existence, including *dukkha* (suffering from unsatisfied desire), and *anicca* (impermanence). Assuming that unsatisfied desires cause suffering, then suffering can be eliminated if its cause (desire) is eliminated. A respectable person, then, according to this ideology, should not work towards the satisfaction of materialistic desires, but should, rather, strive to eliminate the desire itself. A monk, for instance, is specifically prohibited by the religion from tilling fields or raising animals.

Lao folk tales reinforce the belief that a male monk should not labour for material wealth; yet the same folklore conditions women to accept a heavy burden in exchange for honour, protection and security. Even the Lao currency portrays agricultural work being done by women. Numerous

Lao families who farm during the wet season become self-employed gold-diggers during the dry season. Prospectors camp along the Mekong River, especially in the region of Luang Prabang. The women do the heaviest work, digging for dirt and panning it in wooden trays. The men weigh the gold, up to one gram per day.

Writing about the former Kingdom of Modavia, Dana (2005, p. 223) observed,

> Orthodoxy in this kingdom emphasized the respect of authority, along with the importance of guilt. A good Moldavian was expected to obey the religion and work the land. A non-mercantile culture did nothing to encourage the development of entrepreneurship. In 1812, when the kingdom lost Bessarabia to Russia, the tsar's feudal system continued to meet non-conformity with punishment.

Rafiq (1992) suggested that Islam constitutes a barrier to capital access, due to the religious prohibition on interest payments. Metcalf et al. (1996) concluded that Pakistanis were less successful than Indians in self-employment because they were Muslim.

Finally, a religion may encourage entrepreneurship in the broad sense but limit the sectors in which entrepreneurship takes place. Jainism encourages entrepreneurship in trade, but does not allow self-emplyment in agriculture (Iyer, 2004; Nevaskar, 1971). Adherance to this religion thus limits avenues for self-employment, because of its strict pacifism (Iyer, 1999; Nevaskar, 1971).

7. Religions Have Built-in Mechanisms for the Perpetuation of Values

In Jain communities where business and family overlap, a merchant's family and community status is linked to optimal marriage (Bayly, 1983). Marriage takes place among co-religionists and within boundaries, and values are propagated from one generation to the next.

Dana noted co-religionist matchmaking that allowed the perpetuation of religious values:

> Travel was intrinsic to their livelihood and during business trips these frequent travellers would pray, and eat, with co-religionists, and sleep at their homes. The religious duty of allowing animals to rest on the Sabbath (from sunset on Friday until dusk on Saturday) made it impossible to travel with livestock during this time of rest. Therefore, business trips were often extended due to religious obligations, and considerable time was spent with the families of other merchants. During this time, matchmaking was a common occurrence, as the son of a merchant fancied the daughter of another. The co-religionists shared the same language, holidays, belief system and dietary restrictions. All this, in turn, reinforced social networking among this ethnic minority. (2006, p. 589)

Likewise, in a study of Amish entrepreneurship, Dana noted how values – as well as skills – are passed on from one generation to the next:

> From a very young age, Amish children develop a close relationship with their parents. Parents spend almost all of their time with their children, teaching them Amish cultural values. It is not from formal education in school, but rather from their parents that children learn to become self-sufficient in life. Amish boys normally learn a variety of skills on their father's farm. This typically includes cabinetry, carpentry, furniture-making and masonry . . . Most importantly for the Amish, each generation transmits cultural values to the next. This includes asceticism, frugality and thrift . . . Children thus become predisposed towards self-employment, as parents guide them along an almost pre-determined road in life. The young are not encouraged to explore such as to discover themselves, but rather to fit into Amish society, and to feel needed within it. Often, a son learns his trade from his father. Even when a son does not adopt the same profession as his father, it is practical to learn as many manual skills as possible. A son becomes the apprentice of his father at a very young age. Not only does a son learn how to work, but also more importantly according to Amish tradition, he is conditioned into accepting the Amish belief that work is healthy and enjoyable. (2007b, pp. 148–9)

For the Amish – as is the case among some other religious groups – marrying outside the faith is shunned. 'If an Amish woman wants to marry an outsider, she must leave the community, unless he joins Amish society. A deterrent to her leaving is that she is unprepared for secular society, while a stumbling block in the attempt to become Amish is the dialect' (Dana, 2007b, p. 149).

Likewise, but to different degrees, intermarriage is discouraged by other religions. In a study of comparing Indian entrepreneurs in Singapore and their counterparts in the United Kingdom, Hamilton et al. (2008) found that in both countries, most respondents would *not* allow their children to marry outside the faith.

TOWARD THE FUTURE

In a study of mixed marriages and separation, Monahan and Kephart (1954) showed that Jewish families broke up less than non-Jewish ones. Presumably this allowed values to be reinforced and to be passed on from one generation to the next. As society becomes increasingly tolerant of mixed marriages, what will happen to values in the future?

Glazer and Moynihan (1963) found no evidence of convergence among different religions.

> Thus, a Jewish ethos and a Catholic ethos emerge: they are more strongly affected by a specific religious doctrine in the Catholic case than in the Jewish, but neither is purely the expression of the spirit of a religion . . . The important fact is that the differences in values and attitudes between the two groups do not, in general, become smaller with time. On the contrary: there is probably a wider gap between Jews and Catholics in New York today than in the days of Al Smith. (Glazer and Moynihan, 1963, pp. 298–9)

Is this still true almost five decades later?

Linking entrepreneurship to values offers endless possibilities for future research, whether or not these values are promoted by a religion. Some of Rokeach's (1973) values may impact entrepreneurship, and empirical investigation of this could present interesting research opportunities. Amish entrepreneurs value religion over prosperity, but might Rokeach's terminal value of a prosperous life lead to an entrepreneurial start-up? Could it be hypothesized that one who values freedom (independence, free choice) as per Rokeach (1973) might choose to become an entrepreneur?

Likewise, it could be empirically tested whether entrepreneurs exhibit some of Rokeach's (1973) instrumental values. Might there be a relationship between Rokeach's instrumental value of ambition (hard-working, aspiring) and successful entrepreneurship? Does entrepreneurship involve being broadminded (open-minded); capable (competent, effective); or courageous? Examining Rokeach's instrumental value of self-control, might this be linked to Weber's (1930) values of asceticism, frugality and thrift?

FINAL WORDS

Sociologist Max Weber suggested that asceticism, frugality and thrift (Weber, 1930) were values that encourage successful entrepreneurship; these are perhaps necessary but insufficient. I would add that *context* is important. Mennonites value asceticism, frugality and thrift, but Old Colony Mennonites have traditionally been *opposed to the concept of private property*. Hence, among Mennonites, individual entrepreneurs are not flagships of entrepreneurship; instead, entrepreneurial activities take a collective form, as described by Dana and Dana (2007). Indeed, different religions yield unlike patterns of entrepreneurship.

This chapter discussed several observable patterns: (i) various religions value entrepreneurship to different degrees; (ii) different religions yield unlike patterns of entrepreneurship, possibly due to value differences (such as asceticism, frugality and thrift) but also due to specialization (sometimes resulting in a monopoly) and networks; (iii) specialization along religious lines shapes entrepreneurship; (iv) credit networks, employment networks, information networks, and supply networks of co-religionists affect entrepreneurship; (v) religions provide opportunities for entrepreneurship; (vi) religious beliefs may hamper entrepreneurial spirit; and (vii) religions have built-in mechanisms for the perpetuation of values.

Learning about religions, it is evident that each has a set of values. Respect must be paid to the distinctiveness and differences of all.

NOTES

* This chapter is reprinted with permission from *The International Journal of Entrepreneurship and Innovation*, **10** (2), 2009, 87–99. Copyright © 2009 IP Publishing Ltd.

1. The author thanks Professor Ivan Light (UCLA) for interesting discussions leading to this article. The author also thanks the following for comments on preliminary drafts: Dr Garth Cant (University of Canterbury); Dr Sarah Drakopoulou-Dodd (Athens Laboratory of Business Administration Graduate Business School and Robert Gordon University); Professor Gopalkrishnan R. Iyer (Florida Atlantic University); and Professor Richard W. Wright (UCLA).
2. See Young (1991) and Young and Sloman (1986).
3. This is based on Matthew 19:23–4.
4. Rath and Kloosterman (2003) revisited this theme. They noted that 'The arrival of Jews from the Iberian Peninsula in the sixteenth century and later from Eastern Europe, and of Roman Catholics from Westphalia throughout the nineteenth century, greatly influenced the Dutch economic landscape as their business acumen enhanced the nation's economic and cultural wealth' (pp. 123–4).
5. Today, Grahams are manufactured by Nabisco and certified as Kosher by the Union of Orthodox Rabbis.
6. Altinay (2008) distinguished among religious Muslims and secular Muslims. Other studies have treated Muslims as a homogenous group, and did not distinguish between religious and non-practising individuals (see Basu and Altinay, 2002; Dana and Dana, 2008; Metcalf et al., 1996; and Rafiq, 1992).

REFERENCES

Abdullah, Asma (1992), 'The Influence of Ethnic Values on Managerial Practices in Malaysia', *Malaysian Management Review*, **27** (1), 3–18.

Ackrill, Margaret and Leslie Hannah (2001), *Barclays: The Business of Banking, 1690–1996*, Cambridge: Cambridge University Press.

Aldrich, Howard E. (1979), *Organizations and Environments*, Englewood Cliffs, NJ: Prentice Hall.

Aldrich, Howard E. and Gabriele Weidenmayer (1993), 'From Traits to Rates: An Ecological Perspective on Organisational Foundings', in Jerome Katz and Robert H. Brockhaus (eds), *Advances in Entrepreneurship, Firm Emergence and Growth*, Greenwich, CT: JAI Press, vol. 1, pp. 145–95.

Altinay, Levent (2008), 'The Relationship Between an Entrepreneur's Culture and the Entrepreneurial Behaviour of the Firm', *Journal of Small Business and Enterprise Development*, **15** (1), 111–29.

Anderson, Alistair R., Sarah L. Drakopoulou-Dodd and Michael G. Scott (2000),

'Religion as an Environmental Influence on Enterprise Culture: The Case of Britain in the 1980s', *International Journal of Entrepreneurial Behaviour & Research*, **6** (1), 5–20.

Aristotle (1924), 'The Politics', (trans. B. Jowett), in Arthur Eli Monroe (ed.), *Early Economic Thought*, Cambridge, MA: Harvard University Press, pp. 3–29.

Armstrong, Christopher and H.V. Nelles (1977), *The Revenge of the Methodist Bicycle Company: Sunday Streetcars and Municipal Reform in Toronto, 1888–1897*, Toronto: Peter Martin Associates.

Arslan, Mahmut (2000), 'A Cross-cultural Comparison of British and Turkish Managers in Terms of Protestant Work Ethic Characteristics', *British Ethics: A European Review*, **9** (1), 13–19.

Badawi, Abdullah Ahmad (2006), 'Islam and Development', *Global Agenda 2006*, Davos: World Economic Forum, pp. 208–9.

Baldacchino, Godfrey and Léo-Paul Dana (2006), 'The Impact of Public Policy on Entrepreneurship: A Critical Investigation of the Protestant Ethic on a Divided Island Jurisdiction', *Journal of Small Business and Entrepreneurship*, **19** (4), 419–30.

Basu, Anuradha and Eser Altinay (2002), 'The Interaction between Culture and Entrepreneurship in London's Immigrant Businesses', *International Small Business Journal*, **20** (4), 371–94.

Bayly, Christopher Alan (1983), *Rulers, Townsmen and Bazaars: North India in the Age of British Expansion, 1770–1870*, Cambridge: Cambridge University Press.

Becker, Howard (1956), *Man in Reciprocity*, New York: Praeger.

Boissevain, Jeremy and Hanneke Grotenbreg (1987), 'Ethnic Enterprise in the Netherlands: The Surinamese of Amsterdam', in Robert Goffee and Richard Scase (eds), *Entrepreneurship in Asia: The Social Processes*, London: Croom Helm, pp. 105–30.

Borjas, George J. (1992), 'Ethnic Capital and Intergenerational Mobility', *Quarterly Journal of Economics*, **107**, 123–50.

Brammer, S., Geoffrey Williams and John Zinkin (2007), 'Religion and Attitudes to Corporate Social Responsibility in a Large Cross-country Sample', *Journal of Business Ethics*, **71** (3), 229–43.

Candland, Christopher (2000), 'Faith as Social Capital: Religion and Community Development in Southern Asia', *Policy Sciences*, **33** (3–4), 355–74.

Corley, Thomas Anthony Buchanan (1998), 'Changing Quakers' Attitudes to Wealth, 1690–1950', in David J. Jeremy (ed.), *Religion, Business and Wealth in Modern Britain*, London: Routledge, pp. 137–50.

Cousins, Lance S. (1996), 'The Dating of the Historical Buddha: A Review Article', *Journal of the Royal Asiatic Society*, **6** (1), 57–63.

Dana, Léo-Paul (1991), 'Bring in More Entrepreneurs', *Policy Options*, **12** (9), 18–19.

Dana, Léo-Paul (1995a), 'Entrepreneurship in a Remote Sub-Arctic Community: Nome, Alaska', *Entrepreneurship: Theory and Practice*, **20** (1), 55–72.

Dana, Léo-Paul (1995b), 'Small Business in a Non-Entrepreneurial Society: The Case of the Lao People's Democratic Republic (Laos)', *Journal of Small Business Management*, **33** (3), 95–102.

Dana, Léo-Paul (2005), *When Economies Change Hands: A Survey of Entrepreneurship in the Emerging Markets of Europe from the Balkans to the Baltic States*, Binghamton, NY: International Business Press.

Dana, Léo-Paul (2006), 'A Historical Study of the Traditional Livestock Merchants of Alsace', *British Food Journal*, **108** (7), 586–98.
Dana, Léo-Paul (2007a), *Asian Models of Entrepreneurship – From the Indian Union and the Kingdom of Nepal to the Japanese Archipelago: Context, Policy and Practice*, Singapore and London: World Scientific.
Dana, Léo-Paul (2007b), 'Humility-based Economic Development and Entrepreneurship among the Amish', *Journal of Enterprising Communities: People and Places in the Global Economy*, **1** (2), 142–54.
Dana, Léo-Paul and Teresa E. Dana (2007), 'Collective Entrepreneurship in a Mennonite Community in Paraguay', *Latin American Business Review*, **8** (4), 82–96.
Dana, Léo-Paul and Teresa E. Dana (2008), 'Ethnicity & Entrepreneurship in Morocco: A Photo-ethnographic Study', *International Journal of Business and Globalisation*, **2** (3), 209–26.
Drakopoulou-Dodd, Sarah and Alistair R. Anderson (2007), 'Mumpsimus and the Mything of the Individualistic Entrepreneur', *International Small Business Journal*, **25** (4), 341–60.
Drakopoulou-Dodd, Sarah and George Gotsis (2007), 'The Interrelationships between Entrepreneurship and Religion', *International Journal of Entrepreneurship and Innovation*, **8** (2), 93–104.
Dundas, Paul (1992), *The Jains*, New York: Routledge.
Durkheim, Émile (1912), *Les formes élémentaires de la vie religieuse: Le système totémique en Australie*, Paris: Felix Alcan.
Enz, Cathy A., Marc J. Dollinger and Catherine M. Daily (1990), 'The Value Orientations of Minority and Non-minority Small Business Owners', *Entrepreneurship, Theory and Practice*, **15** (1), 23–35.
Farmer, Richard N. and Barry M. Richman (1965), *Comparative Management and Economic Progress*, Homewood, IL: Richard D. Irwin.
Feuerbach, Ludwig (1855), *The Essence of Christianity* (trans. Marian Evans), New York: Calvin Blanchard.
Fishberg, Maurice (1911), *The Jews: A Study of Race and Environment*, London: Walter Scott.
Gadgil, Dhananjaya Ramchandra (1959), *Origins of the Modern Indian Business Class*, New York: Institute of Pacific Relations.
Galbraith, Craig Scott (2007), 'The Impact of Ethnic-religious Identification on Buyer-seller Behaviour: A Study of Two Enclaves', *International Journal of Business and Globalisation*, **1** (1), 20–33.
Galbraith, Craig Scott, Donald R. Latam and Jacqueline Benitez-Galbraith (1997), 'Entrepreneurship in the Hispanic Community of the Southeastern United States', *Frontiers of Entrepreneurship Research*, Wellesley, MA: Babson College.
Galbraith, Craig Scott, Curt H. Stiles and Jacqueline Benitez-Bertheau (2004), 'The Embryonic Development of an Ethnic Neighbourhood: A Longitudinal Case Study of Entrepreneurial Activity', in Curt H. Stiles and Craig Scott Galbraith (eds), *Ethnic Entrepreneurship: Structure and Process*, Oxford: Elsevier, pp. 95–112.
Galbraith, Craig Scott, Curt H. Stiles and Carlos Rodriguez (2003) 'Intra-Enclave Trade: Hispanic and Arab Small Businesses', *Journal of Small Business and Entrepreneurship*, **16** (3/4), 18–29.
Glazer, Nathan and Daniel Patrick Moynihan (1963), *Beyond the Melting Pot:*

The Negroes, Puerto Ricans, Italians and Irish of New York City, Boston, MA: MIT.

Guiso, Luigi, Paola Sapienza and Luigi Zingales (2003), 'People's Opium? Religion and Economic Attitudes', *Journal of Monetary Economics*, **50** (1), 225–82.

Hamilton, Robert T., Léo-Paul Dana and Camilla Benfell (2008), 'Changing Cultures: An International Study of Migrant Entrepreneurs', *Journal of Enterprising Culture*, **16** (1), 89–105.

Hawley, Jana M. (1995), 'Maintaining Business While Maintaining Boundaries: An Amish Woman's Entrepreneurial Experience', *Entrepreneurship, Innovation, and Change*, **4** (4), 315–28.

Hiebert, Paul G. (1976) *Cultural Anthropology*, Philadelphia, PA: J.B. Lippincott.

Hofstede, Geert (2001), *Culture's Consequences*, 2nd edn, Beverly Hills, CA: Sage.

Iyer, Gopalkrishnan R. (1999), 'The Impact of Religion and Reputation in the Organization of Indian Merchant Communities', *The Journal of Business & Industrial Marketing*, **14** (2), 102–17.

Iyer, Gopalkrishnan R. (2004), 'Ethnic Business Families', in Curt H. Stiles and Craig Scott Galbraith (eds), *Ethnic Entrepreneurship: Structure and Process*, Oxford: Elsevier, pp. 243–60.

Iyer, Gopalkrishnan R. and Jon M. Shapiro (1999), 'Ethnic Entrepreneurial and Marketing Systems: Implications for the Global Economy', *Journal of International Marketing*, **7** (4), 83–110.

Jenkins, Richard (1984), 'Ethnicity and the Rise of Capitalism in Ulster', in Robin Ward and Richard Jenkins (eds), *Ethnic Communities in Business: Strategies for Economic Survival*, Cambridge: Cambridge University Press, pp. 57–72.

Juteau, Danielle, and Sylvie Paré (1996), 'L'entrepreneurship ethnique', *Interfaces*, **17** (1), 18–28.

Klandt, Heinz (1987), 'Trends in Small Business Start-up in West Germany', in Robert Goffee and Richard Scase (eds), *Entrepreneurship in Europe: The Social Processes*, London: Croom Helm, pp. 26–38.

Kluckhohn, Clyde K. (1949), *Mirror for Man*, Toronto: Whittlesey House.

Kluckhohn, Clyde K. (1951), 'Values and Value Orientations in the Theory of Action: An Exploration in Definition and Classification', in Talcott Parsons and Edward A. Shils (eds), *Toward a General Theory of Action*, Cambridge: Harvard University Press, pp. 388–443.

Kluckhohn, Florence R. and Fred L. Strodtbeck (1961), *Variations in Value Orientations*, Evanston, IL: Row, Peterson.

Kraybill, Donald B. and Carl F. Bowman (2001), *On the Backroad to Heaven: Old Order Hutterites, Mennonites, Amish, and Brethren*, Baltimore, MD: Johns Hopkins University Press.

Kraybill, Donald B. and Steven M. Nolt (1995), *Amish Enterprise*, Baltimore, MD: Johns Hopkins University Press.

Kroeber, Alfred Louis and Clyde K. Kluckhohn (1952), *Culture: A Critical Review of Concepts and Definitions*, Cambridge, MA: The Museum.

Laidlaw, James (1995), *Riches and Renunciation: Religion, Economy, and Society among the Jains*, Oxford: Clarendon.

Lasry, Jean-Claude (1982), 'Une Diaspora Francophone au Quebec: Les Juifs Sépharades', *Questions de Culture*, **2**, 113–38.

Lee, Jennifer (1999), 'Retail Niche Domination among African-American, Jewish and Korean Entrepreneurs', *American Behavioral Scientist*, **42** (9), 1398–417.

Lewis, W. Arthur (1955), *The Theory of Economic Growth*, Homewood, IL: Richard D. Irwin.
Liuhto, Kari (1996), 'The Transformation of the Enterprise Sector in Estonia: A Historical Approach to Contemporary Transition', *Journal of Enterprising Culture*, **4** (3), 317–29.
Lumpkin, G.T. and Gregory G. Dess (1996), 'Clarifying the Entrepreneurial Orientation Construct and Linking It to Performance', *Academy of Management Review*, **21** (1), 135–72.
Metcalf, Hilary, Tariq Modood and Satnam Virdee (1996), *Asian Self-employment: The Interaction of Culture and Economics in England*, London: Policy Studies Institute.
Minkus-McKenna, Dorothy (2007), 'The Pursuit of Halal', *Progressive Grocer*, **86**, 1 December, 17.
Monahan, Thomas P. and William M. Kephart (1954), 'Divorce and Desertion by Religions and Mixed Religious Groups', *American Journal of Sociology*, **59** (5), 454–65.
Nevaskar, Balwant (1971), *Capitalists Without Capitalism: The Jains of India and the Quakers of the West*, Westport, CT: Greenwood.
Norcliffe, Glen (2001), *Ride to Modernity: The Bicycle in Canada 1869–1900*, Toronto: University of Toronto Press.
Porter, Kenneth Wiggens (1937), *The Jacksons and the Lees: Two Generations of Massachusetts Merchants, 1765–1844*, Cambridge, MA: Harvard University Press.
Rafiq, Mohammed (1992), 'Ethnicity and Enterprise: A Comparison of Muslim and Mon-Muslim Owned Asian Businesses in Britain', *New Community*, **19** (1), 43–60.
Raistrick, Arthur (1950), *Quakers in Science and Industry*, London: Bannisdale.
Raphaël, Freddy (1980), 'Les Juifs de la campagne alsacienne: les marchands de bestiaux', *Revue des Sciences Sociales de la France de l'Est*, **9**, 220–45.
Rath, Jan, and Robert Kloosterman (2003), 'The Netherlands: A Dutch Treat', in Robert Kloosterman and Jan Rath (eds), *Immigrant Entrepreneurs: Venturing Abroad in the Age of Globalization*, Oxford: Berg, pp. 123–46.
Reynolds, Paul D. (1991), 'Sociology and Entrepreneurship: Concepts and Contributions', *Entrepreneurship Theory and Practice*, **16** (2), 47–70.
Rokeach, Milton (1968), *Beliefs, Attitudes, and Values*, San Francisco, CA: Jossey-Bass.
Rokeach, Milton (1973), *The Nature of Human Values*, New York: Free Press.
Rosen, Amy (2008), 'Kosher Quality: A Rabbi, a Newfoundlander and a Fish Walk into a Bar . . .', *enRoute*, (November), 105–08.
Sayigh, Yezid A. (1952), *Entrepreneurs of Lebanon*, Cambridge, MA: Harvard University Press.
Schwartz, Shalom H. (1992), 'Universals in the Content and Structure of Values: Theoretical Advances and Empirical Tests in 20 Countries', in Mark P. Zanna (ed.), *Advances in Experimental Social Psychology*, book 25, Orlando, FL: Academic Press, pp. 1–65.
Shapero, Albert (1984), 'The Entrepreneurial Event', in Calvin A. Kent (ed.), *The Environment for Entrepreneurship*, Lexington, MA: D.C. Heath, pp. 21–40.
Sombart, Werner (1911), *Die Juden und das Wirtschaftsleben,* Leipzig: Duncker und Humblot.

Specht, Pamela Hammers (1993), 'Munificence and Carrying Capacity of the Environment and Organizational Carrying Capacity', *Entrepreneurship: Theory and Practice*, **17** (2), 77–87.

Stewart, Alex (1991), 'A Prospectus on the Anthropology of Entrepreneurship', *Entrepreneurship: Theory and Practice*, **16** (2), 71–91.

Stiles, Curt H., Carlos L. Rodriguez, and Craig S. Galbraith (2007), 'The Impact of Ethnic-religious Identification on Buyer-seller Behaviour: A Study of Two Enclaves', *International Journal of Business and Globalisation*, **1** (1), 20–33.

Taft, William Howard (1919), 'The Progressive World Struggle of the Jews for Civil Equality', *National Geographic*, **36** (1), 1–16.

Thatcher, Margaret (1993), *The Downing Street Years*, London: HarperCollins.

Thomas, William Isaac and Florian W. Znaniecki (1918), *The Polish Peasant in Europe and America*, Boston, MA: Badger.

Weber, Max (1904) 'Die protestantische Ethik und der "Geist" des Kapitalismus. I. Das Problem', *Archiv für Sozialwissenschaft und Sozialpolitik*, **20** (1), 1–54.

Weber, Max (1930), *The Protestant Ethic and the Spirit of Capitalism* (trans. Talcott Parsons), New York: Charles Scribner's Sons.

Woodrum, Eric M. (1985), 'Religion and Economics among Japanese Americans: A Weberian Study', *Social Forces*, **64**, 191–204.

Young, Hugo (1991), *One of Us*, London: Macmillan.

Young, Hugo and Anne Sloman (1986) *The Thatcher Phenomenon*, London: BBC.

Zingales, Luigi (2006), 'Gods and Mammon', *Global Agenda 2006*, Davos: World Economic Forum, pp. 228–9.

PART I

Old Values

1. Religious merchants?

Edwina Pio

INTRODUCTION

Religion is carved into the lives of Indians and finds expression in multifarious ways in day-to-day practices such as morning prayers, offerings to deities and religious observances. Religion is also a driving force for entrepreneurship among certain sections of Indian society, based on caste affiliation. India is a secular democratic republic where 80.5 per cent of Indians are Hindus, 13.4 per cent are Muslim, 2.3 per cent are Christian, 1.9 per cent are Sikh, 0.8 per cent are Buddhist, 0.4 per cent are Jain, 0.6 are other religious persuasions (e.g. Jews and Parsis/Zoroastrians), and 0.1 per cent are those who have not stated a religion (Census India, 2001). Through interaction, research and observation in India, as well as through extant scholarship, it can be argued that there is a strong nexus between the temple and the bazaar for India's entrepreneurs. In this chapter, religion and spirituality will be intertwined, for religion is seen as the outward expression of value systems that are deemed spiritual which emanate from charity (*dana*), devotion (*bhakti*), destiny (*karma*), duty (*dharma*), non-violence (*ahimsa*), the meritless deed (*nishkamakarma*) and service (*seva*).

Noble Prize winner Amartya Sen's (2005; 2006) arguments concerning the portrayal of India by the West indicate that the creation of the image of India changed as the British consolidated their power in colonial times. Thus from an early image of Indian's having tremendous knowledge with an ancient civilization rich with philosophy, advances in medicine, astronomy and mathematics, it changed to that of the native as being inferior, illiterate and needing to be lifted up. In other words the white man's burden was given credence, as well as images of Indians as being other worldly and exotic, ascetic and believers in destiny, hence opposed to change or efforts towards change. Thus through the nineteenth and twentieth centuries, the conceptions of India were discursively institutionalized through images of poverty, ignorance and illiteracy which were foregrounded. There seemed to be an international amnesia about the richness of Indian civilization with its architecture, sculpture, numerals, philosophical treatises and universities of reputation which drew travellers from distant parts of the world to partake of India's intellectual wealth, and seafaring traditions. Some exceptions to this portrayal in the twentieth century were the Indians who were in the USA and later the moguls of Silicon Valley and a few Indian industrialists in India.

Closer to our historical times, India's emergence as an economic superpower to be reckoned with can be traced to a number of complexities, depending on one's vantage point. Undoubtedly it was the political climate which led to the opening up of the economy in the 1990s and India's ascendance in the contemporary world market. But as political, economic and social pundits repeatedly espouse, it was also the people who were prepared to seize the opportunity and push the boundaries of new horizons, to create an amazing wealth for large sections of the Indian population. Yet this wealth distribution continues to leave approximately 25 per cent of Indians below the poverty line despite the fact that India houses some of the richest individuals in the world, for India is a land of tremendous contrasts. The country consists of a total land mass of 3 287 590 square kilometres or an area slightly more than one-third the size of the United States, 28 states and 7 union territories, an estimated population of 1.1 billion as of July 2007, with a life expectancy of 68.59 years, and a literacy rate of 73.4 per cent for males and 47.8 per cent for females based on the 2001 census (CIA, 2008).

Besides English which is the most important language for national, political and commercial communication, Hindi is the national language, along with 21 other official languages. Thus for instance the word entrepreneur is *vyapari* in Hindi, *karobaari* in Urdu, *uduyogpati* in Marathi and *vyavasthapakudu* in Telugu. The gross domestic product (GDP) per capita is US$2700, with a labour force of 516.4 million, based on a 2007 estimate (CIA, 2008). Services are the major source of economic growth, besides traditional/modern agriculture, handicrafts and a range of modern industries, with an average growth rate of more than 7 per cent in the decade since 1997 (CIA, 2008). India, the world's largest democracy, is the fourth largest economy in the world in terms of purchasing power parity, with the most liberal and transparent policies on foreign direct investment among major world economies (Indian Embassy, 2008).

This chapter presents information pertaining to entrepreneurship and religion in India through a cartography of India's business history which serves to set the scene for an understanding of the complexities undergirding religious affiliation and economic prowess. This is followed by a description and analysis of the contemporary scenario of entrepreneurship, where it is argued that religion is a deep motif in the layered practice of entrepreneurship. The chapter ends with suggestions for future research and some thought-provoking concluding comments.

BUSINESS HISTORY AND RELIGION

Religious and philosophical concepts continue to have practical applications in Indian businesses, for Indian culture often does not segment the sacred from the secular, as a person's duty (*dharma*) is interpreted through one's role in life, and every role has certain expectations of *dharma* to be fulfilled (Pio, 2005a; 2005b; 2007a; 2007b). Destiny or *karma* is common parlance in daily life and this is the belief that the fruit of one's actions is the consequence of deeds both in this life and in previous lives, as well as *purushartha* or one's own effort. *Bhakti* or devotion is omnipresent through worship of over a thousand deities, and this can be translated into the world of work where the work site becomes the *shram mandir* or temple of work. *Bhakti* has the power to bind together the human and divine, in a relationship of loving protection on the divine side and loving service by the human being concerned (Matchett, 2003). Learning is greatly valued and the *guru* or revered teacher is accorded a place of importance in the minds and behaviour of Indians and the *guru–shishya* or teacher–student relationship is given much value.

An individual is born into a caste and the four traditional castes are: (1) Brahmins or priests; (2) Kshatriyas or warriors; (3) Vaishyas or merchants/entrepreneurs; and (4) Shudras or those at the bottom rung of the social hierarchy who do menial tasks. The untouchables or harijans fell out of this system and they did the tasks no one else was prepared to do such as waste disposal or garbage removal and cleaning toilets (today's parlance would be waste management!)

Recorded history indicates that during the golden age of the Guptas (fourth century AD) the merchants were organized into collectives, for example the *nigama*, the *pani* and *sreni* (Khanna, 2005). The early entrepreneurs developed intricate systems for credit and forward trading to further their entrepreneurial activities such as buying ships, goods such as indigo, spices, silk, cotton and textiles and investing in cargo and land. The Vaishya caste was largely the source for subcastes such as the Marwaris, Khatris, Banias in northern, eastern and western India, and in southern India, the merchants were primarily the Nattukottai Chettiars (Prakash, 2004). In the period AD 1000–1500, the ship-owning merchants known as *nakhudas* and *nauvittakas* occupy a prominent position as elites in the ports of coastal western Indian and were known for their patronage of religious and cultural activities, as well as cooperation, social amity and religious tolerance between the Jewish, Muslim and Hindu ship-owning merchants (Chakravarti, 2000).

Religious communities such as the Jains, Jews, Sindhis, Ismaili and Parsi merchants were also involved in trade, finance and mercantile entrepreneurship (Das Gupta, 2001; Dobbin, 1996; Pluss, 2005). Thus for example, the Ismaili community from the Indian Kutch region in Gujarat were enterprising merchants in East Africa between 1841 and 1939. The Ismailis are an Indian Muslim community, commonly known as the Khojas, Bhoras or Kutchi merchants who were involved in the rise of the Sultanate of Oman, as well as mercantile success and financing of the caravan trade in and around Zanzibar (Dobbin, 1996; Markovitz, 1999). These merchants traded in raw silk, sugar, cotton yarn, beans and spices between China and India in the nineteenth century (Pluss, 2005).

The Nattukottai Chettiars are Savivaite Hindus from Madras Presidency (today's Tamil Nadu), and were the big merchant bankers, whose commercial involvement had a religious blend based on gift-giving to temples by merchant guilds. The gift-giving was similar to licence fees and financial investments, and gradually led to trustworthiness as a moral basis for credit for merchant activities, which included forward loans and transmission of bills of exchange, where the god was a divine witness to the commercial transactions (Dobbin, 1996). The temple often served as the 'Chettiar exchange' where interest rates were determined, commercial information disseminated, business disputes handled, and capital drawn from temple funds 'was felt to have a special religious significance, as it drew the major deity of the temple into direct participation in business' (Dobbin, 1996, p. 147). The Nattukottai Chettiars in the nineteenth century dominated the pearl fisheries in the Ceylon Straits, as well as major coastal trade in arak and coconut products from Ceylon (Sri Lanka) to Madras. In the early twentieth century the Chettiars' money lending firms had considerable economic success in Burma.

The Sephardic Jews who had settled in Bombay (Mumbai) and Calcutta (Kolkatta) and the Sasoons led the trade between Indian and the Arabian Gulf and also had mercantile businesses in China in the nineteenth century (Pluss, 2005). These Jews maintained their Jewish traditions and synagogues and conducted business using Hebrew and Arabic, besides English.

With the advent of the European powers in India, and eventually the colonial supremacy of the British, trade was monopolized with the colonial powers initially trading in pepper, cinnamon, opium, indigo, gold, silver and gems. The occupational specialization of the caste system ensured that the Vaishya class became the merchants, the overland traders, the maritime investors for waterborne trade and intermediaries between the European powers. Today their scions form the top management and owners of many of the large industrial organizations and conglomerates in India. The merchant communities engaged in activities such as marketing of agricultural products, financing of inland trade through bills of exchange and mobile credit known as *hundi* and through the *arhat* or indigenous form of commission agency (Ray, 1992). Their enterprises complemented those of the English entrepreneurs who allowed them to become prominent in a diversified industrial economy.

The Parsis, by aligning themselves with the Europeans in the China trade, etched a strategic position for themselves (Ray, 1992). The Parsis were the middlemen and the brokers for the British in India and the Portuguese, French and Dutch all employed Parsis as their chief brokers, and in fact prior to the European powers, the Mughal Emperors had granted some Parsis the right to collect customs duties (Dobbin, 1996). The Parsis of the nineteenth and twentieth century also had considerable trading businesses in raw cotton and opium to China, as well as ships trading between London, Calcutta and China (Pluss, 2005). The Parsis built ships for European companies and the Bombay dockyards were instrumental in translating a mercantile mindset into that of an industrial one. The Parsis were also pioneering cotton mill entrepreneurs (Dobbin, 1996). Among Parsi entrepreneurs the most famous is Jamshedji Tata who set up the Indian iron and steel industry in India; and Jamsetjee Jejeebhoy who was the first Indian and the first Parsi to receive the honour of knighthood from Britain in 1842 (Pluss, 2005). The Parsis are also known for their philanthropy through the setting up and endowment of numerous schools, hospitals, libraries and centres for art and culture (Palsetia, 2005). The Parsi religion encourages its adherents to see material reward as proof of their good deeds and intentions in shaping the world.

Other merchant communities were the Bhatias, the Khojas, the Memons and the Multanis who traded not only with China but also with the Arabian Gulf countries. During the 1800s, the British discriminated against those communities who competed with English entrepreneurs in international commerce, pushing many out of the business realm, and local firms with established reputations were defrauded by British partners, leading to more withdrawals from the business sector. Consequently Nafziger (1971) writes that 'the lack of indigenous entrepreneurship . . . stems in part from the discrimination and duplicity of the British in the 19th century' (p. 30). India was the jewel in the crown for the British. The British were assured of cheap raw materials from India, as well as a captive market for finished goods, for India was a major supplier of raw materials such as cotton to the British mills and India's millions were the market for the textiles produced.

Yet the balance sheet is mixed as to the impact of the British in India. The formal Raj (British rule) lasted from 1757 to 1947 and resulted in the building of roads, railways, the postal system, telephone/telegraph lines, dams and bridges as well as English as a medium of instruction

(Ferguson, 2002). There were restrictions on Indian-owned industries and hence on the growth of the Indian economy, and there was an emphasis on cash crops, resulting in the great famines in the late 1800s. However, the British are also said to have reduced local warfare and unified the country despite the British divide and rule policy and the splitting of the subcontinent into India and East and West Pakistan. But the British brought with them systems of governance and financial institutions that are still in use in India today. In the contemporary world there is a strong need for interdependency, and globalization often thrusts this need for co-creating the future into the forefront. When one considers that a butterfly in Benares (India) can create a rainstorm in Chicago (USA), then surely it is of great import that contemporary entrepreneurs move consciously with the knowledge that their strategies and actions need to be sourced from a power that is beyond the mundane; a power that in many instances must of necessity emanate from a value system which is the basis of the world religions, and which in the ultimate analysis leads to wealth creation for current and future generations.

CONTEMPORARY RELIGIOUS MERCHANTS

The economic reforms of the 1990s included: significant industrial and trade liberalization, financial deregulation, improvements in supervisory and regulatory systems, and policies more conducive to privatization and foreign direct investment (Gopinath, 2008). Today's merchant princes include the Ambanis, Birlas, Tatas, Premjis and Narayanamurthys and Indians of Silicon Valley such as Kanwal Rekhi. Many of these princes are India based and are now expanding internationally, whereas others are returning to India to invest and manage start-ups as well as top-performing information technology (IT) companies. 'Indian family-run business[es] have been developing rapidly from firms with limited goals that valued loyalty more than ability into dynamic professionally-managed corporates capable of taking on global competition' (Skaria, 2006, p. 48).

Economic liberalization took effect in 1991 and Pedersen (2000) writes of the silent revolution whose impetus came from a new breed of Indian entrepreneurs who initiated and gave the thrust to the implementation of the economic reforms of 1991. These entrepreneurs were involved in the small, medium and large-scale technology industries which form the modern segment of Indian business, through a system of professional management, rather than a traditional family-based system as compared to many of the established large family-owned conglomerates who have historically dominated the industrial sector (Dossani and Kenney, 2002;

Pedersen, 2000). Changes in the economic environment since the early 1990s reduced state involvement in the use of national capital, and entrepreneurship was galvanized through venture capital from Silicon Valley Indians who utilized the potential of a large English-speaking population with IT skills in India (Dossani and Kenney, 2002). The software industry is a good exemplar of entrepreneurship in India's economic development (Arora and Athreye, 2002). In fact, ex-employees of some of the more famous Indian IT organizations such as HCL and WIPRO have become active entrepreneurs of their own companies, due to low capital requirements and large venture interest in India, resulting in a change towards entrepreneurship which is becoming lucrative and a less insecure source of income in comparison to employment (Arora and Athreye, 2002; Economist 2006/07).

Wani et al. (2003; 2005), in emphasizing the importance of technology-based entrepreneurship, suggest effective interaction of academic institutions with small and medium enterprises (SMEs). In India since its political independence from the British in 1947, it has been crucial to broadly base entrepreneurship and to this end the Entrepreneurship Development Institute has been seeking to create an entrepreneurial mindset with skills and competencies in a varied range of individuals such as young Indian men and women (Dana, 2000). While India continues to be a patriarchal society, today there are a number of Indian women entrepreneurs many of whom are highly educated and run their own business, as well as the larger segment of Indian women who are starting their own micro-enterprises through micro-financing schemes (Ghosh et al., 1998; Porter and Nagarajan, 2005). The Self Employed Women's Association (SEWA) is an organization of poor, self-employed women workers and the SEWA's main goals are to organize women workers to achieve full employment and self-reliance through the strategy of struggle and development in organizing for social change (SEWA, 2008). The SEWA follows the principles of truth (*satya*), non-violence (*ahimsa*), integrating all faiths, all people (*sarvadharma*) and propagation of local employment and self-reliance (*khadi*). Such initiatives are important in a country where caste continues to restrain certain sections of society, for despite untouchability being abolished, just like dowry practices, the legacy of certain customs remain daunting and continue to be practised in various parts of India.

In India, religion continues to be omnipresent. The importance of religion for Indians is exemplified in a study done in the eastern part of India to examine the possible links between growth of entrepreneurship and sociocultural factors such as caste, religiosity and perceived family support (Shivani et al., 2006). Utilizing 200 participants this study found that almost 90 per cent of the respondents have high to medium religiosity and 'all respondents said they had faith in the power of God' (ibid., p. 70). The respondents felt that their religious practices and God's power helped them in their discipline and confidence, and in overcoming difficulties.

Taking the aspect of religion and linking it to the caste system, it can be argued that religion seems to underscore the headstart that members of business castes persist in having based on the legacy of their networks and early socialization processes in creating business acumen. Thus, for example, in a study based upon the perceptions of 66 entrepreneurs hailing from a northern region of India, 72.7 per cent came from business families, thus underscoring the importance of being part of a business caste (Sabbarwal, 1994). In a study of 54 Indian industrialists in south eastern India, it was found that high Hindu castes and Muslims were over-represented among the entrepreneurs and there is a significant positive relationship with caste ranking and education, income, occupational status and perceived class and status (Nafziger, 1975). Moreover, 'the large business families, because of their wealth and financial security, have the latitude to provide the training, education, travel and business experience of their sons, and the spending on plant and equipment that is most appropriate for the entrepreneurial development of their sons' (Nafziger, 1975, p. 139). And 'marriage may be arranged in part to further an economic alliance with another large business family' (Nafziger, 1975, p. 139). Another example of the importance of the caste system, is that of the caste-specific *padu* system of community-based fisheries management in south India which defines the group of rights holders and resource boundaries and fishing sites (Lobe and Berkes, 2004). For example in Tamilnadu the *padu* consists of members of the fishing caste, the Pattanavar, who are Christians as well as Hindus; and in Kerala, all of the fishers are Hindu and members of the Dheevara caste.

However, specific castes linked to entrepreneurship can change. Such shifting of the locus of entrepreneurship to different castes is exemplified in a study on terrorism and rural entrepreneurship in Punjab (Bal and Judge, 2001). In their study, the authors show the linkages between caste, religion, business and terrorism wherein, based on the political situation and the terrorist activities, some families such as the Sodhis who belong to the Hindu Khatri caste and some Brhamins moved out of Punjab and their businesses were taken over by the Jat Sikhs or the traditional cultivating caste. Moreover, the 'displacement of the traditional business community motivated a number of backward castes, specially the Tarkhan, Suniara, Chamar, Thathiar, Chhimba, Kumhar and Nai to take up these new positions' (Bal and Judge, 2001, p. 198), even though the Jats were able to make better use of the entrepreneurial opportunities.

Thus, in considering India's large population where the majority are Hindus, the caste system can be seen as restricting mobility and opportunity, particularly for Hindus. Perhaps this is the reason for the findings of Audretsch et al. (2007), based on data from nearly 90 000 works in India. These scholars note that religions such as Islam and Christianity are found to be conducive to entrepreneurship, while others such as Hinduism seem to inhibit entrepreneurship, and the caste system is seen to influence the propensity to be an entrepreneur. The study focuses on the impact of religion on the economic decision-making process of individuals, and their findings indicate that the class structures of Hinduism continue to influence occupational choice. Thus, individuals from the Hindu religion, barring those from the Vaishya class, are less likely to be entrepreneurs as compared to individuals from other religions. Hindus from the lower class are the least entrepreneurial people and it is possible that the caste system restricts mobility of such individuals.

A raft of organizations and individuals are involved in social entrepreneurship, through throwing off the shackles of caste and instead being impelled by motivations such as a more even distribution for wealth creation, wealth sharing and empowerment. Moreover a case could be made for claiming that the impetus for such entrepreneurial activities stems from Indian values of *ahimsa*, *sewa* and *nishkama karma* where entrepreneurs help to re-engineer society while earning profits at the same time. Social entrepreneurs in India (Noronha, 2007), such as Stan Thaekkaekara of Just Change, work with the tribes of Nilgiris in Tamil Naidu on issues of health, education and livelihood as well as helping these tribes reclaim land. Just Change expands the concept of fair trade and works towards a system of production for the common man by the common man. Vishal Talreja of Dream a Dream builds life skills for over 500 children in Bangalore. Shalabh Sahai and Rahul Barkatky of Mitra Technology Foundation have created iVolunteer which is a volunteer placement initiative. Other examples of social entrepreneurship are the SEWA, Just Change, Childline, Fair Trade Forum, Barefoot College and Aravind Eye Care. Noronha (2007) writes of individuals like Anil Gupta of the HoneyBee network who argue that besides social, natural and intellectual capital, ethic capital or the guiding forces from within us are crucial to power change in the community.

A number of large businesses are also deeply involved in imbuing 'spirit', 'values', 'religiosity', 'spirituality' and 'goodness' into their entrepreneurial activities. Such organizations are not manifestations of fundamentalist tendencies or proselytizing machines for their religions, but rather present a much more eclectic mix of doing good in order to live as a microcosm of the macrocosm that is the universe. For example, the Tata Group is one of India's oldest, largest and most respected business conglomerates with businesses spread over seven business sectors, 98 companies, operating in six continents, and employs some 289,500 people (Tata, 2008). The Tata Group's values and purpose stem from integrity, understanding, excellence, unity, responsibility and a heritage of returning to society what the organization earns. Established in the second half of the nineteenth century, this group has grown into one of India's biggest and most respected business organizations, due to its entrepreneurial vision, commitment to ideals that put people before profits and its fortitude in the face of adversity. The lives and achievements of some of the group's pioneer entrepreneurs such as Jamsetji Tata, JRD Tata and Naval Tata bear witness to the enterprising spirit emanating from a religion whose essence is *Humata, Hukta, Huvarsta* – good thoughts, good words, and good deeds. This spiritual core is the bedrock of the Tata edifice. The Tata Group epitomizes the concept of trusteeship and the philanthropic tradition of the Parsi community. Another Parsi business family is the Godrej group. Interestingly, Parsis form only 0.0069 per cent of India's population (Noble, 2007).

The Bajaj group, another Indian business house, strives for the common good with a number of philanthropic activities for rural development, education, women, Gandhian studies, health and the environment (Bajaj Group, 2007). This group has a number of businesses including electricals, automobiles and finance.

The Birla conglomerate consists of a number of groups such as the Aditya Birla group, the M.P. Birla group and the Yash Birla Group. The Aditya Birla Group (2008), which has the world's largest aluminium rolling company and is a leader in viscose staple fibre, is involved in transformational work in 3700 villages reaching out to 7 million people annually. The M.P. Birla Group which owns over 500 factories in a range of industries such as textiles, cables, automobiles, paper and cement, is known for its philanthropic and educational activities (M.P. Birla Group, 2008). And the Yash Birla group dealing in auto components, infrastructure and real estate and power solutions, calls on its employees to reflect on the conch to find the sublime presence of Lord Ganesha to bless the movement called move ahead and stay ahead (Yash Birla Group, 2008).

Information technology moguls such as Narayana Murthy's Infosys Technologies believes in 'Beyond Business' and stresses the aspect that as corporate citizens with conscience, initiatives must contribute toward making efforts to make a difference to the global community in a spirit of responsibility (Infosys, 2008). Azim Premji the founder of Wipro Limited, India's biggest and most competitive IT company, has a foundation whose vision of influencing the lives of millions of children in India is facilitated through the importance given to the universalization of primary education and programmes which cover over 5000 rural schools (Wipro, 2004a). The company encourages its employees to reflect on the following: 'I am the litmus tests for my integrity. For integrity is the manifestation of conscience' (Wipro, 2004b). Another example of the mix of religious values in action is that of Sunil Bharti Mittal, the group chairman and Chief Executive Officer (CEO) of Bharti Enterprises, who has transformed the telecommunications industry through its world-class services built on leading edge technologies (Bharti Enterprises, 2007). The company is involved through the Bharti Foundation in helping underprivileged children and young people of India realize their potential.

Thus a cogent case can be made for the interweaving of religious values with that of business, based on examples of modern-day entrepreneurs, or contemporary religious merchants, whose merchandise is not religion, but whose products, processes, strategies and wealth spill over into a desire to be of service to the larger community, in a spirit of service which also results in a positive reputation for good corporate social responsibility. And in the recent Indian budget, a risk capital fund is being created in the Small Industries and Development Bank of India (Indiabudget, 2008), which can cushion new and small entrepreneurs as they seek to shed the trappings of the past which prevented their movements into entrepreneurship.

In India, the drivers of growth continue to be services and manufacturing, which are estimated to grow at 10.7 per cent and 9.4 per cent respectively (Indiabudget, 2008). The India Vision 2020 (Gupta, 2002) stresses that the future should be both comprehensive and harmonious, and it should serve to awaken in all Indians 'a greater awareness of our cultural and spiritual strengths – which formed the bedrock of our past achievements and should form the foundation of our future accomplishments. Some of our traditions must change, but knowledge, in essence, is our greatest endowment' (p. 1). The India Vision states that by 2020 the people of India will be more numerous, better educated, healthier and more prosperous than at any time in India's long history, and it visualizes a nation bustling with energy, entrepreneurship and innovation (Gupta, 2002). It is projected that 'SMEs will play a crucial role in ensuring India's international competitiveness and its rapid assimilation of new technologies' (Gupta, 2002, p. 37). It is extremely heartening that pundits of India's future write that 'health, education and employment opportunities for all, and awareness of our rich spiritual and cultural heritage are the essential bases for fostering self-respect and self esteem' (Gupta, 2002, pp. 96–7).

CONCLUDING COMMENTS

This chapter has presented a broad spectrum view of entrepreneurship in India, linking the sacred with the secular, through a historical and contemporary context. The sacred or religious is expressed not only through specific religious castes or adherents of various religions whose entrepreneurship was linked to the fact that the individual was born into a particular caste or business family, but also through community activity and a value system whose anchor is religion or the spiritual values deeply enmeshed in an individual. Examples of entrepreneurship from various religions in India have been offered, and it seems apparent that in India there is a strong meshing of God and mammon where one gives to both 'Caesar and God' in the practice of entrepreneurship in India.

There are numerous areas of research that require more fulsome attention, such as the creation of young entrepreneurs, transfer of learning from enterprises in a particular community and state to other states and communities in India, transfer of international knowledge and immersion in entrepreneurship of other countries which can be transferred to India, women entrepreneurs' understanding of the mix of the sacred and secular, longitudinal studies on the effect of training and opportunities of members of lower/backward castes, and the impact of entrepreneurship programmes in tertiary institutes on students as future entrepreneurs.

In pulling together the various strands of this chapter, some broad principles for consideration with reference to entrepreneurship and religion in India are the following:

1. India is a pluri-religious nation and its people tend to be intrinsically and extrinsically religious and spiritual.
2. The outward expression or exteriority of the interiority or value systems is approached in various ways by individuals in various contexts, articulated through different trajectories and with a range of outlets for the linkage of entrepreneurship with religion. Proselytization of a particular religion is not linked to business interests.
3. By far Indians do not seem to have political expansionist tendencies as evidenced by India's history through the millennia. However, there seems to be a strong merchant ethos which stimulates and inspires individuals towards scanning the environment and seeking entrepreneurial opportunities for wealth creation and wealth sharing.
4. Entrepreneurship and religion are intertwined and their reciprocal play is evidenced in various manifestations such as the business castes and families, as well as the need for empowering individuals who fall outside this privileged circle, and may be trapped in aspects of caste which prevent economic mobility. Propelling 'lower/backward' caste members into a range of employment and enterprise continues to be a major challenge.

5. Indian entrepreneurs by far do not seem to broadcast their religiosity but rather seem to express it through social entrepreneurship and other reputation-enhancing deeds. However, for some entrepreneurs the convergence of their business and religion results in the construction of edifices of worship such as temples. Progressive religious merchants increasingly realize the need to plough back into Indian society their entrepreneurial gains in seeking a more equitable distribution of wealth, skills and knowledge. Thus a cyclical process is set in motion where wealth creation leads to a spiral of betterment for surrounding villages and its people, as well as for employees of the enterprise.
6. Spirituality is like an invisible cloak and a deep anchoring force in many Indian entrepreneurs. One could in fact cogently put forward the notion that there seems to be a collective unconscious, not a fundamentalist version, but the middle path of moderation – Buddha's *majjhima patipada* in the intertwining of religious sentiment with entrepreneurship in India.

It is these religious merchants who can ensure that while India moves forward with speed on the world stage its speed and activities continue to be moderated by minds and hearts, which in seeking to create wealth, catch a glimpse of the infinite. For, paradoxically, in living one's life and facing one's demons, a life well lived is often defined by what one gives back – to society, the nation, the world. Perhaps it is the mix of the temple and the bazaar, or the contemporary religious merchants who can weave a happier and more harmonious world as they control, generate and distribute wealth.

ACKNOWLEDGEMENTS

My gratitude for input into this chapter to: Atul Sinha, Cate Bain, Léo-Paul Dana, Kaushikbhai Patel, Meena Talim and Uday Halankar. However my greatest asset and thankfulness is to my son Isaac for his comprehension of my status quo.

REFERENCES

Aditya Birla Group (2008), 'Global Vision Indian Values', retrieved 28 March 2008 from http://www.adityabirla.com/social_projects/overview.htm.

Arora, A. and Athreye, S. (2002), 'The software industry and India's economic development', *Information Economics and Policy*, **14**, 245–73.

Audretsch, D., Boente, W. and Tamvada, J. (2007), 'Religion and Entrepreneurship', retrieved 24 March 2008 from http://www.iza.org/conference_files/worldb2007/tamvada_j3400.pdf.
Bajaj Group (2007), 'Beyond Profits', retrieved 29 March 2008 from http://www.bajajelectricals.com/t-philan.aspx.
Bal, G. and Judge, P.S. (2001), 'Terrorism and rural Entrepreneurship in Punjab', *Journal of Entrepreneurship*, **10** (2), 191–208.
Bharti Enterprises (2007), 'Bharti Enterprises', retrieved 29 March 2008 from http://www.bharti.com/117.html.
Census India (2001), 'Religious Composition', retrieved 25 March 2008 from http://www.censusindia.gov.in/Census_Data_2001/India_at_glance/religion.aspx.
Chakravarti, R. (2000), 'Nakhudas and Nauvittakas: Ship-Owning Merchants in the West Coast of India (c. AD 1000–1500)', *Journal of the Economic and Social History of the Orient*, **43** (1), 34–64.
Central Intelligence Agency (CIA) (2008), 'The World Factbook – India', retrieved 25 March 2008 from https://www.cia.gov/library/publications/the-world-factbook/print/in.html.
Dana, L. (2000), 'Creating Entrepeneurs in India', *Journal of Small Business Management*, **38** (1), 86–91.
Das Gupta, A. (2001), *The World of the Indian Ocean Merchant 1500–1800*, New Delhi: Oxford University Press.
Dobbin, C. (1996), *Asian Entrepreneurial Minorities: Conjoint Communities in the Making of the World-Economy 1570–1940*, Richmond: Curzon Press.
Dossani, R. and Kenney, M. (2002), 'Creating an Environment for Venture Capital in India', *World Development*, **30** (2), 227–53.
Economist (2006/07), 'Face Value: Delhi Dreams', *The Economist*, 23 December–5 January, 104.
Ferguson, N. (2002), *Empire: The Rise and Demise of the British World Order and the Lessons for Global Power*, London: Allen Lane.
Ghosh, R., Gupta, M. and Dhar, S. N. (1998), 'Women and Entrepreneurship in India', in R.N. Kanungo (ed.), *Entrepreneurship & Innovation: Models for Development*, New Delhi: Sage, pp. 156–75.
Gopinath, S. (2008), 'Development through Planning, Markets or Decentralisation', retrieved 26 March 2008 from http://www.rbi.org.in/scripts/BS_ViewBulletin.aspx?Id=9160.
Gupta, S. (2002), 'India Vision 2020', Planning Commission, Government of India, New Delhi, retrieved 26 March 2008 from http://www.planningcommission.nic.in/reports/genrep/pl_vsn2020.pdf.
Indiabudget (2008), 'Key features of Budget 2008–2009', retrieved 26 March 2008 from http://indiabudget.nic.in/ub2008-09/bh/bh1.pdf.
Indian Embassy (2008), 'Doing Business in India', retrieved 26 March from http://www.indianembassy.org/newsite/Doing_business_In_India.
Infosys (2008), 'Beyond Business', retrieved 27 March 2008 from http://www.infosys.com/beyond-business/default.asp.
Khanna, V. (2005), 'The economic history of India of the corporate form in ancient India', retrieved on 17 February 2007 from http://papers.sssrn.com/sol3/papers.cfm?abstract_id=796464.
Lobe, K. and Berkes, F. (2004), 'The padu system of community-based fisheries management: change and local institutional innovation in South India', *Marine Policy*, **28**, 271–81.

M.P. Birla Group (2008), 'M.P. Birla Group', retrieved 29 March 2008 from http://www.mpbirla.com.

Markovitz, C. (1999), 'Indian Merchant Networks Outside India in the 19th and 20th Centuries: A Preliminary Survey', *Modern Asian Studies*, **33**, 883–911.

Matchett, F. (2003), 'The Puranas', in G. Flood (ed.), *The Blackwell Companion to Hinduism*. Oxford: Blackwell, pp. 129–43.

Nafziger, E.W. (1971), 'Indian Entrepreneurship: A Survey', in P. Kilby (ed.), *Entrepreneurship and Economic Development*, New York: Free Press, pp. 287–316.

Nafziger, E.W. (1975), 'Class, Caste and Community of South Indian Industrialists: An Examination of the Horatio Alger Model', *Journal of Developmental Studies*, **11** (2), 131–48.

Noble, T. (2007), 'Counting Parsis', retrieved 29 March 2008 from http://www.himalmag.com/2007/january/report4.htm.

Noronha, F. (2007), 'Social entrepreneurs set out to change India', retrieved 24 March 2008 from http://www.indiaenews.com/business/20070107/34879.htm.

Palsetia, J.S. (2005), 'Merchant Charity and Public Identity Formation in Colonial India: The Case of Jamsetjee Jejeebhoy', *Journal of Asian and African Studies*, **40** (3), 197–217.

Pederson, J. (2000), 'Explaining Economic Liberalization in India: State and Society Perspective', *World Development*, **28** (2), 265–82.

Pio, E. (2005a), 'Eastern Karma: Perspectives on Corporate Citizenship', *Journal of Corporate Citizenship*, **19** (Autumn), 65–78

Pio, E. (2005b), 'The *Guru-shishya* Process for Radiating Knowledge in Organizations', *Knowledge and Process Management*, **12** (4), 278–87.

Pio, E. (2007a), 'Gurus and Indian Epistemologies: Parables of Labour Intensive Organizations', *Journal of Management Inquiry*, **16** (2), 180–92.

Pio, E. (2007b), 'HRM and Indian Epistemologies: A Review and Avenues for Future Research', *Human Resource Management Review*, **17** (3), 319–35.

Pluss, C. (2005), 'Globalizing Ethnicity with Multi-local Identifications: The Parsee, Indian Muslim and Sephardic Trade Diasporas in Hong Kong', in I.B. McCabe, G. Harlaftis and I.P. Minoglou (eds), *Diaspora Entrepreneurial Networks: Four Centuries of History*, New York: Berg, pp. 245–68.

Porter, E.G. and Nagarajan, K.V. (2005), 'Successful Women Entrepreneurs as Pioneers: Results from a Study Conducted in Karaidudi, Tamil Nadu, India', *Journal of Small Business and Entrepreneurship*, **18** (1), 39–52.

Prakash, O. (2004), 'The Indian Maritime Merchant, 1500–1800', *Journal of the Economic and Social History of the Orient*, **47** (3), 435–57.

Ray, R. (ed.) (1992), *Entrepreneurship and Industry in India, 1800–1947*, Delhi: Oxford University Press.

Sabbarwal, S. (1994), 'Determinants of Entrepreneurial Start-ups: A Study of Industrial Units in India', *Journal of Entrepreneurship*, **3** (1), 69–80.

Sen, A. (2005), *The Argumentative Indian*, London: Penguin.

Sen, A. (2006), *Identity and Violence: The Illusion of Destiny*, London: Allen Lane.

Self Employed Women's Association (SEWA) (2008), 'About Us', retrieved 26 March 2008 from http://www.sewa.org/aboutus/index.asp.

Shivani, S., Mukherjee, S.K. and Sharan, R. (2006), 'Socio-cultural Influences on Indian Entrepreneurs: The Need for Appropriate Structural Interventions', *Journal of Asian Economics*, **17**, 5–13.

Skaria, G. (ed.) (2006), *India 2006: Taking India to the World*, London: World Link.
Tata (2008), 'About Us', retrieved 27 March 2008 from http://www.tata.com/0_about_us/index.htm.
Wani, V.P., Garg, T.K. and Sharma, S. (2003), 'Developing a Techno-entrepreneurial Workforce for Effective Technological Innovation: Its Necessity for the Sustainable Development of SSEs in India', *International Journal of Entrepreneurship and Innovation Management*, **3** (5/6), 492–508.
Wani, V.P., Garg, T.K. and Sharma, S. (2005), 'Engineer as Entrepreneur: A Necessity of Successful Product Innovation in the Small-scale Industry Sector in India', in J.R. McIntyre and I. Alon (eds), *Business and Management Education in Transitioning and Developing Countries: A Handbook*, Armonk, NY: M.E. Sharpe, pp. 39–57.
Wipro (2004a), 'Wipro Cares', retrieved 26 March 2008 from http://www.wipro-corporate.com/wiprocares/summercamp.htm.
Wipro (2004b), 'Spirit of Wipro', Retrieved on 26 March 2008 from http://www.wiprocorporate.com/Spirit/spiritofwipro-index.asp.htm.
Yash Birla Group (2008), available at http://www.yashbirlagroup.com/.

2. Promethian Values in New Mexico*

Léo-Paul Dana and Robert Brent Anderson[1]

We were and still are a communal society in architecture and thought. (Tessie Naranjo, quoted by Roberts, 1996, p. 93)

INTRODUCTION

A distance of 72 miles from Santa Fe (the oldest seat of government in the United States), or 123 miles from Albuquerque, Taos is a small municipality in New Mexico. It was formerly known as Don Fernando de Taos, and also as Fernandez de Taos.

Three miles north, 7112 feet above sea level, at the base of the Sangre de Cristos Mountains, is Taos Pueblo, also known as the Place of the Red Willows (as it sits on both banks of Red Willow Creek). In Spanish, *pueblo* means village or town and in English Pueblo has become a general name for sedentary (in contrast to nomadic, as was the case with Apache and Navajo) American Indians who traditionally dwelt in sun-dried adobe or stone buildings in the North American Southwest. (Adobe is a mixture of earth, straw and water poured into forms and dried under the desert sun; the bricks are bonded together with the same mixture.) Taos Pueblo is considered to be the oldest continuously inhabited community in the United States.

Goddard (1913) classified the Pueblo peoples as a special group, apart from other American Indian groups. Dozier observed, 'Pueblo communities are set apart from their indigenous neighbors by two main criteria: (1) farming as a principal basis of subsistence, and (2) residence in compact villages' (1964, p. 79). Vlasich (2005) noted that the practice of irrigational agriculture always set the Pueblo Indians apart from other groups of New Mexico. A communal building of a pueblo is a solid structure of adobe bricks or stone set in clay and mortar. Rooms are square, built in terraced storeys. The thick flat roof of one storey is accessible by a moveable ladder from the level below. In former times, access to the interiors was by ladders to trapdoors in the roofs, as outer walls had neither windows nor doors; this was a precaution against intruders. Stirling explained, 'At Taos the structure consists of a terraced pyramid built by erecting a large rectangular building with five stories, each smaller by the width of a room than the one below it' (1940, p. 565). The two main buildings in Taos Pueblo are the oldest continuously occupied structures in the United States. An adobe wall surrounds Taos Pueblo, serving as a boundary around a settlement where traditional cultural beliefs are nurtured.

Laxalt wrote of three ways of life in New Mexico, 'New Mexican life is a mélange of three cultures – Spanish, Indian, and Anglo (the local idiom for anyone not Spanish and not Indian)' (1970, p. 299). The objective of this article is to give an account of the Indian community of Taos Pueblo, a sovereign Native American community. This settlement is the only living Native American community that is designated both a World Heritage Site and a National Historic Landmark.

Simpich referred to Taos Pueblo people as 'lords of the Southwest in Coronado's day' (1929, p. v). As will be discussed below, Taos is one of the eastern pueblos.

THE NEED FOR RESEARCH ABOUT EASTERN PUEBLOS

Taos Pueblo is one of 19 pueblos in New Mexico. The others are: Acoma; Cochití; Isleta; Jémez; Laguna; Nambé (traditionally a primary religious centre for Pueblo people); Picurís (the smallest and most secluded of the pueblos); Pojoaque (home of the Cities of Gold Casino); Sandia (which operates a buffalo preserve as well as a hotel and casino); San Felipe; San Ildefonso; San Juan (host to the Oke-Owingeh Arts Cooperative); Santa Ana;[2] Santa Clara (long known for glossy black pottery made by local women); Santo Domingo; Tesuque;[3] Zia; and the successor to the pueblo of Hawikuh, namely Zuñi, one of few groups among whom traditional weaving survived after the arrival of machine-woven textiles. The Zuñi people hunted wild turkeys until 1938 (Simpich, 1938). Today, the Zuñi community is well-known for needlepoint, inlay jewellery, and stone carvings.

The pueblos are classified according to three language groupings: (i) Keresans; (ii) Tanoans; and (iii) Zuñis, who speak a language of Zufiian linguistic stock that is spoken only among this community. Keres speakers reside in Acoma, Cochití, Laguna, San Felipe (the most conservative Keresan pueblo), Santa Ana, Santo Domingo, and Zia. There are three Tanoan subcategories: (i) Tewa (the focus of Creamer and Haas, 1991); (ii) Tiwa; and (iii) Towa. Tewa can be heard in Nambé, Pojoaque, San Ildefonso, San Juan, Santa Clara, and Tesuque. Northern Tiwa is spoken in Picurís and Taos. Southern Tiwa is spoken in Isleta and Sandia. Jémez is the only remaining Towa-speaking pueblo. Dozier noted, 'Tanoan village communities have a *Katcina* cult or some vestige of an organization concerned with supernatural beings' (1964, p. 86). As noted by Hodge (1896), a fourth linguistic stock once existed, namely Shoshonean, which is now extinct.

The above are grouped according to geographic location as well as along linguistic roots. Located in the region of the Rio Grande drainage, the eastern pueblos are Cochití, Isleta, Jémez, Nambé, Picurís, Pojoaque, San Felipe, San Ildefonso, San Juan, Sandia, Santa Ana, Santa Clara, Santo Domingo, Taos, Tesuque, and Zia. The western group (see also Eggan, 1950) consists of Acoma, Laguna and Zuñi. Hawley (1937) classified the pueblos of Acoma and Laguna as transitional, rather than specifically eastern or western. Among the western pueblos, spirits called *Kachinas* are revered as deliverers of good, and dolls depicting them are given to children.

There has long been a wealth of literature about the western pueblos of New Mexico (Judd, 1923). Espinosa (1918) studied all three. Other scholars focused on one:

- *Acoma Pueblo*: A classic study of Acoma is White (1928); today, Acoma is well-known for its Sky City Cultural Center, open since May 2006, as well as the Acoma oil, cattle and commercial enterprises.
- *Laguna Pueblo*: Garloch (1944) provided an economic analysis of the Laguna agricultural sector. Today, where the world's largest open-pit uranium mine used to be, the Pueblo of Laguna developed one of the state's largest enterprises, a hi-tech manufacturing and technical services company, called Laguna Industries.
- *Zuñi Pueblo*: An early account of the Zuñis appears in Judd (1923). Benedict (1935b) focused on Zuñi mythology. Li (1937) also researched the Zuñis. Today, tribal business ventures include: Zuni Entrepreneurial Enterprises; Zuni Forest Products & Services Enterprise; and Zuni Technologies Inc.

There is also a rich literature about western pueblos elsewhere in the Southwest (Brandt, 1954; Thompson, 1950; Thompson and Joseph, 1944; Wall and Masayesva, 2004; 2007). The western pueblos continue to be a subject of considerable research (Damp et la., 2002; Norton et al., 1998).

The eastern pueblos have given rise to some fascinating articles, but relatively fewer than their western counterparts. The role of economics in Cochití Pueblo is examined by Lange (1953). Simpich compared pueblos, and suggested that Isleta Indians were 'far more sophisticated and progressive' (1938, p. 536) than Zuñis. Ellis (1954) wrote about Jémez with a focus on the Corn Dance. A classic study of San Felipe is White (1932). Whitman (1947) researched San Ildefonso, which has long been known for glossy black pottery made by local women. Laxalt (1970) discussed his experience in Santo Domingo. Ellis (1966) provides a history of Zia Pueblo. Ellis et al. (1943) analyzed the Zia economy. Why have the eastern pueblos provided relatively fewer articles than was possible in the west? Dozier proposed an explanation, suggesting:

> No single Pueblo community among the Keresan and Tanoan Pueblos has received the attention and study accorded the Hopi and Zuñi Pueblos. The reason for this is obvious. The Eastern Pueblo Indians resent being studied and hence it is difficult for an investigator to get information out of them. Adverse contact with the Spanish is undoubtedly the cause of this reticence; the Western Pueblos were not as long or as intimately associated with Spanish rulers. It is understandable, therefore, why we have so much more information about the Pueblos most remote from former Spanish control, the Zuñi and Hopi. (1964, p. 84)

Grant wrote:

> Every now and then, some one, pencil in hand, comes to Taos, stays a few days, bent on questioning the Indians . . . To these the red man gives an easy affirmative, . . . Not long ago, one of the older men was heard to give such answers. 'What did you tell that fellow all those lies for John,' said a bystander later. 'Oh,' said the Indian with a faint smile, 'He likes it'. (1925, p. 5)

HISTORICAL OVERVIEW

Legend tells us that Taos Pueblo was founded by a great chief who followed an eagle and led his people up a stream to the mountains. The eagle dropped two feathers, one on the north side of the stream, and the other on the south. At this place, the women built adobe homes on both banks of Red Willow Creek (see Figure 2.1). The homes are physically next to one another resulting in two big structures, *Hlaauma* (North House, shown in Figure 2.2) and *Hlaukkkwima* (South House).

As noted by Reno (1963), Taos Indians know their history through two sources, firstly from ceremonies, songs and oral accounts, and secondly through research. Sutherland wrote that the Pueblo Indians were the 'most advanced aboriginal culture surviving in North America' (1949, p. 783). Descendants of the Anasazi culture, the Pueblo people have the oldest culture north of Mexico. For discussions of the Anasazi, see Reed (1946) and Roberts (1996).

Figure 2.1 Wooden bridge across Red Willow Creek (photograph by Léo-Paul Dana)

The Taos Pueblo people are successors of the Basket Makers who inhabited the American Southwest over 2000 years ago (Coze, 1957). Francisco Vásquez de Coronado and his conquistadors came to this region looking for gold (see Newman, 1993) and with his soldiers he discovered the Taos community in 1540. In the wake of Franciscan missionaries, colonists followed in 1598 and that year Don Juan de Oñate 'standing among old cottonwoods along the Rio Grande, solemnly claimed this land for King Philip II of Spain. The kingdom was called New Mexico' (McDowell, 1987, p. 614). Laxalt recounted, 'In 1598 Spanish settlers began moving northward from Mexico. They founded Santa Fe – La Villa de Santa Fé de los Españoles – in the winter of 1609–1610' (1970, p. 304). The Spanish introduced cattle, goats, horses, and sheep (Simpich, 1938) to the Pueblo communities, and wool eventually replaced cotton as the principal textile.

Until the mid-seventeenth century, priests whipped Pueblo people who practiced their traditional religion (Scholes, 1937). Working from Taos, a spiritual leader from San Juan Pueblo led a bloody revolt in 1680 and this drove Spanish rule from New Mexico. As noted by Stirling, 'In the face of growing colonization of the Southwest, the Pueblo Indians rebelled in 1680 and killed or drove out all the Spaniards. However, the Spanish

Figure 2.2 North House (photograph by Léo-Paul Dana)

soon reconquered the region' (1940, p. 550). Sutherland wrote, 'In 1821 Mexican rule succeeded Spanish; in 1846 the United States took over' (1949, p. 824). Laxalt reported, 'In 1847 the Taos Pueblo Indians joined with dissident Mexicans to resist a new invader, the Anglo. They shot US Governor Charles Bent full of arrows and scalped him while he was still alive' (1970, p. 335).

After the armistice of the Mexican War, in 1848, the Treaty of Guadalupe Hidalgo formally placed New Mexico under US jurisdiction. Laxalt noted, 'the last of the magnificent Apache warriors were vanquished in 1886' (1970, p. 304). By then, traders introduced vegetable-dyed yarn and life for Indigenous people was changing rapidly as the number of immigrants was escalating. German immigrants constituted one of the largest immigrants groups to New Mexico. Those who came before the railroad in 1880 were more interested in acculturation than in preserving their German heritage; those after kept their German identity (Tomas, 2005).

In 1906, land was taken from Taos Pueblo to be preserved as part of the Carson National Forest. As such, the land was placed under management of the US Forest Service, which proclaimed the supremacy of man over Nature. This was very problematic for the Taos Pueblo people who disagreed with that viewpoint. Blue Lake was, and continues to be, considered sacred. Trosper noted an account:

> There is nothing the human hand has made. The lake is our church. The mountain is our tabernacle. The evergreen trees are our living saints. . . . We pray to the water, the sun, the clouds, the sky, the deer. Without them we could not exist. They give us food, drink, physical power, knowledge. (1995, p. 86)

In January 1912, New Mexico became the forty-seventh state of the United States; the Pueblos maintained an aloof independence (Belknap, 1964). Dozier noted that, in 1913, Pueblo Indians were given the same status as other American Indians in the United States, and cited the 1913 decision of the Unites States Supreme Court,

> The people of the Pueblos, although sedentary rather than nomadic in their inclinations and disposed to peace and industry, are nevertheless Indians in race, customs and domestic government, always living in separate and isolated communities, adhering to primitive modes of life, largely influenced by superstition and fetishism, and chiefly governed according to the crude customs inherited from their ancestors. They are essentially a simple, uninformed, and inferior people. (1964, p. 85)

In recognition of their contribution to World War I, in 1924 American Indians were given American citizenship (Reno, 1963).

A few years later, Simpich wrote about Taos, 'It has only about 2000 inhabitants now; it had about that many in 1680 . . . For its size, Taos may well be the most interesting town in America. Its unspoiled aboriginal life, its odd communal houses' (1929, p. 248). Parsons (1939) discussed the overestimation of population in the pueblos.

According to Vlasich (2005), Taos Pueblo had 401 people in 1890, 414 in 1900, and 773 in 1936. Siegel (1949) reported the population of Taos in 1947 as 913, and stated, 'Taos, therefore, is one of the most rapidly expanding pueblos. The continuing population increase has begun to make serious inroads into the previous subsistence economy, and has enmeshed more and more individuals in the money economy of their neighbors' (1949, p. 567).

The census in 2000 counted 4484 people at Taos Pueblo. About 150 of these live within the pueblo all year, and many of these are elderly (see Figure 2.3). Choosing to retain their tradition, members of the old pueblo do not use electricity or indoor plumbing.

Many owners of homes in the North or South buildings of the pueblo actually reside in homes near their fields, or in modern homes on Taos Pueblo land but outside the old walls of Taos Pueblo. In the pueblo, tribal

Figure 2.3 Among the elderly (photograph by Léo-Paul Dana)

members have decided not to use electricity or indoor plumbing. Whereas life in Taos Pueblo is traditional, outside the pueblo walls, residents use modern conveniences. Alcohol is prohibited on the entire reservation.

RELIGION

Benedict (1935a) noted the absence of Dionysian values among Pueblo Indians. A possible explanation is that religion encouraged a Promethean mindset. Traditionally, Pueblo religion was pantheistic and deeply spiritual. It constituted an important part of daily life, as Pueblo society was founded on a set of divine instructions from the Great Spirit. The people were told to plant and harvest in order to survive. Rather than have dominion over Nature, the Pueblo people were instructed by the Great Spirit to be a component of it and to obey the laws of Nature, under the leadership of a spiritual guide referred to as a Cacique.

Taos Pueblo people explained to the author that they have preserved their traditional culture throughout history, often adopting superficial changes but maintaining the old ways and beliefs in secrecy. Genesis, according to Pueblo belief, was as follows: 'At the beginning of all beginnings our ancestors came up out of the earth, until they were living beneath Sandy Place Lake to the north. The world under the lake was like this one, but dark. Spirits, people, and animals lived together; death was unknown' (Ortiz, 1991, p. 7). The Pueblo tribes developed a complex mythology and religion, some aspects of which continue to be observed, in addition to adopted Western religion. Stirling wrote:

> When the Pueblo wears about his neck a small stone image of a mountain lion, it represents much more than meets the eye. The mere carving of the image is but the first step in the preparation of his fetish. The priest of the proper society must perform over it a long ceremony involving hours of prayer and offerings and the placing of the figure on the altar of the hunting society. Here amid sacred objects filled with supernatural powers it becomes charged with the spirit of the Mountain Lion God, the master deer hunter.
>
> When worn by the hunter, the fetish thus impregnated transmits its power to him. Whenever he starts out for deer, he prays over his little fetish, offering pollen and tobacco to the ancestral Mountain Lion. (1940, p. 572)

As reported by Sutherland, 'Pueblo Indians, baptized as Christians, accept the white man's saints even while carrying out their old tribal rites' (1949, p. 817). Alongside Catholicism, Pueblo people retain ancient beliefs and many Indigenous rituals are practiced, often in secrecy and in sacred religious shrines that serve as ceremonial chambers known as *kivas*. Each pueblo has at least two *kivas*, and many are underground. It is believed that all mankind descended from ancestral twins, and in the centre of each *kiva* is a small hole in the floor, representing the *sipapu*, the sacred place wherefrom the mythological ancestral twins are believed to have emerged.

Coze explained, 'Pueblo Indians of Arizona and New Mexico venerate a multitude of spirits ranking just below the major gods. They call these supernatural beings Kachinas, from the Hopi words meaning father of life' (1957, p. 219). For a discussion of Kachina dolls, see Colton (1949).

Coze elaborated, 'At festival times the Kachinas make visits to the pueblos, bringing the blessings of rain and fertility, teaching discipline, and rewarding good' (1957, p. 219). Indeed, according to Pueblo beliefs, life and blessings – such as the cycle of seasons, rain, and crops – are gifts of Kachinas, who are said to live in the snow and ice of the San Francisco Mountain, an eroded strato-volcano near Flagstaff, Arizona. Coze went into further detail, 'Borrowing the bodies of living men, these lesser gods visit the villages to distribute presents and receive prayers to the gods. He who wears the mask of a Kachina believes he loses his personal identity and assumes that of the spirit' (1957, p. 219). In her book *Taos Pueblo*, Parsons (1936) reported that unlike other pueblos, Taos had neither a masked Kachina, nor a curing society. This book was reviewed by Titiev (1937).

In 1978, a federal law guaranteed the religious freedom of American

Figure 2.4 Remains of original San Geronimo Chapel (photograph by Léo-Paul Dana)

Indians. Although Christianity has not replaced traditional religion, pueblos have churches as well as *kivas.* St. Jerome is the patron saint of Taos Pueblo, and this pueblo has a chapel named after him. San Geronimo Chapel was completed in 1850 to replace the original church destroyed during war. Of the original, only the bell tower still stands (see Figure 2.4).

Vlasich (2005) argued that given the high risk involved in self-employed agricultural activities, the Pueblo Indians developed a sophisticated religious ceremonialism to accompany labour in the field.

In Taos Pueblo, Native rituals persevere in daily life. Many youths who have left Taos return from time to time to regain contact with the social and religious values of their tradition. One young interviewee told the author that religion is less important for her generation than was the case among others, especially among those who had strayed away from farming. Yet ceremonialism is very much enjoyed.

WHERE THE ECONOMY MEETS RELIGION

During the mid-nineteenth century the Taos Indians had an annual buffalo hunt to procure meat. The last group buffalo hunt of Taos Indians took place in 1884 (Grant, 1925). During the early 1920s, Grant wrote, 'There are still a few Indians living who can tell of buffalo hunts though each year their number is less' (1925, p. 83).

Coan (1925) estimated that 75 per cent of the sheep in New Mexico in 1880 were controlled by 20 families, of whom 80 per cent were Indigenous. Focusing on Pueblo Indians, Simpich elaborated, 'These Indians own and farm much near-by land, have their own herds, vehicles, and work animals' (1940, p. 713).

Stirling wrote about the pueblos, 'These communities are primarily dependent upon farming. To maize, beans, and squash have been added many introduced crops, such as wheat, watermelons, and various vegetables. Wild plants are used to some extent for food, and hunting adds variety to the diet' (1940, p. 565). During the following decade, McClelland and Friedman suggested:

> that cultures which are concerned with achievement are likely to stress independence training in childhood, which in turn produces a higher level of achievement motivation in members of the culture, at least as reflected in their folk tales. These stories in turn reinforce the achievement orientation which leads to a stress on independence training and so on in a chain of mutually reinforcing events which illustrates nicely what anthropologists mean by such terms as 'culture pattern' or 'cultural value' orientation. (1952, p. 249)

Dozier (1964) wrote about change and Westernization of the pueblos; he distinguished between two types of changes that can occur in an Indigenous community: (i) Indigenous changes arising from within a community or due to contact with other Indigenous people; and (ii) acculturation, resulting from contact with whites. About the pueblos, he observed, 'The first major change was the shift from subsistence farming to a credit system . . . The second dramatic shift, from credit buying to a cash economy, was brought about by the influx of tourists and the operators of craft shops who bought the handicrafts directly from the Indians, paying cash' (Dozier, 1964, p. 92).

Laxalt compared, 'Unlike the Navajos and Apaches, the 960 Indians of Taos Pueblo . . . do not welcome the Anglos' wealth or ways' (1970, p. 335). In particular, Taos Pueblo people have had difficulty with the US Forest Service assumption that man has supremacy over Nature. Trosper wrote that Taos Pueblo religion requires:

> people to adapt their lives and activities to our natural surroundings so that men and nature mutually support the life common to both. The idea that man must subdue nature and bend its processes to his purposes is repugnant . . . Our religion is based upon the unity of man with nature in the Rio Pueblo watershed. Any outside interference with natural conditions of the watershed interferes with our religion. (1995, p. 85)

Figure 2.5 Selling to the tourists (photograph by Léo-Paul Dana)

The pueblo economy today includes art, handicrafts, tourism (see Figure 2.5), retailing, gambling and wages, as well as agriculture. Livestock rearing is important as are several crops including chilli peppers, cotton and squash. Each pueblo cultivates fields in common. The fields are generally attended to by the men. Pueblo men also continue to be skilled weavers, producing cotton clothing and woollen goods including blankets as well as garments. Women are responsible for the preparation of meals; they tend to children and they are often involved in making pottery. Selling handicrafts supplements income.

At Taos Pueblo, there are families who continue to farm. Tribal members plant beans, corn, and squash, along with various vegetables that are part of the traditional diet. Taos Pueblo people supplement subsistence income through hunting in the mountains.

Taos Pueblo also thrives on tourism. Many of the Taos Pueblo tribal people are artists and have shops in the village. Admission is charged to visitors and revenues collected support administrative entities of the governing bodies.

The pueblo operates Taos Mountain Casino (the smallest one in New Mexico) with a café, a gallery, a gift shop, and a video arcade. This is not unique to Taos Pueblo. Sandia Pueblo, for instance, owns the

Sandia Resort & Casino, built on the Sandia reservation, just outside Albuquerque. As well, Tesuque Pueblo operates the Camel Rock Casino.

Individual tribal people work in various career fields on their tribal lands, including education, forestry, health care, and law enforcement. Although many Pueblo people have shifted occupations away from farming, agriculture will remain central to their culture.

CONCLUSION

Both Lasswell (1935) and Parsons (1936) mentioned a conflict between ideal and actual patterns, as strongly valued collectivism was strained by individualism. Lasswell (1935) suggested that Pueblo Indian religion was preserving the integrity of communal life. In contrast, Parsons (1936) predicted the disappearance of ceremonialism and assimilation into American life. During the following decade, Siegel wrote, 'Because of frequent and marked overt manifestations of individualism among its members, Taos has evoked special interest among the students of pueblo society' (1949, p. 562).

Over seven decades later, we observe that both Lasswell (1935) and Parsons (1936) were partially correct in their predictions. Ceremonialism has not disappeared, but it may have less religious meaning than in the past, and possibly more entertainment value. Vlasich wrote, 'A half-century ago some experts predicted the demise of Pueblo religion, but these projections have proven to be false . . . there has been a revival of ceremonial life' (2005, p. 293). Yet, observing the young generation, one sees that Pueblo Indian values have evolved, with individualism having become socially acceptable, as a *complement to communalism rather than a replacement.*

Nevertheless, ethnic boundaries remain highly pronounced. Externally obvious ethnic markers include phenotype, style, dress, values, and manner. Although cultural content has been evolving, a focus on boundary maintenance is evident. To a degree, ethnic identity appears to be reactive to inter-group contact as opposed to a feature of isolation, while ethnic boundaries represent strategies to exercise claims over resources. Barth's thesis is relevant here as co-existence of groups within one ecological niche can be stressful, 'Different ethnic groups will establish themselves in stable co-residence in an area if they exploit different ecologic niches, and especially if they can thus establish symbiotic economic relations' (1956, p. 1088). In the area surrounding Taos, Rodriguez (1987) noted that control over land and water was the primary source of contentions in the relations among Pueblo people and other groups. With regards to the

Figure 2.6 *Adobe* horno *(photograph by Léo-Paul Dana)*

Taos Pueblo's water rights claims to the Rio Hondo and the Rio Pueblo de Taos, the Draft Taos Pueblo Water Rights Settlement Agreement was only released in 2006.

Laxalt wrote,

> As protection against enemies, Indians built their pueblos, or villages, as high as five stories, with no openings on the ground level . . . Taos stands little changed . . . Women still perform such daily cores as sweeping the dirt plaza and baking in beehive ovens. Unlike other New Mexican pueblos, Taos resists modernization, banning electricity and running water. (1970, p. 316)

Roberts confirmed, 'Among Native Americans, the Pueblo peoples have been especially successful at retaining their ties to the past, maintaining their ancestral religion, and keeping their communities intact' (1996, p. 93). Nevertheless, as discussed by Tiller (1997), through increasing access to capital and to markets, tribes throughout New Mexico have been discovering new entrepreneurial opportunities, taking an active role in policy debates affecting industries, and using profits to improve infrastructure.

Taos Pueblo still resists modernization and Westernization. Bread is still baked in a beehive-like cedar-burning *horno*, made of adobe (see Figure 2.6). A cedar fire heats the oven and the hot ash is removed before

Figure 2.7 Baking (photograph by Léo-Paul Dana)

loaves are placed to bake, just as was done centuries ago (see Figure 2.7). More importantly, traditional Pueblo Indian values have survived.

Regardless of how religious a person is, values perpetuated by religion can transcend to a generation that is less practising than is the case among elders. In this case, traditional Promethean values are being perpetuated, including a highly disciplined work ethic.

NOTES

* This chapter first appeared as Léo-Paul Dana and Robert Brent Anderson (2007), 'Taos Pueblo: An Indigenous Community Holding on to Promethean Values', *Journal of Enterprising Communities: People and Places in the Global Economy*, **1** (4), 321–36. Reproduced with permission.

1. The authors thank the following for assistance: Stephanie Hainsfurther, Editor, *New Mexico Business Journal*; Melanie LaBorwit, Education Coordinator, Indian Pueblo Cultural Center, Albuquerque; and Marcie Winters, Taos Pueblo Tourism. Kind thanks also to Diane Pearson, Ethnic Studies Department, University of California, who offered helpful comments on the first version of this paper.
2. This pueblo's star enterprises include its casino and Santa Ana Agricultural Enterprises.
3. Located in the red-brown foothills of the Sangre de Cristo Mountains, near Santa Fe, Tesuque Pueblo operates the Tesuque Pueblo Flea Market.

REFERENCES

Barth, Frederik (1956), 'Ecologic Relationships of Ethnic Groups in Swat, North Pakistan', *American Anthropologist*, **58** (6), 1079–89.

Belknap, William (1964), '20th Century Indians Preserve Customs of the Cliff Dwellers', *National Geographic*, (February), 196–211.

Benedict, Ruth (1935a), *Patterns of Culture*, London: George Routledge and Sons.

Benedict, Ruth (1935b), *Zuñi Mythology*, New York: Columbia University Press.

Brandt, Richard B. (1954), *Hopi Ethics: A Theoretical Analysis*, Chicago, IL: University of Chicago Press.

Coan, Charles F. (1925), *A History of New Mexico*, Chicago, IL: American Historical Society.

Colton, Harold S. (1949), *Hopi Kachina Dolls*, Albuquerque, NM: University of New Mexico Press.

Coze, Paul (1957), 'Kachinas: Masked Dancers of the Southwest', *National Geographic*, **112** (2), 219–36.

Creamer, Winifred and Jonathan Haas (1991), 'Search for the Ancient Ones: Pueblo', *National Geographic*, **180** (4), 84–99.

Damp, Jonathan E., Stephen A. Hall and Susan J. Smith (2002), 'Early Irrigation on the Colorado Plateau Near Zuni Pueblo, New Mexico', *American Antiquity*, **67** (4), 665–76.

Dozier, Edward P. (1964), 'The Pueblo Indians of the Southwest: A Survey of the Anthropological Literature and a Review of Theory, Method, and Results', *Current Anthropology*, **5** (2), 79–97.

Eggan, Fred (1950), *Social Organization of the Western Pueblos*, Chicago, IL: University of Chicago Press.

Ellis, Florence Hawley (1954), 'Spanish-Indian Acculturation in the Southwest: Comments', *American Anthropologist*, **56** (4), 678–80.

Ellis, Florence Hawley (1966), 'The Immediate History of Zia Pueblo as Derived from Excavation in Refuse Deposits', *American Antiquity*, **31** (6), 806–11.

Ellis, Florence Hawley, Michael Pijoan and C.A. Elkin (1943), 'An Inquiry into Food Economy and Body Economy in Zia Pueblo', *American Anthropologist*, **45** (1), 547–56.

Espinosa, Aurelio M. (1918), 'All-Souls Say at Zuñi, Acoma, and Laguna', *The Journal of American Folklore*, **31** (122), 550–52.

Garloch, Lorene A. (1944), 'Agricultural Economy of the Laguna Region', *Economic Geography*, **20** (4), 296–304.

Goddard, Pliny E. (1913), *Indians of the Southwest*, New York: American Museum of Natural History.

Grant, Blanche C. (1925), *Taos Indians*, Glorieta, NM: Rio Grande Press.

Hawley, Florence M. (1937), 'Pueblo Social Organization as a Lead to Pueblo History', *American Anthropologist*, **34**, 504–22.

Hodge, Frederick Webb (1896), 'Pueblo Indian Clans', *American Anthropologist*, **9** (10), 345–52.

Judd, Neil M. (1923), 'Pueblo Bonito, the Ancient', *National Geographic*, **64** (1), 99–108.

Lange, Charles (1953), 'The Role of Economics in Cochiti Pueblo Culture Change', *American Anthropologist*, **15**, 674–94.

Lasswell, Harold D. (1935), 'Collective Autism as a Consequence of Cultural Contact: Notes on Religious Training and the Peyote Cult at Taos', *Zeitschrift für Sozial Forschung*, **4**, 232–47.
Laxalt, Robert (1970), 'New Mexico: The Golden Land', *National Geographic*, **138** (3), 299–345.
Li, An-Che (1937), 'Zuñi: Some Observations and Queries', *American Anthropologist*, **39**, 62–76.
McClelland, David C. and Gerald A. Friedman (1952), 'A Cross-cultural Study of the Relationship between Child-training Practices and Achievement Motivation Appearing in Folk Tales', in Guy E. Swanson, Theodore. M. Newcomb and Eugene L. Harley (eds), *Readings in Social Psychology*, New York: Holt, pp. 243–9.
McDowell, Bart (1987), 'New Mexico: Between Frontier and Future', *National Geographic*, **172** (5), 602–33.
Newman, Cathy (1993), 'The Pecos: River of Hard-won Dreams', *National Geographic*, **184** (3), September, 38–63.
Norton, Jay B., Roman R. Pawluk and Jonathan A. Sandor (1998), 'Observations and Experience Linking Science and Indigenous Knowledge at Zuni, New Mexico', *Journal of Arid Environments*, **39**, 331–40.
Ortiz, Alfonso (1991), 'Origins', *National Geographic*, **180** (4), 4–13.
Parsons, Elsie Clews (1936), *Taos Pueblo*, Menasha, WI: George Banta.
Parsons, Elsie Clews (1939), *Indian Religion*, Chicago, IL: University of Chicago Press.
Reed, Erik (1946), 'The Distinctive Features and Distribution of the San Juan *Anasazi* Culture', *Southwestern Journal of Anthropology*, **2**, 295–305.
Reno, Philip (1963), *Taos Pueblo*, Chicago, IL: Swallow Press.
Roberts, David (1996), 'The Old Ones of the Southwest', *National Geographic*, **189** (4), 86–109.
Rodriguez, Sylvia (1987), 'Land, Water, and Ethnic Identity in Taos', in Charles L. Briggs and John R. Van Ness (eds), *Land, Water, and Culture: New Perspectives on Hispanic Land Grants*, Albuquerque, NM: University of New Mexico Press, pp. 313–403.
Scholes, Frank V. (1937), 'Troublous Times in New Mexico', *New Mexico Historical Review*, **12**, 407–9.
Siegel, Bernard J. (1949), 'Some Observations on the Pueblo Pattern at Taos', *American Anthropologist*, **51** (4), 562–77.
Simpich, Frederick (1929), 'The Santa Fe Trail, Path to Empire', *National Geographic*, **56** (2), 213–52.
Simpich, Frederick (1938), 'New Mexico Melodrama', *National Geographic*, **73** (5), 529–69.
Simpich, Frederick (1940), 'Seeing Our Spanish Southwest', *National Geographic*, **77** (6), 711–56.
Stirling, Matthew W. (1940), 'Indian Tribes of Pueblo Land', *National Geographic*, **78** (5), 549–88.
Sutherland, Mason (1949), 'Adobe New Mexico', *National Geographic*, **96** (6), 783–830.
Thompson, Laura (1950), *Culture in Crisis: A Study of the Hopi Indians*, New York: Harper.
Thompson, Laura and Alice Joseph (1944), *The Hopi Way*, Chicago, IL: University of Chicago Press.

Tiller, Veronica E. (1997), 'Indian Enterprise: American Indian's Economic Participation in New Mexico', *New Mexico Journal*, (February) 46–7.
Titiev, Mischa (1937), 'Taos Pueblo' (Book review), *American Anthropologist*, **39** (2), 335–7.
Tomas, Jaehn (2005), *Germans in the Southwest, 1850–1920*, Albuquerque, NM, University of New Mexico Press.
Trosper, Ronald L. (1995), 'Traditional American Indian Economic Policy', *American Indian Culture and Research Journal*, **19** (1), 65–95.
Vlasich, James A. (2005), *Pueblo Indian Agriculture*, Albuquerque, NM: University of New Mexico Press.
Wall, Dennis and Virgil Masayesva (2004), 'People of the Corn: Teachings in Hopi Traditional Agriculture, Spirituality, and Sustainability', *American Indian Quarterly*, **28** (3&4), 435–53.
Wall, Dennis and Virgil Masayesva (2007), 'People of the Corn: Traditional Hopi Agriculture & Sustainability', in Léo-Paul Dana and Robert Brent Anderson (eds), *International Handbook of Research on Indigenous Entrepreneurship*, Cheltenham, UK and Northampton, MA, USA: Edward Elgar, pp. 404–12.
White, Leslie A. (1928), 'Summary Report of Field Work at Acoma', *American Anthropologist*, **30**, 559–68.
White, Leslie A. (1932), *The Pueblo of San Felipe: Memoirs of the American Anthropological Association N° 38*, Washington, DC: American Anthropological Association.
Whitman, William (1947), *The Pueblo of San Ildefonso*, New York: Columbia University Press.

3. The Mizrahim: Anglicized Orientals with transnational networks and 'ethics capital'

Léo-Paul Dana*

INTRODUCTION

In 597 BC, 10 000 inhabitants of Jerusalem – then capital of the Kingdom of Judaea – were taken to Babylonia by the Babylonian ruler, Nebuchadnezzar. Following a siege, the Judaean capital was defeated by the Babylonians in 586 BC. Godspeed wrote:

> Nebuchadnezzar bestirred himself and advanced in strong force as far as Riblah on the middle Orontes. Thence he sent out a division against Judah, that overran the country and besieged the three strongholds which held out, Azekah, Lachish, and Jerusalem . . . The defence of Jerusalem was particularly desperate; only after a siege of one and a half years was it taken (586 BC). The usual punishments were inflicted. The king was blinded by Nebuchadnezzar's own hand; his sons and counsellors were slain, the citizens deported, the city was demolished, and the booty carried away. (1902, p. 280)

Weche elaborated, 'Nebuchadnezzar had also mercilessly ransacked Canaan and expelled the Israelites from their land' (2000, p. 623). Exiled to the region of Mesopotamia (from the Greek 'between the rivers' and referring to the land between the Euphrates River and the Tigris River) the Judaeans were 'segregated in Babylonia and left practically to themselves, preserved their national spirit' (Godspeed, 1902, p, 285). In time, the Babylonian Empire ceased to exist and the region of Mesopotamia was occupied by various foreign empires, including the Ottoman Empire.

In 1865, the Alliance Israélite Universelle established what is reputed to have been the best school in Baghdad. Graduates were usually fluent in several languages, including French and Arabic. During the Great War of 1914 (later known as the First World War), the Ottoman Empire sided with the Central Powers, resulting in declaration of war by the Triple Entente (alignment of France, Great Britain and Russia). With over 400 000 men (mostly from India), the United Kingdom captured 45 000 prisoners of war and triumphed during the Mesopotamian campaign, resulting in the British Mandate of Mesopotamia, combining the Ottoman *vilayets* (provinces) of Baghdad, Basra and Mosul. For a map of the region immediately after the fall of the Ottoman Empire, see Simpich (1919, p. 374). London granted independence to Iraq in 1932.

Together with neighbouring communities of co-religionists in Muslim countries, the descendants of Judaeans who were exiled to Babylonia are known as 'Arab Jews', 'Oriental Jews', or Mizrahim (plural of Mizrahi), from the Hebrew word *מזרח* (pronounced *mizrah*) meaning east. Many authors, including Betta (2003) and Cernea (2007) refer to these people by using the term 'Baghdadi' although Baghdad is not necessarily their place of origin. Cernea wrote, 'Although they are known collectively as "Baghdadis", and the majority did depart from Baghdad or Basra, in fact their numbers included many with ancestry not from ancient Babylonia' (2007, p. xvii).

Distinct from Ladino-speaking Sephardim of Western Europe and North Africa who trace their origins to Spain and Portugal, and very different from Yiddish-speaking Ashkenazim of Eastern Europe, Mizrahim developed a Judaeo-Arabic tongue, written using Hebrew script. Other languages once common among Mizrahim include: Bukhori; Dzhidi (Judaeo-Persian); Gruzini; Judaeo-Aramaic; Judaeo-Kurdish; Judaeo-Marathi; Juhuri (Judaeo-Tat); and Kurdish. Cernea noted that, 'their common languages – Judeo-Arabic, Judeo-Persian, and Hebrew – provided them with "secret languages" with which to conduct business' (2007, p. xix).

Many studies about entrepreneurship, including Fishberg (1911) and Sombart (1911), have treated Jews as a homogenous group and did not consider ethnicity. Others have focused on Ashkenazi entrepreneurship (see for example, Raphaël, 1980), or on Sephardi Jews (see for example Lasry, 1982). Much has been written about Ashkenazi Jews including entrepreneur Mayer Amschel Rothschild (1743–1812)[1] son of banker Moses Amschel Bauer (Leese, 1940); political activist Karl Heinrich Marx (1818–83), son of lawyer Heinrich Marx; tailor and manufacturer (Loeb) Levi Strauss (1829–1902) son of Hirsch Strauss, trader of dry goods; physician and psychologist Sigmund Freud (1856–1939), son of wool merchant Jakob Freud; sociologist Émile Durkheim (1858–1917), son of Chief Rabbi Moïse Durkheim and author of *Les formes élémentaires de la vie religieuse* (Durkheim, 1912); physicist Albert Einstein (1879-1955), son of Hermann Einstein, who operated an electrical technology business; and Metro-Goldwyn-Mayer (MGM) motion-picture icon Louis Burt Mayer (1885–1957) (born Eliezer) whose father was a scrap metal dealer in New Brunswick, Canada, while his mother peddled chickens door to door.

Among the successful Mizrahi entrepreneurs in London are Baghdad-born Maurice Saatchi, Baron of Staplefield, and his brother Charles, co-founders of the advertising firm Saatchi & Saatchi, which became Britain's largest advertising agency in 1979, the largest in Europe in 1981, and in 1986 the world's largest. In 1995, the brothers founded M & C Saatchi, employing over 1000 people in 2009.

The purpose of this chapter is to contribute to knowledge about the Mizrahim. The chapter was researched while I was in the process of conducting research for other books (Dana, 1999a; 2002; 2007a) and I came across Mizrahi entrepreneurs, in China, India, Indonesia, Japan, Malaysia, Myanmar, New York and Singapore; I took the time to interview them and discovered patterns that reflect beliefs and values affecting entrepreneurship. I later searched for and interviewed more Mizrahim in Australia, Canada and the United States, to learn more. This chapter will give an overview about what I have learned about this ethnic group, from the literature, and while conducting field research. Sections on specific countries will be followed by a discussion of Sassoon families, based on interviews and on secondary sources where indicated.

NETWORKS

Until the mid-twentieth century, an important network of multilingual Mizrahi entrepreneurs included hubs in London and in several cities across Asia, among them Bombay and Calcutta (India), British Hong Kong, Kobe (Japan), Penang (Malaya at the time), Rangoon (Burma at the time), Shanghai (China), Singapore and Surabaya (Indonesia). Cohen wrote that Mizrahim 'were almost as familiar with each other as the Jews of Manchester with those of Liverpool' (1956, p. 195). Betta confirmed, 'Baghdadis in Shanghai, Hong Kong, Singapore, Surabaya, Rangoon, Calcutta and Bombay were in constant contact with each other' (2003, p. 1002). Cernea elaborated:

> Like points in a silken cobweb, the Baghdadi Jewish diaspora once spread throughout Southeast Asia, from Bombay to Shanghai. Woven into the web were distant, but never isolated, communities in Singapore, Calcutta, Rangoon, Karachi, Dacca, Penang, Hong Kong, Yokahama, and Surabaya[2] . . . The threads of the cobweb were far from fragile; they were active communication lines that belied and defied the physical distances and wove these dots on the map into a coherent community. Along these lines flowed trade, information . . . and marriage partners, all enabled by a common language, a common world view . . . This richly textured community maintained its vitality and integrity while living in a vast sea of Chinese, Indians, Burmese or Malays. (2007, p. xv).

Cernea continued, 'Such were the spiritual and communal ties among Baghdadi Jews that though physically separated, they were never apart' (2007, p. xvi).

Although numerous families continued speaking Arabic and/or Judaeo-Arabic, most of the Mizrahi emigrants from Iraq learned English and many eventually discarded their traditional dress while living a culturally hybrid lifestyle in Westernized circles. They were described as Oriental in origin and appreciation while English in their objects and associations (Rolland, 1989). Their community did not mingle with Ashkenazi Jews, who formed a separate social circle. Betta wrote that Ashkenazi Jews in Shanghai tended to be financially less well off. 'Many of them endured severe economic deprivation, in stark contrast to the wealthy Baghdadi traders, who lived privileged existences marked by social events within the British community. The economic contrasts between Baghdadi and Russian Jews exacerbated relations between the two communities and led to the rise of mutual misunderstandings' (Betta, 2003, p. 1011).

It appears that the success of Mizrahi entrepreneurship networks was influenced by: (i) fluency in several languages; (ii) values common to Mizrahim (including family cohesion, a disciplined work ethic, respect for others and being benevolent toward employees); and (iii) networking with co-religionists. Trans-national Mizrahi networks facilitated *credit; employment* and *information exchange.*

Credit networks, as observed by Geertz (1962), have existed among co-ethnics who shared the same language, such as Japanese entrepreneurs in the United States (Light, 1972), Chinese Entrepreneurs in Papua New Guinea (Wu, 1974), Chinese entrepreneurs in New York (Wong, 1987), or Korean entrepreneurs in the United States, studied by Light and Bonacich (1988) and later by Iyer and Shapiro (1999), and among co-religionists, such as in the case of Jewish credit networks, studied by Juteau and Paré (1996). Dana (2006) noted that Jewish cattle dealers relied heavily on other Jews for financing, and that co-religionists provided finance when needed, 'A network of livestock merchants, across the region, facilitated the dissemination of knowledge and availability of finance among co-religionists. In the event of bankruptcy, an individual was given assistance by other merchants' (Dana, 2006, p. 594). Discussing Jewish and Muslim entrepreneurs in Morocco, Dana and Dana noted that 'Merchandise was often purchased on credit, thereby requiring a relationship of trust between supplier and peddler' (2008, p. 215). In a study of Catholic Hispanics, Galbraith et al. (2004) suggested that a co-ethnic capital market appears to be the last dimension developed within an ethnic community. The Mizrahim were co-religionists as well as co-ethnics, who spoke Judaeo-Arabic because they shared common origins.

Employment networks have also been widespread and documented. Betta wrote, 'in the late 1920s . . . the majority of Baghdadi Jews were either self-employed or were working for other Baghdadis' (2003, p. 1004). Porter (1937) noted that entrepreneurs were giving preference to members of their immediate circle rather than giving equal opportunity to outsiders. Raistrick (1950) found Quakers to be clannish and nepotistic. In contrast to Bonacich (1973), who suggested that exploitation takes place in enclaves, Wong (1987) found labour conflicts to be reduced in the enclave. Galbraith et al. (1997) found that successful Hispanic entrepreneurs were actively finding employment for other recent immigrants. Networks can benefit entrepreneurs, employees or both.

Min and Jaret (1985) noted that networks *benefited an entrepreneur* by serving as a source of manpower. In Malaysia, Abdullah (1992) found that Muslim Malays expressed strong preference for employing Muslim candidates over non-Muslims. Galbraith et al. (2003) and Stiles et al. (2007) suggested that Catholic Hispanic and Muslim Arab entrepreneurs were dependent on co-ethnic business in their respective enclave, relying upon co-religionists for labour, especially at the start-up phase. In a study of Turkish entrepreneurs, Altinay (2008) likewise found a strong relationship between the religion of an entrepreneur and recruitment.

Among the Amish, co-religionist employment networks have *benefited entrepreneurs and employees*. Kraybill and Nolt (1995) observed that Amish entrepreneurs gave preference in business to co-religionists; Dana explained the reason behind this: 'While the Amish people believe that a community of voluntary believers is the context for life, the fundamental unit of Amish society and of their economy is the family . . . home-based enterprises allow family members to work together, reinforcing the Amish family unit' (2007b, p. 150).

Betta wrote, 'Under (David) Sassoon's paternal guidance scores of indigent Jews, especially from Mesopotamia, found employment in his firm and were also able to secure an elementary education for their children at the David Sassoon school' (2003, p. 1001). Cernea elaborated, 'All students in the Sassoon schools sang "God Save the Queen" in English, Hebrew and Arabic' (2007, p. xxiii). Betta noted that employees 'could constantly rely on the support of Baghdadi Jewish networks . . . brides were found, in other communities of the Baghdadi trade diaspora' (2003, p. 1002).

Information networks are also found in the literature. In their ethnic study of Surinamese in Amsterdam, Boissevain and Grotenbreg (1987) suggested that access to a network of contacts is an entrepreneurial resource. They noted that networks can provide introductions to wholesalers and warning of government inspection, among other things. Boissevain and

Grotenbreg observed, 'Hindustanis appear to have a larger network . . . than do Chinese and Creole businessmen. Given the value they attach to family loyalty, this seems to indicate that Hindustanis have access to a wider information and support network' (1987, p. 117). Likewise, a co-religionist information network has existed in Alsace: 'They managed the link between the rural and urban economies, providing cash for farmers and a source of meat for consumers. In addition, they spread information as required. If one farmer needed a bull, temporarily, for breeding purposes, a livestock merchant could source this need' (Dana, 2006, p. 590).

There were also individuals who specialized in information:

> Some Jews did not themselves deal with livestock, but served as brokers, or informers who simply sold information which would lead to transactions. These entrepreneurs were called *Schmüsser*, and their commission was referred to as *Sassergeld.* Operating informally, these individuals mingled with the villagers, identified needs and opportunities and then waited by the side of a road, knowing that livestock merchants would be passing by eventually. The *Schmüsser* then sold their information to livestock merchants. (The word they used for this activity was *vermassere*, literally meaning 'to inform'.) In order to reduce time spent away from their own villages, the transient merchants preferred to pay for this market research, rather than to conduct this time-consuming task themselves. The *Schmüsser* thus formed an integral part of the business network. (Dana, 2006, pp. 592–3)

Likewise in his study of 1200 Muslim entrepreneurs in London, Altinay (2008) found a strong relationship between religion and advice-seeking practices. One interviewee stated, 'If people from the same religion and the background do not help and support each other, who else would do so' (Altinay, 2008, p. 120). Altinay (2008) also found that Muslims who practise their religion rely more on advice from co-ethnics.

CHINA

Early Jewish traders travelled overland from the eastern shores of the Mediterranean, to Baghdad, Samarkand, Kashgar, Dunhuang and the Pacific Rim. A document found along the Silk Road in Dunhuang indicates the presence of Jews in China, during the year 718. Another document, from the year 877, mentions (in Arabic) the Jews of Guangzhou (Canton), next to the island of Hong Kong. About 1000 years ago, some 70 Jewish families moved to Kaifeng, the capital of the Sung Dynasty. Cernea suggested, 'it was from Baghdad that the ancestors of the Jews of Kaifeng, China, most likely departed' (2007, p. xviii). Many of these people were entrepreneurs, mostly involved in the silk trade. They adapted to Chinese society, they bound the feet of their daughters, they wore pigtails and spoke the local dialect. Yet they did not give up their own cultural values, and they did maintain a strictly kosher[3] diet. They built the earliest known synagogue in China, in the year 1163. Some Jewish families, in China, were granted the right to adopt prestigious last names, for instance Ai, Chu, Li, Tsang, and Tsu. One Jew was given the name of the emperor, Zhao.

In 1605, the Jesuit priest Matteo Ricci became the first Westerner to meet the Jews of Kaifeng and to see their Torah scrolls. Here were entrepreneurs who prospered until 1644 when the Yellow River flooded, destroying the city. Despite the flood, the community survived. After their last spiritual leader died in 1811, the synagogue was not maintained and by 1860, it fell into decay; a hospital was subsequently built on its site, near the street called Teaching Scriptures Lane North. The sculptured lion and lotus stone bowls which formerly adorned the synagogue courtyard were transferred to the Tung Ta mosque, where they remain. Bainbridge (1907) documented these Chinese Jews up to that time.

In 1942, Bishop Williams Charles White, a Canadian from the Church of England, published a three-volume work about these people (White, 1942). In 1957, Czech sinologist Timoteus Pokora counted 100 Indigenous Jewish families in Kaifeng, 'mainly businessmen and tradesmen' (Leslie, 1972, p. 74). Interested in this Indigenous[4] community, in 1991 Professor Xu Xin introduced a Centre for Jewish Studies at Nanjing University.

Forming a community apart from the Indigenous Chinese Jews discussed above, prominent Mizrahi merchants from Baghdad (who had sojourned in India) settled in Hong Kong, Ningbo, Shanghai and Tianjin during the nineteenth century. Betta wrote,

> The Sassoons presence in the Middle Kingdom dates back to 1843–44 when Elias David (1820–84), the second son of David Sassoon sailed to Canton . . . During his sojourn in China Elias David Sassoon established the first two offices of David Sassoon, Sons & Co., respectively in Hong Kong in 1843 and in Shanghai in 1845. (Betta, 2003, p. 1001)

Elias David Sassoon later created a new venture, for further expansion, namely E.D. Sassoon & Co. (Betta, 2000). The Sassoons were an influential Mizrahi family in Hong Kong and in Shanghai. (A separate section, below, discusses the Sassoon family in more detail.)

In Hong Kong, the Ohel Leah Synagogue was built during 1901 and 1902, part-way up Victoria Peak, and named after Leah Sassoon (wife of Elias David Sassoon), on land donated by her sons. Born in Paddington, England, to entrepreneur Jonah Nathan and Miriam Jacob Nathan,

Lieutenant-Colonel Sir Matthew Nathan, who served as governor of Hong Kong under the reign of King Edward VII, became honorary president of Ohel Leah. The main street in Kowloon was subsequently named after him, that is, Nathan Road. In 1925, a cantor was brought to Hong Kong from Baghdad. The community continued speaking Judaeo-Arabic, which they wrote using Hebrew script; as well, they learned English and Chinese. In 1963, a reform rabbi from St. Louis became the community's spiritual leader. In 1974, a German friar, Father Herbert Vogt, discovered four Torah scrolls at the 'Thieves Market' on Cat Street, in Hong Kong. These were assumed to have once belonged to the Chinese Jews of Kaifeng, and were acquired by Sir Lawrence Kadoorie to be placed in Ohel Leah. In the vicinity of Ohel Leah, I asked Chinese residents in the neighbourhood what they could tell me about the people 'who come to this church'. Replies included, 'They work very hard'; 'They never rip you off'; 'It is very good to do business with them because they are so honest'; 'They are rich because everyone trusts them'; and 'Suppliers give them credit because these people are always honest and reliable'.

In Shanghai, Sir Jacob Elias Sassoon funded Ohel Rachel, a synagogue in memory of his wife, Rachel, on Seymour Road, in Shanghai; it was completed in 1920. The building still stands, as does the Hebrew school next door. The synagogue serves as the headquarters of the Shanghai Education Bureau and its address has been changed to 500 Shaanxi Beilu (Figure 3.1). I asked elderly people in the area whether they had any recollections of its members. Only one person did. 'Very honest people,' he said, 'with honest business ethics.'

A prominent Mizrahi family in the People's Republic of China (PRC) today is the Kadoorie family, who migrated from Baghdad via Bombay. Born in 1865, Ellis Kadoorie shifted from Bombay to Shanghai in 1880, as an employee of David Sassoon & Sons. His younger brother, Elly Kadoorie, was born in 1867 and also came from Bombay to Shanghai in 1880. The brothers were entrepreneurs in Shanghai and in Hong Kong. In 1901, Elly founded, in Hong Kong, the China Light and Power Company Limited (a family business that later grew into the CLP Group, one of the leading power companies in the world). Ellis was knighted in 1917 and died in 1922. During the Second World War, his brother Elly was taken away from his Shanghai home (Figure 3.2) and died in a Japanese prison camp during 1944; he was survived by his sons Lawrence and Horace. Sir Lawrence Kadoorie was born in 1899 in Hong Kong; his brother, Sir Horace Kadoorie was born in 1902. They both worked for Victor Sassoon in Shanghai, and also for their father's China Light and Power Company. (It was not uncommon for entrepreneurs to learn by working for entrepreneurs.) A successful hotelier, industrialist and philanthropist, in 1981

Figure 3.1 *Former Ohel Rachel (photograph by Léo-Paul Dana)*

Figure 3.2 *Shanghai home of Sir Elly Kadoorie (photograph by Léo-Paul Dana)*

Sir Lawrence Kadoorie was made Baron Kadoorie of Kowloon and the City of Westminster; he died in 1993, followed by his brother in 1995. The son of Sir Lawrence Kadoorie, Sir Michael David Kadoorie was born in 1941 and lives in Hong Kong with his wife and three children. The family's hotel chain operates under the name Peninsula.

I interviewed Mizrahim in Hong Kong, and asked what they believed to be the causal variable contributing to the success of their entrepreneurial community. Typical responses related to: (i) family cohesion; (ii) a disciplined work ethic; (iii) networking with co-religionists with similar values particularly with regards to family cohesion and work ethic; and (iv) fluency in several languages, the latter confirming Betta who stated, 'In Shanghai, Baghdadis with Indian links could also converse in Hindustani. Fluency in the language was useful for commercial purposes' (2003 p. 1013).

INDIA

Gadgil (1959) noted that Jews were among the chief traders of Kerala, in South India, but their origins are uncertain and these people were not necessarily Mizrahim.

In Bombay, the first Mizrahi to settle was Shalom ben Ovadiah HaCohen, a merchant who arrived from Aleppo (*Halab*) in 1790. He was soon followed by others from Baghdad and Basra. Yet others came from Iran and Yemen. Cernea suggested, 'British-ruled India was an attractive destination because of its open economic and religious climate and its heterogeneous society' (2007, p. xix).

Betta wrote,

> in 1830 . . . David Sassoon (1792–1864), the scion of Baghdad's most eminent Jewish family, chose the city as his permanent commercial base . . . On the basis of his lineage Sassoon, who remained throughout his life an 'Oriental' merchant-prince, proud of his Judaeo-Arabic heritage, imposed himself as the charismatic head of the local community. (2003, p. 1001)

Here, David Sassoon became a magnate of the cotton industry. His son Abdullah[5] revolutionized the weaving industry in Bombay, contributing to Bombay becoming an important manufacturing centre. Some Mizrahi families spread to Calcutta, New Delhi and even Rangoon, Burma. Cernea wrote, 'In a relatively short time after arriving in India, the Baghdadis commanded trading networks throughout Southeast Asia' (2007, p. xix).

Betta observed, 'Baghdadi Jews . . . in Bombay and Calcutta were neither colonizers nor colonized' (2003, p. 1000). The term Baghdadi, in the context of Indian Jewry, refers to Mizrahim tracing their origins to Baghdad or Basra, and also to others from Aden, Afghanistan, Persia (known as Iran since 1935) and Syria. These people usually spoke Arabic, and sometimes Persian. They published periodicals in Arabic, using Hebrew script. Being white foreigners in India, the Mizrahim enjoyed a special standing under the Raj, and this helped them flourish.

As was the case in China, Mizrahi entrepreneurs in India dealt with international networks of Mizrahim, but had little contact with Indigenous Jews in their host society. Mizrahi institutions enabled Mizrahim to stay apart from the Indigenous Bene Israel, who are ethnic Indians.

In 1861, David Sassoon funded the Magen David Synagogue (Figure 3.3) in Bombay. This synagogue was enlarged in 1910 by Sir Jacob Elias Sassoon (1848–1916). With an imposing tower, the structure exhibits Gothic influence. Daily services are conducted here, and several men are each paid a monthly honorarium to attend prayers, after which a warm breakfast is served, under the supervision of Flaoori Barouk, a woman of Baghdadi descent.

Among the regulars who network here are Jacob Solomon and Bensyon Ghosalker, the *shamash* (parnass) of Bombay's other Baghdadi congregation, Keneseth Eliyahoo, commissioned by the Sassoon family in 1884 and completed in 1885, in Bombay's Fort neighbourhood (not far from the place where the Prince of Wales museum would be built some years later). In 1985, the Bombay community celebrated the centennial of the Keneseth Eliyahoo Synagogue. The festivities, during February 1985, were graced by the President of India, Giani Zail Singh, and the postal service issued a stamp on this occasion. The building stands at the corner of Dr V.B. Gandhi Marg (formerly Forbes Street) and Motiwani Path, but is no longer a hub of a trans-national network. The lavish sanctuary is up a staircase. Seats are settees with cushions. Up another flight of stairs is a balcony with hand-carved balustrades made of wood.

Around the corner from Keneseth Eliyahoo (Figure 3.4), and facing the David Sassoon Library and Reading Room, 152 Mahatma Gandhi Road (Figure 3.5), the Jewish Club, on the second floor of the Jeroo Building at 137 Mahatma Gandhi Road (Figure 3.6) was established by Mizrahim, as a gambling centre and restaurant. Specialties on the menu include: basmati rice; dhal; mushroom soup; pan-fried potato chips; yellow eggs; lassi; and Duke's Mangola, a mango-based beverage originally prepared by a small family business and now under the wings of PepsiCo. Vice-chairman and honorary secretary of the club, Mr E.J. Mashal said to me, 'I am one of the last four Iraqi-born Jews in India.' He was born in 1925, and came to India in 1931. The other three, he explained, were Nessim and Renée Ezair of Bombay, and Mrs Saeeda Kollet (née Haskel) of Delhi. Under the fans that were suspended from the high ceiling, he explained that the transnational networks of Mizrahim facilitated information exchange, international finance, travel and even employment and entrepreneurship training, but most of all he emphasized the Mizrahi work ethic. 'If you have networks and people are ready to help you, but you do not want to work, then you do not make money. We worked well and we made money

Figure 3.3 *Magen David Synagogue at 340 Sir JJ Road, Byculla, Mumbai (photograph by Léo-Paul Dana, exhibited at the National Museum of Singapore)*

Figure 3.4 *Keneseth Eliyahoo, 55 Dr V.B. Gandhi Marg, Fort Mumbai (photograph by Léo-Paul Dana, exhibited at the National Museum of Singapore)*

Figure 3.5 David Sassoon Library and Reading Room, completed in 1870 in Venetian Gothic style (photograph by Léo-Paul Dana)

and this attracted more money and so our neighbourhood became quite exclusive.'

Mizrahi traditions are closely observed in Bombay. Freddie Sopher explained to me that he continues to observe Mizrahi traditions specific to those of Babylonian ancestry. On Friday night, for instance, *bamya* (okra) is intrinsic to the Kiddush meal. For Passover, Freddie boils dates to make *halek*, the Passover version of *seelan*; after the juice begins to thicken, it is sprinkled with bits from giant walnuts. During our talks, he stressed the importance of networks with co-religionists abroad. He confirmed that

Figure 3.6 Networking venue for Mizrahim in Bombay (photograph by Léo-Paul Dana)

although the latter lived in different unlike host societies, these people had similar values.

Jacobs and Ezekiel wrote that Mizrahim in Calcutta lived, 'in the best part of the town, the Chowrunghee, their habits and costumes being European in every respect, though their vernacular is Arabic' (1902, p. 497). Today, five synagogues remain from a once-thriving community in Calcutta. The oldest is Naveh Shalome (Abode of Peace), completed in

Figure 3.7 *Calcutta Maghen David (photograph by Léo-Paul Dana exhibited at the National Museum of Singapore)*

Figure 3.8 Mizrahi Torah scrolls (photograph by Léo-Paul Dana)

1831. It has been abandoned, but on the same grounds is Maghen David with an impressive clock tower (Figure 3.7), built in 1884 by Elias David Joseph Ezra. Every two weeks, on Saturday morning, prayers are held here, following Mizrahi *minhag*. Networking continues with people discussing prices and opportunities. The same is true, fortnightly, at Calcutta's Beth-El, built in 1856 and later enlarged by Elias Shalome Gubbay, who raised the centre on massive columns with lofty arches, enlarged the synagogue by three chambers, and added ornamental windows as well as marble floors. Beth-El once had over 100 hand-written Mizrahi (encased) Torah scrolls (see Figure 3.8 for Mizrahi Torah scrolls). Calcutta's Shaare Rason, established in 1897, and Maghen Aboth organized in 1933, are both closed, but interviewees smiled as they remembered the networking that once took place here. 'Very, very big deals were discussed in several languages', explained one respondent.

Next door to Shaare Rason (which has become a clothing shop) I visited the home of Rahmah Cohena and interviewed her and her servants. In her absence, one of the latter emphasized to me, 'It is very good to work for people like her; she is very good to us.' Rahmah's cousin resides across the street and networking could be seen on a daily basis.

Among other prominent families of the Calcutta community are the

Nahoums. In 1902, the patriarch Nahoum founded Dainty Confectionery, at New Market (formerly Hogg Market). His grandson David Nahoum inherited Nahoum & Sons Private Ltd, and continues operating the bakery, at the same location since 1916 (Gupta, 2007). Specialties here include caca rings and sambousek, enjoyed in former times by travelling Mizrahim who appreciated foods with which they were familiar. Employees are Hindu.

During my time in Calcutta, David Nahoum told me that the observance of the Biblical commandment of *Lo Tashchit* (you shall not waste) was a key to success in business. Another key to successful entrepreneurship, he explained, was fluency in several languages and he reminisced that Calcutta once had a wealthy community of entrepreneurs fluent in several languages. His narrative was consistent with Betta, who wrote, 'As Orientals, Baghdadis born or raised in India could also communicate in Hindustani, a lingua franca used in India's ports. According to Jael Silliman, middle-class Jews in Calcutta in the late nineteenth century spoke at home not only Judaeo-Arabic but also Hindustani' (2003, p. 1013).

During our discussions, David Nahoum also emphasized: (i) family cohesion among Mizrahim; (ii) a disciplined work ethic among Mizrahim; and (iii) how Mizrahim networked with co-religionists abroad, because although these lived in different unlike host societies, these people had similar values with regards to family cohesion, languages, work ethic and networking.

MALAYSIA

During 1786, in exchange for British protection from raiders and pirates, the Sultan of Kedah granted to the East India Company a virtually uninhabited island off the west coast of the Malay Peninsula. It was here, on Prince of Wales Island (also known as the island of Betelnut, or Penang) that Georgetown, the first of the British Straits Settlements, was established. Whereas in Melaka, further south along the Malay Peninsula, the Portuguese and the Dutch had monopolistic intentions, policy in Penang – one of the Straits Settlements – was one of free trade. This attracted Mizrahi and other enterprising and industrious traders to Penang, transforming Georgetown into a prosperous port. Figure 3.9 illustrates what was formerly a home in the Mizrahi neighbourhood of Penang.

Up to 1867, the Straits Settlements were governed from British India. Their status was then changed to that of Crown Colony and Penang no longer relied on India for government; however, business networks with India were maintained and trade grew. The Jewish community which

Figure 3.9 Formerly home of a Mizrahi family (photograph by Léo-Paul Dana)

evolved in Penang added to the multicultural nature of the island. By the turn of the twentieth century there were Ashkenazi as well as Mizrahi families in Georgetown: Bernstein, Brambier, Charkas, Cohen, Grand, Grimberg, Grutz, Horn, Houfswang, Lazarus, Leiberman, Marcus, Silverman, and so on.

During a visit to the Jewish cemetery in Georgetown I noticed that the inscription on a 1888 tombstone was engraved by hand in Penang, but those of 1896 and thereafter were often carved in Calcutta. When I asked the keeper to comment, he said, 'Those people buried here had very developed connections with people like them in India. They had the same religion and the same language, actually same languages because they spoke many languages'. Even tombstones were bilingual, with Hebrew as well as Latin characters. The tombstone of Abraham Reuben Ezekiel Abdullah Gubai (d. 1920:12:25) is partially inscribed in Arabic. It should be mentioned that records were not always kept with great precision. For example, Rahamin David Akarib died Tuesday, 10 May 1921, 'age about 38'.

Until 1938, Manesseh Mordecai (1878–1938) lived at 3 Nagore Road. The official address of Hyam Abraham Heyam (1876–1939) was 28 Nagore Road. David Mordecai (1873–1950) and Mozelle Mordecai (1889–1951) resided at 24 Nagore Road. More imperial style residences include the stately mansion at 384 Burma Road, not far beyond Mandalay Road; it was the home of Mozzett Manasseh (1874–1949), Aaron Manasseh (1898–1957) and Ezra Ezekiel Manasseh (1896–1958). On an afternoon during which coconuts were being harvested from the row of majestic palms in the gardens, the current occupant of the villa told me, 'Manasseh was very popular with local people. He was always very good with employees and very fair in business dealings.' Mizrahi entrepreneurs employed Indigenous Muslims and Hindus who traced their origins to British India.

By the timc Malaysia became a country in 1963, only a handful of Jews remained in Penang. On 22 April 1964 Haya Jacob died (1912–64). The next Jewish death in Malaysia was that of economist Sason Hai Jacob (1945–72).

The synagogue of Penang, known as *Yahoudi Gameh* (literally 'Jewish mosque') still stands at 28 Nagore Road near Lorong Ceylon. In former times, the premises were rented from the family of Ng Huang Lim, an elderly Chinese gentleman whom I had the pleasure to interview in his home next door. He smiled as he remembered fondly,

> When we were small we loved to watch through the swinging doors, especially on Monday, Thursday and I think on Saturday . . . They spoke many languages and they knew people everywhere in the Empire, because you know, we were part of the British Empire . . . They had many languages used for business and they also had a language among themselves and I think they wrote it from right to left . . . Respect was always very important for them. They respected others and they were always fair in business, very generous to their employees.

He also mentioned 'their respect for nature, which they said was because of their holy writings'. (I assumed this was in reference to Deuteronomy 20:19 that commands not destroying trees 'for you may eat from them, but you shall not cut them down'. Later, I learned that based on the passage of Deuteronomy 11:15, stating 'I will give grass in your fields for your cattle, and you shall eat and be satisfied' the Babylonian Talmud derives the law that one is prohibited from eating before providing food for his or her animal (Berachot 40a).) Finally, Ng Huang Lim said to me, 'You know, they were very fair in business, so we all trusted them'.

Born in Penang in 1910, a prominent member of the *Yahoudi Gameh* was Barookh Ephraim, the son of Aboudi Ephraim Nahob who had come to British Malaya from Baghdad. The passing away of Barookh Ephraim, in 1976, resulted in the closing down of Malaysia's only synagogue. The building was transformed into the medicine factory of Khoo Ching Leng and in 1992 it was converted into a florist shop. Muslim music still streams out of minarets five times a day, mingling with the smells of curry and sweet tea; Indian music is still heard in the streets but the sounds of Jewish prayer are gone from Penang. The wife and younger son of Barookh Ephraim have moved to Sydney, Australia. The elder son, Charlie, and daughter, Tefaha, were until recently residing in Penang along with their cousin Mody Mordecai. These were the last three Mizrahim in Malaysia. Mody and Charlie retired. I had fascinating talks with Tefaha who married a Malay and worked as a telephone operator. She proudly told me that she spoke 'Hockien Chinese, Malay, English and some Hebrew'.

MYANMAR (FORMERLY BURMA)

Beginning in the mid-nineteenth century, Mizrahim from Iraq, who traded in teak, coffee, gold, jade and rice, were encouraged by British colonial authorities to settle in Burma. A wooden prayer hall was built in Rangoon in 1854, and it became the meeting place for Mizrahim to network. The wooden building was replaced in 1893 by a more elaborate Musmeah Yeshua Synagogue that stands today in the heart of Yangon, as Rangoon is now called. The Synagogue Trust owns apartments and shops, the rent from which is used to maintain the synagogue. A major restoration took place from 1993 to 1994.

Cernea (2007) wrote that Burma provided a hospitable home for Jews since the first settlers arrived, and that their cohesive community within Burma was in close contact with Jewish settlements abroad, including Bombay, Calcutta, Singapore, Shanghai and Surabaya. She described the Baghdadi Jews in British Burma as shaped by loyalty to Jewish tradition as well as by the pervasive influence of British culture. She noted that their elites strove to assimilate British notions of class, and she emphasized the fact that the British Empire acted as an agency for promoting free markets, the rule of law, investor protection and relatively incorrupt government. Cernea wrote, 'Baghdadis . . . lived in the heart of Rangoon, employing Bene Israel, Cochini Jews, and Hindustanis in their stores, and Hindustanis and Muslims in their homes' (2007, p. 21). She elaborated, 'Through the years, the wealthiest families of Rangoon have included the Solomons, Meyers, and Sofaers, as well as Aslan Benjamin, A.J. Cohen, who became rich in the early 1920s by investing in rice shares, and Charles Joseph' (2007, p. 22). She also wrote about multilingualism among the Baghdadis in Burma: 'The Burmese language they learned at school . . . they spoke Hindustani to the servants, English in school, Arabic to their parents . . . and Hebrew in synagogue' (Cernea, 2007, pp. 39–40).

The Mizrahim of Burma were worldly people, travelling and moving to other countries under the Union Jack, and also to Mizrahi communities beyond the Empire. In 1935, Victor Kelly departed for Kobe

(Dana, 1999b). When Japan occupied Burma, there was a mass exodus of Mizrahim from Burma. Although many were born here, they were not considered local, and unlike the Burmese who were denied passage on British ships, many Mizrahim were able to escape by sea and relocate in other communities of their trans-national network.

The independence of Burma, in 1948, made Judah Sassoon (now living in Los Angeles) feel like 'a stranger in the land of my nativity' (Cernea, 2007, pp. 46–7). Cernea commented on this, 'Yet the land he is talking about – Burma – was never truly his home; his home existed within the international community of Burma, the transnational community of Baghdadis, and within an England he had never visited' (Cernea 2007, p. 47). Of the few Mizrahim who remained in Burma after independence, most departed when the military seized power in 1962 and nationalized businesses.

Moses Samuels, caretaker of the synagogue and entrepreneur, discussed with me the usefulness of information obtained when networking here. His son, Sammy Samuels, who is fourth-generation Burmese and uses the name Aung Soe Lwin studied in New York and has been keeping in touch with me via e-mail.

SINGAPORE

In 1830, a group of Mizrahi entrepreneurs came to Singapore from Ottoman Iraq, to work in the spice trade. Many followed, and Singapore became home to a thriving community of Mizrahi entrepreneurs.

Born in Baghdad and educated in Calcutta, Menasseh Meyer arrived in Singapore in 1861, returning to Calcutta in 1864, to learn Arabic and Hebrew and work with his uncle. Learning from an entrepreneur was perhaps more effective than learning at a school. At the age of 21, he relocated to Rangoon where he launched his own business and returned to Singapore in 1873, where he founded an international business operation operating between India and Singapore.

In 1878, the Maghain Aboth Synagogue was consecrated on Waterloo Street (Makepeace et al., 1921). Menasseh Meyer began investing in Singapore real estate in 1885. Among his assets was the Teutonia Club, built in 1900, and converted in 1929 into the Goodwood Park Hotel. In 1905, Menasseh Meyer established another synagogue, the late-Renaissance style Chessed El, on Oxley Rise (Makepeace et al., 1921). Meyer was knighted in 1906.

Many Mizrahim lived along Short Street and in the adjacent area south of the Rochor Canal. In 1924, the Ellison Building (Figure 3.10) on Selegie Road became the tallest building in the neighbourhood. Between

Figure 3.10 Ellison Building (photograph by Léo-Paul Dana)

the Ellison Building and the Maghain Aboth Synagogue, the David Elias Buildings (Figure 3.11) were erected in 1928, on Middle Road, at the corner of Short Street, facing Selegie Road. When Menasseh Meyer died in 1930, he was reputed to be the richest Jew in the Far East.

A Mizrahi by the name of David Saul Marshall (born in 1908) – member of the Maghain Aboth Synagogue on Waterloo Street – led the movement for Singapore's independence and became the Chief Minister of Singapore. In April 1956, he led a delegation (including Lee Kuan Yew) to London to ask for internal self-government; on 23 April 1956, David Saul Marshall showed Herbert Morrison signatures of 167 000 people requesting independence for Singapore. In 1959, when self-government was granted, Lee Kuan Yew became the nation's prime minister. David Saul Marshall later served as Singapore's ambassador to France, Spain, Portugal and Switzerland. When he died in 1995, Dr. Marshall was Chevalier de la Legion d'Honneur of France. The programme for his memorial service cited a few lines from an interview conducted shortly before his death: 'Human warmth is perhaps a very real and basic element of a Jew . . . Then there is family cohesion, a healthy ethos of work, and a perpetual struggle for a better life for oneself and posterity.'

Figure 3.11 David Elias Buildings (photograph by Léo-Paul Dana)

A theme, re-occurring in interviews I conducted with Mizrahim living in Singapore, related to the importance of *treating employees well, and paying wages promptly*. Jacob Ballas reminded me that it is stated in the Bible, 'Do not withhold that which is due to your neighbour, and you shall not steal; the wages earned by a day labourer shall not remain overnight with you until the morning' (Leviticus 19:13). This is subsequently elaborated upon, 'You shall pay his hire on its day; the sun shall not set upon him, for he is poor, and his life depends upon it; let him not call out against you to the Compassionate One, for a sin would be upon you' (Deuteronomy 24:15).

'Baghdadi Jews,' said Jacob Ballas, 'always pay on time what they owe, so people trust them and this helps them be successful entrepreneurs . . . The importance of paying a debt is emphasised in the *Book of Psalms*.' I later read the *Book of Psalms* and noted this passage: 'One who borrows and does not repay it is the same whether one borrows from man or from the all-present God; as it is said, The wicked borroweth and payeth not again, but the righteous dealeth graciously' (Book of Psalms, xxxvii:21).

Several interviewees in Singapore attributed entrepreneurial success to the observance of *Lo Tashchit*, the prohibition against destroying or wasting resources. The *Babylonian Talmud* consists of the Mishnah and the Babylonian Gemara that represents 300 years of analysing the former. The *Babylonian Talmud* condemns the wasting of lamp oil, the tearing of garments, the chopping up of furniture for firewood, or the unnecessary killing of animals (*Babylonian Talmud*, Talmud Shabbath 67b, Tractate Hullin 7b, Kiddushin 32a). Kiddushin (32a) elaborates that a person who breaks vessels, vandalises a building, or does away with food in a destructive manner violates the commandment of *Lo Tashchit*, referred to as Commandment 529, in the *Sefer Ha-Chinuch* (*Book of Education*). This book teaches that the righteous and those who improve society love that which is good and worthwhile and to cling to it, so that good becomes a part of mankind and that nothing, not even a grain of mustard, should be lost to the world; therefore, people should prevent any destruction that they can.

THE SASSOONS

Born in Baghdad in 1750, Sheikh Saleh Sasson was a prosperous merchant. He had several children, the eldest one of whom was Daud (David), born in Baghdad in 1792 (Hyams, 1906), also 'a wealthy Mesopotamian merchant' (Jacobs and Hyams, 1906a, p. 67). David's son Abdullah ibn

Daud Sassoon (1817–96) was also born in Baghdad (Jacobs and Lipkind, 1906a), followed by Eliyahoo (1819–80), whose name was Anglicized to Elias. The family emigrated from Ottoman Baghdad to Persia, where David opened a trading office. David already spoke Arabic and Turkish. Jacobs and Hyams wrote, 'He had a fair knowledge of Hebrew, Arabic, Persian, Turkish and Hindustani, but not of English' (1906a, p. 67). Sheikh Saleh Sasson died in Bushire, Persia (nowadays Iran), in 1830.

David Sassoon subsequently shifted his family to Bombay. Cernea explained,

> When he arrived in Bombay in 1832, British and Parsee merchants dominated the import-export business. He began by exporting textiles to Persia, Baghdad, and the Gulf states and importing goods that could be resold to England. Then he began to buy the wharfs, offering dock space and storage space to small merchants arriving from Afghanistan or Russia. In return, he had the first choice of the exotic goods they brought . . . His success was due . . . also to his ability to speak Arabic, his knowledge of the conditions within the countries he was dealing with . . . and his absolute trustworthiness. (2007, p. xx)

In 1833, David established the banking and mercantile enterprise David Sassoon & Co., the firm that built the Sassoon Dock, an innovation in its day in that it was the first wet dock in western India (Jacobs and Lipkind, 1906a). The Sassoon factories of silk and cotton goods, in Bombay, provided considerable employment (Jacobs and Lipkind, 1906a). The Sassoons became the wealthiest family in India, 'with branches at Calcutta, Shanghai, Canton and Hongkong' (Jacobs and Hyams, 1906a, p. 67).

Having funded Bombay's Magen David Synagogue in 1861, in 1863 David Sassoon paid to build Ohel David, in Puna. Both synagogues became hubs of a co-ethnic network where entrepreneurs could exchange information and discuss opportunities with one another. Cernea wrote, 'Like other first generation Baghdadis, David Sassoon wore Arabic dress to the end of his life, setting himself visually as well as mentally apart from the populations among whom he lived. Like other Baghdadis, he spoke Arabic, Judeo-Arabic and Hebrew' (2007, p. xxiii).

When David Sassoon died in 1864 (Jacobs and Hyams, 1906a), his first-born son Abdullah David Sassoon (1817–96) inherited the family business David Sassoon & Co, by then a great banking and mercantile enterprise (Jacobs and Lipkind, 1906a). Abdullah David Sassoon diversified into textiles and built docks; in recognition for his contribution to the industrialisation of India, he was knighted in 1872. From his profits, Abdullah David Sassoon sent funds to Baghdad to build a school (Alliance Israélite Universelle) that he donated to the Mizrahi community there (Jacobs and Lipkind, 1906a). He moved to England in 1876, and in 1890 Queen

Victoria named him baronet (Jacobs and Lipkind, 1906a). He died in Brighton in 1896, as Sir Albert Sassoon, First Baronet of Kensington Gore. He was survived by his son, Bombay-born Second Baronet of Kensington Gore, Sir (Edward) Albert Sassoon (1856–1912),[6] spouse of Aline Caroline de Rothschild (1867–1909), daughter of Baron Gustave de Rothschild (Jacobs and Lipkind, 1906b). Sir (Edward) Albert and Aline had a son Philip Albert Gustave David Sassoon[7] (1888–1939) who became Third Baronet of Kensington Gore, and a daughter Sybil Rachel Betty Cecile Sassoon born in London (1894–1989).[8]

In 1867, Abdullah's younger brother, Eliyahoo, using the name Elias David Sassoon (1819–80), established a new firm in India, E.D. Sassoon & Co., which had branches in Hong Kong and Shanghai (Jacobs and Hyams, 1906b). Elias died in Ceylon, during 1880. His eldest son Jacob Elias Sassoon (1848–1916) a banker, mill-owner and merchant (Jacobs and Hyams, 1906c) and his third son Edward Elias Sassoon (1853–1924) together funded a synagogue in his memory, Keneseth Eliyahoo, opened in 1884, in the Fort neighbourhood of Bombay.

Jacob Elias Sassoon was married to Rachel Isaacs (1857–1911); a serial entrepreneur, he established several mills and dye works in Bombay and expanded his enterprises to Calcutta and to Karachi. He became First Baronet of Bombay, in 1909. Given that he had no children, his title was passed on to his younger brother Edward Elias Sassoon (1853–1924), who was married to Leontine Levy of Cairo; she lived in Bournemouth until 1955. Edward and Leontine had a son, Ellice David Sassoon (1881–1961), who was born in Naples in 1881 and became Third Baronet of Bombay.

Ellice David Sassoon (1881–1961) inherited the company (and title) of his uncle, Sir Jacob, and he moved to Shanghai in 1923. Henceforth known as Sir Victor (Ellice) Sassoon, between 1926 and 1929, he built the Sassoon House, which housed the Cathay Hotel on Shanghai's Bund; the tenth floor was Sir Victor (Ellice) Sassoon's residence. This later became the Peace Hotel and is now the Fairmont, featured in Figure 3.12.

In 1930, the Sassoon Banking Corporation was registered in Hong Kong to take over banking interests of the E.D. Sassoon merchant company. In 1952, the E.D. Sassoon Banking Company was registered in the Bahamas and it became a merchant bank. Sir Victor (Ellice) Sassoon lived at his home on Cable Beach in Nassau until he died in 1961. With him disappeared the title Sassoon Baronet of Bombay that had been crested in 1909 for Victor's uncle, Jacob Elias Sassoon and passed on to Jacob's brother Edward Elias Sassoon, who was Victor's father. A driver in Nassau happened to mention to me that he had met Sir Victor Sassoon. I wanted to know more. 'A nice man,' he said. 'He was very honest and most generous.

Figure 3.12 Former Sassoon House (photograph by Léo-Paul Dana)

I think his religion forced him to treat everybody well, but I cannot recall what religion that was.'

Among David Sassoon's other sons was Solomon David Sassoon (1841–94), also a successful banker and merchant. Jacobs and Lipkind wrote about him, 'He went to China as an assistant in his father's business house, and afterward became the head of the firm of David Sassoon & Co., remaining in charge of it until his death. Sassoon was director of the Bank of Bombay . . . He was chairman of the Sassoon Spinning and Weaving Co., of the Sassoon and Alliance Silk Co' (1906c, p. 68).

In 1903, the Sassoon family built the Sir Jacob Sassoon School, next to the Magen David Synagogue, in a predominantly Jewish neighbourhood of Bombay. In 1909, Jacob Elias Sassoon was awarded the title Baronet of Bombay. Sir Jacob's business had branches in Hong Kong, Kobe, London, Manchester and Shanghai.

David Sassoon & Co. included a banking wing and later, the E.D. Sassoon Banking Company became a branch of the E.D. Sassoon & Co. (Ji, 2003). The E.D. Sassoon Bank and Trust Ltd, was based in the

Bahamas until 1972 when it was acquired by Wallace Brothers, and it became the Wallace Brothers Sassoon Bank Ltd. This supplemented informal credit networks existing among Mizrahim. The phenomenon of credit networks exists among many ethnic communities and this has been well documented.

Not directly related to the Sassoons of India is the family of Haroun Sasson, born in Persia to a Mizrahi whose name was Sasson, at a time when family names were not mandatory; it was the custom for the eldest son to take his father's first name for his surname. Sasson had several children, each of whom selected a different last name. The family migrated from Persia to Ottoman Iraq, and during the late nineteenth century moved from Basra, in Ottoman Iraq, to Cairo.

The eldest of Sasson's children was Shaoul Agamy (brother of Haroun Sasson), who continued to wear traditional Mizrahi dress – including a full-length kaftan robe for men, usually made of rich fabric, and traditionally wrapped turban head-cover (in Arabic known as *ema*, pronounced with the first letter being guttural) – in Egypt, until the 1930s. This is similar to the case of David Sassoon who 'stressed his Judaeo-Arabic identity by wearing traditional clothing, whilst his sons often wore Western dress' (Betta, 2003, p. 1009).

Haroun was Sasson's second son and he adopted the family name Sasson, in honour of his father. Haroun came to Egypt at a young age, but unlike his brothers, Haroun wore Western fashions, perhaps influenced by his wife, Salha.

Haroun's younger sister was Chakhla, who married Cesar Nathan and took his family name; they had a daughter Jeanne who married into the Azubel family. Jeanne Azubel's daughter Judith married Freddie Kiel from Alsace, and lived in Maryland until the late twentieth century.

Haroun's younger brother was Morad Mizrahi, who resided in Egypt and continued wearing traditional dress, with a full-length kaftan and turban. The last son of Sasson was Yaacob (Jacob) Hagami (literally meaning Persian, in Arabic); he also wore a full-length kaftan and turban. A rich man, Yaacob (Jacob) Hagami lived in Daher (a neighbourhood of Cairo); his daughter Marie became a midwife. In summary, each of Haroun Sasson's siblings had a different last name.

Haroun had seven multilingual children: (i) Shaoul; (ii) Simha; (iii) Yaacob; (iv) David; (v) Israel; (vi) Rose; and (vii) Rahmin. The first-born son, Shaoul lived in Ottoman Palestine where he had a son Haroun Sasson, born at the time of the Great War (The First World War). The eldest daughter Simha had two sons (Zaki and Albert) from her first husband. She remarried into the Emano family and had seven children: (i) Jacques living in New York and later Florida; (ii) trilingual Esther,

Figure 3.13 From left to right, Elio (Eliyahoo) Sasson, the author, daughter of Elio and Elio's wife Claire

married to Sabatino Argy and mother of several children, including entrepreneur Ninette Green of Haifa (whom I interviewed in three languages); (iii) Haroun; (iv) Henriette, single, living in New York; (v) Sophie of Nahariya (whom I interviewed in three languages); (vi) Elie Emano of Paris; and (vii) quadrilingual entrepreneur Zaki Emano.

Yaacob was a resident of Jerusalem, in British Palestine. He had a son Haroun, whom I could not find trace of. David had five sons who lived in Israel: (i) Léon, who died in Ashqelon during the mid-1970s; (ii) Elio, an entrepreneur in Ramat Eliyahoo, Rishon LeTzion (married to a cousin of Mrs. Dora Sassoon); (iii) trilingual Haroun (Rico) in Ofakim, in the Negev; (iv) Moïse (married to Daisy) in Beer Sheva (whom I interviewed in four languages); and (v) Solomon who died in Beer Sheva during the early 1970s. See Figure 3.13.

Israel Sasson's younger sister Rose married Aharon Abignoli and had a daughter, Fifi. This daughter married her cousin, Zaki Emano (mentioned above), and lived in Israel; their son Ronnie became a successful industrialist in New York. Marriage to a relative was not uncommon among Mizrahim. Cernea noted, 'The prohibition against inter-marriage meant that communities were often linked through extensive kinship ties' (2007, p. xix). Israel Sasson also had a younger brother, Rahmin Sasson, who moved to England where he used the Anglicized name, Clement Sasson and raised a son Edouard (Anglicized to Edward).

Israel Sasson (Figure 3.14) was born in the Basra *vilayet* of the Ottoman Empire, in 1883. At a young age, he moved to Egypt, nominally Ottoman at the time, but administered by the United Kingdom (until independence was proclaimed in 1922). He was originally set up for an arranged marriage with Loulou Akerib (Figure 3.15), eldest daughter of Habiba and Shlomo Selim Akerib who was prosperous merchant from Basra. Israel Sasson actually married Loulou's younger sister, whose Arabic name was written in Hebrew characters *נעמה* – pronounced Na-ee-ma – and Anglicized to Naomi (Figure 3.16). Israel and Naomi had eight children (see Figure 3.17), all born in Egypt and all educated in Arabic, English, French and Hebrew.

Israel Sasson was a grain and cotton merchant in Cairo (Fields, 1974). Later, he became a retailer in partnership with his brother-in-law Aharon Abignioli, the husband of his younger sister Rose. For head-cover Israel Sasson wore a brimless red tarbouche, made of felt, with a silk tassel, along with a Western suit (Figure 3.18), reflecting an openness to Westernization. This is consistent with the situation in Shanghai, as described by Betta, 'In Shanghai Baghdadi traders and their families shed their Oriental heritage gradually and underwent a process of Anglicization, along similar lines to those experienced by their co-religionists in Bombay, Calcutta, Rangoon, Singapore and Hong Kong' (2003, p. 1014).

Israel Sasson died on 1 January 1943. He was survived by his three sons, all of whom Anglicized their family name to Sassoon: (i) Selim; (ii) Haroun (Westernized to Rico and Anglicized to Henry); and (iii) Menashe (Anglicized to Robert); and five daughters: (i) Habiba (Westernized to Aimée); (ii) Sophie Charlotte; (iii) Rahma (Westernised to Clemy); (iv) Loulou; and (v) Helène (Anglicized to Helen). The entire generation emigrated from Egypt, the last of them (Sophie Charlotte Tadros) in 1962. Notice that most Anglicized their names. This is similar to the situation Cernea described in Burma, where 'Eliahu Sofaer became Elias and then Ellis; Saleh Saul became Charlie Saul; Ramah Aaron, Rose Aaron, and her brother Ezekiel Aaron, Edward Aaron' (2007, p. 46).

Henry Sassoon (Figure 3.19) established himself as an entrepreneur in post-war Montreal, building rows of homes as well as an apartment complex on McGregor Street (renamed 'avenue Docteur Penfield', in 1978). He left Montreal in 1957, and took up residency in Bel Air, in southern California. In 1963, he began construction of the Long Beach Towers, at 600 East Ocean Boulevard, in Long Beach; this was completed in 1964 (Brownell, 1966). At 666 East Ocean Boulevard (later changed to 700 East Ocean Boulevard), Henry Sassoon built the 27 storey International Tower (originally Tower Sixes), at a cost of US$7 million. This circular high-rise was engineered by Tung-Yen Lin, Professor emeritus of civil engineering

Figure 3.14 Israel Sasson, wearing Eastern dress during early twentieth century (photograph courtesy of Daniel Nathan Scharf)

at the University of California, and considered among the greatest structural engineer of his times. In July 1964, the newspaper *Long Beach Press Telegram* predicted this would be 'one of the most unusual structures ever erected'.[9] Wooden forms were airlifted to position and concrete was poured 24 hours a day. The tower rose about 24 feet per day (Figure 3.20). When completed, Henry Sassoon claimed that this was the tallest pre-stressed-concrete structure in the world. Brownell (1966) evaluated

Figure 3.15 Loulou Akerib (1890–1968)

Figure 3.16 Naomi Sasson in Heliopolis during 1938

the building to be worth US$10 million, and Henry Sassoon sold it to California Savings and Loan. Roberts Consolidated Industries, Inc. used Henry Sassoon to endorse their doors in an advertisement: 'Henry chose Roberts Bi-Fold metal doors for The Tower – and saved $4.00 on every wardrobe – 960 doors in all . . . they come pre-finished . . . in a flawless, baked semi-gloss Navajo white.'

Henry also established Sassoon Development Inc., based in Beverly Hills, which built Country View Estates. Henry died in March 2001, a few days before his ninetieth birthday. Tung-Yen Lin died in 2003 at the age of 91.

Henry's younger brother Robert was also a very successful entrepreneur. He left Egypt for France where he was the owner–manager of the Rex Agency, in Marseilles. There he adopted Marcel Merle and Robert Merle. Robert Sr spent some time in London (Figure 3.21), acquired British citizenship and subsequently moved to Canada where he worked with his brother Henry and launched his own developments. In 1961, he married Anne-Marie Pross, who had been born in Germany in 1929; together they raised a family and remained in Dorval, a suburb of Montreal, and he mastered German.

DESCENDANTS OF ISRAEL SASSON

Israel Sasson (Basra, Ottoman Empire, 1883 – Cairo, Egypt, January 1943)
Married to **Naomi Akerib** (Basra, Ottoman Empire, 1892 – Montreal, Canada, January 1968)

Selim Sassoon	**Haroun (Henry) Sassoon**	**Habiba (Aimée)**	**Sophie Charlotte**	**Rahma (Clemy)**	**Menashe Reuben (Robert) Sassoon**	**Loulou**	**Helène (Helen)**
Born: 1909	**Born:** 1911	**Born:** 1913	**Born:** 1914	**Born:** 1919	**Born:** 1921	**Born:** 1924	**Born:** 1925
Married: Dora (Bat Esther) Cohen in 1943	**Married:** Ines Fontenance in 1944	**Married:** Edmond Shmuel (Ben Moshe) Hirsch in 1937	**Married:** Fayez Tadros in 1942	**Married:** Alberto di Leone d'Ana in 1946	**Married:** Ann-Marie Pross in 1961	**Married:** Herbert Leo Scharf in 1946	**Married:** Henri Zelnick in 1942
Father of: Claude 1944 Josette 1948		**Mother of:** Nadine 1937 Yrielle 1939-1960 Alain Raymond 1946	**Mother of:** Sobhi 1946	**Mother of:** Léo-Paul 1958	**Father of:** Marcel 1942 Robert 1946 Marie-Louise 1958 Kathleen 1961 Margaret 1962 Natasha 1980	**Mother of:** Isabel Jean 1952 Daniel Nathan 1954	**Mother of:** Serge 1943 Percy 1947 Michel Roger 1955
Deceased: 1997 in Toronto	**Deceased:** 2001 in Montreal	**Deceased:** 1966 in flight	**Deceased:** 2002 in Montreal				

Note: Name at birth followed by Anglicized name in brackets.

Figure 3.17 Family tree compiled by the author

Figure 3.18 *Israel Sasson, wearing tarbouche (photograph courtesy of Daniel Nathan Scharf)*

Figure 3.19 *Henry Sassoon standing beside the author in San Fernando Valley, 4 July 1988 (photograph by Ines Sassoon)*

Figure 3.20 Henry's tower, in May 1965 (photograph courtesy of Henry Sassoon)

Figure 3.21 *Robert Sassoon in London during 1951 (photograph courtesy of Robert Sassoon)*

Figure 3.22 Edmond Shmuel Ben Moshe Hirsch (1910–74) with spouse Aimée (1913–66) (photograph courtesy of Nadine Pekar)

Aimée (Figure 3.22) married Edmond Shmuel Ben Moshe Hirsch (1910–74) in 1937. They left Egypt in 1956 and settled in Montreal. Edmond worked for some time with a brother-in-law in Canada, and also freelanced in Europe.

Sophie Charlotte married Fayez Tadros. They remained in Egypt until

Figure 3.23 Clemy

1962, when they relocated to Montreal where Fayez was self-employed until the 1990s.

Clemy (Figure 3.23) was married to serial entrepreneur Alberto di Leone d'Ana (Figure 3.24) in January 1946 and they departed for Italy in 1951. She gave birth in Lausanne, Switzerland, in April 1954. They moved from Switzerland to Canada in 1958 where they had a second son. She was

Figure 3.24 Alberto di Leone d'Ana

Figure 3.25 From left to right, Loulou Scharf, Naomi Sassoon and Herbert Leo Scharf

an active philanthropist in Montreal; in 1983 she contributed towards a Chair in Musicology at the Hebrew University. She also provided funding for two chairs in cancer research.

Loulou married Herbert Leo Scharf (Figure 3.25), who after graduating

Figure 3.26 Helen Zelnick in Australia

Harvard Law School in 1951 set up his practice focusing on anti-trust and trade regulation. While he was a student, she taught Arabic. Once her children were grown up, Loulou set up a cooking school (Arum, 1981). Herbert died 6 August 2002.

Helen (Figure 3.26) married into the very wealthy and respected Zelnick family, and with her husband Henry lived in Australia, Canada and the United States, where he was an entrepreneur.

In summary, entrepreneurship prevailed among the children of Israel Sassoon. Most were either entrepreneurs and/or married to entrepreneurs. Likewise, most of the grandchildren of Israel Sassoon were founders of corporations, otherwise self-employed or working for a business owned by a family member. After several years in southern California, Sobhi Fayez Tadros is a successful developer in Montreal. Alain Hirsch founded Alain Hirsch Construction, Corp, of Los Alamitos, California. Marcel Merle, son of Robert Sassoon, became successfully self-employed in Montreal. Robert Sassoon's daughter Marie Louise Lloyd became a successful entrepreneur in Manchester. Isabel Jean Kurek (born Scharf) established Isabel J. Kurek Photography, based in Maryland. Her photographs appear in: *American Express Black Ink*; *Maryland Life Magazine*; *W Magazine*; *Horse of the Delaware Valley*; *In and Around Horse Country*; *Chesapeake Life Magazine*; *John Lyons Magazine*; *Covertside Magazine*; Maryland Tourism Ad; *Maryland Million Program*; *The Equiery*; and *The Chronicle of the Horse*. Her brother Daniel Nathan Scharf is a self-employed artist. Michel R. Zelnick has been president of the Zelnick Group since 2001.

REFLECTIONS

In New York, one interviewee gave me to read a quotation from Simons:

> more than any other immigrant group, Jews have found their way into almost every interstice of American life, have taken just about every opportunity this nation has to offer, and have given back to America in enriching ways that are wondrous. I think the Jewish immigrants, from the very beginning of their time and America's time, have come closer to realizing the American Dream than have any other group. The Jewish premium on family and religion, hard work and education, charity and public service, *is* the American Dream. (1988, p. 7)

He then explained to me that in his opinion, premium on family, religion, hard work and education, charity and public service was the lifeline of Mizrahi networks.

Empirical findings discussed above confirm that the ethnic resources of Mizrahi entrepreneurs have included credit networks, employment networks, information networks and supply networks. Mizrahim benefited from social capital and this facilitated access to financial capital.

In addition, Mizrahi entrepreneurs appear to have benefited from a feature that could be termed 'ethics capital', related to the reputation they had based on their business ethics. Consider some of the comments about these people:

- 'They never rip you off.'
- 'It is very good to do business with them because they are so honest.'
- 'They are rich because everyone trusts them.'
- 'They were very fair in business, so we all trusted them.'
- 'His absolute trustworthiness.'

From this we might understand that they benefited from having a good reputation, or 'ethics capital'. This supports Cernea, who suggested that

Mizrahim were 'prospering . . . especially because of the economic benefit derived from the extensive ties of trust afforded by their religion and family networks' (2007, p. xvii).

CONCLUSION

Neither colonists nor colonized, Mizrahim immigrated to several hubs across Asia, developing strong entrepreneurship networks, helping them succeed in the realm of business – out of all proportion considering their small population.

Common values across Mizrahi communities included family cohesion, a disciplined work ethic, respect for others and benevolence toward employees. Ethics were emphasized and this earned these people a reputation, resulting in ethics capital. Sharing these values facilitated networking, and the transnational networks in turn facilitated credit, employment and information exchange. Learning from network members was an effective substitute for academic credentials.

Mizrahi networks became an ethnic resource helping entrepreneurs launch new start-ups that added jobs to the aggregate job supply. In contrast to ethnic ownership literature that focuses on co-ethnic employment, this study showed that Mizrahi entrepreneurs employed non-co-ethnic immigrants.

Fluency in several languages allowed Mizrahi entrepreneurs to communicate effectively among themselves, with suppliers, with buyers, and with non-co-ethnic employees in their host societies. This had a mutually beneficial result: enhanced economic opportunities for co-ethnics and for their host societies, including other immigrant groups.

Network-driven immigration concentrated Mizrahim in selected neighbourhoods. While networks expanded the efficiency of searches and increased the supply of housing, geographic clustering of Mizrahim put pressure on the price of land, making Mizrahi neighbourhoods quite exclusive.

NOTES

* The author thanks Distinguished Professor Richard W. Wright for comments on an earlier draft of this chapter.

1. Source: Mosley (2003).
2. A photo of the Mizrahi synagogue in Surabaya appears in Dana (2007a).
3. A kosher diet respects the dietary laws from the Bible, including: 'Ye shall therefore put difference between clean beasts and unclean, and between unclean fowls and clean:

and ye shall not make your souls abominable by beast, or by fowl, or by any manner of living thing that creepeth on the ground, which I have separated from you as unclean' (Leviticus 20:25). Leviticus 3:17 prohibits observers from eating blood or fat. Leviticus 22:8 elaborates, 'That which dieth of itself, or is torn with beasts, he shall not eat to defile himself therewith: I am the LORD'. This is understood to mean that it is not kosher to eat food from animals that die themselves or that are killed by another animal. Leviticus also provides details as to what species the Bible allows observers to eat or not. It is not permitted to eat camel, 'he is unclean onto you' (Leviticus 11:4). The hare (Leviticus 11:6); pork (Leviticus 11:7); eagles (Leviticus 11:13); vultures (Leviticus 11:14); ravens (Leviticus 11:15); owls (Leviticus 11:16); cormorants (Leviticus 11:17); swans, pelican and eagles (Leviticus 11:18) are specified as not allowed. The same is true of the stork, the heron and the bat (Leviticus 11:19). Leviticus 11:29 states, 'These also shall be unclean unto you among the creeping things that creep upon the earth; the weasel, and the mouse, and the tortoise after his kind'. Leviticus 11:30 adds, 'And the ferret, and the chameleon, and the lizard, and the snail, and the mole'. It is not allowed to eat scavengers and predators; for this reason, observers refrain from eating catfish, clams, lobsters, oysters, and shrimp.

4. An upper case I is used for the word Indigenous, as per the convention of Hindle and Lansdowne (2005, p. 132).
5. Jacobs and Lipkind (1906a) spelled his name 'Abdallah' as pronounced; more recently, Abdullah is used, corresponding to literary Arabic.
6. Source: Mosley (2003).
7. Source: Hyams (1906).
8. Source: Hammond (1998).
9. Source: Mullio and Volland (2004, p. 218).

REFERENCES

Abdullah, Asma (1992), 'The Influence of Ethnic Values on Managerial Practices in Malaysia', *Malaysian Management Review*, **27** (1), 3–18.

Altinay, Levent (2008), 'The Relationship Between an Entrepreneur's Culture and the Entrepreneurial Behaviour of the Firm', *Journal of Small Business and Enterprise Development*, **15** (1), 111–29.

Arum, Nancy (1981), 'A Full Menu of Classes in the Cuisine of Your Choice', *New York Times*, 13 September A10.

Bainbridge, Oliver (1907), 'The Chinese Jews', *National Geographic*, **18** (10), 621–32.

Betta, Chiara (2000), 'Marginal Westerners in Shanghai: The Baghdadi Jewish Community', in Robert Bickers and Christian Henriot (eds), *New Frontiers, Imperialism's New Communities in East Asia 1842–1953*, Manchester: Manchester University Press, pp. 38–54.

Betta, Chiara (2003), 'From Orientals to Imagined Britons: Baghdadi Jews in Shanghai', *Modern Asian Studies*, **37** (4), 999–1023.

Boissevain, Jeremy and Hanneke Grotenbreg (1987), 'Ethnic Enterprise in the Netherlands: The Surinamese of Amsterdam', in Robert Goffee and Richard Scase (eds), *Entrepreneurship in Asia: The Social Processes*, London: Croom Helm, pp. 105–30.

Bonacich, Edna (1973), 'A Theory of Middleman Minorities', *American Sociological Review*, **38**, 583–4.

Brownell, Keith W. (1966), *Appraisal Report: International Tower, Long Beach*, Glendale, CA: Keith W. Brownell Co.

Cernea, Ruth Fredman (2007), *Almost Englishmen: Baghdadi Jews in British Burma*, Lanham, MA: Lexington Books.

Cohen, Israel (1956), *A Jewish Pilgrimage: The Autobiography of Israel Cohen*, London: Valentine, Mitchell.

Dana, Léo-Paul (1999a), *Entrepreneurship in Pacific Asia: Past Present & Future*, Singapore, London and Hong Kong: World Scientific.

Dana, Léo-Paul (1999b), 'The Iraqi Community of Burma', *La Voix Sépharade*, **28** (2), 52–3.

Dana, Léo-Paul (2002), *When Economies Change Paths: Models of Transition in China, the Central Asian Republics, Myanmar, and the Nations of Former Indochine Française*, Singapore, London and Hong Kong: World Scientific.

Dana, Léo-Paul (2006), 'A Historical Study of the Traditional Livestock Merchants of Alsace', *British Food Journal*, **108** (7), 586–98.

Dana, Léo-Paul (2007a), *Asian Models of Entrepreneurship – From the Indian Union and the Kingdom of Nepal to the Japanese Archipelago: Context, Policy and Practice*, Singapore and London: World Scientific.

Dana, Léo-Paul (2007b), 'Humility-based Economic Development and Entrepreneurship among the Amish', *Journal of Enterprising Communities: People and Places in the Global Economy*, **1** (2), 142–54.

Dana, Léo-Paul and Teresa E. Dana (2008), 'Ethnicity & Entrepreneurship in Morocco: A Photo-ethnographic Study', *International Journal of Business and Globalisation*, **2** (3), 209–26.

Durkheim, Émile (1912), *Les formes élémentaires de la vie religieuse: Le système totémique en Australie*, Paris: Félix Alcan.

Fields, Sidney, (1974), 'Kitchen Crasher', *Daily News*, New York, 4 March, p. 55.

Fishberg, Maurice (1911), *The Jews: A Study of Race and Environment*, London: Walter Scott.

Gadgil, Dhananjaya Ramchandra (1959), *Origins of the Modern Indian Business Class*, New York: Institute of Pacific Relations.

Galbraith, Craig Scott, Donald R. Latam and Jacqueline Benitez-Galbraith (1997), 'Entrepreneurship in the Hispanic Community of the Southeastern United States', *Frontiers of Entrepreneurship Research*, Wellesley, MA: Babson College.

Galbraith, Craig Scott, Curt H. Stiles and Jacqueline Benitez-Bertheau (2004), 'The Embryonic Development of an Ethnic Neighbourhood: A Longitudinal Case Study of Entrepreneurial Activity', in Curt H. Stiles and Craig Scott Galbraith (eds), *Ethnic Entrepreneurship: Structure and Process*, Oxford: Elsevier, pp. 95–112.

Galbraith, Craig Scott, Curt H. Stiles and Carlos Rodriguez (2003) 'Intra-Enclave Trade: Hispanic and Arab Small Businesses', *Journal of Small Business and Entrepreneurship*, **16** (3/4), 18–29.

Geertz, Clifford (1962), 'The Rotating Credit Association: A "Middle Rung" in Development', *Economic Development and Cultural Change*, **10**, 241–63.

Godspeed, George Stephen (1902), *A History of the Babylonians and Assyrians*, New York: Charles Scribners' Sons.

Gupta, Gargi (2007), 'An Era of Bakes from a Kitchen in India', *Business Standard*, 20 October.

Hammond, Peter W. (ed.) (1998). *The Complete Peerage or a History of the*

House of Lords and All its Members from the Earliest Times, vol. 14: *Addenda & Corrigenda*, Stroud: Sutton.

Hindle, Kevin and Michele Lansdowne (2005), 'Brave Spirits on New Paths: Toward a Globally Relevant Paradigm of Indigenous Entrepreneurship Research', *Journal of Small Business and Entrepreneurship*, **18** (2), 131–43.

Hyams, J. (1906), 'Pedigree of the Sassoon Family', in Isidore Singer (ed.), *The Jewish Encyclopedia*, New York: Funk & Wagnalls, p. 66.

Iyer, Gopalkrishnan R. and Jon M. Shapiro (1999), 'Ethnic Entrepreneurial and Marketing Systems: Implications for the Global Economy', *Journal of International Marketing*, **7** (4), 83–110.

Jacobs, Joseph and Joseph Ezekiel (1902), 'Calcutta', in Isidore Singer (ed.), *The Jewish Encyclopedia*, New York: Funk & Wagnalls, p. 497.

Jacobs, Joseph and J. Hyams (1906a), 'David Sassoon', in Isidore Singer (ed.), *The Jewish Encyclopedia*, Funk & Wagnalls, p. 67.

Jacobs, Joseph and J. Hyams (1906b), 'Elias David Sassoon', in Isidore Singer (ed.), *The Jewish Encyclopedia*, Funk & Wagnalls, p. 68.

Jacobs, Joseph, and J. Hyams (1906c), 'Jacob Elias Sassoon', in Isidore Singer (ed.), *The Jewish Encyclopedia*, Funk & Wagnalls, p. 68.

Jacobs, Joseph and Goodman Lipkind (1906a), 'Sir Albert Abdallah David Sassoon, Bart', in Isidore Singer (ed.), *The Jewish Encyclopedia*, Funk & Wagnalls, pp. 66–7.

Jacobs, Joseph and Goodman Lipkind (1906b), 'Sir Edward Albert Sassoon, Bart.', in Isidore Singer (ed.), *The Jewish Encyclopedia*, Funk & Wagnalls, pp. 67–8.

Jacobs, Joseph and Goodman Lipkind (1906c), 'Solomon David Sassoon', in Isidore Singer (ed.), *The Jewish Encyclopedia*, Funk & Wagnalls, p. 68.

Ji, Zhaojin (2003), *A History of Modern Shanghai Banking: The Rise and Decline of China Finance Capitalism*, Armonk, NY: M.E. Sharpe.

Juteau, Danielle and Sylvie Paré (1996), 'L'entrepreneurship ethnique', *Interfaces*, **17** (1), 18–28.

Kraybill, Donald B. and Steven M. Nolt (1995), *Amish Enterprise*, Baltimore, MD: Johns Hopkins University Press.

Lasry, Jean-Claude (1982), 'Une Diaspora Francophone au Québec: Les Juifs Sépharades', *Questions de Culture*, **2**, 113–38.

Leese, Arnold (1940), *Gentile Folly: The Rothschilds*, Guildford: White House.

Leslie, Donald Daniel (1972), *The Survival of the Chinese Jews: The Jewish Community of Kaifeng*, Leiden: E.J. Brill.

Light, Ivan H. (1972), *Ethnic Enterprise in America*, Berkeley and Los Angles, CA: University of California Press.

Light, Ivan H. and Edna Bonacich (1988), *Immigrant Entrepreneurs: Koreans in Los Angeles*, Los Angeles: University of California Press.

Makepeace, Walter, Gilbert E. Brooke and Roland St.J. Braddell (eds) (1921), *One Hundred Years of Singapore*, London: John Murray.

Min, Pyong Gap and Charles Jaret (1985), 'Ethnic Business Success: The Case of Korean Small Business in Atlanta', *Sociology and Social Research*, **69** (April), 412–35.

Mosley, Charles (ed.), (2003), *Burke's Peerage, Baronetage & Knightage*, 107th edn, Wilmington, DE: Burke's Peerage.

Mullio, Cara and Jennifer M. Volland (2004), *Long Beach Architecture: The Unexpected Metropolis*, Santa Monica, CA: Hennessey & Ingalls.

Porter, Kenneth Wiggens (1937), *The Jacksons and the Lees: Two Generations of Massachusetts Merchants, 1765–1844*, Cambridge, MA: Harvard University Press.
Raistrick, Arthur (1950), *Quakers in Science and Industry*, London: Bannisdale.
Raphaël, Freddy (1980), 'Les juifs de la campagne alsacienne: les marchands de bestiaux', *Revue des Sciences Sociales de la France de l'Est*, **9**, 220–45.
Rolland, Joan G. (1989), *Jews in British India: Identity in a Colonial Era*, Hanover, CT: University Press of New England.
Simons, Howard (1988), *Jewish Times: Voices of the American Jewish Experience*, Boston, MA: Houghton Mifflin.
Simpich, Frederick (1919), 'The Rise of the New Arab Nation', *National Geographic*, **36** (5), 369–93.
Sombart, Werner (1911), *Die Juden und das Wirtschaftsleben*, Leipzig: Duncker und Humblot.
Stiles, Curt H., Carlos L. Rodriguez and Craig S. Galbraith (2007), 'The Impact of Ethnic-religious Identification on Buyer-seller Behaviour: A Study of Two Enclaves', *International Journal of Business and Globalisation*, **1** (1), 20–33.
Weche, Meres J. (2000), *Planet of the Greeks: The Great Time Warp of History*, Ottawa: Amun-Ra.
White, William Charles (1942), *Chinese Jews: A Compilation of Matters Relating to the Jews of K'ai-fêng Fu*, Toronto: University of Toronto Press and Department of Chinese Studies, Royal Ontario Museum.
Wong, Bernard P. (1987), 'The Role of Ethnicity in Enclave Enterprises: A Study of the Chinese Garment Factories in New York City', *Human Organization*, **46** (2), 120–31.
Wu, David Y. (1974), 'To Kill Three Birds with One Stone: The Rotating Credit Association of the Papua New Guinea Chinese', *American Ethnologist*, **1**, 565–84.

PART II

Christian Communities

4. Greek Christian Orthodoxy and entrepreneurship

Dimitri Tassiopoulos

INTRODUCTION

The Hellenic Republic (or more colloquially, Greece) is a constitutional republic and multiparty parliamentary democracy. Greece is a mountainous country in the south-eastern European Union, with a landmass of 132 100 square kilometres, which is bordered by various Balkan countries in the north and hemmed in by nearly 2000 islands on its eastern, southern and western borders. Traditionally, Greeks refer to themselves as 'Hellenes' and to the country as Hellas. It is further noted that the word 'Greek' comes from the Latin *Graeci*, and is a name given to the people of this region by the Romans (Jurgens, 2008).

The Greek flag, continues Jurgens (2008), features a white cross in the left upper corner flanked on the right and bottom by alternating white and blue stripes. The white cross symbolizes the Greek Christian Orthodox religion, whilst the blue strips represent the sea and the sky, and the white stripes depict the valour and purity of the Greek struggle for independence. All in all, government, church and society 'constitute' a holy amalgamation.

Greece: The Geography of its Religions

Greece has an estimated population of 10.9 million. Approximately 98 per cent of citizens identify themselves, at least nominally, with the Greek Orthodox faith. There are also approximately 500 000 to 800 000 Old Calendarists throughout the country. With the exception of the Turcophone Muslim community (some of whose rights and privileges, as well as related government obligations, are covered by the 1923 Treaty of Lausanne), the government does not keep statistics of religious groups; censuses do not ask for religious affiliation. Ethnic Greeks account for a sizeable percentage of most non-Orthodox religions. The remainder of the citizens of Greece is composed of Muslims (officially estimated at 98 000, although some Muslims claim up to 140 000 countrywide). Accurate figures for other religious groups are not available. Members of Jehovah's Witnesses are estimated at 50 000; Catholics at 50 000; Protestants, including evangelicals, at 30 000; and the Church of Jesus Christ of Latter-day Saints (Mormons) at 300. Scientologists claim to have 500 active registered members. The Jewish community numbers approximately 5000, of whom 1000 are citizens and reside in Thessalonica. Approximately 250 members of the Baha'i Faith, the majority of whom are citizens of non-Greek ethnicity, are scattered throughout the country. There are also small populations of Anglicans, Baptists and non-denominational Christians. There is no official or unofficial estimate of atheists. The majority of non-citizen residents are Albanians (approximately 700 000 including legal and illegal residents) and are not Greek Orthodox; a nominal number are Muslim, Orthodox or Roman Catholic, but the majority of whom are non-practising. Some religious groups, such as the Evangelicalists and Jehovah's Witnesses, consist almost entirely of ethnic Greeks. Other groups, such as Mormons and Anglicans, consist of an approximately equal number of ethnic Greeks and non-Greeks (US State Department, 2003).

Greek Religious Practice in Ancient Times

In Ancient Greece, violations of norms arising from pre-Christian religious customs created the possibility of divine sanctions with misfortunes of all sorts sometimes attributed to the gods' righteous indignations. A norm was that temples, sanctuaries and other religious buildings were not to be disturbed and was seen first depicted in the Homeric period, and, according to Lanni (2007), the destruction of sacred buildings and objects, even during wartime, was not tolerated, even in retaliation. There are many examples concerning warring forces that took care to avoid disturbing religious buildings and sites. Most notably, Alexander the Great took vengeance on states who desecrated sacred buildings and objects. He, himself, carefully avoided destroying sacred buildings and objects during his campaigns. The immunity of priests and other religious functionaries was a strong norm first depicted in the Homeric period. Making war during religious festivals was considered contrary to the laws of war. This norm was not only applied to pan-Hellenic festivals, such as the Olympic Games, but states were also banned from attacking a city that was observing a local festival. Ultimately, the religious basis of such laws helped foster compliance amongst the citizens of Ancient Greece. The fear of divine sanctions provided incentives to comply with the law. Furthermore, according to Anderson et al. (2000), in Ancient Greece, entrepreneurship was viewed as illegitimate by some (for instance, Aristotle) as it was viewed as an unnatural mode of conduct whereby one man stood to gain from another.

Religious Freedoms and Practices

Religious activities are strictly controlled by the Ministry of Education and Religion. The traditional hostility of Greece to all religions other than Orthodoxy and Judaism has recently given way to greater tolerance, especially since the removal of religious affiliation from national identity cards.

Religious instruction in Orthodoxy in public primary and secondary schools is mandatory for all Greek Orthodox students. Non-Orthodox students are exempt from this requirement; however, non-Orthodox students have reported some instances of discrimination related to attendance at religious education classes or other celebrations of religious or nationalistic character (Baldwin-Edwards, 2005).

The Christian Orthodox Church

It is estimated, by Berger (2005, p. 437), that there 'is about 350 million Orthodox Christians in the world. The term is somewhat flexible, as it sometimes is used only to refer to the churches that are affiliated with the Patriarch of Constantinople, sometimes also (includes) the so-called non-Chalcedonian churches, such as the Armenian and the Coptic.' The Christian Orthodox Churches, states Jurgens (2008), nonetheless share a common liturgy (a prescribed form of public religious ceremony), worship and tradition. In their beliefs, the church is considered largely conservative, resistant to change and allows little flexibility.

Early Christianity, according to Berger (2005), existed as a voluntary association both in the Greek and Latin speaking regions of the Western world. Following the Constantinian establishment (not to be confused with the rule of Constantine the Great), Eastern Christian Orthodoxy existed in four social forms: (a) as a state church, first in the Byzantium, then in Russia, then in the independent states emerging from the slow disintegration of the Ottoman Empire; (b) as a more or less tolerated minority under Muslim rule, as in the Ottoman millet system (refers to legally protected religious minority groups in the Ottoman Empire); (c) as a persecuted community under Communist rule; and, (d) as a Diaspora community, principally in ethnic enclaves in Western Europe, the Americas and elsewhere. For a prominent number of Christian Orthodox followers, there has been a taken-for-granted unity between religion and community.

Where Christian Orthodoxy existed as the official church of the society, this unity was enforced by the power of the state. The only option for voluntary action was by the way of dissidence. The Christian Orthodox followers under the Ottoman Empire millet system were more or less comfortable, although Ottoman policies changed from time to time, and there was little choice, although converting to Islam was a distinct choice. Embracing Christian Orthodoxy under communist rule required voluntary action of a courageous kind as it involved great personal cost. The church went underground and certainly could not be taken for granted. Finally, Christian Orthodoxy in the Diaspora depends on the strength of ethnic identification, for example, for many Russian-Americans or Greek-South Africans, being Christian Orthodox is still a matter of course as ethnic ties weaken with assimilation; this taken-for-grantedness comes under increasing pressure. The Christian Orthodox churches are organized in ethnically defined jurisdictions and are increasingly functioning as de facto voluntary organisations (Berger, 2005).

Eastern Orthodox Church Organization

The Eastern Orthodox Church is the second largest single Christian communion in the world and is considered by its adherents to be the very same Church established by Christ and his Apostles. It is composed of numerous theologically unified autocephalous ecclesiastical bodies each led by a synod of independent bishops whose duty it is to preserve the inner beliefs and practices (Traditions) of the Church. All Orthodox bishops can trace their lineage back to one of the 12 Apostles through the process of apostolic succession.

The Eastern Orthodox Church is a union comprising the 14 or 15 separate autocephalous (or self-governing) hierarchical churches that recognize each other as 'canonical' Orthodox Christian churches, although, there is essentially a political disagreement over the autocephaly of one of the churches – the Orthodox Church in America.

There is no single earthly head of all the Orthodox Churches comparable to the Pope of Rome. The highest-ranking bishop of the communion is the Patriarch of Constantinople, who is also primate of one of the autocephalous churches. These organizations are in full communion with each other, so any priest of any of those churches may lawfully minister to any member of any of them, and no member of any is excluded from any form of worship in any of the others, including reception of the Eucharist. Each local or national Orthodox Church is a portion of the Orthodox Church as a whole. The autocephalous hierarchical churches (ranked in order of seniority) are:

1. Church of Constantinople, under the Ecumenical Patriarch
2. Church of Alexandria (sometimes called the Greek Orthodox Patriarchate of Alexandria to distinguish it from the Coptic Orthodox Patriarchate of Alexandria)
3. Church of Antioch
4. Church of Jerusalem
5. Church of Russia (est. 1589)
6. Church of Serbia (est. 1219)
7. Church of Romania (est. 1925)
8. Church of Bulgaria (est. 927)
9. Church of Georgia (est. 466)
10. Church of Cyprus (est. 434)
11. Church of Greece (est. 1850)
12. Church of Poland (est. 1924)
13. Church of Albania (est. 1937)
14. Church of Czech and Slovak lands (est. 1951)
15. Orthodox Church in America (est. 1972). (Autocephaly though not universally recognized.)

Autocephaly in hierarchical Christian churches and especially Eastern Orthodox (and Oriental Orthodox churches), is the status of a hierarchical church whose head bishop does not report to any higher-ranking bishop. When an ecumenical council or a high-ranking bishop, such as a patriarch or other primate, releases an ecclesiastical province from the authority of that bishop while the newly independent church remains in full communion with the hierarchy to which it then ceases to belong, the council or primate is granting autocephaly. For example, the Cypriot Orthodox Church was granted autocephaly by the Council of Ephesus and is ruled by the Archbishop of Cyprus, who is not subject to any higher ecclesiastical authority, although his church remains in full communion with the other Eastern Orthodox churches. Similarly, the Georgian Orthodox Church was granted autocephaly (independence) in 466 by the Patriarchate of Antioch.

The Church of Greece (or the Eastern Orthodox Church of Christ) is one of the 15 autocephalous Eastern Orthodox churches which make up the Eastern Orthodox Communion. Today it is one of the most important autocephalous, or ecclesiastically independent churches of the Eastern Orthodox communion. Its canonical territory encompasses the pre-1833 borders of Greece, approximately half of Greek territory (the rest of Greece is subject to the Ecumenical Patriarchate in Constantinople, however, due to an arrangement agreed between the churches of Athens and Constantinople, most of those dioceses are de facto administered as part of the Church of Greece for practical reasons). The Church was formerly a part of the Ecumenical Patriarchate of Constantinople. It was declared autocephalous in 1833 in a political decision of the Bavarian Regents acting on behalf of King Otto, who was a minor at the time. It was only recognized as such by the Patriarchate in 1850, under certain conditions with the issue of a special 'Tomos' decree which brought it back to a normal status. As a result, it retains certain special links with the 'Mother Church'. The Church of Greece was established by the Greek constitution as the 'prevailing' religion of Greece, it is financially supported by the government and exercises significant political and economic influence. By virtue of its status, as the prevailing religion, the canon law of the Church is recognized by the Greek government (Wikipedia, 2008).

The Greek Christian Orthodox Church, thus, has a significant political and economic influence on its followers. Anderson et al. (2000) as well as Drakopoulou Dodd and Seaman (1998) refer to one aspect of environmental munificence (or benevolence), that is, the role of religion as a support for enterprise culture in an environment which is abundant in appropriate resources. The overall aim of this study is to explore the role of the Greek Christian Orthodox religion as a support for enterprise culture amongst the Greek people. Thus, the primary research aim of this study is to develop a better understanding of the relationship between Greeks, entrepreneurship and the values that are represented by the Greek Orthodox Church. This research has been undertaken because of the gap in knowledge concerning this subject area.

METHODOLOGY

Desktop research was conducted involving the rapid review research methodology. The process involved the review of relevant literature concerning the relationship between Greeks, entrepreneurship and the values that are represented by the Greek Orthodox Church. The research period spanned from April to June 2008. A literature review, according to Taylor and Procter (2001), is an account of what has been published on a topic by accredited scholars and researchers with the purpose of conveying what knowledge and ideas have been established on a topic. A literature rapid review is defined by a guiding concept (that is, the research objective, the problem or issue being researched), and is not only a descriptive list of the material available, or a set of summaries.

The aim of the literature rapid review was to be organized around the main research aim and to synthesize the results into a summary of what was and what is not known; to identify areas of controversy in the literature; and to formulate questions that needed further research.

FINDINGS

After Christ's disciples, according to Haralambos (2005), were given the authority to spread the gospel throughout the region, they travelled extensively over the land that now includes present-day Greece, establishing churches along the way. Christians, including those of the Greek Orthodox faith originate from these early Churches. Today the customs, traditions and beliefs of the then Greek Christian Orthodox churches remain strictly intact. The early church communities, particularly of the Hellenistic-Pauline Diaspora, according to Drakopoulou Dodd and Gotsis (2007), tended to draw their members from amongst the less privileged. Thus, the antagonism towards wealth of the earlier church leaders, including Jesus and James, has always been noticeable. The Jesus Movement in rural Palestine exhibited considerable hostility to the pursuit of wealth, and the stance became even more pronounced in the Jerusalem Love Community, who rejected individual property holdings, entrepreneurial risk-taking and even labour itself. The Apostle Paul began the process of justifying the strength of this theology which became the so-called Pauline School that introduced both a strong work ethic and the importance of self-sufficiency, to Christianity. In the second century, even more wealthy people joined the Church. A way of dealing with their prosperity needed to be found, however, most Church leaders continued to support the Jerusalem Community's opposition to the pursuit and retention of wealth. It was felt that private property was the root of human dissension as the struggle for individual possessions destroyed the original good order of the world since all had an equal share in God's gifts. For instance, John Chrysostom stated 'the everlasting desire to accumulate goods in excess of what is needed for self-support, to be the source of all human evil' (Drakopoulou Dodd and Gotsis, 2007, p. 137).

Partial mitigation, however, was found in the influential work of Clement of Alexandria who proposed that the rich could join the church provided that they used their wealth to assist the poor. It was viewed that Christ could not possibly have intended that the rich give up all their possessions, for if they did, they would no longer be able to accomplish the good that can only be accomplished by those who have resources at their disposal. It was thus viewed that the affluent were not sinful because of their riches, as poverty could also not be considered a virtue in itself. In the conditional justification of wealth, a state of moderate prosperity was envisaged, in which one possessed sufficient goods to meet one's own needs and to effectively help the poor. In this respect, Clement's compromise, although not universally accepted by later Fathers, was encouraging for the entrepreneurial aspects of economic life, as Christians were allowed to participate in the process of accumulating capital. However, the strictures remained firmly in place that these rich Christians could not become attached to wealth for its own sake and had to live modestly.

In 312, Constantine (not to be confused with Constantine the Great) won the battle of Milvian Bridge, according to Drakopoulou Dodd and Gotsis (2007), becoming emperor of Rome and subsequently founding Constantinople as the capital of what became ultimately the Eastern Roman Empire. He developed a new relationship between the State and the Church, claiming that divine intervention had assisted his victory. Under Constantine, the Christian Church became the accepted faith of the whole Roman Empire. The concept of Christendom, the unity of the Church and the State which prevailed until the late Middle Ages and afforded so much influence in the church, stems from Constantine and his explicit and formal creation of the Church State.

With regards to work ethic, highlights Drakopoulou Dodd and Gotsis (2007), the Church Fathers followed an essentially Pauline view, arguing that labour increased production and reduced injustice and sinfulness, provided for physical exercise and generated funds for charity. The excess of riches and earthly prosperity could be morally justified through generous giving of alms. This was further emphasized by John Chrysostom who stated that 'work permits man to echo the creativity of God, by joining in the act of shaping the created world and its resources' (Drakopoulou Dodd and Gotsis, 2007, p. 138). Linked to the positive view of labour was an emphasis on self-sufficiency, or autarchy. Autarchy was seen to progress the Pauline view of justifying labour and production and extending it to include consumption. This period also saw a return to Ancient Greek writings to supplement the biblical canon, most especially among the Eastern Fathers in the third and fourth centuries AD, many of whom had received a Greek education based on Aristotelian conception of the sterility of money. This is evident, according to Drakopoulou Dodd and Gotsis (2007), in the language used by many of them to condemn money. It also explains some of their developments in the area of enterprise values; a recognition of the creative aspects of work, the positive benefits of redistribution of resources to areas of need and a Stoic emphasis on ascetic autarchy (or frugal self-sufficiency).

Greek Christian Orthodoxy and Entrepreneurs in Greece

Introduction

Bitros and Minoglou (2006) state that at the beginning of the nineteenth century developments within the Greek mercantile communities situated within the Ottoman Empire instigated the creation of a new moral order. Namely, in 1806 Sultan Selim granted commercial privileges to the 'Greek nation' which led to the creation of a self-regulating Greek Traders' Coalition formally recognized by the Ottoman authorities, which was based on a system of legal decrees, an amalgam of the 1807 Napoleonic Commercial Code and the body of Greek Customary Law that had evolved spontaneously since the Byzantine Era. The Greek Traders' Coalition was not simply a legal entity. It played an important role in the dissemination of the new moral order, acting as an enlightenment of the Greek world of traders via the twin procedure: transplantations of modern (*read* Western) commercial techniques and the strict adherence to Christian Orthodox virtues within the Greek merchant communities (or *Paroikies*). Namely, scientific and moral enlightenment were advocated as a *sine qua non* for the material progress and success of the Greek business community. In essence, within the Greek mercantile communities there were now two cultural influences at play: the reality of the so-called 'Levantine' unreliable and parochial business practices versus the vision of modernity. The latter, a combination of new Western business techniques, the ethos of enlightenment, and the Eastern (orthodox) Christian values, prescribed a new moral order, which some may argue is the cornerstone of success of the Greek business networks.

Modern era of Greece

The Church of Greece wields significant political and economic influence. The government, under the direction of the Ministry of Education and Religion, provides some financial support to the Orthodox Church by, for example, paying for the salaries and religious training of clergy, and financing the construction and maintenance of Orthodox Church buildings (Bureau of Democracy, Human Rights and Labor, 2002). The Greek Constitution establishes the Eastern Orthodox Church of Christ (Greek Orthodoxy) as the 'prevailing' religion, but also gives the right for all citizens to practice the religion of their choice. The government generally respects this right; however, at times non-Orthodox groups face administrative obstacles or legal restrictions on religious practice. The Constitution prohibits proselytizing and stipulates that no rite of worship may disturb public order or offend moral principles.

The Church plays a role as an educational institution in Greece. From the historical past of Greece, the Orthodox Church has been of necessity 'the school of the nation'. The priest, specially hired teachers, or other members of the community, teach the role of Orthodoxy, Greek civilization and accounts of Hellenic history. The history of the early Church and that of Byzantine Greece are constantly promulgated as synonymous. Learners are expected to take pride in the role of Greeks in the expansion of Christianity and the fact that the records of the early Church were written in Greek. The supremacy of Orthodoxy is continually emphasized, together with the underlying cultural superiority of the Hellenic tradition. The prevalent ethnocentrism about the role of Greeks in the world and the general interpretation of history is exemplified in the continuity of Greece: from Ancient Greece through the Byzantine period to Modern Greece.

The Greek market, according to Karopoulos and Lazaretou (2006), is mostly dominated by family controlled businesses. As a typical Southern European economy, according to Petrakis (1997, p. 401), the Greek economy is notable for having the highest density of small and medium-sized businesses per 1000 inhabitants in the European Union. It is further noted that these businesses find it difficult to transform themselves into larger more advanced ventures. 'In other words, there seems to be a high density of entrepreneurial talent appearing (indeed, it may even be facilitated) but which later fails to find fertile ground in which to grow and create the conditions for a strong entrepreneurial sector' (ibid.). Numerous factors are cited as reasons for this state of affairs, amongst others, the labour market, technological factors, access to public commodities, and costs related to the public finance system, which are affecting the scope for growth. Furthermore, the oligopolic structuring of the market (a market characterized by a small number of producers who often act together to control the supply of a particular good and its market price), which facilities growth of creative entrepreneurial events, seems to exert negative pressure on such events.

The many religious festivities in Greece, most notably during Easter, the Assumption of the Blessed Virgin Mary (15 August) and Christmas, provide for participation in impressive rituals and ceremonies, which help in the reaffirmation of the faith in Orthodoxy and Hellenism. The religious calendar of events of the Greek Orthodox Christian Church has a direct impact on business operations, whose owners organize their business affairs around such events. New businesses routinely undergo inauguration/consecration ceremonies (*egenia*) that are performed by a priest to bless the new business for long-term prosperity. The priest, emphasizes Adendorff (2005), is thus an indispensable part in the life of the Greek community. In so doing, the church is affirming that no gift, event or human responsibility is secular or detached from God. For the Orthodox

Christian, all good things have God as their origin and goal. Nothing is outside of God's love and concern.

Societal attitudes

Citizens tend to link religious affiliation very closely to ethnicity. Many attribute the preservation of national identity to the actions of the Greek Orthodox Church during approximately 400 years of Ottoman rule and the subsequent nation-building period. The Church exercises significant social, political, and economic influence and it owns a considerable, although undetermined, amount of property.

Many citizens consider an ethnic Greek also an Orthodox Christian (US State Department, 2003). To be Greek, states McNall (1974) means more than being a resident of certain territory. One subscribes unconsciously to the idea of a people and a nation. Hellenism was developed during the many years under Ottoman domination as an ideology used by Greeks to maintain their cultural integrity. During the period of Ottoman occupation, the Orthodox Church was the sole centre of Greek power where the Church carried the responsibility for the religious life of Greeks as well as acting as the intermediary between the Ottoman authorities and the Greek population. The relationship of the Orthodox Church to Hellenism is complex. Hellenism stresses a classical education, which was anticipated to return Greece to her golden Age. Civil servants were educated along classical lines and received their appointments because of the classical aligned education. The Greek population tended to emulate the strata of society, placing the highest value on white-collar positions. This emulation often militates against vocational programmes and any deviation from classical training even though classical education has become non-functional for adaptation to modern society.

The Ottoman occupation produced a reliance on a system of patrons. Patronage, states McNall (1974), becomes a way of controlling one's destiny and reducing the uncertainties dealing with a still largely Byzantine bureaucracy. One could advance on the basis of who one knows, not based on merit and individual effort. The world of the Greek populace is anthropomorphized, so that the universalistic definitions are not called for. Greek Orthodoxy is a particularistic religion, because the individual can locate all problems, solutions and explanations for events outside of him or herself. It is the miraculous icon that can heal or the saint that will answer the prayer. Although the Greek populace is aware of rational explanations, it takes time for the population to give up entirely the notion that Fate controls one's destiny. Orthodoxy is a syncretic religion that fuses the magical beliefs and practices of ancient cults with modern Christianity. Research conducted by McNall (1974) found that members of the Greek populace tended to score highly on closed-mindedness. Many were unwilling to accept variation of opinion and tended to see issues in terms of black and white. Their ideological perspective is a traditional one, allowing for little diversity of opinion as they see no need for diversity. The religious system supports this position as it does not encourage change. Patronage thus replaces group action as a means of accomplishing anything. Greece is, furthermore, characterized by 'shame culture' behaviour where such behaviour is regulated almost exclusively by the dominant group to ensure conformity to the demands of this group. In the 'shame orientated culture', notes McNall (1974), failure to achieve in the larger world is the fault of someone else. Failure at economic enterprises, at school or life in general is due to the trickery and deceit of others. The shame culture is viewed as maladaptive (faulty or inadequate adaptation) to modern society because it prevents the belief in the efficacy of the individual initiative and in personal worth (with much behaviour considered moral being apparently maladaptive).

Networks and clans

Greek business, according to Harlaftis and Minoglou (2001), is a business based on the formation of networks and is based on trust and common culture. The cohesive force of the Greek network is the common origin or kinship of an extended family enclave; *Greekness* is entirely connected with the Greek language, Greek Orthodoxy and the Greek family. Culture is embedded in Greek-owned businesses and has proven pivotal in their structure and function. Networking and cooperation are usually based on common business culture, as this minimizes the risk and cost of transactions where a network is defined as a set of high trust relationships which directly or indirectly link together everyone in a social group.

Emigration

Greek emigration, according to Adendorff (2005), to the Diaspora was a result of the perpetual structural crisis of Greek society, from the establishment of the first independent state after 1828 to the present. The structural crisis and its consequences, social and economic, resulted in the primary push favouring emigration; the crisis stems from the devastation of rural Greek areas and increasing urbanization (which is not based on long-term planning). This has forced the Greek economy to face the problem of unemployment not only in the rural agricultural areas but also in the urban areas.

Greek Christian Orthodoxy and Entrepreneurs in the Diaspora

During the long history of Hellenism, Greek life has unfolded into two geographic areas: Greece proper, and the many communities that Greeks have formed outside of Greece proper. In ancient times, according to Constantinou (2007) and Harlaftis and Minoglou (2001), Greek colonizers established a presence along the Mediterranean coastline to the Black Sea region, with further large concentrations along the coastal area of western Asia Minor. It is emphasized by Harlaftis and Minoglou (2001) that the entrepreneurship of the Diaspora resulted in very successful international business operations (particularly because of the use of networks, culture, religion and family) and preceded the so-called globalization of the modern world economy. In modern times, 1700s and later, Greek emigrants once again established merchant communities in many European countries as well as in Egypt, China and India. As a result of the political upheavals in the eastern Mediterranean, as well as the Balkans, there had been a gradual dispersion of the Greek populations from the modern nation-state of Greece as it evolved territorially during the nineteenth and twentieth centuries. This scattering of the Greek population being due to economic, political and warfare reasons.

Introduction

'Diaspora' is historically, according to Harlaftis and Minoglou (2001), used for those people that have left their countries for various reasons, either voluntarily or involuntarily, and have established themselves in other countries and regions but who have kept ties or identify with their homeland. It is however further emphasized that the Diaspora is seldom, if ever, referred to in Greece other than in the sense of recent groups of emigrants in industrialized countries. For Greeks who live out of Greece, the word *homogeneia* is commonly used which means 'men of common breed'. This notion of 'breed' may be the result of the 'space-less' linguistic, cultural and religious communities that existed within the former Ottoman Empire which formed the Ottoman millet system and this 'imagined community' of *genos*, or breed, has now evolved into the modern notion of nation. Consequently, the Greeks that were dispersed within the territories of the Ottoman Empire, which used the former territories of the Byzantium Empire, were not considered until the early twentieth century as 'Diaspora' because Greeks have always lived there.

The closing decades of the nineteenth century saw the Greek Diaspora spread around the world in three waves. During the first wave, from 1880 to 1924, Greeks immigrated to the USA in large numbers. During the second wave from 1924 to 1950, Greeks emigrated to South America, Africa and Australia while fewer numbers immigrated to the USA due to new more restrictive emigration policy of that country. The third wave occurred in the 1960s with emigration destinations in Australia, Canada and Germany, according to Harlaftis and Minoglou (2001), Constantinou

(2007) and Burnley (2005). The USA was once again a popular emigration destination for Greek émigrés in the mid 1960s. As economic conditions in Greece gradually improved from the 1980s, immigration to the various Diaspora countries declined sharply. Given the difficulties with defining Greek ethnicity, only estimates of the total number of Greeks living outside Greece can be determined. The Greek authorities estimate the number of Hellenes abroad to be about 5.5 million whilst the World Council of Hellenes Abroad estimated the Hellenes to be 7 million. On the basis of the latter figure, the total number of Hellenes living abroad is estimated to be 64 per cent of the total population of Greece which was just under 11 million in 2001. It is further noted that citizens of Greek origin live in more than 140 countries, with the largest communities being found in USA, Australia, Germany, Canada and South Africa. Constantinou (2007) further notes that wherever Greeks have settled, once they reached a certain critical mass, they have formed distinct communities centred on the Greek Christian Orthodox Church. The Greek Christian Orthodox Church, states Jurgens (2008), has helped meet the emotional and spiritual needs of the Greek Diaspora across the world. Hellenism and Greek Christian Orthodoxy are intertwined and serve as the cord that has kept the Greek Diaspora attached to the mother country, nourished patriotic appetites and helped preserve the faith and the language of the forbears of the Diaspora. The religious practices, that is, the liturgy (a type of formalized church service) of the Greek Christian Orthodox Church helps keep alive the Greek ethnic cultural traditions of the Greek Diaspora with ethnicity being seen as synonymous with the church. One is considered a Greek not because one is an Hellene (or Greek) by birth; indeed many of Greek parentage have abandoned their identities and have disappeared into the mainstream societies of their adopted countries. One is considered Greek rather because one has elected to remain part of the Greek community and an individual who is a member of the Greek community by virtue of the attachment to the Greek Christian Orthodox Church on which the community is based. Consequently, most Greeks consider the Greek Christian Orthodox Church to be the centre of community life.

The first immigrants of the pre-Second World War period who settled in the various countries of the Diaspora, states Jurgens (2008) and Constantinou (2007) were, for the most, single men who were searching for better economic opportunity and who had no intention of remaining permanently away from Greece. Their goal was to earn enough capital and then return to their homeland in order to support their families and provide dowries for their sisters. (When in 1981 Greece entered the European Community (now the EU), at about the same time the dowry system became outlawed, although it is still informally practised by some

Greek families.) They went to work in the large industrialized cities of the various Diaspora countries as factory labourers, busboys, and bootblacks. Others went to mill towns and worked in textile and shoe factories, whilst others found work in mines and on the railroads, states Jurgens (2008). Most of the Greeks that went to the USA were subject to the *padrone* system, a form of exploitative indentured servitude employed in many of the larger industrial cities of the North and in the large mining corporations of the West. Nonetheless, the Greeks stressed individual effort and talent and, with a long tradition of entrepreneurship, many who were pedlars and street merchants became owners of small businesses. In the 1920s Greeks owned thousands of confectionary shops across the USA and usually owned the candy-manufacturing businesses that supplied the stores. When the candy business collapsed, Greeks became restaurant owners. By the late 1920s several thousand Greek restaurants were scattered across the USA. Many Greek immigrants of the 1950s and the 1960s went into the fast-food restaurant business. The Greek professional class remained small until the 1940s. Unlike the previous immigrants, the new immigrants of the 1960s were graduates of Greek high schools or universities (Constantinou, 2007). Today many of the Greeks in the Diaspora engage in many professional endeavours. Instead of remaining in family held businesses, third- and fourth-generation Greeks in the Diaspora are increasingly pursuing professional careers (Jurgens, 2008).

Generations

It is proposed by Burnley (2005) that for ethnic immigrant groups, such as the Greeks, that do not speak English on arrival in their adoptive country, it is a three-generation process. The first generation speak their own ethnic language at home and learn English to communicate at work; the second generation learn fluent English, but communicate with their parents in the mother tongue; and the third generation has only had partial ancestral language use. While living conditions and means vary considerably over time between generations, economic and cultural linkages to the older community foci remain with many second-generation Greeks living within a 10–15 minutes drive from their parents and the Greek Orthodox Church. Caravelis (2007, p. 7) writes the following concerning the role of the Greek Orthodox Christian Church and the role it plays in promoting the ethnic cohesiveness of the Greek community:

> The Greek Church has come to symbolise for (the Greek Diaspora) the sense of belonging, which Greek society as a whole did for Greeks living abroad. This is why we have today the seemingly unexplainable, if not contradictory phenomenon, of completely anglicised third and fourth generation Greeks zealously supporting the Greek Orthodox Church; their church touches them deeply, or

> as completely, as does one's place of birth, or even country of origin. This is why Greek churches in the (Diaspora) have traditionally been more than just places of worship, they are veritable small-nations-within-a–nation, complete with Greek schools, large halls for lunches, dinners, dances and conferences, annual festivals and ceremonies, communal and camouflaged political activities and elections, sport events and study groups.

It is further noted by Caravelis (2007, p. 13) that the Greeks have never created contiguous ethnic communities because they rather felt connected with other Greeks through their affiliation with the Greek Orthodox Church. It is, however, emphasized that ethnic communities are necessary vehicles to ethnic cultural preservation.

> The maintenance of the ethnic culture is easier when there are substantial numbers of an ethnic group within a host country. The chief cultural survival interest of most host minority groups is to maintain links with their native country's shared belief systems. Once the community is established, community institutions become an important site to perpetuate and reinforce a sense of ethnicity. Consequently, the creation of an ethnic community, the maintenance of cultural ties, the preservation of the native language, and in many cases, the continuation of native religious institutions in the new setting, promote the survival of the ethnic group (ibid.).

Network or niche formations

The Diaspora people, once settled in their adoptive countries, developed enclave networks based on their own cultures that have proven pivotal for their financial survival (Stiles et al., 2007). 'Niche formation', according to Adendorff (2005), is a logical outcome of migration and is a process by which entrepreneurs who share a religious or other common background, cluster together in an economic sector, furthermore, it is considered to be a common phenomenon. Migrant groups that produce a strong entrepreneurial group, according to Sahin et al. (2007), can be of great economic significance for the migrant business community as well as the total community through job creation and opportunity creation. Migrant entrepreneurs can thus satisfy the special needs of co-migrant clients, since they share the same language, culture and religion, and can therefore communicate better. It is stated by Anagnostatou (2003, p. 289) that participation in 'ethnic networks' is a way of 'reaffirming their tribe . . . it is totally cultural; it is anthropological'. It is however noted by Adendorff (2005) that not all entrepreneurial activities of immigrants can be considered ethnic. Entrepreneurs can be considered ethnic if they have major advantages or disadvantages as a result of their ethnicity. Ethnic entrepreneurs may benefit from co-ethnic loyalty (from buyers and sellers) and co-ethnic employment. Entrepreneurs become ethnic entrepreneurs when ethnic resources become more important than the non-ethnic resources commonly used in entrepreneurial activity. Ethnic entrepreneurs need to develop socially meaningful relationships in order to start a business. To start a business, ethnic entrepreneurs draw on 'co-ethnics' to help them, but these ties are not a given. They have to activate their networks for them to become social capital. Over time, people reach a point where they recognize each other of the same ethnic grouping by defining them as belonging. Shared cultural indicators, according to Adendorff (2005, p. 84), include 'language and religion. Identifying features may embrace physiology and demeanour whilst dress, food, and other familiar consumer items become cultural markers.' People draw on such indicators to define themselves as culturally similar. As a result, the enclave economy would be a part of the social structure of families, neighbours, friends and acquaintances. Entrepreneurs from the same ethnic group would get easier access to business networks in the enclave than would outsiders. They would be in an advantageous position to utilize those ethnic networks. A business that depends on ethnic relations would typically establish value chains within such an ethnic community.

The first-generation Greeks in the USA who were fruit and vegetable pedlars became owners of grocery stores and flower vendors became florists' shops. Coffee houses were opened to serve the needs of the immigrants and were particularly important and were located in the heart of the ethnic area or locale. The immigrants gathered in the coffee houses to socialize, to discuss the politics of the homeland, exchange news about friends and relatives in the homeland, discuss community politics in their adoptive country and raise funds in support of the church and other commercial causes (Constantinou, 2007).

In Australia, according to Burnley (2005), the majority of Greek immigrants arrived in the country between 1950 and 1971. Most had emigrated as permanent residents, were from rural and town proletariats and knew little English on arrival. The migration process in Australia was network-mediated chain migration and the initial community formations involved familial, village and regional ties, institutions and small businesses. The ethnic enclave, however, does not imply ethnic segregation, but rather ethnic concentrations in particular locales (Razin and Langois, 1996). Stiles et al. (2007) and Caravelis (2007) indicate that these new networks provide the ethnic groups with the means to raise their economic standards and establish roots in their new environments. Historically, most such immigrants settled in ethnic neighbourhoods and in some cases where the dense concentration of immigrants arose and strong ethnic economies developed, these groups become embedded as ethnic enclaves. The accumulation of ties within a co-ethnic community could create a number of opportunities for immigrants with entrepreneurial skills and initiative to start their businesses. Moreover, according to Bitros and Minoglou (2006), the embeddedness of the branches of the networks in the Greek communities abroad, called *Paroikies*, is where the Greek Christian Orthodox Church provided moral leadership and maintained the community ties, reinforced the adherence of network partners to the rules of ethical business conduct. The influence of group characteristics (Razin and Langlois, 1996), particularly the size of the ethnic community in a locale, did have an influence on enhancing entrepreneurship; where a large ethnic community which offered a large co-ethnic clientele and well-developed community-based entrepreneurial networks could be expected to greatly enhance prospects for entrepreneurship and consequently improved prospects for self-employment. Razin and Langois (1996) and Vouyouka Sereti (1999) further note that Greeks in the Diaspora were characterized as immigrant niches that had high rates of self-employment. Many maintained ethnic ties and possessed some skills and resources, but lacked formal qualifications or contacts to advance as employees. Hence they formed ethnic entrepreneurial networks in the distribution and blue-collar niche industries, with numerous Greek immigrants gravitating towards the restaurant business because it required relatively little investment and a minimal command of the English language. It is, however, emphasized by Razin and Langois (1996) that later generations of this ethnic group tended to progress towards white-collar industries and occupations as the influence of opportunities outside the ethnic locales grew, diminishing the influence of internal group characteristics and external group-specific obstacles for advancement. For example, many Greek South Africans, according to Adendorff (2005, pp. 84–5), who seemed similar to outsiders did not, themselves, feel that they shared a common background that warranted ongoing ties. This 'drifting apart' was seen to lessen the range of others with whom new immigrants could exchange support in a foreign country.

Cultural distancing

Social reality, according to Stiles et al. (2007), is seen as the composition of what is defined as 'ethnic'. Ethnicity is conventionally accepted to refer to four characteristics of a person: race, nationality, language, and religion. Anagnostatou (2003, p. 306) states that cultural distancing is a direct cultural outcome of immigration and is accomplished by aligning the self (of the Greek Diaspora) with the values of Occidentalism (individualism, discipline, order and equality). Thus, images of Zorba the Greek, the embodiment of undisciplined emotionality and unproductive (in the capitalist sense) abandon is repeatedly tempered by an emphasis of the Greek

Diaspora work ethic. Statements such as 'we are good at work, great at play', 'at the root, we're all about hard work' and 'Greeks, as much as we like to have fun, we're also workaholics' point toward the taming of the Orientalist stereotype through the appropriate use of Occidental values.

Conversely, Greek individualism has consistently been used as argument for Greek immigrant fitness in the Diaspora, the 'negative variety' of *eghoismos* (competitive self-regard or egoism) bring to the fore disruptive atomism. In some instances, immigration as a new beginning is associated with particular interpretation of *eghoismos* and it captures at once two meanings: positively valued individualism and negatively valued, disruptive atomism. This semantic coherence fractures into the Occidental and Orientalist model of nationalist identity once the cultural orientation of Greece (Western or Eastern?) is at stake. In the Greek Diaspora, *eghoismos* is criticized as 'the Greek ego, our Achilles heel'. Threatening collective action, it becomes an element of unruliness and uncivil divisions. As a result, it is singled out as the unwanted anomaly in the Greek Diaspora according to Anagnostatou (2003, p. 306). The singling out of *eghoismos* points towards an incomplete Occidentalization of the Greek Diaspora. It draws a boundary between the Greek Diaspora and the Greeks in Greece proper. Unlike the latter, whose Western-self is confronted by an internal 'oriental' Other – marking historically constituted ambivalence that makes Greeks less-than-authentic Occidentals – Greeks in the Diaspora are constituted as emerging Occidentals whose identity is constructed in relation to Western norms and values.

Religious events and the role of women

Greek women in the Diaspora, according to Ebaugh and Salzmann Chafetz (1999), have played a fundamental role in reproducing the traditional culture in Greek immigrant congregations in three distinctive ways: by preparing and serving ethnic foods for social events that occur both at central religious sites and at home for religiously connected practices; as teachers of children in congregation-supported ethno-religious classes (for example, Sunday School), and as leaders of youth groups. It is further noted that women provide most, if not all, of the work of securing the supplies and preparing, cooking and serving the food. In the light that traditional foods are closely linked to religious and ethnic identities, which are indistinguishable for many immigrants, women often go to great lengths to procure the necessary ingredients for the traditional meals. The preparation and consumption of ethnic foods also reinforce traditional religious and ethnic identities within the family and friendship networks. For instance, traditional meals after weekly church services can take on religious meanings. In many cases, the preparation of traditional foods provides women with the opportunity to instruct their daughters in the meanings of ethnic customs while teaching them culinary skills. The following is noted by Caravelis (2007, p. 131): 'food has long ceased to be merely about sustenance and nutrition. It is packed with social, cultural and symbolic meaning. Every mouthful, every meal, can tell us something about ourselves, and about our place in the world'.

The development of the Greek Orthodox Church's women's social service groups/clubs, whose primary function was social service delivery, is proposed to be one of the initial catalysts of numerous Greek immigrant families becoming involved in service-related, restaurant, fast-food and catering businesses in the Diaspora. In general, as emphasized by Stiles et al. (2007), religious behaviour, such as the involvement in religious institutions and family religiosity (or being pious) tend to influence the nature of entrepreneurial behaviour usually defined as the number of start-ups within an ethnic group.

CONCLUSION

Culture is defined by Adendorff (2005) as 'the core values and beliefs of individuals within society, which are formed in complex knowledge systems during childhood and reinforced throughout life'. Culture thus shapes the organizations that evolve and the nature of social structures as they grow and adapt. Fogel et al. (2005, p. 26) further add that

> the supply of entrepreneurs depends not only on reward and status, but also on personality, culture and life experiences. An entrepreneur will often find his opinion is in conflict within the majority view. He needs the self-confidence that, even though in a minority, he is right . . . in identifying profitable opportunities the entrepreneur needs to synthesise information from different sources.

Family, religion, education, pride, honour and a strong work ethic is what defines the Greeks from any other culture (Haralambos, 2005). The pattern that has emerged is that the Greek Diaspora, regardless of where they were born, has retained a strong attachment to their ethnic background. Their attachment is aided by their membership of the Greek Christian Orthodox Church and formal ethnic organizations. Participation in church-sponsored cultural activities, especially the Greek festivals, is considered a very important part of the Greek identity. The Greek Christian Orthodox Church symbolises for the Greek Diaspora its ethnic background and provides the only visible link with the homeland, providing at the same time a clear group identity. 'The Greek is born into his religion, and Church affiliation symbolizes for him the way of life' (Adendorff, 2005, p. 191). When a Greek asks 'Is he an Orthodox Christian?' it is usually implied 'Is he Greek?' As a repository of Greek values and one of the conservative agents, the Greek Orthodox Church, with its continuous emphasis on Orthodoxy and Hellenism, has been one of the important resistant blocks to assimilation of the Diaspora (Adendorff, 2005, p. 193).

Many authors have conducted research concerning ethnic networks and the Greeks in Greece or abroad. The historical role of the Greek Orthodox Christian Church and how this has influenced the entrepreneurial processes of Greeks has also been extensively analysed. The role of the Greek Diaspora women in the entrepreneurial creative process, however, is not as well researched and needs further analysis. An in-depth analysis is also needed of the role of the entrepreneurial creative process and the Greek Orthodox Christian Church in the post-1981 (more secular) period when Greece became the tenth member of the European Union. Various EU policies have seen a gradual separation of the State from the Church, in particular, the removal of religious affiliation from state identity cards which is considered an assault on Greek nationalism and identity by the Greek Orthodox Christian Church. The Church, according to Stanley (2000), is furthermore concerned about the country's plans to institute a separation of State and Church, which among other things could drastically reduce church income.

ACKNOWLEDGEMENTS

This research was supported by Walter Sisulu University. The researcher wishes to acknowledge the invaluable contribution made by Louise Roberts concerning language editing.

REFERENCES

Adendorff, C.M. (2005), 'The Development of a Cultural Family Business Model of Good Governance for Greek Family Businesses in South Africa', unpublished doctoral thesis, Rhodes University. Available at: http://eprints.ru.ac.za/192/ (accessed 23 April 2008).

Anagnostatou, Y. (2003), 'Model Americans, Quintessential Greeks: Ethnic Success and Assimilation in Diaspora', *Diaspora*, **12** (3), 279–327.

Anderson, A.R., S. Drakopoulou Dodd and M.G. Scott (2000), 'Religion as an Environmental Influence on Enterprise Culture: The Case of Britain in the 1980s', *International Journal of Entrepreneurial Behaviour & Research*, **6** (1), 5–20.

Baldwin-Edwards, M. (2005), 'The Integration of Immigrants in Athens: Developing Indicators and Statistical Measures', available at: www.mmo.gr/pdf/publications/mmo_working_papers/Migrants_in_Greece_Report_Eng.pdf (accessed 25 April 2008).

Berger, P.L. (2005), 'Orthodoxy and Global Pluralism', *Demokratizatsiya*, **15** (3), 437–47.

Bitros, G. and I. Minoglou (2006), 'Entrepreneurship and Market Order: Some Historical Evidence', *Munich Personal RePEc Archive (MPRA)*, available at: http://mpra.ub.uni-muenchen.de/573/ (accessed 6 May 2008).

Bureau of Democracy, Human Rights, and Labor (2002), 'Greece: Country Reports on Human Rights Practices – 2001', available at: http://www.fas.org/asmp/profiles/greece/greece-hr-01.htm (accessed 23 April 2008).

Burnley, I.H. (2005), 'Generations, Mobility and Community: Geographies of Three Generations of Greek and Italian Ancestry in Sydney', *Geographical Research*, **43** (4), 379–92.

Caravelis, M. (2007), 'Unbounded Ethnic Communities: The Greek-Canadian Culturescape of South Florida', unpublished doctoral thesis, University of South Africa.

Constantinou, S.T. (2007), 'Ethnic residential shifts: The Greek population of Akron, Ohio, 1930–2005', *GeoJournal*, **68**, 253–65.

Drakopoulou Dodd, S. and G. Gotsis (2007), 'Labour Is Holy but Business Is Dangerous: Enterprise Values from the Church Fathers to the Reformation', *Journal of Enterprising Culture*, (June), 133–63.

Drakopoulou Dodd, S. and P.T. Seaman (1998), 'Religion and enterprise: an introductory exploration', *Entrepreneurship Theory and Practice*, (Fall), 71–86.

Ebaugh, H.R. and J. Salzman Chafetz (1999), 'Agents of Cultural Reproduction and Structural Change: The Ironic Role of Women in Immigrant Religious Institutions', *Social Forces*, **78** (2), 585–613.

Fogel, K., A. Hawk, R. Morck and B. Yueng (2005), 'Institutional Obstacles to Entrepreneurship (August 2005 Draft)', in M. Casson, B. Young, A. Basu and N. Wadeson (2006), *Oxford Handbook of Entrepreneurship*, Oxford: Oxford University Press.

Haralambos, P. (2005), 'Greek Customs in Modern America', available at: http://www.peteharalamos.com/essays/greeks.pdf (accessed 6 May 2008).

Harlaftis, G. and I.P. Minoglou (2001), 'Greek Diaspora Entrepreneurship 18–20th centuries: A Comparative and Methodological Analysis', proceedings from the 13th International History Congress, Buenos Aires 2002.

Jurgens, J. (2008), 'Greek Americans', available at: http://www.everyculture.com/multi/Du-Ha/Greek-Americans.html (accessed 6 May 2008).

Karopoulos, P. and S. Lazaretou (2006), 'Corporate Ownership Structure and Firm Evidence from Greek Firms (Paper 37)', Bank of Greece, Economic Research Department – Special Studies Division, available at: www.bankofgreece.gr (accessed 25 April 2008).

Lanni, A. (2007), 'The Laws of War of Ancient Greece: Paper No 07-24', *Harvard Law School Public Law Research*, available at: http://ssrn.com/abstract=1069874 (accessed 6 May 2008).

McNall, S.G. (1974), 'Value Systems that Inhibit Modernisation: The Case of Greece', *Studies in Comparative International Development*, **9** (3), 47–63.

Petrakis, P.E. (1997), 'Entrepreneurship and Growth: Creative and Equilibrating Events', *Small Business Economics*, **9**, 383–402.

Razin, E. and A. Langlois (1996), 'Metropolitan Characteristics and Entrepreneurship among Immigrants and Ethnic Groups in Canada', *International Migration Review*, **30**, 703–27.
Sahin, M., P. Nijkamp and T. Baycan-Levant (2007), 'Multicultural Diversity and Migrant Entrepreneurship: The Case of the Netherlands', *ITU A/Z*, **4** (1), 20–44.
Stanley, A. (2000), 'The World: An Inseparable Church and State; on Greeks Playing the Euro Card', *The New York Times*, 25 June, available at: http://www.nytimes.com (accessed 1 June 2008).
Stiles, C.H., C.L Rodriguez and C.S. Galbraith (2007), 'The Impact of Ethnic-Religious Identification on Buyer–Seller Behaviour: A Study of Two Enclaves', *International Journal of Business and Globalisation*, **1** (1), 20–33.
Taylor, D. and M. Procter (2001), 'The Literature Review: A Few Tips on Conducting It', available at: http://www.utoronto.ca/writing/litrev.html (accessed 25 April 2008).
US State Department (2003), 'Report on International Religious Freedom', available at: http://www.state.gov/g/drl/rls/irf/2003/24411.htm (accessed 25 April 2008).
Vouyouka Sereti, M. (1999), 'Entrepreneurship and Ethnicization: The Greek Community of Astoria in Transition', unpublished doctoral thesis, State University of New York at Stony Brook.
Wikipedia (2008), 'Eastern Orthodox Church', available at: http://en.wikipedia.org/wiki/Eastern_Orthodox_Church (accessed 25 April 2008).

5. Economics and spirituality in the entrepreneurial development strategy of the Franciscan California missions: the historical case of San Diego

Craig S. Galbraith, Curt H. Stiles and Jacqueline Benitez-Galbraith

INTRODUCTION

There has been increasing interest in the developmental entrepreneurship, economic sociology, and institutional economics literature regarding the role that pre-colonial institutions, hierarchy, and government structures had upon the development of indigenous populations upon intense contact with the colonizing nations. Acemoglu et al. (2001), and others (for example, La Porta et al., 1999) have argued that one of the major factors determining post-colonial economic development is the quality of the institutional arrangements that the colonizing power brings to a particular region. Acemoglu et al. (2001), for example, found that on the average, regions where the colonial powers established strong institutional and legal frameworks, then the post-colonial indigenous population probably benefited by various social, health, and economic measures. However, in regions where the colonial effort was primarily extractive, with little or no attempt to establish strong institutions, then the post-colonial situation became stagnant or even declined. Others (for example, Boone, 2003; Gennaioli and Rainer, 2007; Mamdani, 1996) have argued that the quality and characteristics of the existing pre-colonial indigenous institutions is also important in understanding post-colonial development. Certain pre-colonial institutional frameworks, for example, might lend themselves to more or less integration with the colonial institutional frameworks, and it is really the combination, and the integration, of colonial institutions and pre-colonial indigenous institutions that ultimately determine the economic trajectory of various regions, such as Africa. This argument is echoed by Peruvian economist, Hernando de Soto's analysis of the failures and successes seen in modern-day Latin and South America (De Soto, 2000; 2006).

The basis for our discussion of the Catholic mission entrepreneurial strategy in California and its impact on local economic development (including the development of an entrepreneurial class) is grounded in this institutional argument, particularly the concept of public good spillovers and 'capture' effects, and the differences in transaction costs associated with institutional weaknesses and ethno-linguistic differences.

Centralization, Public Goods, and 'Capture'

'Capture' addresses the activity of elites in developing and distributing public and quasi-public goods to society, and is tied to the notion of centralization. This issue is highly debated within the political economy literature on centralized institutions and government (see Bardhan, 2002; Bardhan and Mookherjee, 2000).

Two different notions of 'capture' effects have been offered. Tiebout (1956), invoking the now classic argument of 'voting with one's feet' showed that a quasi-spatial adjustment mechanism could, under certain assumptions, lead to an efficient equilibrium or Pareto optimality for local public goods. Thus, individual households, each attempting to maximize their own utility, will tend to congregate with similar households in geographical areas where local jurisdictions offer cost-competitive public goods that cater to those particular preferences. This should result in smaller, more homogeneous municipal constructs. As Heikkila observes, 'an irresistible metaphor is a giant shopping mall with countless "municipality boutiques" offering specialized products or services for a well-defined clientele' (Heikkila, 1996, p. 205). This results in the notion of a 'central capture' view, in that decentralization results in the accountability of local elites – an argument for localized authority and institutions.

On the other hand, others (for example, Mamdani, 1996) have argued that decentralization in pre-colonial societies most often evolved into simple 'decentralized tyranny', and that centralization of institutions and government within pre-colonial society actually resulted in greater development and distribution of public goods, such as health, education, and welfare within these indigenous societies. This argument lies within the notion of 'local capture' (Riker, 1964). Under the 'local capture' scenario, upon interaction with intense colonial settlement, it can be argued that centralized, strong pre-colonial institutions were better able to adapt to both colonial technologies and colonial centralized institutions.

Gennaioli and Rainer (2007) expand the notion of 'capture' by arguing that rigidity of indigenous pre-colonial stratification is also important to understanding the impact of colonial contact. The key finding relevant to our analysis is the Gennaioli and Rainer mathematical proof, with empirical supporting evidence from Africa, that under decentralization in stratified societies few public goods are provided. In other words, there is no incentive to support the general population. On the other hand, in more egalitarian groups, decentralization results in the production of local public goods that directly benefit that particular group (such as localized welfare, health benefits to the community, and so on) but not in goods that 'spillover' or would benefit a larger portion of the region, such as better roads, or agreements for water sharing, and so on. On the other hand, pre-colonial centralization does result in the creation and 'spillover' of public goods that benefit pre-colonial society in general.

Carry Capacity and Stratification

Another important factor, and one often ignored in the political economy literature when looking at North American indigenous pre-colonial societies, is the notion of the 'carrying capacity' of the environment. 'Voting with one's feet', an assumption behind much of the economic arguments of development, implies having some degree of intergroup mobility. However, we argue that high density to the point of reaching carry capacity, particularly with static horticultural indigenous populations, made intergroup mobility extremely difficult if not impossible. Thus stratification increases and efforts to control population growth, particularly among the lower classes, become culturally necessary or starvation occurs. Under these conditions, the primary mechanism to increase the carry capacity of a particular environment becomes either the entrepreneurial development of new productive technologies, or the adoption and integration of introduced technologies. However, when indigenous populations are mobile, once carrying capacity is reached in one area, then it might be more economic to simply (a) raid surrounding communities to bring back resources, or (b) migrate to other areas, peacefully if there are not other populations within the region, or forcibly if other, possibly weaker, populations inhabit the targeted region.

Differences in the way economically important assets were owned and managed also impact the basic societal and entrepreneurial fabric of these tribes. The horticulturists were governed by an extreme class stratification that was unshakably rigid and that drew all wealth upward into the hands of the upper class, particularly if intergroup mobility was difficult. Labor was sedentary, and warfare was low status, avoided by the upper class, and, for commoners, not a guaranteed route to success. In contrast, the nomadic hunters had a leadership system that rewarded individual initiative and provided substantial status mobility for those in the lower economic strata that were willing to be entrepreneurial. Wealth acquisition was encouraged, rewarded, and pursued with aggression.

Institutional Failures

Institutional sophistication – or at the other end of the spectrum, failures – will also affect the ability to centralize. As the whole body of institutional economics literature argues (for example, North, 1990; Teece, 1982; Williamson, 1975), the basis for economic institutions must be found in those enforceable formal and informal contractual systems that ultimately make the costs of transacting within organizations competitive with market transaction costs. Nevertheless, a structured legal system sophisticated enough to allow efficient economic organization among non-related members (such as employees, owners, customers, suppliers, and financiers) is not easily developed. The problem becomes even more difficult as the tradable assets become less-product or region-specific (Galbraith and Kay, 1986; Kay, 1997). Without the advantages offered by these tight structural and language related institutional mechanisms, the boundaries of the economic organization will remain limited, ill-defined, and economically inefficient.

This is important when understanding many indigenous, pre-colonial economies. For example, there is much made of the family-based economic traditions of Native American tribes, however this phenomenon must be placed within the context of pre-colonial technology. In other words, the more primitive technology, such as stone axes and flint tools, used by the pre-colonial populations demanded cooperative strategies to achieve some level of economic efficiency. That is, groups had to work together rather than as individuals. However, due to a lack of an institutional framework to effectively organize these cooperative strategies among unrelated entities, the Native American people, like the highland Scottish clans, had to access the social capital derived from related parties in the form of clans and families. Because of network complexity, however, social capital typically has substantial diminishing returns to scale; the larger the radius of the network that is required to access social capital, the weaker the ties among its members. This naturally results in relatively small, fragile cooperative organizations that will rapidly dissolve and be replaced as technology or demand/supply conditions change – as they did when the entrepreneurially inclined Iroquois people of the Northeastern United States, for example, adopted the European trapping, farming and trade technologies. In these situations, the weak pre-colonial property-right regimes and institutions are easily abandoned and new ones quickly established as productive technologies become more efficient.

In fact, this understanding of the role of market institutions in societal evolution is a key area where anthropologists and institutional economists/business theorists often diverge. Anthropological research has certainly long recognized that kinship ties, extended families, and tribal networks have functioned as economic transaction points where markets 'are either absent or of limited importance' (Chibnik, 2005, p. 207; see also Sahlins, 1972); however, what is difficult for anthropology research to acknowledge is that kinship ties, extended families, and tribal networks are relatively inefficient institutional frameworks for complex economic transactions, and thus economic development. Rather they exist primarily as a result of institutional failures due to some underlying limiting factor, such as a proliferation of minority languages within a region, lack of sophisticated written languages among trading groups, or endemic warfare between neighboring factions. The priority of economic institutions over kinship markets is clearly seen in world history (for example, Rodrik et al., 2004). Once innovative technologies are introduced, often by contact with other, more advanced expanding societies, the old, fragile kinship related market frameworks of pre-colonial societies are usually quickly abandoned, and new institutional frameworks adopted. And in those situations where the old networks are maintained, they are usually converted into either simple cooperative economic agencies similar to a corporate charter that benefit from local endowments, such as the 'fair trade coffee cooperatives' in Africa, or economic clubs that take advantage of government sanctioned monopolies, such as reservation-based tribal casino gaming in North America (Galbraith and Stiles, 2003)

Similarly, there is often mention of communal property when discussing pre-colonial indigenous economics, but it is well recognized that that communal property inevitably results in large economic externalities, most notably, the free-rider problem. Among pre-colonial Native Americans, in the instances where there appeared to be some type of collective tribal ownership of assets, it almost always involved ceremonial buildings (Oberg, 1973), a type of asset where externalities can be easily managed (Miller, 2001). Or if the communal property was a grazing field, then inevitably there would be a highly localized stratified system of government (chieftains) that could manage any negative externalities, such as overgrazing, since pre-colonial indigenous institutional frameworks were usually not sufficiently sophisticated to allow multiple, unrelated parties to contractually manage externalities.

It is also interesting to note that, like today, pre-colonial war was also a collective effort, often with both economic and institutional overtones.

However, without efficient economies of organization, centralized control was relatively weak, as evidenced by the competition between multiple spiritual shamans and war chiefs, the generally disorganized line of battle, and the fact that many tribal members would act as 'free-riders' by electing not to participate but still benefit from a victory by robbing the vanquished or dead (Mishkin, 1940; Secoy, 1953).

Ethnolinguistic Diversity, Transaction Costs, and Entrepreneurial Behavior

Language, almost by definition, is a core component of human development. In a broad historical sense, there has always been a close relationship between the complexity of civilization and the complexity of language. Over the past several decades, several important theoretical models have emerged to describe the relationships between language and economics. One of the most dominant themes in both ethnic entrepreneurship and economic sociology is that a common language shared by co-ethnics contributes to the development of social capital within an ethnic community. While other aspects of social capital, including shared traditions, cultural trust, tacit knowledge, implicit habits and behavioral norms, have certainly been discussed, language is certainly believed to be one of the most important social capital building blocks (for example, Fearon and Laitin, 2000, 2003; Fishman, 1999; Grin, 2002; Menzies et al., 2007). This package of relationship-building factors creates powerful economic, social, and political boundaries that ultimately define an ethnic enclave or community (Adler and Kwon, 2002; Light, 2004; Light and Bhachu, 2004; Piore, 1979). A common language, it is argued, will generally reduce transaction costs, resulting in more sophisticated and stronger institutions, greater agreement regarding property rights, increased cross-group trade, and ultimately more economic growth. On the other hand, two groups with vastly dissimilar languages may result in increased cross-group transaction and organizing costs to the point where joint institutional arrangements, and even trade, may be impossible. In addition, as Bryson (1990) argues, multiple languages may decrease social and economic mobility since language differences make it easier to establish and institutionalize rigid class structures, thus increasing the transaction cost between these groups.

There is greater debate, however, regarding the impact of language on economic development (Arcand, 1996; Grin, 2001; Nettle, 2000). A long history of development research has found support for the 'Fishman–Pool' hypothesis that linguistic heterogeneity leads to lower economic growth due to the higher levels of government instability, institutional failures, and economic transactions costs associated with high language and ethnic diversity (Coulmas, 1992; Easterly and Levine, 1997; Fishman, 1972; Pool, 1991).

But we can also look at ethnolinguistic diversity from an entrepreneurial perspective. If language or cultural diversity is high in a region, mobility barriers between ethnic or indigenous groups increase and the opportunity to expand outside the group becomes more costly. In this situation, the business community will likely pool (typically as a large number of marginal micro-enterprises) within the ethnic or indigenous market boundaries, resulting in 'congestion', increased competition, and ultimately elevated small business failure rates – particularly as new ethnic enterprises also enter the enclave seeking benefit from the social capital (Galbraith and Benitez-Galbraith, 2009; Galbraith et al., 2007).

In concluding this section, as previously mentioned, while there is a voluminous literature debating Spanish colonial activities in the vast region that currently makes up the southwestern region of the United States and northern Mexico, very few researchers or historians have approached the issue from an economic perspective examining pre-colonial structural limitations, if any, and whether or not the mission system offered some solutions to these problems. Based upon the recent literature in developmental economics and entrepreneurship, we therefore consider centralization, stratification, carrying capacity, intergroup mobility, institutional sophistication, and ethnolinguistic diversity as critical drivers for a more accurate understanding of the economic and entrepreneurial implications of the contact between the early Spanish and the indigenous populations.

CALIFORNIA MISSION ACTIVITY

The eighteenth-century Spanish Catholic missionary efforts within the vast regions of the southwestern United States and Northern Mexico, particular Baja California and the Sonora region of the Mexican frontier, were somewhat unique within world history. Unlike that vast majority of colonial intrusions, where missionary and Church activity took a secondary role to more secular economic speculation, political conquest, or mass immigrant settlement, in these sparsely populated and weakly controlled Spanish claimed areas the Catholic orders of Franciscans, Dominicans, and Jesuits took the lead role of settlement, administration, and cultural interaction with the local indigenous populations on a large scale. In fact, the other two agencies, *presidio*s (forts) and government supported *pueblos* (towns), the Spanish used to colonize were simply not important in the earliest settlement period of California. Presidios were established to protect the missions, and were typically manned by about 10 poorly equipped soldiers commanded by a corporal. Independent secular pueblos were generally non-existent in the colonial periods of our investigation.

Prior to the eighteenth-century missions system Spain was quite aware of the importance of California and the Southwestern United States. Hernán Cortés landed at Santa Cruz bay, near current day La Paz on 3 May 1535. In the following two centuries there were several small-scale, poorly funded, and ultimately failed attempts to establish missions in Baja California, first led by the Franciscans and later the Jesuits.

Confronted by the threat of foreign occupation, and lack of government resources, the Spanish government on 5 February 1697 formally authorized the Jesuits to take control of California (and the Sonora region of Old Mexico, now split between the State of Sonora in modern Mexico and the State of Arizona in modern USA) using their Order's funds, but with authorization to enlist a cadre of soldiers for protection and to take possession of lands in the name of Spain. In essence, the Jesuits were to have a somewhat unique combination of both governmental authority and spiritual authority. By the end of 1767, some 14 missions remained in Baja California (the peninsular states of Baja California Norte and Baja California Sur in modern Mexico), with several others abandoned due to epidemics and extremely difficult environmental conditions (Herberman, 1908). Since few records were kept, it is difficult to measure the success of the Baja California missions, or the economic situation of the native populations during this colonial period in Baja California.

In 1767, for reasons unrelated to the California mission activities, Carlos III, King of Spain issued a decree expelling the Jesuits from Spanish territories, and confiscated their assets (the *Extrañamiento*). Soon after the expulsion of the Jesuits, Viceroy de Croiz of New Spain requested that the Franciscan friars of the Apostolic Missionary College of San Fernando in Mexico City take over the missionary activity in California. They immediately took possession of the abandoned missions in Baja California, and subsequently established many new missions. Around 1770 the Dominicans within Mexico sought permission to establish a parallel set of missions in California, but a friendly agreement was reached between the two orders to reduce redundancy – the missions of Baja California were ceded to the Dominicans while the Franciscans then turned their attention to Alta California.

Alta California (the State of California in modern USA) was initially explored by Juan Rodriguez Cabrillo in 1542, and later by Sebastian Vizcaino in the early 1600s. By the mid-eighteenth century, Alta California was beginning to attract the attention of the Russians, who had established fur trading settlements in the Pacific Northwest, down to Point Reyes just north of modern-day San Francisco. Prior to the ceding of the Baja

California missions to the Dominicans, the Superior of the Baja California missions was the Franciscan friar, Fr. Junipero Serra. In response to the perceived threat of the Russians, the Spanish representative Jose de Galvez, approached Fr. Serra about settling Alta California.

Fr. Serra immediately agreed, and an expedition was organized under the encouragement of Viceroy de Croiz and Jose de Galvez. Two ships sailed in 1769, one from La Paz and one from Cabo San Lucas, and two land expeditions were launched, one with Fr. Serra. They converged in San Diego between April and July 1769, and established the first mission settlement in Alta California in San Diego on 16 July 1769. A series of explorations and mission establishment occurred up the coast of California, to Sonoma about 600 miles north of San Diego.

THE ENTREPRENEURIAL SPIRIT OF THE FRANCISCANS

An important aspect of understanding the economic and entrepreneurial strategy in the Mission process is grounded in the overall spiritual orientation of the Franciscan Order,[1] established in 1209 by St Francis of Assisi (1181–1226). The Franciscans were founded as a 'mendicant' order whose members take strict vows of poverty, do not own property either as individuals or a group, tend to work as individuals or small groups in isolated areas, and depend directly on charity. With this orientation, the Franciscans are different from other monastic orders, all of which have their own distinct spiritual and economic orientation, such as the community entrepreneurial orientation of the Benedictines, the reclusiveness and individual labor requirements of the Trappists, and the educational and scholastic aspects of the missionary Jesuits (for example, Galbraith and Galbraith, 2004).

This orientation clearly framed the Franciscan efforts in both Baja and Alta California. First, the Franciscans were willing to go as small groups (typically two friars to establish a mission), or even individuals into the most remote situations, and live under extremely impoverished circumstances. Letters from the mission friars describe the most impoverished conditions for the early friars, but without complaining due to the Franciscan orientation. In modern terms, entrepreneurial self-efficacy must have been extremely high within this Franciscan group of New Spain missionaries

Second, from inception, the missions that the Franciscans established and operated were to be temporary. There was never any plan that the mission would hold land or property in the long run, but rather that after a period of time, mission property would be turned over to the local indigenous population, and the Church functions alone would become the responsibility of the local parish priest – this was known as a strategy of 'secularization'. Simply put, according to Franciscan economic and theological philosophy, they did not own the missions but simply managed them as legal agents for the local indigenous population who would ultimately inherit the property and assets. This attitude was always made clear in the writings of the missions' friars; for example, as late as 1827 Frs Zalvidea and Barona of Mission San Juan Capistrano wrote to the Governor Echeandia of California, 'all these lands did and do now belong to the Indians' (Letter, 22/12/1827).[2] The notion of a land 'trust' for the native population was supported under the laws of Spain.[3] One can also note that this Franciscan lack of interest in land ownership is exactly why the Franciscans ceded the Baja California missions to the Dominicans and turned their attention to Alta California.

Thirdly, due to the historical Franciscan 'mendicant' philosophy regarding charity, they felt that the missions should also be charitable to the local population, therefore when Indians came to the mission to be baptized, they would be given food in exchange. In fact, there were many instances when whole Indian communities would come to be baptized but be turned away due to the lack of supplies to give them in return. In many missions, particularly in Baja California, only those near death would be baptized due to the lack of exchange provisions.

And finally, with respect to the California Franciscans, all were highly educated, having studied abroad and at the Apostolic Missionary College of San Fernando in Mexico City where they received detailed instruction in local language, culture, and transferable technologies and crafts, such as tool making, horticultural sciences, and appropriate ranching techniques. In fact, after the expulsion of the Jesuits in 1767, the Franciscans were for almost 80 years the most educated group of individuals in all of California[4] (for example, Davis, 1993).

The missionary fathers, particularly Father Serra who was quite familiar with the problems in Baja California, appeared to immediately see the problem later described in more theoretical terms by modern development economic theorists (for example, Boone, 2003; Gennaioli and Rainer, 2007; Mamdani, 1996). In order to achieve economic and spiritual development within the region, the mission strategy had to be designed to overcome the structural limitations existing in the local indigenous communities. Examining the histories, letters and diaries of the early friars clearly shows they had four, somewhat related objectives within this framework. First, to 'save souls', that is the conversion of the 'Indios barbaros' to Christianity; second, to reduce the extent of 'immoral behaviors', such as thievery and sexual promiscuity that was prevalent among some California native groups; third, in the mission of Christian charity, to reduce poverty, increase the protection of females, decrease infant mortality, increase health care, and enhance the economic productivity of the Indians, and fourth, to hold in trust as protectors, and ultimately develop the economic base and value of the mission holdings for the native population.

SOCIO-ECONOMIC CONDITIONS OF PRE-COLONIAL SAN DIEGO

The socio-economic conditions of the Native population in Alta California at the time of the San Diego's mission establishment in 1769 were somewhat different from most of the Spanish colonial experience, even in Baja California. From an economic perspective the commonly held image of pre-colonial Southern Californians as simple hunters and gathers has been enhanced by more modern anthropological and archeological efforts.[5] In the San Diego region, research by Florence Shipek (1982; 1986; 1987) and Richard Carrico (1986), in particular, has shown a somewhat more agriculturally oriented economic system (with hunting activities) combined with a primitive land tenure system often seen among other pre- and post-colonial North American permanent horticultural societies. In particular, the Southern Californian indigenous economic system was based upon: (a) private (individual and family) land, structure, tool, and water ownership; (b) private ownership of certain intangible assets, such as songs and medicinal formulas; (c) inheritance and assignment rights of the assets; (d) agricultural methods including primitive ditch-based irrigation, fire clearing of brush, and some broadcasting of grain-grass seed in fields; and (e) a highly stratified, decentralized, and static political system of 'bands' and chieftains that managed disputes, declared war, and might have enforced local land management regimes (Shipek, 1987, pp. 12–18). As Carrico (1986) notes, in pre-colonial San Diego, 'Indian people . . . were actively controlling and enhancing their environment and were not the passive foragers often portrayed as "Digger Indians". In more modern terms, the native people of San Diego might be best described as forager-horticulturists, with protein food sources obtained from hunting.

However, the land tenure and political system, while similar to other static horticultural Native American populations, was probably made even more rigid and stratified by the high population density of the area. Best estimates are that approximately 17000 individuals lived in the San

Diego region in 1769, for a land density of three to five person per arable acre, considered one of the highest among indigenous populations in pre-colonial United States.[6] Since arable land was scarce in the region's dry climate, the productive land was primarily located in lower altitude valleys and stream beds with water sources and in the mountain glens with permanent small lakes fed by snow melt. It is generally accepted that the population was nearing, or had reached, its maximum population carrying capacity density by 1767.

Under these high-density situations, combined with the low intergroup mobility between the numerous Native bands in the region, static farming becomes dominant and social structure rigidity and asset ownership becomes critical. As previously mentioned, horticulturists under these static conditions are often governed by an extreme class stratification that drew all wealth upward into the hands of the upper class or elites, that is, a 'decentralized tyranny' to use Mamdani's (1996) phraseology. This stratification is noted by Shipak (1986; 1987), in describing the social classes in the San Diego *Kumeyaay* indigenous populations, where the upper class and leaders held the best land, owned slaves, and employed other unlanded, poor natives. In these situations, the poor classes typically live on the fringe of society, often by begging, or as the Spanish explorers and setters constantly noted, by an 'addiction to stealing' (for example, Costanso, 1770, 24 January; Diaz, 1774, Diaries). Even the Spanish military officer Pedro Fages, later governor of California, noted very early that the local natives often killed the Spanish pack animals for 'satisfying their hunger than by way of insult or of taking revenge' (Fages, 1769). These types of statements, and incessant well-documented thievery of food items from the Spanish in the 1767 to 1774 period, clearly indicate a subsistence economic lifestyle at best, at least for a significant portion of the population.

Pre-colonial native life expectancy was low. The earliest explorers and friars rarely report of older inhabitants in the villages, seeing primarily younger men and women. Infant mortality was probably very high due to malnutrition. This is not surprising. As Johansson (1982) notes, 'Before contact with Europeans had begun, the native peoples of North America were varied in their demographic characteristics; nevertheless, available evidence indicates that, on an average, their life-expectancy-at-birth values fell into the same low ranges typical for other groups at similar levels of technological development.' Since there were no written records in pre-colonial periods, the best estimates probably come from similar forager-horticulturist or hunter-gatherer tribes with similar technology studied in more modern times, such as the Tsimane tribes in north-central Bolivia, that have remained isolated from colonial contact. These studies point to a very low life expectancy, somewhere between 15 years and 25 years (Gurven, 2006; Walker et al., 2006). Given the difficult chaparral terrain, the low levels of technology development, the arid region's drought cycles, and the higher density of pre-colonial people in Alta California, it is our opinion that the likely average life expectancy for the immediate pre-colonial contact period would be more in the 15 to 20 year range for the population in general, compared to a life expectancy of over 40 years for Europeans during the same time period (see discussion of disease management below).

Not surprisingly, warfare has low status in these stratified, local horticultural hierarchies. Localized chiefs simply won't act warlike unless they are absolutely certain they will win – there is simply too much to personally lose, and little to personally gain from war for the elites within a stratified, static society. This is well documented by a number of early Spanish land explorers who trekked over vast regions of California and the Sonora districts (such as in the first Anza expedition in 1774) and who noted the lack of sophisticated weapons, particularly among those indigenous people living in less productive regions. Not surprisingly, the bands described by the Spanish as having more centralized political structure and organization were also the wealthier native communities, occupying the best agricultural land, such as the Yumas near the Colorado River in California (Anza, 1774). They also, the Spanish noted, had the best weapons of the tribes encountered.

The rigid horticultural-based social structure and land tenure system, combined with the high population density and limitations of having approached the carrying capacity of the environment under current technology, had several implications. First, at the time of first colonial contact, it was clear that a large portion of the population was barely maintaining itself at subsistence levels. There is no indication that the early missionaries or explorers, in spite of their small population, were able to trade with the local people to obtain food simply because the local populations had no excess food to trade (with the exception perhaps of recently caught surplus prey or fish).

In fact, because of the lack of food trade with the local population, most critical to the survival of the mission and presidio population during the first 10 years after 1769 in Alta California were the occasional supply ships from San Blas. These ships brought critical food and manufactured items to the missions. Second, typical when the carrying capacity of land is reached, population control becomes necessary or starvation ensues.[7] As a number of contemporaneous letters suggest the earliest Spanish considered some of the social customs of the local population exceedingly immoral. Infanticide is sometimes mentioned (Mooney, 1911), and according to early historian Hubert Howe Bancroft (1874), in some central California tribal groups such as the Gallinomeros, the ritualistic killing of the elderly by their children was evident. Young unmarried women were particularly susceptible to sexual abuse (Fages, 1769). Third, with the exception of woven baskets, and some pottery items, there were no manufactured goods or trade items.

The technology of the area was essentially of a primitive Stone Age nature. Most of the native bands encountered were described by the first Spanish explorers as having a 'low grade of culture' (for example, Diaz, 1769, Diary AGI 88-1-22), often living in the open without any shelter (Costanso, 1770, Diary, 8 September 1769), albeit most lived in 'huts' located in villages that Spanish called 'rancherias.' Approximately 60 established rancherias are believed to have been scattered around the San Diego region. Trades and crafts knowledge was low, even when compared with other North American tribes. Various letters, for example, suggest that the indigenous people knew very little of well construction, land tilling, hide tanning, masonry, cloth making (other than netting) or food preservation. In fact, there is little evidence of significant technological advancement among the San Diego population in the 200 years from Juan Rodriguez Cabrillo's visit in 1542.

Finally, ethno-linguistic diversity was extremely high within the region. In the relatively small San Diego region, four different language groups have been identified (Carrico, 1986). This high ethno-linguistic diversity is further emphasized in the Juan Bautista de Anza diary describing the first land expedition in 1774 from Sonora to Alta California, where a variety of languages were encountered among the numerous Alta California tribes along the way.

Based upon the best modern archeological and written first-hand account information available (see also, Hackel, 2006; Jackson and Castillo, 1996; Maynard and Meighan, 1976), Table 5.1 provides a summary of the important structural socio-economic characteristics of the San Diego indigenous people upon initial contact with the San Diego mission system in 1769.

Not surprisingly, in line with received economic theory, there is little evidence that the Alta California tribes developed any significant public or semi-public goods, either at the local level, such as an educational system, community based irrigation, common water rights extending to poor tribe members, or even a crude health system,[8] or at a broader level, such as maintained trade roads between tribes. In essence, given the structural characteristics described above, as Gennaioli and Rainer (2007) argue, under 'decentralization tyranny', in stratified societies, few public goods are provided, and there tends to be few, if any, spillover effects. This appears to be exactly the case at the dawn of mission contact.

Table 5.1 Socio-economic characteristics of the pre-colonial indigenous population in San Diego

Stratification Relatively rigid class structure	High stratification
Centralization Political power centralized versus localized with village elites and chiefs.	High localization
Technology level Degree of technology adoption and usage	Low technology usage
Ethnolinguistic diversity Number of different languages or variants spoken within a relatively small area, or among different strata of society.	High linguistic diversity
Carrying capacity	Near environmental carrying capacity
Intergroup mobility	Low intergroup mobility
Slave ownership Slave owners and/or unlanded segments working for elite segments	Possible slave ownership by elite
Poverty level	General subsistence level economy
Institutional sophistication Contract law, land tenure, ability to organize unrelated parties, recourse mechanisms	Low institutional systems

After the founding of the San Diego mission, Frs Jayme and Fuster were left in charge of its operation. The first year was extremely difficult. Originally the crude wood, mud, and straw San Diego mission was built next to the small presidio. Unfortunately most of the sailors that arrived in 1769 either died, or were extremely sick from scurvy during the first year. Thus the mission's diverted attention to tending the Spanish sick, plus the intimidating proximity of the presidio to the mission, at first made it difficult to baptize the natives. In addition, the crops failed in the first year due to lack of water and poor land, and there were few supply ships, as several were damaged in storms. The situation did not improve much in the second year.

Fr. Serra soon saw the economic development problems inherent in the structural problems of the existing indigenous economy. In addition, there were several important social problems that had arisen with the Spanish soldiers that were clearly going to undermine the mission effort. By 1773, the Alta California entrepreneurial strategy needed to become more comprehensive and refined. And it is this strategic vision that framed the mission entrepreneurial strategy for the following 50 years. In particular:

1. The missions needed to provide centralized government to the Indian population in order to generate what Gennaioli and Rainer (2007) refer to as 'public goods with spillover effects', and overcome the stratified 'decentralized tyranny' of the multiple local elites controlling the region's Rancherias. In essence, the Franciscan friars discovered that they needed to follow a strategy of 'local capture' (Riker, 1964) that, given the structural failures within the indigenous economy, the authority and responsibility for 'public good' generation and distribution needed to be centralized.
2. An important component of this broad 'public good' needed to focus on formal education to facilitate 'technology transfer', in particular, training the Indians in various crafts and trades, such as tanning, higher quality pottery making, candle making, metal working, woodworking, horse riding and herding.
3. All the missions, particularly the San Diego mission that was initially built on less productive land, needed to obtain a regular schedule of supplies until the missions could become self-sufficient, not only for the survival of the mission and presidio personnel, but also as charity 'exchange goods' to assist in the conversion of the local population.
4. The presidio Spanish soldiers needed to be tightly controlled and prevented from abusing Indian females.
5. The San Diego mission had to be moved away from the adjacent San Diego presidio in order to become less intimidating, and closer to the local, indigenous Rancherias (villages).
6. Productivity of the land, low under Indian technologies, needed to be increased. Productivity could be enhanced by (a) developing agriculturally oriented public goods, such as building reservoirs, a local police to control thievery, and a transportation system, (b) that grazing livestock (sheep and cattle in particular) would provide better protein food sources than occasional hunting of game, and could be grazed on non-agriculturally productive land, (c) that agricultural productivity could be increased with mules, horses, and plows, (d) that new crops, such as grapes, corn, wheat, barley, and fruit trees would flourish in the Alta California microclimates, and (e) that various crafts, such as food preservation and centralized flour milling, would increase productivity due to scale and food storage advantages.
7. Encouraging settlement by established Mexican families could help demonstrate the importance of family traditions and moral behavior.

Fr. Serra knew that this all had to happen fast or the entrepreneurial mission project would fail. By 1773 he was in Mexico City to plead his case and got a commitment from Spanish authorities on all of the above (26 Articles of Memorandum, #1, February, 1773). In response to Fr. Serra's efforts, the first overland 'Anza' expedition was organized in 1774 by Juan Bautista de Anza to bring not only supplies but also herds, technology, skilled craftsmen, crop specimens, and a few families to the missions. Fr. Serra also got a commitment for more reliable supply shipping from San Blas, as well as authorization that education and administration of the native population would be centralized and be the responsibility of the friars. And finally, Fr. Serra received a new, revised set of authorizations, including the right to demand that any soldier who exhibited 'licentious or cruel' behaviors toward the Indians would be immediately recalled.[9]

In 1774, the San Diego mission moved to a spot approximately 6 miles from the presidio, to be closer to the Indian villages. Land was more arable, so crops were better and a few small herds had been established. Baptisms increased dramatically.

Around this time, the San Diego mission developed a strategy somewhat different from the other Alta California missions. The core Alta California mission strategy was deep centralization, which is to house, educate, and train the baptized natives within or immediately surrounding the mission property. In San Diego, however, since land was less productive in the immediate mission location, newly baptized people would be given a couple of days (or less) instruction, then rotated back to their villages. They would then come in to the mission periodically for education and training in the crafts, or to work the land. Only the unmarried young women and the more established neophytes, primarily the families, would stay on mission central property in San Diego.

In 1775, a not-unexpected attack occurred.[10] The elites and chiefs from approximately 40 of the more remote rancherias organized an attack on the mission and the presidio. In spite of some recent attempts to paint the attack as a response against Christianity or mission abuses (that is, Carrico, 1997), the attack fits exactly with the response one would expect from a highly stratified, localized system of elites when confronted with an expanding centralized mission government that is starting to provide important 'public goods' to the community. Also, most of the poorer Indians within the 'attacking force' probably simply saw an opportunity to steal food and supplies from the mission; thievery of food supplies was one of the biggest problems in the early missions and guards had to be placed on the supply stores constantly. In addition, it was well known by the Spanish that economics provided the main motivation for uprising in the Sonora and California districts, and they specifically tracked the number of 'thefts' as a primary leading indicator of uprising since it indicated increasing desperation by the poorest subset of the local population. Finally, since warfare was unattractive to already established, localized elites, it was only pursued when these elites felt that there is no chance of losing. This was exactly the situation in 1775.

Although the San Diego presidio had only about 10 soldiers, and the San Diego mission had 11 Europeans/Mexicans (friars plus skilled workers), the organizers of the attack waited until several of the soldiers were out of the region on other activities. Approximately 500 natives attacked the basically unarmed mission and another 500 natives were to attack the presidio's remaining handful of soldiers some 6 miles away. The presidio attack never materialized. The mission attack, however, burned most of the mission buildings and immediately killed two people, including the beating and mutilation of Fr. Luis Jayme. Interestingly, the majority of the mission attacking force quickly got distracted early by the spoils of the attack, carting off the few relics and supplies of the mission, and tried, mostly unsuccessfully due to their stone weapons, to slaughter the herd animals. Even though being outnumbered over 50 to 1, the remaining nine mission personnel, which included only one capable soldier, one family including two children, and the remaining friar, fended off the attacking force for several hours.[11] One of the wounded died later.

The attacking force finally lost their cohesion and will, and wandered back to their villages. Armed groups from the more local 'Christian' villages quickly started to send men to protect the mission, and the native families (who were unarmed) living at the mission village came out of their barricaded homes to assist the wounded mission personnel.

In spite of overwhelming numbers of the attacking force, the abysmal failure of the 1775 attack essentially ended the native elite's power among San Diego's more distant rancherias. Within a few months a small squad of Spanish soldiers arrested the instigators without incident, and returned the stolen materials to the mission. In 1780 the mission was rebuilt under the supervision of Fr. Serra,[12] but this time with the adobe walls and a chapel now seen as the traditional mission style of architecture.

No more violence occurred after the 1775 incident. In 1784, at the age of 70, and after traveling over 24 000 miles mostly by foot, Father Junípero Serra died at Mission San Carlos Borromeo in Monterrey, California; however, the entrepreneurial strategy envisioned by Fr Serra continued in force for several more decades.

By 1800, the San Diego Mission, along with the other Alta California missions, was firmly established, with irrigated farmlands, reservoir systems, deep wells, dedicated food processing, curing, and preservation as well as various trade and craft production activities, such as pottery, tanning, candle making, cloth weaving, and blacksmithing. Sheep and cattle ranching became dominant. In addition, a variety of new agricultural products, such as grapes, wheat, figs, barley, and corn were introduced to the region. The road system was improved between the native Rancharias, and distant mission properties were now connected. According to Duggan (2005) the California missions started to produce substantial economic surpluses between 1800 and 1810. San Diego reported 1797 as its most successful year in terms of 'baptisms'. Around this time, important trade markets also started to develop, initially with the local presidio and governmental agencies.

Problems started to develop around 1810 as the war for Mexican independence developed. Spain, already struggling financially, could no longer support its troops in California. These local troops, as well as corrupt government officials, started to levy and tax the missions. Yet some of the missions, including San Diego, continued to grow and prosper. The primary reason for this continued expansion was the opening of the export trade market. Although exporting was essentially illegal under Spanish rule, by the mid-1820s Spain could no longer enforce this ban, and may privateer trading vessels started to visit the missions to acquire export products. Due to its attractive and safe harbor, San Diego was one of the missions that benefited from the export market.[13]

The situation declined significantly after Mexican independence from Spain in 1821. Although the native population investment in mission lands was protected under Spanish law, Mexican law did not provide the same protection, and the Mexican government did not support the mission strategy. In 1834–35 the Alta California mission lands, including those of San Diego, were secularized by the Mexican government, the remaining native mission population drifted away since there was no more protection for them, and the best mission farm and ranch land was confiscated by local Mexican officials, speculators, and ranchers, many of whom were retired presidio soldiers.[14] Under secularization, the missions were to give one half of their movable property to the mission natives, and each head of a mission family was to be given 400 square yards (simply a large house and garden plot). Everything else — lands, movable properties, property of all classes — was to be transferred to the Mexican administrators. Native families were given the opportunity to leave the mission, or work as laborers for the Mexican government. In San Diego, only about 10 per cent of the remaining mission populations chose to work for the Mexican administrator (Jackson, 1902).

California ceded from Mexico in 1848 and gold was discovered near San Francisco, forever changing California history. The population of California exploded overnight, and the native population became an increasingly small minority of the total population. California entered the United States in 1850, and between 1850 and 1880, under the control of the United States at the time, the demise of the Indian population accelerated. Ultimately those natives that did not assimilate into the broader population were ultimately resettled on reservation lands similar to the rest of the United States.

Was the mission strategy successful? Success can be analyzed from many different perspectives.

Economic Outcome

Without question, from an entrepreneurial point of view, the Alta California mission strategy, including the San Diego mission, was successful. While by modern standards overall production was tiny, according to official mission records the San Diego mission at its peak had over 50000 acres.[15] Crops included corn, barley, kidney beans, chick peas, and wheat (for example, Hackel, 1998; Magnaghi and Magnaghi, 2005). The San Diego mission livestock herds included approximately 20000 sheep, 10000 cattle, and 1250 horses. This is a somewhat remarkable level of productive activity considering that the vast majority of the San Diego region is an arid chaparral receiving less than 15 inches of annual rainfall. The mission produced economic surpluses for many years, and resulted in an active trade market with the local Spanish, and later Mexican governments. Being a well-sheltered port city, San Diego also benefited from the export trade market. As with all the California missions, after 1821 with Mexican independence, conditions declined rapidly in San Diego. However, from its inception in 1769 until 1830, for almost 60 years the mission generally created the vast majority of economic output for the region.

Public Goods Outcome

During the near half century of initial growth and stability, a whole generation of natives benefited from a variety of public goods supplied by the San Diego mission. The road system between the interior and coast communities and between various valleys and rancherias was developed. Welfare and public health systems were established at the mission. Education of the native population, particularly in the productive crafts and skilled trades, was undertaken. In San Diego alone, a large irrigation system was built, including a stone dam and a 6 mile brick and stone irrigation conduit. The development and spillover of public goods is exactly what would be expected under the Gennaioli and Rainer (2007) theorem.

Most of these 'public goods' subsequently ceased, or fell into disrepair, with the fall of the mission system.

Technology Transfer

Land productivity, through enhancement of tilling and gravity fed irrigation, and crop diversity increased exponentially during the mission period, not only in the San Diego area, but throughout California. Essentially, all the major groups of grain currently raised in California, plus the vast majority of grown fruits, such as apples, oranges, peaches, pears, plums, prunes, lemons, grapes, pomegranates, olives, and nuts, were introduced by the Franciscans. Grapes and wine making was also introduced, particularly in the central area of California, providing the seed capital and crops for the modern wine industry. Most importantly, the Franciscans introduced livestock to the area, establishing ranching as the major industry utilizing previously unproductive land. Overall, the mission system was able to sustain both the local native population and the growing Spanish presidio and pueblo populations. The Mexican war of independence stalled any further expansion. It wasn't until the huge population explosion during the 1848 gold rush period that livestock numbers in California exceeded their peak mission levels (Johnston and McCalla, 2004).

Economic Buffering

The missions, including San Diego, expanded their land holdings by securing farm and ranching tracts as the local population converted. This land, as previously discussed, was held in trust by the Franciscan under Spanish law, the *Recopilacion de leyes de los Reynos de las Indias* of 1680 and was clearly understood as a 'trust' by the friars' own writings throughout the mission period – this was the Franciscan strategy, and one that is argued today in various legal cases. By holding land, technically in the name of the Indians who converted and now worked the land, the missions provided a protective economic buffer to the increasing pressure during the early 1800s from both retiring Spanish military personnel and new Spanish immigrant speculators that wanted to acquire the best land. Duggan (2005) notes that the friars' effort to discourage and dislodge Spanish land squatters from mission land is often misinterpreted as protecting ownership, rather than protecting the 'trust'.

Of course, after the mission system collapse in 1834, the lack of enforcement of earlier Spanish laws by the Mexican government, and then the ceding of California to the United States, combined with the population explosion starting in 1848, and without the centralized mission counterbalance, new immigrant land speculators, ranchers, and military routinely forced the natives off the best land.

Assimilation and Labor Force Advantages

Unlike the majority of indigenous people in the United States who essentially had to assimilate, usually unsuccessfully, by their own means into the advancing colonial framework, or retreat to isolated lands and later reservations, during the peak mission periods over 50 per cent of California's indigenous population were directly associated with the mission system. Many natives became quite skilled in important construction, agricultural and production trades and crafts. This had important advantages. First, it potentially created a basis for successful assimilation for those natives that chose that direction, and second, for those that returned to their native villages, it potentially provided a basis for local development. For example, an important 1852 government report by the Honorable B.D. Wilson of Los Angeles, one of the first American settlers in Southern California, noted,

> These same Indians had built all the houses in the country, planted all the fields and vineyards. Under the Missions they were masons, carpenters, plasterers, soapmakers, tanners, shoemakers, blacksmiths, millers, bakers, cooks, brickmakers, carters and cartmakers, weavers and spinners, saddlers, shepherds, agriculturists, horticulturists, vineros, vaqueros; in a word, they filled all the laborious occupations known to civilized society.

In particular, the natives became skilled and highly prized 'cowboys' in the post-mission period as the large secular ranches developed (often on old mission property). Wilson continues by noting that Indians constituted 'the majority of the laborers, mechanics, and servants' of San Diego and Los Angeles, and 'they all spoke the Spanish language, and a not inconsiderable number could read and write it . . . They had built all the houses in the country, had taught the new whites [authors' note: Wilson is referring to the white immigration to California during the population explosion of the late 1840s] how to make brick, mud mortar, how to use asphalt on roofs; they understood irrigation, and were good herders.'

However, the labor force advantage that the former mission Indians had in California during the 1820s to the 1840s was starting to evaporate by 1850, as the massive American, European and Chinese immigration also brought highly skilled tradespeople, the primary language rapidly shifted from Spanish to English, and the former mission Indians could not obtain title to their lands. Wilson noted this 'title' problem in 1852 when he wrote to the US Department of Interior making a case for action regarding the former mission Indian's land rights, 'It is not natural rights I speak of, nor merely possessory rights, but rights acquired and contracts made, acquired and made when the laws of the Indies had force here, and never assailed by any laws or executive acts.'

Spiritual Success

With the exception of a few isolated mountainous villages, by the 1834 secularization period the vast majority of the indigenous population had been baptized into Christianity. Today, the Catholic parish priests continue to minister to the remaining native people on the present day reservations with 16 different missions, including the Santa Ysabel mission, which was founded as a sub-mission of San Diego in 1818. The San Diego mission itself was occupied in 1892 by the Sisters of Saint Joseph of Carondolet, who conducted an American Indian children's school until 1909. In 1931, the mission was rebuilt to reflect the design of the 1813 church. It is currently an active Catholic parish. The Diocese of San Diego also operates Mission San Luis Rey, another of the 21 original missions founded in 1798, and its various sub-missions also serving the indigenous community, such as Mission San Antonio de Pala founded in 1816.

Disease Management

One of the major criticisms often leveled at the mission effort was the introduction of epidemic diseases into the indigenous population. There is no question that introduced disease severely impacted the Native American populations throughout the United States, sometimes in devastating proportions, sometimes less so depending on the region and period being examined. In California, the native population was clearly affected by introduced diseases. One line of current thought is that these diseases entered California overland from Sonora prior to 1797. Another more traditional model is that the diseases were brought during the initial mission expeditions to California, most probably by the soldiers and sailors. In addition, there is no doubt that venereal disease was spread by the mistreatment of native women by some early Spanish soldiers.

In examining the issue of disease, one must remember that the colonial process would have happened no matter what, with or without the mission system, and diseases most certainly would have been introduced regardless.

Many modern critics of the mission system argue that life expectancy was actually made worse by the policy of using dormitories for the neophyte population. Almost always this argument is grounded by examining mission records of births, deaths, and baptism to determine mortality and life expectancies. Based on these records, it is often remarked that the life expectancy of a mission Indian was less than 15 years.[16] However, this figure is misleading, and must be put into an appropriate context.

First, it must be remembered that the pre-colonial indigenous life expectancy in California was probably between an average of 15 and 20 years at best, based upon current research, something that most modern critics of the mission system fail to mention.[17] Second, it is now known from medical forensic analysis of skeletal remains that pre-colonial contact indigenous populations within North America suffered from a variety of debilitating diseases, including tuberculosis and pneumonia (for example, Larsen, 1994; Russell, 1980; Ubelaker, 1992). Third, paleoanthropologists have also now documented increasing levels of malnutrition, poor health, and war among indigenous people in the decades prior to colonial contact, which in turn resulted in a precipitous drop in indigenous life expectancy throughout much of the pre-colonial United States. This situation was exacerbated by the overall crowded living conditions, poor sanitary practices, and generally promiscuous behavior (leading to more rapid transmission of infectious diseases) of pre-colonial native populations (Larsen, 1994; Steckel and Rose, 2002). Many have attributed these events to population levels within the pre-colonial Americas reaching the carrying capacity of the environment, a situation that most likely existed in the mission region of California.

Fourth, since the mission system clearly represented a 'welfare' state including providing shelter and food for a 'baptism', given the heavily stratified structure of indigenous society, the mission most certainly first attracted the poorer, unlanded classes, rather than the landed, more affluent elites. This is well supported by the descriptions of the early friars. Statistics regarding the relationship between class structure and life expectancy in pre-1900 United States (before the 'public good' of government health support) indicate that the difference in life expectancy between high and low income levels is close to 33 per cent, and that the difference increases in more historical periods (Finlay, 1981; Steckel and Rose, 2002). In addition, research of the pre-colonial stratified indigenous populations in Meseoamerica and the Andes also indicates a large disparity in health, nutrition, and life-expectancy, with the poorer strata of society suffering greatly (Steckel and Rose, 2002). Using this argument, one might expect the original pre-colonial life expectancy of those indigenous people who most likely entered the mission system would be between 11 and 15 years, thus the analysis of the mission population suggests no real difference (death rates of about 54 per 1000 reported by the San Diego Mission statistics are within the range typically seen in poor forager-horticultural pre-colonial societies), or in fact, the mission system might have actually increased life expectancy among the lower strata populations it attracted.

However, even the often cited mission life expectancy is probably biased too low. First, the missions attracted a large number of unmarried women attempting to escape an indigenous society that held women in very low esteem, and the friars protected them under lock and key in dormitories, but with strict rules regarding pregnancies. In fact, for several decades, unmarried women outnumbered men in the missions by approximately 40 per cent, later dropping to parity in the later mission period. Under these highly controlled conditions the 'birth rates' on the missions would expect to be lower than in the surrounding community. Second, since exchange goods were offered for 'baptism', in the early years, if no goods were available whole villages might be turned away from a baptism. Under these scarce conditions, a baptism might occur only when death is near, thus inflating the mission death rates.[18]

Regardless, the key economic determination is that no indigenous person was ever forced to be baptized, participate in the mission system, or move onto mission property. It was completely voluntary. Clearly, every native that entered the mission system made a rational choice suggesting that the mission life, for them, was better than the option of not associating with the mission, in other words, they 'revealed their preference' for the mission strategy over their native culture, health status, social condition and economic status. This appeared particularly the case for the young women in indigenous California societies. In other words, weak institutional regimes are easily abandoned and new ones quickly established as productive technologies become more efficient, institutional arrangements become stronger, and ultimately people benefit.

CONCLUSION

The founding of the San Diego mission in 1769 can be viewed to be the opening of a final chapter of economic development activities that had begun exactly 250 years earlier, with the arrival of Cortés on the coast of Mexico in 1519. This final chapter can be argued to be the end of the era of Spanish colonial economic development efforts, the end of the era of Catholic Church sponsored and funded economic development, and, maybe most dramatically, the last opportunity for the native population to develop an economy of their own making before being exposed to the powerful buffeting of rapid and unconstrained growth and globalization. The dwindling resources of both the Spanish government and the Franciscan Order worked to lend an air of inevitability to the two dramas of State and Church. But the remote location of California and its isolation only accentuate the stark drama of the beleaguered native population bracing for the onslaught to come.

If the period of economic development is seen to run from 1769 to 1827, when Franciscan Fathers Zalvidea and Barona wrote to Governor Echeandia in protest, then the economic development opportunity for the indigenous people can be said to have lasted for about 60 years. This is a very short period for a people to raise themselves from essentially a subsistence, Stone Age economy to being able to compete on a global stage. Given the brevity, Fr. Serra's sense of urgency expressed in 1773 is understandable. And given how much was accomplished in so little time, the Franciscan entrepreneurial development strategy in Alta California seems remarkable.

There were other possible development strategies, and several of them were put forward during the 60-year period of the mission success. For example, the governor of California, Pedro Fages, urged a strategy of small freehold farms with private ownership by Indian families. This recommendation by Fages was mentioned in the journal of French naval officer and explorer Jean Francois de la Perouse during his 1786 visit to Monterey and Mission San Carlos Borromeo. Another possible economic strategy, large-scale plantation-style production of agricultural products for export to China and the Orient, was urged by Spanish merchant Vicente Vasadre y Vega, also attested to by de la Perouse. Both of these strategies, and others, were rejected by the Franciscans in favor of the strategy described in this chapter. It is our judgment that neither of these strategies would have been as effective in addressing the pre-colonial problems of public goods capture, institutional weakness, social stratification, and high transactions costs due to ethnolinguistic diversity.

NOTES

1. Duggan (2005) is one of the few researchers who have specifically examined the inherent dilemma of Scholastic Economic Theology, Franciscan attitudes toward poverty, and their management of the California missions, essentially as entrepreneurs, manufacturers, and exporters.
2. As Duggan (2005) notes, there was some minor disagreement as some Franciscan writers argued that communal land, that is mission land, should be managed more like monastic lands, communally owned and worked by all, rather than as a trust for future private ownership by the natives. This attitude is actually more in line with the Benedictine community model of productivity and land tenure.
3. As codifed in the *Recopilacion de leyes de los Reynos de las Indias*, 1680.
4. There is a commonly repeated myth that the California mission friars attempted to employ inappropriate European agricultural techniques, however, there is simply no evidence for this conclusion. For the San Diego mission, only the first couple of years'

harvest proved difficult, but this was due primarily to the poor location of the first mission and the extremely poor land of the region. In fact, the evidence clearly points to a program to transfer highly appropriate technologies to the Indian population. The Franciscans had over 100 years of experience in Mexican mission management, all the friars had university educations, the Apostolic Missionary College of San Fernando in Mexico City, in particular, had an excellent education program of local environments, plus most of the friars, including Father Serra, had decades of professional experience in managing mission agricultural activities in various regions of Mexico.

5. Early Spanish explorers, such as Cabrillo, interacted almost exclusively with coastal and island tribes, who tended to be transient fishing and game-hunting societies, versus the inland, more horticultural societies (Allen, 1998)
6. The best estimates place the pre-colonial California indigenous population at about 135 000, which was approximately 9 per cent of the total indigenous population in the lower United States (estimated about 1.5 million in pre-colonial times). However, they occupied only 4 per cent to 5 per cent of the livable land mass, suggesting a substantially higher density than average.
7. There are many different theories of population, and there is considerable debate regarding how humans, and other advanced biological organisms, respond to carrying capacity issues. The important aspect of this issue for our purposes is to note that by the mid-1700s, the pre-colonial carrying capacity utilizing native technologies within the San Diego region was being approached.
8. The earliest contact letters (*circa* 1769 and 1770) indicated that hurt or wounded natives would be brought immediately to the Spanish for treatment.
9. The mission friars constantly had problems with misbehaving presidio soldiers, often complaining about this problem to superiors. Unfortunately, although the Franciscans gained the right to demand recall of such soldiers in 1773, this was rarely enforced by the Spanish authorities in Monterey or Mexico. Abusive Spanish soldiers from the presidios remained a problem throughout the history of the California missions, and certainly undermined the progress of the missions.
10. Letters from the San Diego Presidio commanders in 1774 anticipated violence, and requested more military supplies and arms.
11. An account of the attack is described in a letter by Fr. Palou approximately two weeks after the attack.
12. Between 1775 and 1780 the mission had a temporary location near the presidio.
13. Richard Henry Dana's famous novel, *Two Years Before the Mast*, describes the exporting of hides from the missions and surrounding ranches in both San Diego and San Juan Capistrano, during the 1834 to 1836 period, at the final period of decline and decay of the California missions.
14. The crumbling remains of the San Diego mission was sold in 1845. It did not return to the Catholic Church's control (along with a few acres) until 1865.
15. 1797 to 1815 seemed to be the peak economic period for the San Diego mission.
16. In fact, the San Diego mission Indians had a much lower mortality, with a death rate of 56 per 1000 versus the 78 per 1000 for all the California missions (Carrico, 1997). This death rate is similar to the estimated death rates of pre-colonial societies under similar stratified conditions as the pre-colonial contact California indigenous culture (Robson and Kaplan, 2003).
17. As a comparison, historical demographic research suggests that life expectancy in pre-colonial Africa was between 20 and 22 years (see Campbell, 1991). It should be noted, however, that these African populations were more technologically advanced, had better food sources, and more centralized government than the pre-colonial Alta California populations. Studies of isolated modern-day hunter-gatherers and forager-horticulturists groups, including the Tsimane Indians in north-central Bolivia, indicate that 50 per cent never make it to age 15. Jones (2004) also reports that the average life expectancy in pre-colonial rural societies was much less than 25 years, significantly lower than equivalent European societies. For example, in seventeenth-century England

life expectancy is estimated around 40 years (Wrigley and Schofield, 1981), while the life expectancy was even higher among early seventeenth-century New England colonists (Tate and Ammerman, 1979, p. 158). California and other southwestern natives typically lived under much harsher conditions than other natives, and thus probably had much lower life-expectancies than other native groups.

18. There is also some evidence that the main period of epidemic disease and population decrease among the native population in California was not during the mission period, but after secularization of the missions and increased interaction with the general Mexican, and later US populations. For example, in the 1872 document, *The Case of the Mission Indians in Southern California, and the Action of the Indian Rights Association in supporting the Defense of their Legal Rights*, it states that 'Suffering, hunger, disease and vice have cut down more than half of their numbers in the last thirty years' – implying from the early 1840s.

REFERENCES

Acemoglu, D., S. Johnson and J. Robinson (2001), 'The Colonial Origins of Comparative Development: An Empirical Investigation', *American Economic Review*, **91** (5), 1369–401.

Adler, P. and S. Kwon (2002), 'Social Capital: Prospects for a New Concept', *The Academy of Management Review*, **27**, 17–40.

Allen, R. (1998) 'Native Americans at Mission Santa Cruz, 1791–1834: Interpreting the Archaeological Record', *Perspectives in California Archaeology*, vol. 5, Los Angeles: Institute of Archaeology, University of California.

Anza, J. (1774), Jaun Bautiosta de Anza diaries, translated in H. Bolton (1930), *Anza's California Expeditions*, vol. 2, Berkeley, CA: University of California Press.

Arcand, J. (1996), 'Development Economics and Language: The Earnest Search for a Mirage?', *International Journal of the Sociology of Language*, **121**, 119–57.

Bancroft, H.H. (1874), *The Native Races of the Pacific States of North America*, New York: D. Appleton.

Bardhan, P. (2002), 'Decentralization of Governance and Development', *Journal of Economic Perspectives*, **16**, 185–205.

Bardhan, P. and D. Mookherjee (2000), 'Capture and Governance at the Local and National Levels', *American Economic Review*, **90** (2), 135–9.

Boone, C. (2003), *Political Topographies of the African State: Territorial Authority and Institutional Choice*, Cambridge: Cambridge University Press.

Bryson, B. (1990), *Mother Tongue*, New York: William Morrow Co.

Campbell, G. (1991), 'The State and Pre-colonial Demographic History: The Case of Nineteenth-century Madagascar', *Journal of African History*, **32**, 415–45.

Carrico, R. (1986), 'Before the Strangers: American Indians in San Diego at the Dawn of Contact', *The Impact of European Exploration and Settlement in Local Native Americans*, San Diego, CA: Cabrillo Historical Association, pp. 5–12.

Carrico, R. (1997), 'Sociopolitical Aspects of the 1775 Revolt at Mission San Diego de Alcala: An Ethnohistoircal Approach', *Journal of San Diego History*, **43** (3), http://www.sandiegohistory.org/journal/97summer/missionrevolt.htm (accessed 11 December 2008).

Chibnik, M. (2005), 'Experimental Economics in Anthropology: A Critical Assessment', *American Ethnologist*, **32** (2), 198–209.

Costanso, M. (1770), reprinted in F. Teggart (1911), 'The Portolo Expedition of 1769–1770: Diary of Miguel Costanso', *Academy of Pacific Coast History*, **2** (4), 1–67.

Coulmas, F. (1992), *Language and Economy*, Oxford: Blackwell.

Davis, T. (1993), 'A Day in the Life of a Friar', California Mission Studies Association, http://www.ca-missions.org/davis.html (accessed 11 December 2008).

De Soto, H. (2000), *The Mystery of Capital: Why Capitalism Triumphs in the West and Fails Everywhere Else*, New York: Basic Books.

De Soto, H. (2006), 'Trust, Institutions and Entrepreneurship', in C. Galbraith and C. Stiles (eds), *Developmental Entrepreneurship: Adversity, Risk, and Isolation*, Amsterdam: Elsevier Sciences, pp. 3–20.

Diaz, J. (1769), reprinted in H. Bolton (1930), *Anza's California Expeditions*, Berkeley, CA: University of California Press.

Diaz, J. (1774), reprinted in H. Bolton (1930), *Anza's California Expeditions*, Berkeley, CA: University of California Press.

Duggan, M. (2005), 'Laws of the Market vs. Laws of God: Scholastic Doctrine and the Early California Economy', *History of Political Economy*, **37** (2), 343–70.

Easterly, W. and R. Levine (1997), 'Africa's Growth Tragedy: Policies and Ethnic Divisions', *Quarterly Journal of Economics*, **112** (4), 1203–50.

Fages, P. (1769), reprinted in I. Engstrant (1975), 'Pedro Fages and Miguel Costanso: Two Early Letters from San Diego in 1769', *Journal of San Diego History*, **21** (2), http://www.sandiegohistory.org/journal/75spring/fages.htm (accessed 11 December 2008).

Fearon, J. and D. Laitin (2000), 'Ordinary Language and External Validity: Specifying Concepts in the Study of Ethnicity', paper presented at the 2000 Annual Meetings of the American Political Science Association, Washington, DC, 31 August–4 September, http://www.ceu.hu/cps/bluebird/eve/statebuilding/fearon-laitin.pdf (accessed 11 December 2008).

Fearon, J. and D. Laitin (2003), 'Ethnicity, Insurgency, and Civil War', *American Political Science Review*, **97** (1), 75–90.

Finlay, R. (1981), *Population and Metropolis: The Demography of London, 1580–1650*, Cambridge: Cambridge University Press.

Fishman, J. (1972), *The Sociology of Language*, Rowley, MA: Newbury House.

Fishman, J. (ed.) (1999), *Handbook of Language and Ethnic Identity*, Oxford: Oxford University Press.

Galbraith, C. and J. Benitez-Galbraith (2009), 'The Impact of Ethnolinguistic Diversity on Entrepreneurial Activity: A Cross-country Study', *International Journal of Entrepreneurship and Small Business*, **8** (3), 307–31.

Galbraith, C. and N. Kay (1986), 'Towards a Theory of Multinational Enterprise', *Journal of Economic Behaviour and Organisation*, **7**, 3–19.

Galbraith, C. and O. Galbraith (2004), *The Benedictine Rule of Leadership*, New York: Adams Media Publishing.

Galbraith, C. and C. Stiles (2003), 'Expectations of Indian Reservation Gaming: Entrepreneurial Activity within a Context of Traditional Land Tenure and Wealth Acquisition', *Journal of Developmental Entrepreneurship*, **8** (2), 93–112.

Galbraith, C., C. Rodriguez and C. Stiles (2007), 'Social Capital as a Club Good: The Case of Ethnic Communities and Entrepreneurship', *Journal of Enterprising Communities*, **1** (1), 38–53.

Gennaioli, N. and I. Rainer (2007), 'The Modern Impact of Precolonial Centralization in Africa', *Journal of Economic Growth*, **12** (3), 185–234.

Grin, F. (2001), 'English as Economic Value: Tools, Facts and Fallacies, *World Englishes*, **20** (1), 65–78.

Grin, F. (2002), *Using Language Economics and Education Economics in Language Education Policy*, Strasbourg: Language Policy Division, Council of Europe.

Gurven, M. (2006), 'Long-Ago Peoples May Have Been Long in the Tooth', *Science*, **312** (5782), 1867

Hackel, S. (1998), 'Land, Labor, and Production: The Colonial Economy of Spanish and Mexican California', in R.A. Gutierrez and R.J. Orsi (eds), *Contested Eden, California Before the Gold Rush*, Berkeley, CA: University of California Press, pp. 111–46.

Hackel, S. (2006), *Children of Coyote, Missionaries of Saint Francis: Indian–Spanish Relations in Colonial California*, Chapel Hill, NC: University of North Carolina Press.

Heikkila, E. (1996), 'Are Municipalities Tieboutian Clubs?', *Regional Science and Urban Economics*, **26**, 203–26.

Herberman, C. (1908), *The Catholic Encyclopedia*, New York: Catholic University of America Press.

Jackson, H. (1902), *Glimpses of California and the Missions*, Boston, MA: Little, Brown and Company.

Jackson, R. and E. Castillo (1996), *Indians, Franciscans and Spanish Colonization: The Impact of the Mission System on California Indians*, Albuquerque, NM: University of New York, Mexico Press.

Johansson, S.R. (1982), 'The Demographic History of the Native Peoples of North America: A Selective Bibliography', *American Journal of Physical Anthropology*, **25** (S3), 133–52.

Johnston, W.E. and A.F. McCalla (2004), 'Whither California Agriculture: Up, Down, or Out? Some Thoughts about the Future', Paper SR041, Special Report Series, Giannini Foundation of Agricultural Economics, University of California.

Jones, D. (2004), 'The Persistence of American Indian Health Disparities', *American Journal of Public Health*, **96** (12), 2122–34.

Kay, N. (1997), *Pattern in Corporate Evolution*, Oxford: Oxford University Press.

La Porta, R., F. Lopez de Silanes, A. Shleifer and R. Vishny (1999), 'The Quality of Government', *Journal of Law, Economics and Organization*, **15**, 222–79.

Larsen, S. (1994), 'In the Wake of Columbus: Native Population Biology in the Postcontact Americas', *Yearbook of Physical Anthropology*, **37**, 109–54.

Light, I. (2004), 'The Ethnic Ownership Economy', in C. Galbraith and C. Stiles (eds), *Ethnic Entrepreneurship: Structure and Process*, Amsterdam: Elsevier Science, pp. 3–44.

Light, I. and P. Bhachu (2004), *Immigration and Entrepreneurship: Culture, Capital, and Ethnic Networks*, Piscataway, NJ: Transaction Publishers.

Magnaghi, E.B. and R.M. Magnaghi (2005), 'The Agricultural Development of Mission San Fernando, Rey de España', in R.M. Beebe and R.M. Senkewicz (eds), *Architecture, Physical Environment, and Society in Alta California*, Proceedings of the 22nd Annual Conference of the California Mission Studies Association, Bakersfield, CA: California Mission Studies Association, pp. 135–52.

Mamdani, M. (1996), *Citizen and Subject: Contemporary Africa and the Legacy of Late Colonialism*, Princeton, NJ: Princeton University Press.
Maynard, G. and C.W. Meighan (1976), *As the Padres Saw Them: California Indian Life and Customs as Reported by the Franciscan Missionaries, 1813–1815*, Santa Barbara, CA: Santa Barbara Mission Archive-Library.
Menzies, T., L. Filion, G. Brenner and S. Elgie (2007), 'Measuring Ethnic Community Involvement: Development and Initial Testing of an Index', *Journal of Small Business Management*, **45** (2), 267–82.
Miller, C. (ed.) (2001), *Fluid Arguments: Five Centuries of Western Water Conflict*, Tucson, AZ: University of Arizona Press.
Mishkin, B. (1940), 'Rank and Warfare among the Plains Indians', *Monographs of the American Ethnological Society*, No. 3.
Mooney, J. (1911), 'Mission Indians (of California)', in *The Catholic Encyclopedia*, New York: Robert Appleton, available at: http://www.newadvent.org/cathen/10369a.htm (accessed 13 November 2008).
Nettle, D. (2000), 'Linguistic Fragmentation and the Wealth of Nations: The Fishman–Pool Hypothesis Reexamined', *Economic Development and Cultural Change*, **48** (2), 335–48.
North, D. (1990), *Institutions, Institutional Change, and Economic Performance*, Cambridge: Cambridge University Press.
Oberg, K. (1973), *The Social Economy of the Tlingit Indians*, Seattle, WA: University of Washington Press.
Piore, M. (1979), *Birds of Passage: Migrant Labor and Industrial Societies*, Cambridge: Cambridge University Press.
Pool, J. (1991), 'The World Language Problem', *Rationality and Society*, **3**, 21–31.
Riker, W. (1964), *Federalism: Origin, Operation, Significance*, Boston, MA: Little Brown.
Robson, A. and H. Kaplan (2003), 'The Evolution of Human Life Expectancy and Intelligence in Hunter-gather Economics', *American Economic Review*, **93** (1), 150–69.
Rodrik, D., A. Subramanian and F. Trebbi (2004), 'Institutions Rule: The Primacy of Institutions over Geography and Integration in Economic Development', *Journal of Economic Growth*, **9**, 131–65.
Russell, H. (1980), *Indian New England Before the Mayflower*, Hanover, NH: University of New Hampshire Press.
Sahlins, M. (1972), *Stone Age Economics*, New York: Taylor and Francis Group.
Secoy, F. (1953), 'Changing Military Patterns of the Great Plains', *Monographs of the American Ethnological Society*, No. 21.
Shipek, F. (1982), 'Kumeyaay Socio-political Structure', *Journal of California and Great Basin Anthropology*, **4**, 293–303.
Shipek, F. (1986), 'The Impact of Europeans upon Kumeyaay Culture', in *The Impact of European Exploration and Settlement in Local Native Americans*, San Diego, CA: Cabrillo Historical Association, pp. 13–25.
Shipek, F. (1987), *Pushed Into the Rocks*, Lincoln, NE: University of Nebraska Press.
Steckel, R. and J. Rose (eds) (2002), *The Backbone of History, Health and Nutrition in the Western Hemisphere*, Cambridge: Cambridge University Press.
Tate, T. and D. Ammerman (1979), *The Chesapeake in the Seventeenth Century*, New York: W.W. Norton.

Teece, D. (1982), 'Towards a theory of the multiproduct firm', *Journal of Economic Behavior and Organization*, **3**, 39–63.
Tiebout, C. (1956), 'A Pure Theory of Local Expenditures', *Journal of Political Economy*, **64**, 416–24.
Ubelaker, D. (1992), 'Patterns of Demographic Change in the Americas', *Human Biology*, **64**, 364.
Walker, R., M. Gurven, K. Hill, A. Migliano, N. Chagnon, R. Souza, G. Djurovic, R. Hames, A. Hurtado, H. Kaplan, K. Kramer, W. Oliver, C. Valeggia and T. Yanauchi (2006), 'Growth Rates and Life Histories in Twenty-two Small-scale Societies', *American Journal of Human Biology*, **18** (3), 295–311.
Williamson, O. (1975), *Markets and Hierarchies*, New York: Free Press.
Wilson, B. (1852), reprinted in J. Caughey (1995), *The Indians of Southern California in 1852: The B.D. Wilson Report and a Selection of Contemporary Comment*, Lincoln, NB: University of Nebraska Press.
Wrigley, E. and R. Schofield (1981), *The Population History of England 1541–1871: A Reconstruction*, Cambridge: Harvard University Press.

6. The religious ethic of the Protestant ethnics

Ivan Light

A century after its initial publication, Max Weber's *The Protestant Ethic and the Spirit of Capitalism* remains the most influential statement of the relationship between religion and entrepreneurship.[1] In this classic essay, the German economist and pioneer sociologist, Max Weber (1864–1920) proposed the existence of an 'elective affinity' between ascetic, this-worldly Protestantism and the triumph of capitalism in late medieval Europe.[2] In Weber's account, key Protestant theologians such as John Calvin, Martin Luther, and Richard Baxter inadvertently increased the number and quality of entrepreneurs in late medieval Europe by changing the way Europeans thought about business. Instead of condemning wealth and praising charity and poverty, standard recommendations of Roman Catholic theology, the Protestant theologians praised business success, which they interpreted as a sign of God's favor. Signs of divine favor were especially valuable to Protestant laymen, Weber proposed, because the Calvinist doctrine of predestination left Protestant laymen insecure about their eternal salvation, and thus in need of signs of grace such as business success provided. If a person prospered, believers concluded that God prospered the person. Additionally, because the Protestant theologians stressed thrift, hard work, and an ascetic lifestyle, laymen who followed the theologians' lifestyle advice actually enhanced their chances of obtaining success in business, and therewith the coveted reassurance of God's grace.[3]

In the early modern period, before missionaries brought the Protestant message to Latin America, Asia, and Africa, access to the Protestant ethic was restricted to the European nations that embraced the Reformation: Britain, Scandinavia, portions of Germany and Switzerland, the Netherlands, Belgium, and Bohemia. Therefore, Protestantism was at that time part of the ethnic culture of the nations that had embraced the Reformation. Understanding that overlap, Weber also understood that nations and ethnic groups that embraced the Reformation in the sixteenth and seventeenth centuries had previously practiced Catholicism and economic traditionalism, Catholicism's economic partner. Weber nonetheless proposed that the Protestant sects imposed their religious template so deeply on believers that it superseded the prior ecclesiastical and ethnic economic cultures of the newly Protestant nations.[4] Wolfgang Schluchter (1981, p. 143) avers that, in Weber's opinion, ascetic Protestantism did not lead to 'a compromise between economic and moral action' but rather to a 'radical subordination of economic culture to morality'. If so, the ex-Catholics embraced the Protestant ethic without taking along any baggage from their religious past. Precisely this doctrinaire suppression of pre-Reformation ethno-religious heritages supposedly permitted the Reformation to impose its economic template upon the newly Protestant societies, thus providing them a decisive advantage in capitalism's long struggle with economic traditionalism, its predecessor.

Embodied in economic traditionalism and in Catholicism were a multiplicity of practices and beliefs that inhibited the full societal transition to a market economy. Among these residuals were deeply embedded social conventions that obliged merchants to treat kin and co-ethnics better than others rather than treating all the same. A principal way to fulfill this norm was to charge kin and co-ethnics less than one charged others, the so-called dual price system. Another way was fair treatment for some, not for all. To kin and co-ethnics, merchants offered fair treatment and low prices; to others, they offered high prices, guile, and the gyp.[5] In contrast, Protestants were supposed to extend the same price and fair treatment to all, whether friends or not. Weber stressed the universalism of sectarian Protestantism over and against the dual-price tradition that preceded it everywhere, not just in Europe.[6] 'At all periods of history . . . there has been ruthless acquisition, bound to no ethical norms whatever. . . Trade has often been unrestrained in its relations with foreigners and those outside the group. The double ethic has permitted here what was forbidden in dealings among brothers.'[7] Protestants doctrinally rejected the dual-price ethic.[8] In terms of our current thinking about these issues, Weber implied that doctrinaire Protestantism suppressed economic traditionalism within the Protestant nations. The ethical universalism of the Protestants' theology legitimated the price-making universalism of the free market. In a sense, however, the opposite [also] occurred. Becoming Protestants, ex-Catholics became sectarian equivalents of an ethnic minority whose social organization revived the dualism their religious doctrine repudiated: us saints versus the world.

WEBER'S DISMISSAL OF WERNER SOMBART

This issue underlay Weber's polemic with Werner Sombart, an intellectual competitor. Anti-Semites accused the Jews of clannishness, and Weber agreed that Jews were clannish. Of course, Weber added, all traditional trading was fundamentally clannish, and Jewish 'pariah capitalism' was a traditional mode of private enterprise.[9] However, against Sombart, who credited the Jews with inventing capitalism, Weber taught that the clannishness of the Jews, against which anti-Semites fulminated, was the exact reason the Jews *could not* have created 'rational bourgeois capitalism'. By rational bourgeois capitalism Weber meant whole societies that organized their production and consumption around the operation of markets rather than the predecessor, feudal societies that contained capitalistic islands. On these grounds, Weber rejected Werner Sombart's (1863–1941) claim that the Jews had been *as important as* the Protestants in creating modern capitalism during the late Middle Ages (Schluchter, 2005, p. 84). Some years later, in his *General Economic History*, Weber acknowledged the important historical role that the Jews had played in the transition from feudalism to capitalism. But this role, in Weber's opinion, fell short of co-*creating* capitalism as Sombart claimed. To create rational bourgeois capitalism, Weber argued, novel people were necessary who embraced a universalistic trading standard: the same price and equal treatment for all regardless of their kinship or ethno-religious affiliations. The Protestant sectarians embraced this universalistic standard; the Jews did not.[10] Therefore, Weber concluded that Protestants (not Jews) had the distinction or, as the anti-Semites saw it, the opprobrium of having invented full capitalism.[11]

The Protestant theologians had been, Weber showed, quite aware that the temptations of the world could lure entrepreneurs to sin. That is, having worked hard and created value, dour Protestant entrepreneurs would be tempted to enjoy the luxury their high incomes could procure. Should they do so, alas, they succumbed to the lure of wine, women, and song against which their ardent faith had protected them. On the one side stood the Protestant entrepreneurs' faith in God, and the restraints imposed by their membership in disciplined sects that enforced the unique religious ethic of worldly asceticism. On the other side were arrayed all the worldly and materialistic temptations their wealth now permitted. In fact, Daniel Bell (1996) has argued that mature capitalism drew the entire United States into just that trap, making hyper-consumers, and we would now add *obese* hyper-consumers, out of the spiritual descendants of the nation's ascetic Protestant founders.

However, another antinomy of the Protestant ethic has escaped full airing. This is the strain between universalism and particularism in the business practice of the saints as the sectarian Protestant styled themselves. As Weber emphasized, Protestant doctrine required and supported universalism, especially one price universalism that offered all buyers the same fair terms (Weber, 1946a, p. 313). Evaluating the Weber thesis, Jere Cohen (2002, p. 103) declares, 'Puritan ethics required that each transaction be judged in terms of its benefits to all parties affected' rather than its benefit to oneself alone. Similarly, a leading interpreter of Weber, Reinhard Bendix (1960, p. 90) observed that 'collective control and strict exclusion of nonbelievers' usually resulted in a sharp and lasting cleavage between the in-group and the out-group. 'In the case of the Protestant sects, the great paradox was that there was no such cleavage' (ibid.) Indeed, precisely on this ground, Weber argued, the Jews had fallen short because their traditional economic ethic permitted Jewish business owners to offer friends and co-ethnics better terms than were offered others. In contrast, Weber proclaimed, of all the world's religions, only the Protestants approved the aggressive ethical universalism in theology that the market imposed in practice. Reflecting a divine injunction, markets did not discriminate between buyers and sellers in respect of ethnic or family background either; but, during the Reformation, non-Protestants still did. Non-Protestants retained the traditional economic ethic, which discriminated with gusto on the grounds that everyone *ought in justice* to favor kin and co-ethnics in trade and business. Catholics still thought it right to give economic preference to co-ethnics or co-religionists; and wrong and dishonorable to treat kin, co-religionists, and neighbors like strangers in one's economic relations. The market's price-making universalism imposed a nasty cultural shock on traditional people. However, that same market universalism *pleased and gratified* the Protestant business people whose religious ethic entirely approved and even demanded equal treatment of buyers and sellers regardless of religion, ethnicity, or kinship ties.

THE NORM OF UNIVERSALISM

The heritage of this Protestant obsession with ethical universalism is alive today in much of the world, not just in the Protestant countries. The norm of economic universalism has become part of modernization. Its manifestation is the normative expectation that buyers, sellers, contractors, and job seekers *should* be evaluated on their merits, and without penalty or benefit arising from their religion, ethnicity, or kinship ties and, we would now add, their gender, their physical disabilities, and sexual orientation. As a result of this globally shared universalism, a faded heritage of the Protestant ethic, modern people everywhere express disapproval when they learn that business decisions were, in fact, made on the basis of precisely these proscribed ties. It seems to modern people disgraceful that the high bidder got the contract because of family connections to the boss.

It is scandalous that the less competent applicant was hired because her uncle was a major shareholder. To inhibit such deplorable outcomes, and in response to public indignation, modern nation states have legislated search requirements that specify exactly how employers must advertise jobs in order to safeguard themselves against complaints of discrimination. The laws also require and define open bidding policies on external contracts. Discrimination against outsiders is one pole of this protection; discrimination in favor of insiders is the other. Both are prohibited. States have also regulated sexual harassment at work. No one is to suffer or benefit at work because of [gender or] sexual orientation. All must be treated alike, and rewarded or punished only for the work they do. This is the normative universalism that, according to Weber, originated in the Reformation, and buttressed the triumph of capitalism.

Laws against discrimination prove that, despite public professions of support for universalism, an unwanted particularism persists in modern societies. After all, if unwanted particularism did not persist, laws prohibiting discrimination would be unnecessary. Because employers still discriminate against outsiders and in favor of insiders, laws are needed to inhibit this transgression. Managers sometimes really do award contracts or jobs to kin, co-ethnics, and even to sex partners – so laws seek to prevent this abuse. After five centuries of market capitalism, why does economic particularism persist in modern societies that routinely declare it odious and even legislate against it? This question may require more and different scholarly attention than it has thus far received. In answer to this question, people have been satisfied to learn that some misguided and backward individuals, rotten apples in the social barrel, persist in anti-social behavior out of meanness, irrational prejudice, or the hope of personal advantage. They are also informed that these abuses work to the long-term disadvantage of organizations that permit it. Yes, it is claimed, no-bid contracts handed out to cronies injure the company, but it is understandable that cronies would seek illicit advantage. Obtaining this illicit advantage, the cronies take care of themselves and their friends at the expense of the organization's welfare. Ultimately, mediocrities and incestuous loyalties in the board room condemn a business to failure.

This analysis is often correct. However, this popular diagnosis causes people to ignore the possibility of systemic causes. The diagnosis identifies a normative failure, not a systemic problem. Seeing it that way, people comprehend the issue as personal advantage versus system advantage rather than a contest between alternative definitions of system advantage, which would be much harder to deal with. Personal advantage benefits the corrupt decision-makers. System advantage benefits the system. In contrast, systemic causes promote and encourage economic particularism *because* particularism is sometimes more *efficient and profitable for the system than is universalism*. If they exist, systemic causes would refer back to the market economy's *raison d'être*, which is to identify and promote whatever is profitable and efficient, rather than to the normative corruption of individuals. Promoting particularism in these cases, the market would just be doing its job in defiance, where necessary, of law and public opinion.

Arrayed against this systemic possibility is the orthodox logic of the neo-classical economists to which Max Weber, a renegade economist, himself subscribed. This neo-classical logic proclaims that markets, like hard-core Protestants, are consistently universalistic; they reward decision-makers who practice strict universalism, and they punish those who evidence what Gary Becker ([1957] 1971, pp. 8–9) called 'a taste for discrimination'. If they hire co-ethnic incompetents, so the argument proceeds, employers render themselves vulnerable to business competitors who hire the most qualified. Meritocratic hiring would gratify the Protestant conscience, but what matters to Becker are the adverse consequences of discrimination. Discrimination injures the business that discriminates, and will be continued only when decision-makers are willfully blind to the adverse implications of their choices. Thus, 'even slight differences' in wages between blacks and whites, Becker ([1957] 1971, p. 37) claims, 'compel employers' to hire blacks in preference to whites.[12] In the long run, so Becker's argument continues, universalistic employers will produce a better product thanks to the superior qualification of their work force. Non-universalistic employers risk extinction at the hands of universalistic competitors. 'Crony capitalism' consists exactly of these inferior practices, and, while it enriches the cronies, it devastates companies and economies that practice it.[13]

This theoretical argument has considerable force; additionally, the market has manifestly worked to the advantage of socially disadvantaged and disesteemed groups in many famous cases. For example, when male workers were drafted, employers hired women to replace them during the Second World War. The image and experience of 'Rosie the riveter' then energized a whole generation of women to seek equal opportunity in the work force. Similarly, when native miners went on strike in Colorado, nineteenth-century coal-mine owners hired immigrant strike-breakers, thus enabling the despised Slavic and Greek immigrants to penetrate industries otherwise closed to them by nativist prejudice. Finally, during the Second World War, when field hands became scarce, agricultural employers demanded and obtained the right to hire temporary Mexican workers. As a result of this experience, Mexicans became familiar with the United States, learned English, and decided later to become permanent migrants and citizens. In effect, in all these cases, the market gave entry to those once excluded. Although these examples could be multiplied, the point is to concede that markets do often produce universalism and not, churlishly, to cling to the foolish counter-claim that the market's vaunted universalism never promotes efficiency and profitability, nor that, in reverse, profitability and efficiency never recommend a policy of universalism.

That said, the persistence of long-term discrimination in market economies is equally undeniable. The market economy has had 350 years to equalize the treatment of blacks and whites in the United States, but the inter-racial disparities in hiring and pay persist. Reckoning since the beginning of European capitalism in 1500, the market economy has had 500 years to overcome wage discrimination against women, homosexuals, the disabled, and ex-convicts but has signally failed to do so (Light, 2007). If even slight wage discrepancies *compel* employers to hire blacks and women, as Gary Becker maintains, then why has racial and gender equality not yet arrived? Apparently the market economies reduced that discrimination, but they did not *overcome* it. Indeed, this failure to overcome discrimination explains why public indignation has compelled virtually all the nation states of the developed world to introduce laws that restrict the ability of employers to discriminate against women, immigrants, the disabled, and others, seeking to require recalcitrant employers to practice universalism in hiring and procurement. Why did market economies fail to produce equality of opportunity despite centuries of trying?

FROM PROTESTANT ETHIC TO PROTESTANT ETHNIC

Answering that question brings us back to an assumption Max Weber introduced into social theory that, although frequently challenged, has escaped full debate. Jere Cohen (2002, p. 257) declares that, 'Contrary to Weber's claim that Puritanism helped capitalism break through tradition, Puritanism was quite traditional itself, and . . . some of its traditional beliefs retarded capitalist growth'. As Max Weber himself acknowledged (1946a, p. 313), the sectarian Protestants *did favor kin in business*; Cohen is right about that; but it is not clear that their *beliefs* caused their particularism if by beliefs Cohen means their distinctive religious doctrine.[14] Possibly, the Protestants imported some traditional economic beliefs into the reformed religion, in which case their traditional behavior was caused by incomplete digestion of the Protestant ethic. Influenced by the Protestant ethic, Protestants were not governed by it. Possibly also, the in-group/out-group dualism of saints versus sinners reproduced a religio-ethnic preference despite the vaunted universalism of the Protestant ethic. In either case, Max Weber would have exaggerated the Protestants' doctrinaire universalism, overestimating the obliteration of traditional economic ideas by Puritan economic ideas and underestimating the social boundaries that sectarianism imposed. First, there was the traditional economic culture that Protestant nations practiced *before they became* Protestants. Possibly Protestantism's this-worldly asceticism coexisted with this traditional economic culture, and did not fully supersede it. Syncretism usually arises when peoples change their religion. That is how Wotan trees became Christmas trees. In a similar case, the traditional elements within Protestant business culture would surface in the later business practice of the Protestants.

Second, the sectarianism of the ex-Catholics or ex-Anglicans led them to distinguish between the saints, all trustworthy folk, and the God-damned sinful children of the world. Acknowledging this judgmental attitude, Weber (1958: 122) wrote:

> This consciousness of the divine grace of the elect and holy was accompanied by an attitude toward the sin of one's neighbor, not of sympathetic understanding based on consciousness of one's own weakness, but of hatred and contempt for him as an enemy of God bearing the signs of eternal damnation.

This harsh contrast reintroduced into the sectarians' community life a new version of the ancient economic dualism the Reformation had doctrinally rejected. In the Roman Catholic churches, where they had originated, Protestant sectarians had been members of the religious majority as well, of course, as believing Roman Catholics. Catholics had an organizational housing in a socially embedded church organization as well as a doctrinal housing in Catholic doctrine. However, when ex-Catholics became Baptists or Methodists, they became sect members, not church members. Sect members drew and draw a sharper distinction between themselves and outsiders than do church members.(Weber, 1946a, pp. 314, 317). The new ex-Catholic sectarians thus became a religious minority even within Lutheran or Anglican nations.

THE QUAKERS

This counter-argument rests upon two sources of evidence. First, there is the actual business practice of the sectarian Protestants, whether Methodist, Pietist, or Baptist. Of these, Quakers, a Baptist derivative, have the best documented record of entrepreneurial achievement. Seventy years of historical studies of the numerous and influential Quaker entrepreneurs during the eighteenth and nineteenth centuries have proved that these moralistic and disciplined Protestants, core heirs of the Protestant ethic, were *and still are* overrepresented in business in both Britain and North America.[15] That finding supports Weber. However, the same research has also reported that Quakers routinely discriminated in favor of co-religionists and kinsmen when doing business (Jeremy, 1998, p. 15; Porter, 1965; Prior and Kirby, 1998). Historians have considered the British and American Quakers clannish, endogamous, snobbish, exclusive, nepotistic – and successful in business (Ackrill and Hannah, 2001, p. 23; Lamoureaux, 2008, pp. 6–11; Raistrick, 1950, p. 44).[16] These results are not altogether in conformity with the supposed universalism of the Protestant ethic. If they discriminated, why were they also successful in business? Although Weber anticipated the restraining power of kinship upon universalism in general, Weber taught that the Protestant sects had abolished by fervent and doctrinaire enthusiasm the in-group/out-group dualism characteristic of ethnic groups. However, Weber overlooked the possibility that structural features of the Puritans' sectarianism introduced a new boundary between saints and sinners, the trusted in-group and mistrusted out-group. If so, this religious boundary would have mimicked the effects of ethnic boundaries, making Protestant ethnics out of imperfectly doctrinaire adherents of the Protestant ethic. The business history of the Quakers shows this tension.

If anyone should have been strictly universalistic in their business ethic it was the Quaker entrepreneurs of the eighteenth and nineteenth centuries. But they were not. The sincerity of their religious beliefs is impossible to question – so the Quakers' practical rejection of Protestant universalism must have flowed from other sources.[17] What that source was can be inferred now from three decades of research into ethnic economies and social capital.[18] Ethnic entrepreneurs still distinguish between trusted in-group and mistrusted out-group in business. What is more, this research has shown that economic universalism is *not invariably* the most profitable or efficient business decision. Often it is; frequently it is not. When proper account is taken of social capital, a modern concept that neither Weber nor his contemporaries understood, the despised and rejected economic dualism begins to make business sense again (Halpern, 2005, ch. 2). Kenneth Porter states the issue clearly. Evaluating three centuries of business practice in Puritan New England, Kenneth Porter (1965, p. 98) concludes that merchant families 'regarded the comparative security from flagrant dishonesty, resulting from doing business on a family basis, as compensation for possible increased energy and initiative, accompanied by greater risk, which might have been produced by an infusion of fresh blood'. That is, in Porter's evaluation, Puritan business families faced a trade-off between the possible advantages of doing business with dynamic but unknown non-Quakers, who might be dishonest, versus the security of doing business with mediocrities of known probity. Given this choice, Puritan business families usually chose the known insider over the unknown outsider. Saying a doctrinaire yes to one-price and fair treatment for all, the Puritan business families nonetheless discriminated in favor of co-religionists, and so would have been chargeable under current anti-discrimination statutes.

Suppose, for example, that two candidates for the same job presented themselves to a Quaker entrepreneur. One was a co-religionist, married to a kinswoman, and thought modestly competent. The other was a non-Quaker armed with extraordinary technical qualifications. This outsider might do an exceptional job whereas the insider would probably turn in a mediocre performance. On the basis of doctrinaire universalism alone, the Quaker entrepreneur should hire the talented outsider. However, the Quaker entrepreneur must also consider that the insider is of known probity, has a Protestant work ethic, and, if hired, will strengthen his relationship with his kinswoman's influential business clan whose financial assistance he might one day need. The Quaker entrepreneur does not know how honest the outsider is, whether he drinks too much, consorts with low women, or how consistently he works. Moreover, hiring the talented outsider builds no advantageous business connection. Since the insider is moderately qualified, the serious Quaker entrepreneur can hire the less qualified insider in the sincere belief that he has made the best business decision. That decision is the very one that, as Weber pointed out, the popular theologian, Richard Baxter, had recommended two centuries earlier.[19] *Whatever is most profitable is God's will*, and we must do God's will.

When it is considered, additionally, that, thanks to the routine operation of social networks and cultural capital, fellow Quakers learn about the Quaker entrepreneur's jobs and contracts quite easily whereas non-Quakers have trouble accessing this information, the Quaker entrepreneur's particularistic decision is the more understandable. This particularism offends the Protestant ethic's strict universalism, but finds *God's approval anyway* as those who make such decisions wax prosperous. Finally, when it is considered that the Quaker community of Britain and North America contained at that time more than its share of leading business people, we can appreciate the advantageous cultural capital that the Quaker communities had accumulated. Thanks to that cultural capital, Quaker job seekers were among the best workers available anywhere. Quakers knew their stuff and worked hard. In point of fact, non-Quakers were rarely more competent than fellow Quakers. Therefore, the cheapest and easiest job search, hiring through ascriptive social networks, yielded the best candidates (Mayhew, 1968).

CONCLUSION

The Protestant ethic inadvertently created Protestant ethnic economies within which a traditional economic dualism resurfaced as saints versus sinners. Protestant theologians understood that successful entrepreneurs might succumb to the temptations of worldliness to which their economic success exposed them. As Weber abundantly explained, and Daniel Bell has subsequently validated, the Protestant entrepreneurs' shining faith, which sought to do God's work in the world, predictably came up against the seductions of the material world. After all, theologians knew that 'Satan is the lord of this world'. It has not, however, been properly appreciated that when doing God's will in the world, Puritan entrepreneurs often found particularism more advantageous than strict universalism. For this reason, reviewing the business practice of New England merchants in the eighteenth century, Naomi Lamoureaux (2008, p. 11) debunks the 'view that strong family and community ties are antithetical to capitalist enterprise'. As those Puritan merchants' practice displayed, doctrinaire universalism was not always the most advantageous business choice. In many cases, Protestant business owners made particularistic choices in the conscious interest of business advantage; and having done so, they frequently obtained *the business advantage they anticipated.* These advantages were real. Making this particularistic choice, however, Protestant entrepreneurs behaved like Protestant ethnics who trusted the saints, their co-religionists, more than the sinful children of the world, everyone else. If even doctrinaire Quakers of the eighteenth century could make this choice, then how much easier would it be for people less imbued with the norm of universalism?

To the extent that particularism sometimes works to the advantage of organizations, even among those doctrinally committed to strict universalism, we can better appreciate the difficulties that innovators experience. If universalism were always the better business choice, then entrepreneurs would more easily destroy and creatively renew the economic status quo. However, in reality, now as in the past, talented outsiders can fail in competition with mediocre insiders. Even when mediocre insiders fall short in personal performance vis-à-vis talented outsiders, those mediocrities may nonetheless solve some business problems thanks to their known loyalty, their friendship networks, the external support they command, or the past favors they reciprocate. Since the ordinary functioning of organizations requires that these mundane issues receive constant attention, it is unsurprising that they may outweigh the performance advantage that talented outsiders enjoy. A universalistic choice is sometimes, but not always, in the best interest of the organization.

Politically very incorrect, this conclusion has one intellectual advantage.[20] It explains the otherwise bewildering persistence of discrimination in the institutional business world. If particularism's frequent advantageousness is acknowledged, we need no longer attribute discrimination invariably to meanness, sociopathic personalities, blind greed, or blind prejudice. Rather, we infer that organizations confront choices that sometimes contradict a policy of strict universalism. Even the Puritans encountered this counter-pressure. In the modern world, these structural pressures attract the unwelcome attention of states, which, responsive to the outrage of voting publics, seek to curtail the ability of economic decision-makers to discriminate against outsiders or in favor of insiders. In doing so, the state publicly construes its action as seeking to compel prejudiced decision-makers to make more-efficient, more-profitable business decisions in the interest of the shareholders, the community, or the economy, and in deference to an abstract norm of strict universalism embedded in the law. Sometimes that construction is on target. When particularism results from the attempts of decision makers to gain personal advantage at the expense of the organization's interest or even at the expense of the economic system, as it often does, then state-sponsored legal universalism imposes the best interest of society upon recalcitrant decision-makers. Additionally, political and social indignation is real; this popular indignation compels states to take action on behalf of struggling outsiders, like women employees, who want to break the glass ceiling. These political pressures are real; they command legal enforcement. But when economic particularism reflects a prudent decision to prefer mediocre insiders over superior strangers, which sometimes conduces to the organization's welfare, then the state's mandatory universalism undermines the market's *raison d'être*, efficiency and profitability. The market collides with the state. If eighteenth-century prosecutors had compelled the Quakers to employ strictly universalistic rules in business, they would in effect have mobilized the normative structure of the Protestant ethic to *undermine* the real economy of Protestant ethnics. Even ardent Protestants had an ethnic economy!

However, these errors are not fatal to Weber's larger argument. We may concur with Weber that, left to itself, economic traditionalism would not have created rational bourgeois capitalism in the late Middle Ages. If so, then the Reformation's moral universalism supported and encouraged the transition to a more dynamic economic system earlier than would otherwise have happened. We may also concur with Weber that moral universalism encourages a dynamic market economy as opposed to a stagnating one. Entrepreneurship depends upon moral universalism because entrepreneurs are quintessential outsiders; arrayed against the entrepreneurs are the cozy but real advantages of restricting access to trusted insiders with good connections. Yet entrepreneurs introduce market dynamism. If entrepreneurs always lose, and insiders always win, then economies stagnate. Here emerges the *obverse* formula: no Reformation, no ethical universalism; no ethical universalism, no opening to entrepreneurs; no opening to entrepreneurs, no innovation. In short, Weber's corrected formula holds this: no Reformation in the sixteenth century, no dynamic capitalism later. This formula rescues Weber's grand vision from criticisms based upon the actual particularism of the Puritan merchants and bankers. That grand vision rescued, we need not return to the unsound conviction that economic particularism is *never a more profitable* business decision than universalism, nor that economic particularism vanished when nations and ethnic groups embraced the Reformation. Indeed, precisely because particularism is still so frequently profitable, change-seeking entrepreneurs have to fight against a *profitable alternative*, not just against prejudice, corruption, or obtuse reluctance to change. A profitable alternative is a much tougher enemy for innovators to dislodge than are sheer human stupidity and short-sightedness, ubiquitous though those latter two always are.

NOTES

1. Was Protestantism a cause or an effect of capitalism, or possibly both cause and effect? Weber's causality has been debated for a century. For a recent summary and a new perspective, see Forte (2008).
2. Later, Weber expanded his research horizon by examining Hinduism, Buddhism, Confucianism, and Islam (Weber, 1946b). Results suggested that non-Western societies had not developed the distinctive this-worldly asceticism that Weber earlier identified as crucial to the West's transformation to capitalism from feudalism. 'If it can be shown that the Asian tradition hinders inner-world asceticism and that the Near Eastern and Western tradition favors it, we have gained a strong indicator for the religious distinctiveness of ascetic Protestantism. I believe that in his comparative studies Weber in fact follows this line of reasoning' (Schluchter, 1981, p. 162). See also: Swedberg (1998, pp. 133–40). Some contemporary Islamic scholars have been persuaded that Islam's inherent 'Protestantism' has yet to be liberated for economic development (Alatas, 2007, p. 512).
3. For a comparison of Weber's approach to entrepreneurship with those of Joseph Schumpeter and Frank Knight, his approximate contemporaries, see Brouwer (2002).
4. For a critique of Max Weber's treatment of ethnicity and ethnic groups in general see Banton (2007).

5. Rubinstein (1998, p. 173) fails to understand Weber's distinction between rational bourgeois capitalism and traditional business ethics. 'It is not obvious that thrift, hard work, asceticism, etc., lead to entrepreneurial success . . . Such qualities as low cunning, an eye for bargains and untapped potential markets, and an ability to cheat one's suppliers or customers with a straight face and without doing irreparable harm to one's reputation surely come to mind as more relevant qualities for the successful entrepreneur than thrift.' This is a short-sighted view because in the long run, as Benjamin Franklin taught, 'honesty is the best policy'.
6. 'What emerges . . . is how much the Puritan business ethics differed from what Weber calls the "double ethic". Earlier in history, he explains, there had been one ethic for one's family, clan, or community of believers, and another moral code for strangers and outsiders . . . Puritans dramatically broke with this by introducing a new type of ethics into business, according to which every individual should be treated in the same way, regardless of creed or origin' (Swedberg, 1998, p. 129). Earlier, Benjamin Nelson (1969, p. xv) took a similar position: Weber 'insisted that the singular triumph of methodical bourgeois capitalism in the West was exceptionally favored by Occidental priority in completing another and even more impressive advance toward the adoption of a single moral standard for all society – the transcendence of the traditionalist and tribalistic ethic of the Gentile era'.
7. Weber (1958, p. 57).
8. 'The ethic of ascetic Protestantism stands at the beginning of the "world domination of unbrotherliness"' (Schluchter, 1981, p. 156).
9. 'Jewish capitalism was speculative pariah-capitalism, while the Puritan was bourgeois organization of labour' (Weber, 1958, p. 271). Swedberg (1998, p. 142) comments, 'The Jews never developed a rational capitalist spirit; and neither did they contribute to the growth of industrial capitalism. Weber's term for the type of economic activities that the Jewish merchants excelled in was "pariah capitalism," which can be described as a form of traditional commercial capitalism.'
10. 'Another important feature of Jewish economic ethic was its double ethic and how it affected the issue of usury. According to Deuteronomy 23:20, "You may exact interest on loan to a foreigner but not on a loan to a fellow-countryman". This double ethic naturally increased in strength when Judaism became the religion of a fully segregated people – and also when the Jews were met by hostility of other peoples' (Swedberg, 1998, pp. 141–2). For more detail, see Schluchter (1981, p. 69).
11. 'Weber developed his thesis about the Protestant roots of capitalism in part as a response to extreme German conservatives who saw capitalism as "Jewish"' (Waters, 1998, p. 184).
12. 'In a capitalist economy, Weber says one must follow the rules of the market or go under – there is simply no place for *caritas*' (Swedberg, 1998, p. 111). Agreed, but there is no place for discrimination either.
13. Paul Krugman (2002), 'Crony Capitalism', *New York Times*, 15 January.
14. Rubinstein (1998, p. 172) agrees, citing the preferences for kin among early Protestant business owners. 'Among non-religious characteristics of religious or ethnic groups, in particular, the existence of kinship networks, national and sometimes international, typical of such groups as Quakers, Unitarians, Huguenots, and overseas Scots, is perhaps the most important. Kinship networks arguably assisted materially in entrepreneurial success by sharing and diminishing risks, supplying capital and low interest loans, providing honest partners, providing accurate information about marriage partners for dynastic formation.'
15. 'Quakers . . . were not particularly numerous in Britain, totaling between 14000 and 16000 in 1850, or roughly one in 2000 of the UK population, then 27 million . . . Yet during the eighteenth and nineteenth centuries there were a disproportionately large number of Quaker entrepreneurs' (Corley, 1998, p. 140). Ackrill and Hannah (2001) report that Quakers are still overrepresented in business in Great Britain.
16. 'A conspicuous feature of business in early Massachusetts, appearing in all its aspects,

was the dominating influence of family relationships. In the forming of all personal business relationships, from taking on an apprentice to hiring a supercargo or captain, from selecting a commission merchant to choosing a partner, the Massachusetts merchant seems to have regarded himself as bound not to go outside his circle of kinship, so long as there was in it any one desirous of employment' (Porter, 1965, p. 88).

17. True heirs of the Protestant ethic, the Amish entrepreneurs of Pennsylvania still gave preference in life and in business to co-religionists in the 1990s. See Kraybill and Nolt (1995).
18. For a review of ethnic economy literature, see Light (2004).
19. Said Richard Baxter: 'If God shows you a way in which you may lawfully get more than in another way (without wrong to your soul or to any other), if you refuse this, and choose the less gainful way, you cross one of the ends of your calling, and you refuse to be God's steward, and to accept His gifts and use them for Him: you may labour to be rich for God, though not for the flesh and sin' (quoted from Weber, 1958, p. 62).
20. Colin Campbell (2006) attributes contemporary sociologists' lack of interest in pursuing Weber's economic ideas to methodological reservations. To this reservation one might add the politically incorrect conclusions to which Weber's work leads when systematically applied to modern conditions.

REFERENCES

Ackrill, Margaret and Leslie Hannah (2001), *Barclays: The Business of Banking, 1690–1996*, Cambridge: Cambridge University.

Alatas, Farid Syed (2007), 'Contemporary Muslim Revival: The Case of "Protestant Islam"', *The Muslim World*, **57**, 508–20.

Banton, Michael (2007), 'Max Weber on "Ethnic Communities"': A Critique', *Nations and Nationalism*, **13** (1), 19–35.

Becker, Gary (1957 [1971]), *The Economics of Discrimination*, 2nd edn, Chicago, IL: University of Chicago Press.

Bell, Daniel (1996), *The Cultural Contradictions of Capitalism*, 2nd edn, New York: Basic Books.

Bendix, Reinhard (1960), *Max Weber: An Intellectual Portrait*, New York: Doubleday.

Brouwer, Maria T. (2002), 'Weber, Schumpeter and Knight on Entrepreneurship and Economic Development', *Journal of Evolutionary Economics*, **12**, 83–105.

Campbell, Colin (2006), 'Do Today's Sociologists Really Appreciate Weber's Essay *The Protestant Ethic and The Spirit of Capitalism*?', *The Sociological Review*, **54**, 207–23.

Cohen, Jere (2002), *Protestantism and Capitalism*, Hawthorne, NY: Aldine de Gruyter.

Corley, T.A.B. (1998), 'Changing Quaker Attitudes to Wealth, 1690–1950', in David J. Jeremy (eds), *Religion, Business and Wealth in Modern Britain*, London: Routledge, pp. 137–50.

Forte, Juan Manuel (2008), 'Religion and Capitalism: Weber, Marx and the Materialist Controversy', *Philosophy and Social Criticism*, **34**, 427–48.

Halpern, David (2005), *Social Capital*, Cambridge: Polity Press.

Jeremy, David (1998), 'Introduction, Debates about Interactions between Religion, Business, and Wealth in Modern Britain', in David J. Jeremy (eds), *Religion, Business and Wealth in Modern Britain*, London: Routledge, pp. 1–31.

Kraybill, Donald B. and Steven M. Nolt (1995), *Amish Enterprise*, Baltimore, MP: Johns Hopkins University Press.
Lamoreaux, Naomi (2008), 'Rethinking the Transition to Capitalism in the Early American Northeast', *The Journal of American History*, **90** (2), 1–23.
Light, Ivan (2004), 'The Ethnic Economy', in Neil Smelser and Richard Swedberg (eds), *Handbook of Economic Sociology*, 2nd edn, New York: Russell Sage Foundation, ch. 16.
Light, Ivan (2007), 'Women's Economic Niches and Earnings Inferiority: The View from the Ethnic Economy', *Journal of Ethnic and Migration Studies*, **33**, 541–57.
Mayhew, Leon (1968), 'Ascription in Modern Societies', *Sociological Inquiry*, **38**, 105–20.
Nelson, Benjamin (1969), *The Idea of Usury: From Tribal Brotherhood to Universal Otherhood*, Chicago, IL: University of Chicago Press.
Porter, Kenneth (1965), *The Jacksons and the Lees*, New York: Russell & Russell. First published 1937.
Prior, Ann and Maurice Kirby (1998), 'The Society of Friends and Business Culture, 1700–1830', in David J. Jeremy (eds), *Religion, Business and Wealth in Modern Britain*, London: Routledge, pp. 116–36.
Raistrick, Arthur (1950), *Quakers in Science and Industry*, London: Bannisdale Press.
Rubinstein, W.D. (1998), 'The Weber Thesis, Ethnic Minorities, and British Entrepreneurship', in David J. Jeremy (eds), *Religion, Business and Wealth in Modern Britain*, London: Routledge, pp. 170–81.
Schluchter, Wolfgang (1981), *The Rise of Western Rationalism*, Los Angeles, CA: University of California Press.
Schluchter, Wolfgang (2005), *Handlung, Ordnung, und Kultur*, Tübingen: Mohr Siebeck.
Swedberg, Richard (1998), *Max Weber and the Idea of Economic Sociology*, Princeton, NJ: Princeton University Press.
Waters, Chris (1998), 'Ethnicity, Religion and Wealth: A Commentary on the Uses of Max Weber', in David J. Jeremy (eds), *Religion, Business and Wealth in Modern Britain*, London: Routledge, pp. 182–5.
Weber, Max (1946a), 'The Protestant Sects and the Spirit of Capitalism', in Hans H. Gerth and C. Wright Mills (eds), *From Max Weber: Essays in Sociology*, New York: Oxford University, pp. 302–22.
Weber, Max (1946b), 'The Social Psychology of the World Religions', in Hans H. Gerth and C. Wright Mills (eds), *From Max Weber: Essays in Sociology*, New York: Oxford University, pp. 267–301.
Weber, Max (1958), *The Protestant Ethic and the Spirit of Capitalism*, New York: Charles Scribner's Sons.

7. The effects of Methodism on entrepreneurship

Anne White

INTRODUCTION

In 1912 sociologist and anthropologist Emile Durkheim published a seminal work entitled *The Elementary Forms of Religious Life*.[1] In this work, Durkheim detailed a theory which identified a pattern of organization consistent within all human societies and which he named Structural Functionalism. Durkheim's theory described society as being built upon order which incorporated interrelationship and balance among the various parts of its constitution as a means of maintaining the smooth functioning of the whole. He argued that the construction and identity of any given society is based on shared norms and values as the basis of existence. Further, social order was established based on tacit agreements, or consensus of opinion, between groups and organizations within the main system. The structural functionalist perspective also recognized that it was necessary to incorporate change into communal and individual structure as part of an indispensible process through which correction of imbalance or social dysfunction could take place. Ideally, this change or adaptation should occur slowly so that people and institutions could adapt without rapid disorder.

From a structural functionalist perspective the development and contribution of the Methodist movement is a fascinating study in group dynamics, change, innovation and adaptability. Due to its organizational structure and emphasis on journal keeping, Methodist historical records provide a wealth of research information into the formation and dynamics of its goal orientation or spiritual journey.

In keeping with Durkheim's theory, the Methodist community can be identified through the following structural patterns: (i) throughout its variety of global representations or smaller sectarian movements[2] it retains common characteristics or shared values and norms particular to Methodism, thus maintaining group identity; (ii) nurtures social order and group cohesion known as fellowship, through commitment and loyalty to the New Testament, the Christian message, and the teachings of John Wesley; (iii) emphasizes individual and group responsibility and ownership of goals, projects and communication outreach; (iv) possesses the ability to change and recoup according to the needs of the community; (v) due to its organizational and constitutional structure promotes change and innovation through teaching and training, promoting advancement among its membership; and (vi) possesses strong organizational and communication skills through a network of communities. It is interesting to note that these identifiable functional aspects are also indispensible strengths identified as essential to successful entrepreneurial projects. Thus Durkheim's theory and the reality of a spiritual group or denomination, contribute to an understanding of an ethical, relevant, adaptable and successful business dynamic and the resulting business practices.

HISTORICAL BACKGROUND OF METHODISM

To appreciate the contribution of Methodism to the modern global community it is necessary to understand its historical development. From its inception, British Methodist tradition distinguished itself as a spiritual renewal movement, which displayed an innovative spiritual and social approach to the human condition. The movement itself was in part a rebuttal response by the broader religious community to the new era of eighteenth-century Enlightenment which systematically expressed supreme confidence in human perfectibility through autonomous human endeavour without the need or aid of God.[3]

The specific branch of this eighteenth-century renewal movement, which later became known as Methodism,[4] was formed during a period of powerful spiritual renewal commonly referred to as the Eighteenth-Century Evangelical Revival.[5] The strong revival atmosphere fostered by the Methodists in particular, appealed to a broad social spectrum attracting large groups of people, both male and female, from various class structures. This new spiritual and intellectual freedom appealed to many people on both sides of the Atlantic who were drawn to its more egalitarian and progressive nature, and in essence, 'helped to break down the secular barriers of class, race, sex, and ethnicity, and to meld them into one community'.[6]

From records, journals, letters and newspaper articles it is evident that many people were engaged in an intensely serious search for spiritual meaning which they believed was to be found in the salvation afforded through Jesus Christ. As early Methodism had developed during a period marked by Enlightenment rationalism, scientific empiricism, and increased social mobility,[7] the new movement was presented as an answer to societal flux. Methodism offered stability rooted in traditional beliefs, yet incorporated the opportunity to effect positive change and progress, salvation and a better life. These ideas, so successfully embraced by the Methodists, later developed the group into one of the largest Protestant movements for social change in the nineteenth and early twentieth centuries.[8]

Initially, the British revival was led by three spiritually reform-minded Anglican clergymen who sought to stay within the Church of England and bring renewal to the masses. The ministers were George Whitefield, and the brothers John and Charles Wesley. In their early years of cooperation these men developed a community which extended throughout the British Isles.[9] Due to the Methodists' emphasis on free will – known as Arminianism[10] – whereby the individual consciously chose to turn to Christ for salvation; their belief in personal, conscious choice to effect change; and a continuous responsibility to God and one's neighbour, they produced a flexible social movement which lent itself to innovation, change and renewal.

Unfortunately, however, this dynamic movement suffered an internal dispute regarding theological issues over predestination[11] versus free will, and there was a consequent splintering of groups, some of whom followed Whitefield with the majority following the leadership of John and Charles Wesley.[12] The Methodists subsequently became a denomination after John Wesley issued the Deed of Declaration in 1784 through which he announced the official break with the Church of England.

After the death of John Wesley in 1791, the Methodists splintered and amalgamated into various branches, including the Methodist New Connexion (1797), the Independent Methodist Churches (1806), the Primitive Methodists (1807), the Bible Christians (1815), the Protestant Methodists (1827) the Wesleyan Methodists (1836), the United Methodist Free Churches (1857), the Wesleyan Reform Union (1859) and the United Methodist Church (1907). These groups, or sect variations, can be found throughout the modern world with a global Methodist population, according to 2006 data, around 75 million members.[13] The majority of Methodist churches are now connected through the World Methodist Council (WMC), which is part of the larger World Council of Churches. The WMC consists of 500 representatives from the member churches located throughout the world. In addition to this, there are also member churches of the World Methodist Council in Latin America and the Caribbean that have formed a regional Council of Evangelical Methodist Churches; there is an Asian Methodist Bishops' Council; a European Methodist Council, and there are British and North American Sections within the WMC.[14]

Despite the many and varied representations of Methodism that have developed over its 224 years as a spiritual movement there are still many distinct similarities identifiable throughout its groupings. These similarities are due in most part to the continuing significance of John Wesley's teachings as pivotal dogma in the worldwide Methodist traditions.

In the global Methodist community there exists a collection of 44 sermons which are recognized as the theological foundation of the original movement led by John Wesley,[15] and usually referred to as 'the standard doctrines of the Methodist Connexion'.[16] This compendium of Wesley's theological teachings, all based on traditional biblical teachings of the Old and New Testaments is simply known as *The Forty-Four Sermons*. The sermons act as a guidebook for the Methodist lifestyle and address a wide range of issues such as salvation, ethical standards and individual conduct, the Kingdom of Heaven as taught by Jesus (later developing into concepts of a just society), just laws, honesty and humility, the dangers of bigotry, self-denial, and the proper use of money. In writing his preface to his authorized sermon compendium, compiled in 1746, Wesley wrote that 'The following sermons contain the substance of what I have been preaching for between eight and nine years last past [1746]. During that time I have frequently spoken in public, on every subject in the ensuing collection.'[17]

Wesley's teachings were, in fact, established Christian doctrine and therefore not novel; but it was the method of application that proved pertinent and resilient. What John Wesley did was apply these principles to practical, vigorous personal and social application, thus empowering the ordinary, individual Methodist. The spiritual concepts within the Wesleyan revival movement were basic New Testament theology that had been re-emphasized during the Sixteenth Century Protestant[18] Reformation, spearheaded by Martin Luther.[19] The Reformation emphasized a return to the scriptures, faith based on Christ's redemption alone, and the responsibility of all believers to live godly lives as full participants within society. These teachings became known as the three tenets of the Reformation and are known as Sola Scriptura,[20] Justification by Faith[21] and the Priesthood of All Believers.[22]

As a corollary of Christian reform it was self-evident that one's faith called for ethical conduct and the intelligently designed formation of a just society. In essence, these ideas were traditional Christian teachings, however, in the hands of the Methodists and other evangelical[23] Christians, during the eighteenth, nineteenth and early twentieth centuries, the ancient truths became tools to develop campaigns for social reform and social justice that were radical and ambitious in their scope and development.

Ideas about radical change were emphasized particularly in Methodist theology due to the nature of Methodism itself which promoted both an emotional heart religion[24] and a rational, informed methodological approach to understanding and communicating the Gospel.[25] This Methodist trait of being able to confront difficult or delicate issues in a blunt manner was demonstrated eloquently in the interpretation of the use of money. Unlike many other Christian groups who viewed money and its uses as a recipe for disaster, Wesley tackled the 'problem' of greed in his plain speech manner.[26] In the last of his 44 sermons entitled *The Use of Money*,[27] he quoted from the teachings of Jesus regarding the ethical use of money, trade, and business through Christian stewardship. In the Gospel of Luke, chapter 16:1–14, which is often referred to as the 'parable of the talents' Jesus focused on the ethical use of money and the many dangers of entrapment regarding its compromising power. Money, Jesus said, was something one could use as a steward, always remembering accountability to God. On the other hand, greed, or the love of money, was the danger and one could not place its acquisition on par with responsibility to God. There had to be priorities set because one could not serve God and wealth or Mammon with the same allegiance as there would definitely be a conflict of interest.[28] Referring to riches or wealth, Wesley succinctly stated, 'Mammon means riches, or money. It is termed "the mammon of unrighteousness" because of the unrighteous manner wherein it is frequently procured, and wherein even that which was honestly procured is generally employed'.[29]

Speaking to his Methodist followers, Wesley continued with teachings that formed the basis for a broad spectrum of Methodist entrepreneurial ventures throughout the eighteenth, nineteenth and early twentieth centuries. In this forty-fourth sermon he wrote,

> the right use of money, a subject largely spoken of, after their manner, by men of the world, but not sufficiently considered by those whom God hath chosen out of the world. These generally do not consider, as the importance of the subject requires, the use of this excellent talent. Neither do they understand how to employ it to the greatest advantage; the introduction of which into the world is one admirable instance of the wise and gracious providence of God.[30]

Money, according to Wesley, was to be ethically obtained and used in the service of others through philanthropic, charitable endeavours, to noble ends, through the discipline of self-stewardship. In theory, wealth was not to be squandered in ostentatious living or frivolous lifestyles but was to be used to feed the hungry, cloth the poor, provide assistance to widows and children, orphans, the indigent and dispossessed, to heal the sick and protect the powerless. The function of money gained through honest business or honest 'industry' was to provide assistance and care to the less fortunate in order to spread the Gospel of Jesus Christ.

John Wesley also adopted innovative approaches to the use of people power and the delegation of responsibility. What was also interesting was the fact that the movement offered empowerment to those outside the conventional societal systems of authority and power. One of the distinct, identifying features in the foundational early British Methodist system was the inclusion and empowerment of the working class, the poor, and women in all groups. These peripheral groups had opportunity to actively participate in the life of the small Methodist groups through the practice of involved stewardship. As a development of this involvement their active participation and responsibility provided them with access to the organizational structures of their membership and often established these men and women in positions of leadership and influence.

In the fervour of the Evangelical Revival, the Wesleyan movement encouraged community participation with its members acting in various leadership and organizational capacities. This was a practical necessity as the community experienced a rapidly increasing membership and any trained leadership was vastly overworked. Initially, Wesley was reticent to draw on the laity for key leadership roles but as the membership of the Methodist groups known as *societies* increased it became evident that adjustment was needed. As Methodism developed it drew from its own membership and created its own leadership from within its ranks, thus providing opportunities for social advancement and influence.[31] Those who demonstrated initiative and leadership qualities often received free *in situ* training and education within the movement. This was done in order to equip these trainees for participation in the various Methodist society organizations involving stewardship and preaching.

A prime example of this training programme was the Office of Local Preacher[32] which John Wesley established to meet the needs of the many Methodist societies functioning without an ordained minister. These local preachers were delegated to exercise leadership, preach to the congregations, oversee small groups called bands and take charge of the larger weekly class meetings. The meetings were organized to provide guidance, as well as teaching and training for those already within the society or for those expressing interest in the Methodist form of Christianity. The lay leaders were essential to the spiritual community as they facilitated cohesion of the group and acted as mentors and examples of Christian life, thus providing security and continuity.

In delegating leadership to the laity and incorporating training programmes for the societies, Methodism demonstrated a 'natural progression within the context of the Methodist societies',[33] where personal accountability and responsibility were stressed together with community support and guidance. In the societies 'envy, covetousness, hypocrisy, gossip and double-dealing' made Christian fellowship 'impossible'.[34] It was therefore necessary for believers to learn to function both as individuals and collectively, thus learning group dynamics, effectiveness, and loyalty to a greater cause.

As part of this natural progression females demonstrating preaching and leadership talents were also included into the Office of Local Preacher, thus assuming official leadership roles within their religious societies. As the Methodist religious societies worked through group participation, the sharing of ideas, and goal-oriented projects, with input from broad membership representation, it was necessary for there to be clear direction and a wise director in the person of the local preacher. It was simply logical that gifted, spiritual female leadership would be identified and allowed to develop.[35]

LATER DEVELOPMENTS

Under the direction of John and Charles Wesley, together with the intense involvement of like-minded clergy, and the Methodist laity, the movement rapidly expanded into other parts of the British colonial world, Europe, South America, China and East Asia. Its success lay in its ability to adapt to other cultures whilst retaining its evangelical core beliefs. The movement's ability to survive change and challenge is demonstrated by the fact that after the death of John Wesley, Methodism underwent sectarian divisions but always regrouped and continued. Even though its initial unity was splintered, the core beliefs surrounding salvation, ethical conduct, free will and accountability were still integral to its identity. Existing alongside these pivotal doctrinal beliefs were the same Wesleyan practical applications concerning the proper use of money, individual leadership, the delegation of responsibility, and innovative group projects and campaigns. All these spiritual and philosophical ideals would grow into major undertakings such as public education, health care, labour law challenges, the emancipation of women, social justice campaigns, child protection, prohibition, and trade union movements,[36] to name but a few.

Over the next two centuries, precedents such as the inclusion of females into official capacities, together with working-class participation, and a growing awareness regarding the possibility of social equality, gradually developed into a strong Methodist voice for social change. Emotional, deeply troubling issues such as slavery and its abolition, the emancipation of women, exploitation and poverty, voting rights, equality under the law, labour reform, and social justice were to be addressed by the reform minded.

These proposed reforms, however, did not go unchallenged by a broad representation of influential and prosperous Methodists who had vested interests in the status quo. Opposition came from ultra-conservative clergy, religious zealots, slum landlords, exploitive businessmen, avaricious politicians, and women who viewed female emancipation as 'unwomanly'.

These people styled themselves 'Methodist' but had abandoned or reinterpreted many of the original Methodist tenets of individualism, community and social reform. The resistance they mounted to spiritual and social reform was often powerful and eloquent, with generous financial and political aid provided to thwart reform campaigns.

One British Methodist who vehemently challenged the widespread complacency developing in the movement was the Reverend William Booth. Booth decried the exploitation of the poor and the apathy and entrenchment of the Methodist church. He identified the cause of this cruelty as stemming from the conservatism and apathy of a comfortable middle class who had forgotten their spiritual roots which had been founded in radical reform. Booth went on to found the Salvation Army in 1878 and to reintroduce many of the early radical approaches to Gospel communication and social issues and aid for the poor. By seceding from Methodism and establishing the Salvation Army, 'the General', as William Booth was lovingly referred to, introduced competition and a direct challenge to a religious system that had grown lethargic. As a consequence of Booth's active social campaigns, many Methodists and other evangelicals were galvanized into action and were forced to change their protocols and work ethic in order to remain relevant to the communities that they served.[37]

Booth, who considered himself a theological heir to John Wesley's teachings,[38] wrote a highly controversial, but thoroughly researched socio-theological work entitled *In Darkest England and the Way Out* which was published in 1890.[39] In this work Booth addressed issues such as destitution, prostitution, poverty, degradation, crime, punishment, alcoholism, illiteracy, drunkenness, slum living conditions, the need for organized labour unions, and the pain of hopelessness. This research tome became a working document for social reform which was also frequently referred to and acknowledged in reform minded Methodist circles. Further to this, *Darkest England* became a working template for the British Salvation Army Social Work branch and was adopted to meet the needs of Salvationists in various global communities. It is still recognized as 'influential in the delivery of government welfare today' in its scope, identification and analysis of societal problems.[40]

ORGANIZATIONAL ENTREPRENEURIAL FOUNDATIONS

Early in the history of the Evangelical Revival, the Methodists understood that communication and nurture were essential to the revival and to individual spiritual conversion. In the centuries that followed these concepts were more fully identified and developed and it became evident that there was need for organized campaigns to effect social reform. Organization, communication, education and empowerment, together with clear cohesion of religious affiliation, would be necessary to construct group action and these were all concepts of which Methodism had intimate and historical knowledge.

Communication, both verbal and written, was vital in rousing the individual and the group and mass gatherings or revivals, and the distribution of religious tracts were part of Methodist history, so the precedent already existed. There had, however, been many improvements to communication systems since the movement's inception, which included the establishment of educational programmes and affordable reading material for the middle and working classes within Methodist membership, thus raising literacy levels and political awareness. The British-based Epworth Press and the American Methodist Publishing House were established in order to provide easily accessible inspirational and religious literature and information for Methodists and other Christians, thus providing a network of communication. In addition to this, charitable work evolved into organized health care and hospital infrastructures for the poor, children's homes were established, and there was a multitude of 'rescue missions' to help the destitute and women who had fled the sex trade. There was, therefore, an extensive infrastructure in and through which to educate, influence and involve people spiritually and politically.

One of the most successful methods of mass communication, however, was still the mass gathering or conference, which is still a popular means of group communication in the twenty-first century.[41]

In order to facilitate the radical dualistic change of consciousness necessary within the individual and/or society required resilient bonds between small groups who networked and looked out for each other within the larger denomination. Maintaining the practices of the revivalists, including Whitefield and John Wesley, Methodism drew on earlier established large Presbyterian Scots/Irish community meetings known as holy fairs, and adapted them to large open-air religious celebrations for the believers.

It was the Methodists' willingness to adopt and adapt familiar events and turn them into innovative means of mass communication that contributed to the success of the movement. The Methodist leaders recognized that strength lay within an informed grassroots membership who could spread 'the word' quickly. Every person was an emissary for Christ and the whole world was the mission field.[42] Evangelists and missionaries, as official representatives of the Methodist tradition, established societies based on the founding Wesleyan ideas and were well aware of the isolation and rejection that some societies and individual members faced in their particular home and work environments. Isolation led to discouragement and often the hostility that Methodists faced outside of their newly found faith was intense. What was needed was encouragement of the individual through group inspiration and identification. Thus, the practice of camp meetings or camp revivals[43] was introduced to the pioneering communities in order to provide communication and cohesion among smaller isolated groups into a larger religious community. Camp revivals and meetings served as opportunities for spiritual renewal, encouragement and conference opportunities in a time when travel and communication systems were often slow, daunting and/or virtually impossible for many who lived in small communities separated by vast distances.

The Methodists identified many negative social issues and customs that needed to be overturned, and the influence of mass organization or collective groups was seen as the way to challenge entrenched privilege and exploitation. In the instances of campaigns for the abolition of slavery and the 'female franchise' or women equality and right to vote the political and business establishments were very slow to change. The campaigns waged were concerted ones, mounted by a broad variety of concerned Christian groups and social institutions, and these historical events often overshadowed the smaller, grassroots campaigns for individual rights and freedoms and the rights of the farmer, fisherman, miner, labourer and small merchant producer or retailer. However, it is often in these local efforts that the positive nuances of democracy and entrepreneurship are to be appreciated, and in fact applauded for their spectacular success stories of creativity, talents, rights, freedoms and plain gritty tenacity.

Many Methodists espoused labour reform and took their inspiration from the life and writings of John Wesley who recognized the exploitation of the disenfranchised. Describing the grinding misery of the poor and their living conditions, he wrote

> I found them in their cells [hovels] underground, others in their garrets [slum tenements], half starved both with cold and hunger, added to weakness and pain. But I found not one of them unemployed who was able to crawl about the room. So wickedly, devilishly false is that common objection, 'They are poor only because they are idle'. If you saw these things with your own eyes, could you lay out money in ornaments or superfluities?[44]

Shamefully enough, however, there were many Methodists who had made their fortunes by exploiting the poor. Poverty, powerlessness, and lack of education placed people in the lower classes at an enormous disadvantage, forcing them to work long hours, in debilitating conditions, all for meagre wages. Opposition towards reform and a just society came from people within the Methodist ranks who, because of their religious antecedents, knew exploitation ran contrary to Methodism's code of ethics.

It was against this backdrop of exploitation that various groups of working-class and some middle-class Methodists formed an organized labour movement. This movement was not a trade union organization per se, but a cooperative enterprise whereby people produced goods and/or services and marketed them through a main distributor. Fair prices were negotiated for both producer and consumer in order to provide protection against exploitation and exorbitant distribution fees.

Examples of this growing independence of labour and the creativity of the entrepreneurial spirit can be taken from world wide Methodism, especially Britain and the United States. For sake of brevity, however, material will now be presented in a Canadian context.

A variety of middle-class Methodists, comfortably established in business and trade, were somewhat uncomfortable with the growing freedom espoused by ordinary working people. Despite this disapproval from the upwardly mobile or newly affluent, the cooperative movement became a popular means of entrepreneurship in the Atlantic provinces, parts of Ontario, and on the prairies of Western Canada.[45] In the Maritime communities there were cooperatives such as the British Canadian Co-operative,[46] the Co-operative Union of Canada, and the Women's Co-operative Guilds. In Ontario there was the powerful United Farm Workers of Ontario and the United Farmers Organization. Finally, in Canada's western province of Alberta there was the powerful United Farmers of Alberta (UFA) and the United Farm Women of Alberta (UFWA) that held sway from 1909 to 1921. The presence of women as leaders and organizers in these movements was common and, in one instance, sent shock waves through the province of Alberta. In 1917, Louise McKinney, a Methodist local preacher and avid temperance leader, was elected to the Provincial Legislature of Alberta representing the Non-Partisan League which represented the agrarian movement or the UFA/UFWA.[47]

The strength of these cooperatives lay in their ability to collaborate and share resources for the common good, while at the same time making a profit, and providing opportunities for flexible and innovative new ways of marketing product and labour. As entrepreneurial ventures they drew from a pool of talent that was ready to work, was goal oriented, and through hard-earned business acumen, could build successful ventures outside of the traditional.

On a more conventional note, there were successful Methodists who were established in banking, politics, the stock market, and the retail business. There were men like John MacDonald (1824–90) who was known as the 'merchant prince' of Toronto and impressed upon his employees the

Figure 7.1 *T. Eaton signs were common across Canada (photograph by Léo-Paul Dana)*

Figure 7.2 *Made for Simpson's (photograph by Léo-Paul Dana)*

need for discipline, hard work, integrity, frugality, benevolence and patriotism.[48] MacDonald later provided Timothy Eaton with a line of credit to launch his own retail business.[49] Prominent Ontario-based Methodist captains of industry included: Timothy Eaton (1834–1907), founder of the Eaton's Department Store chain (see Figure 7.1); Robert Simpson, founder of the Simpson's Department Store chain (see Photos 7.2), later 'Simpsons' (see Figure 7.3); Joseph Wesley Flavelle (1858–1939), president of William Davis Co. of Toronto and chairman of the Bank of

Figure 7.3 Signature on Simpsons shopping bag after apostrophe removed (photograph by Léo-Paul Dana)

Commerce, the National Trust Company, and also Simpsons Ltd; and the Manitoba-based James Ashdown who was dubbed 'Winnipeg's Merchant Prince'.[50] These men exemplified the ambitions of many upwardly mobile Methodists, who believed that hard work and the right kind of entrepreneurial approach would yield major financial rewards.

Surprisingly, however, these Methodist men of commerce, although often strikingly different in religious philosophy from that of their idealist brethren, shared a common trait. This commonality was the ability to identify a need and fill it. In the context of spirituality, the idealist Methodists had devised missions, organizations and campaigns to fill the void of human suffering and need. The powerful merchants, using their business acumen, identified material needs and the commodity market, and sought to fill the existing commercial need. The other-worldly mission-minded Methodists had used advertising to publicize revivals, social campaigns and fund raisers. The Methodist captains of industry used advertising to promote their businesses and then used some of their financial wealth to fund philanthropic and religious causes. Thus the rich Methodists, still cognizant of Wesley's teachings on the responsibilities of wealth and the function of riches, donated some of their profits towards funding the work of God, while those running the various projects gladly received their donations.

The work of God, according to Methodist interpretation, and for that matter, conventional Christianity in general, accepted the reality of disparity between the rich and poor. Those who were affluent were expected to share their wealth through philanthropy, compassion and dedication. This meant that many wealthy Methodists were generous financial supporters of home and overseas missions, educational facilities – including co-educational colleges, trade schools and hospitals. Yet, as major employers and investors, it was often the failure or reticence of these wealthy men to provide an adequate working wage for the working class. Ironically, through increased education and information, the working class developed their own labour power, organized for higher standards of living, and gradually achieved a somewhat limited but democratic society.

CONCLUSION

Durkheim's observations on social order and consensus are easily identifiable within the dynamics of Methodism, which is based on shared values and norms, interrelationship and balance. Further, the acceptance of change and adaptation are ingrained into the tradition, and this provides opportunity for evolving perspectives to be considered.

In this context, the relevancy of Methodism's contribution to entrepreneurship can further be examined through the process of group dynamics. Noting the six structural patterns within the tradition, the similarities of application to successful business philosophy become evident. Point (i) – If one considers this religious structure comparable to a large business organization, there is group identity. Point (ii) – a constructive business environment will nurture social and group cohesion in order to enhance employee morale and performance. Point (iii) – an employee who is respected and appreciated will be intellectually engaged in her/his company's projects and goals. Point (iv) – a successful company will be highly sensitive to changes in market requirements and will possess the ability to change and adapt accordingly. Point (v) – a business will have a rigorous policy of educational advancement and internal promotion opportunities. This will assist in maintaining expertise. Finally, point (vi) – in order to keep current, there will be an efficient and prompt network of reporting in order to facilitate communication between branches.

Collectively, and by consensus, the Kingdom of Heaven, as the goal of the Methodist, was being constructed through very different and often conflicting approaches. The strength of the movement was and is in its ability to incorporate a broad representation of society in the cause of Christ, and at the same time, meet the needs of the community through efficient organization. Within a secular entrepreneurial context, analysis of the Methodist structural framework provides insight into an alternate but successful reality. Through their ingenuity, adaptability, and approaches to social innovation the Methodists have developed a philosophical and organizational template with which to meet the changing requirements of their cultures. Their main strength is their people and any successful business entrepreneur will appreciate that concept.

NOTES

1. Emile Durkheim, *The Elementary Forms of Religious Life* (New York: Free Press, 1995) trans. Karen E. Fields.
2. *Sect* in the context of Methodism is defined as a party or faction in a religious body that splinters off from the larger system to create its own 'interpretation' of the main tenets of the originating group.
3. Kenneth Cracknell and Susan White, *An Introduction to World Methodism* (Cambridge: Cambridge University Press, 2005), p. 105.
4. The term Methodist was the nickname given to members of the Holy Club established at Oxford University in 1729 by Charles Wesley and led by brother John Wesley. It consisted of a group of students who dedicated themselves to seriously searching for God and living a holy life. They lived by the method, or the practice of the Gospel, regularly participating in the sacrament of Holy Communion, reading of the Bible and visitation of the sick and those in prison. The nickname was then given to members of the Evangelical Revival who followed these holiness practices. John Wesley established groups or societies that met on a regular mid-weekly and Lord's Day basis. As the movement developed it distinguished itself outside of the confines of the Church of England and was known as Methodism.
5. Powerful spiritual movements known as revivals were characterized by positive expressions of spiritual change within the individual. This change would result in following Jesus Christ and a strong commitment to personal holiness life, which would consequently result in social renewal within the broader society.
6. Neil Semple, *The Lord's Dominion* (Montreal: McGill-Queen's University Press, 1996), p. i.
7. Cracknell and White, *An Introduction to World Methodism*, p. 5.
8. Methodism was known as the 'Revivalist Denomination' and was favoured by the poor working class, immigrants, pioneers, as well as the middle class. By 1884, it emerged as the largest Protestant denomination in Canada. See Semple, *The Lord's Dominion*, p. 4.
9. George Whitefield (1714–70), John Wesley (1703–91) Charles Wesley (1707–88). Whitefield was a charismatic preacher who had participated in the first Great Awakening, which was the famous religious revival that occurred in the American colonies. Whitefield then used the same approach of bringing the Word of God to the common people in Britain through field or open air preaching and initiated what was known as the Evangelical Revival. John Wesley followed as another gifted preacher and leader of the revival and later established himself as the founder of the Wesleyan Methodist church. Charles Wesley was a prodigious writer and hymnist, who composed many of the Methodist hymns still in use in the denomination.
10. John Wesley (1770), *The Question 'What is an Arminian?' Answered by a Lover of Free Grace*, Bristol: Gale, referenced from Global Ministries, the United Methodist Church archives, http://new.gbgm-umc.org/ (accessed July 2008). Under Point 7 Wesley states that 'The Calvinists hold, (1.) God has absolutely decreed, from all eternity, to save such and such persons, and no others; and that Christ died for these, and none else. The Arminians hold, God has decreed, from all eternity, touching all that have the written word, "He that believeth shall be saved: He that believeth not, shall be condemned:" And in order to this, "Christ died for all, all that were dead in trespasses and sins;" that is, for every child of Adam, since "in Adam all died."'

11. God chooses who will be saved.
12. There was a final dispute in 1741 which led to the separation between Whitefield and the Wesleys. See Arnold Dallimore, *George Whitefield: the Life and Times of the Great Evangelist of the Eighteenthteeth Century Revival* (Edinburgh: The Banner of Truth Trust, 1990), p. 43.
13. Cracknell and White, *An Introduction to World Methodism*, p. vii
14. Official website of the World Council of Churches, http://www.oikoumene.org/en/member-churches/church-families/methodist-churches/wmc.html (accessed July 2008).
15. John Wesley, *Sermons on Several Occasions* (London: Epworth Press, 1967). 'Consisting of forty-four discourses, published in four volumes, in the years 1746, 1748, 1750 and 1760.'
16. Preface to Wesley's *Sermons on Several Occasions.*
17. Ibid.
18. In 1529 Luther and his followers formally protested the decision of the Roman Catholic Church and the Emperor Charles V at the Diet of Spires. The Diet had officially denounced the reform movement also known as the Reformation.
19. Martin Luther (1483–1546) led a movement for change with Roman Catholicism with his re-emphasis on scriptural teachings. There had been many earlier reformers, such as John Wycliffe, known as 'the morning start' of the Reformation (mid-1320s to December 1384); Jan Hus (*c.*1372–1415); and William Tyndale (1484–1536), but it was Luther who later orchestrated the reform movement.
20. Scripture alone was sole authority. Any teaching that was merely a tradition and not based in scripture was to be rejected.
21. One did not earn God's redemption or forgiveness. One's salvation was based on the redemptive atonement of Christ and through faith.
22. Every believer had a responsibility to Christ to live ethically and to live the teachings of Jesus in the world. Thus, everybody, in a spiritual context, was equal in God's sight. Religious leaders were not spiritually superior in God's sight.
23. Historically, Evangelicals confessed a belief in the truth of the five solas: Sola gratia, Sola fide, Solus Christus, Sola Scriptura, Soli Deo Gloria. In short, they confessed that salvation is by grace alone, through faith alone, in the Person and work of Christ alone as revealed in the Scripture alone, to the glory of God alone.
24. The revivalists taught that heart religion or new birth was imperative to salvation.
25. George M. Thomas, *Revivalism and Cultural Change* (Chicago: University of Chicago Press, 1989), p. 142.
26. He believed in preaching in a straight forward way so that people could understand him. Wesley, *Sermons on Several Occasions*, p. v,
27. Ibid., p. 576.
28. Ibid.
29. Wesley, *Sermons on Several Occasions,* pp. 577–8.
30. Ibid. p. 577.
31. Paul Wesley Chilcote, *John Wesley and the Women Preachers of Early Methodism* (London: Scarecrow Press, 1991), p. 67.
32. This recognized order was established in 1744.
33. Chilcote, *John Wesley and the Women Preachers of Early Methodism*, p. 3.
34. Cracknell and White, *An Introduction to World Methodism*, p. 125.
35. Once Wesley conceded the necessity of using lay preachers, he saw no reason to exclude women. A number of these women established themselves as very eloquent preachers in Britain, as well as in many parts of the world, including British North America. See Wesley's essay on 'Thoughts Concerning the Origin of Power', taken from *Political Writings of John Wesley* (Bristol: Thoemmes Press, 1998), p. 45.
36. Robert F. Wearmouth, *Methodism and the Working-Class Movements of England, 1880–1850* (London: Epworth Press, 1937), p. 254. The famous case of the Tolpuddle Martyrs describes a group of agricultural labours, some of whom were Methodist lay preachers, who tried to organize a trade union. Some of the organizers were deported

to Australia via the prison transports (hulks). Later, many working-class Methodists developed strong trade union affiliations and contributed to labour rights for the poor.

37. Phyllis D. Airhart, 'Ordering a New Nation and Reordering Protestantism, 1867–1919', *The Canadian Protestant Experience, 1760–1990*, ed. George A. Rawlyk (Montreal: McGill-Queen's University Press, 1990) p. 119.
38. The Wesley Centre on Line, Wesley Centre for Applied Theology,
39. William Booth, *In Darkest England and the Way Out* (Montclair, NJ: Patterson Smith, 1975) reprint of original 1890 text.
40. Official Salvation Army website, re *In Darkest England and the Way Out*: http://www.salvos.org.au/about-us/our-history/in-darkest-england.php (accessed 30 July).
41. Employing the North American vernacular of the period, Protestant mass gatherings were known as camp revivals or camp meetings where people would travel often long distances to a religious gathering. During this time they would camp out in tents or wagons and there would be preaching, religious services, group and individual prayer, singing, discussion and networking. This means of socialization, involving the group dynamics of defined focus, purpose, inspiration, and exchange of ideas, is still an effective tool in both religious and secular organizations today.
42. John Wesley had voiced this sentiment in one of his journal entries, dated 12 August 1738, when he recorded, 'I look upon the world as my parish'.
43. The origin of the camp meeting was the holy fair, a Scottish Presbyterian practice dating from the late sixteenth century. The holy fair was a common phrase used to describe a large sacramental gathering. 'In them religion and culture, communion and community, piety and sociability commingled.' See Leigh Eric Schmidt, *Holy Fairs: Scottish Communions and American Revivals in the Early Modern Period* (Princeton, NJ: Princeton University Press, 1989), p. i.
44. John Wesley (1938), *The Journal of John Wesley*, standard edition, Vol. 4, Bicentenary Issue, ed. Nehemiah Curnock, London: The Epworth Press, 8 February 1753, p. 52.
45. Semple, *The Lord's Dominion*, p. 411.
46. In 1930 the British Canadian Guild participated in the Canadian Fair Wage Hearings. The Guild described 'the advantages enjoyed by cooperative workers compared with those of workers in private enterprises'. See Rusty Neal, *Brotherhood Economics* (Sydney: UCCB Press, 1998), p. 68.
47. Bradford J. Rennie, *The Rise of Agrarian Democracy* (Toronto: University of Toronto Press, 2000) p. 132.
48. Semple, *The Lord's Dominion*, p. 335. MacDonald was also appointed to the Canadian Senate.
49. Airhart in *The Canadian Protestant Experience*, p. 105.
50. James Ashdown (1844–1924). Created a wholesale hardware company in Western Canada, with branches in Saskatoon, Calgary and Nelson, which supplied individual merchants with goods until the rise of department store chains and mail order businesses. Later he was appointed a Justice of the Peace for Manitoba in 1871. In 1873 he was chairman of the committee which obtained Winnipeg's incorporation as a city in 1874.

REFERENCES

Airhart, Phyllis D. (1990), 'Ordering a New Nation and Reordering Protestantism, 1867–1919', in George A. Rawlyk (ed.), *The Canadian Protestant Experience, 1760–1990*, Montreal: McGill-Queen's University Press.

Booth, William (1975), *In Darkest England and the Way Out*, Montclair, NJ: Patterson Smith. Reprint of original 1890 text.

Chilcote, Paul Wesley (1991), *John Wesley and the Women Preachers of Early Methodism*, London: Scarecrow Press.

Cracknell, Kenneth and Susan White (2005), *An Introduction to World Methodism*, Cambridge: Cambridge University Press.
Dallimore, Arnold (1990), *George Whitefield: The Life and Times of the Great Evangelist of the Eighteenth Century Revival*, Edinburgh: The Banner of Truth Trust.
Durkheim, Emile (1995), *The Elementary Forms of Religious Life*, trans. Karen E. Fields, New York: Free Press.
Neal, Rusty (1998), *Brotherhood Economics*, Sydney: UCCB Press.
Rennie, Bradford J. (2000), *The Rise of Agrarian Democracy*, Toronto: University of Toronto Press.
Schmidt, Leigh Eric (1989), *Holy Fairs: Scottish Communions and American Revivals in the Early Modern Period*, Princeton, NJ: Princeton University Press.
Semple, Neil (1996), *The Lord's Dominion*, Montreal: McGill-Queen's University Press.
Thomas, George M. (1989), *Revivalism and Cultural Change*, Chicago, IL: University of Chicago Press.
Wearmouth, Robert F. (1937), *Methodism and the Working-Class Movements of England, 1880–1850*, London: Epworth Press.
Wesley, John (1770), *The Question, 'What Is an Arminian?' Answered by a Lover of Free Grace*, Bristol: Gale, referenced from Global Ministries, the United Methodist Church archives, available at: http://new.gbgm-umc.org/ (accessed July 2008).
Wesley, John (1938), *The Journal of John Wesley*, standard edition, Vol. 4, Bicentenary Issue, ed. Nehemiah Curnock, London: The Epworth Press, 8 February 1753, pp. 279–80.
Wesley, John (1967), *Sermons on Several Occasions*, London: Epworth Press.
Wesley, John (1998), 'Thoughts Concerning the Origin of Power', in *Political Writings of John Wesley*, Bristol: Thoemmes Press.

8. The Hutterite Brethren: old world values and new age technologies

Robert L. Malach and Sandra Malach

INTRODUCTION

Hutterites have been living successfully in collective agricultural colonies for over 400 years. They are profoundly religious, applying their belief in community ownership of property, pacificism (separation of church and state), and communal agrarian lifestyle as God's directions for proper living. Each community is symbolic of Noah's Ark. While the outward appearance of the Hutterite Brethren appears old fashioned, a closer look reveals how up to date and competitive their economic model is and how well it is poised to meet twenty-first-century challenges.

Outward appearances can often be misleading and nowhere more so than when one first encounters members of the Hutterite Brethren. The men with their beards, straw or black hats, dark pants and suspenders and the women with their long dresses, aprons and polka dot bandanas look similar to the Amish or Mennonite brethren. While there are some similarities, it would be a serious mistake to base assumptions regarding how Hutterites live, worship and work based on knowledge of the Amish or Mennonites. The most significant differences are the communal lifestyle of the Hutterites and the early adoption of agricultural innovations.

To understand the Hutterites communal lifestyle and business model one must first have some knowledge of how their history and religious beliefs are integrated into their communal lifestyle. Hutterites have practiced their faith and lifestyle in self-contained communities for over four centuries (Hostetler, 1974). Important aspects of their faith include: (1) a belief in the Community of Goods, not personal ownership of property, (2) pacificism – the total separation of church and state resulting in a non-involvement in state politics or conflict, (3) adult baptism and (4) a communal agricultural lifestyle where the faithful worship and work together for their collective well being (Hostetler, 1965). While having some similarity to Amish and Mennonite beliefs, Hutterite differences lie in how the community applies itself to the task of making a modern-day agricultural community prosper in both an economic and social way.

There are several different sects (Leuts) of Hutterites in North America – Dariusleut, Lehrerleut and Schmiedeleut. The authors visited the Hillview Colony, which is part of the Dariusleut Leut. At the colony we visited with the Hofer family and they helped give us a more personal perspective of day-to-day life in a Hutterite colony.

TRADITIONAL LIFESTYLE

About 93 people live at the Hillview Colony near Rosebud, Alberta, Canada. Most of the colony members are related in the 10 families that live and work on the colony. Each family lives in their own housing unit, six units forming a long house. The homes are very plain and furnished only with necessary furniture, most of which is built on the colony. There are few decorations or pieces of art on the walls. The colourful rag rugs placed at the doorway were also made by the women of the colony. Hutterite beds are also covered with their famous down duvets made from the breast feathers of geese.

Community members take their meals together in a communal dining room where the men, women, older and younger children are seated in separate groups, the children in their own dining rooms. The food is prepared in a spotless community kitchen that rivals the most modern commercial kitchens. One woman is the head cook but all women rotate through a schedule as kitchen assistants. Certain days of the week are dedicated to specific tasks that vary with the season, that is, Tuesday is baking day and the responsibility for kitchen clean-up is every third week. The women also preserve vast quantities of fruits and vegetables and freeze meat produced by the colony. As a result, the colony's food is substantially derived from their land and animals.

In addition the women run the kindergarten, work in the gardens, maintain their homes, make the family clothing and linens, and finish household furnishings. Women do not take part in colony elections or the business of the colony, as gender roles are clearly defined. The role of women in the Hutterite colony is very traditional; this is signified by girls receiving a sewing machine as a gift from the colony when they are baptized and make the transition from the role of girl to woman and assume adult duties.

The children help their mothers and fathers with daily chores, learning first hand many of the necessary tasks required to maintain the community. They have fun as well. They sled and skate in the winter, ride horses in the summer, sing songs and enjoy the many animals that also live on the colony. Hutterite children attend school at their colony, which is taught by a non-Hutterite teacher and a Hutterite teacher who provides the children with instruction in their German dialect, teaching them how to write, speak and sing in their native tongue. Education is not highly sought after, and most children leave school at grade 9, the mandatory minimal educational requirement in Alberta and the highest level of education available at the colony school.

The men are the spiritual leaders of the family, but do not have any significant duties related to the maintenance of the home.

PROGRESSIVE BUSINESS

The men manage the colony and provide the labour for all of the agricultural operations. All of the colonies pursue mixed farming; the production of grain and the raising of a variety of animals, including pigs, cows, sheep, chickens and geese. Products and by-products are utilized by the colony or sold at the wholesale or retail level. This provides Hutterites with competitive advantages arising from both vertical and horizontal integration of the agricultural products distribution chain.

Colony Management and Labour

Hutterite colonies are able to achieve efficiencies in their human resources through the method by which leaders are selected and the optimal utilization of labour. With the exception of the garden, only the men work on the farm. Thus the colony is run as a patriarchal-democracy (Hostetler, 1965) where the men elect the leaders and make important business decisions by voting.

All of the colony men participate in the election of their leaders and those who have a management role. The community leader is the Preacher, of which there may be more than one. Preachers are nominated by members of the colony, then a vote occurs and any nominee with more than five votes has his name placed in a hat for a lottery; the man whose name is pulled will become ordained for life as the Preacher (Hutterites.org, 2005). In addition to conducting a daily church service before supper, the Preacher is also responsible for conducting religious ceremonies (baptisms, marriages and funerals) and for motivating, disciplining and providing guidance to colony members. In this regard he is responsible for human resources. The Colony Boss is also elected and works with the Preacher and the other bosses to provide general and financial management. The Colony Boss is responsible for maintaining community funds and overseeing the sale and purchase of community goods (Hostetler, 1965). A major responsibility is that of receiving all earnings and expenditure receipts from the other bosses. He also carries out an internal audit function, watching out for missing funds. Other elected positions are the Field Boss, who is responsible for grain production, the Pig Boss, the Cow Boss, the Poultry Boss, the Gardener and the German Teacher. Men may hold more than one position. It is interesting to note that there is no Sales Boss, but each boss is responsible for the product through the entire distribution system from production to final sale. Large transactions are handled by five or six elders elected from the group, who form an executive committee.

Individuals do not choose their jobs but are selected to work with particular bosses according to their abilities and the colony's labour requirements. Individuals may work for various bosses according to seasonal labour requirements (that is, during seeding and harvest men who normally work for the Poultry, Cow or Pig Boss will also work for the Field Boss). This is part and parcel of the subjugation of self to the community. Community needs and values supersede those of the individual and in exchange the community provides for those individuals who serve it.

Needless to say, harmony and productivity are prized and community leaders, who have often lived and worked with their fellow men for their entire lives, are adept at recognizing each individual's personality and skill set so that these selections usually confirm what everyone, including the individual concerned, believed was best for that person and for the community at large.

From an outsider's perspective, we were curious how the focus on colony goals and objectives dealt with the differences in individual colony members' abilities to contribute. This curiosity is somewhat misplaced when one remembers that individuals do not work for personal gain or recognition, and their personal allowance is a meagre $10 per month. Colony work is God's work and all gain belongs to the collective, which in turn supplies each individual according to their needs and their personal wants. We were reminded that day-to-day issues of harmony in this community could and sometimes were dealt with expeditiously through appropiately subtle or direct lessons from the Preacher at daily worship services which are held before supper every day. Other issues are handled again, subtly or directly, by community bosses or elders as needs be.

Technology and Productivity

While visiting at Hillview Colony, this pride of colony productivity was subtle but evident. While it would be improper to call a colony member boastful, pride surrounded the adoption of technology and best practices in all aspects of their agricultural operation. Colony members are very business-like and focused on maximizing efficiencies and increasing profitability. It was evident that these efficiencies were pleasing to all in their furtherance of colony and not individual ambitions. The example given to us was the progress made by the Hillview Colony in the pig operations when the new colony split off from the Rosebud Colony. The Hillview Colony was a first-mover in the adoption of technological advances in the pig barns, resulting in increased profitability from this segment of the operation. This financial success allowed the colony to quickly get on its feet, ensuring its survival as a new and viable community.

We were reminded that diversity was important and that the colony recognized that overdependence on any one agricultural commodity was a vulnerability to be avoided. The colony has viable grain, pig, poultry, cattle, and garden operations that supply colony needs for both sustenance and revenue generation. Everywhere you look on the colony you see evidence of the latest equipment, including farm machinery, facilities and computer technology and knowledge of best practices. The colonies adopt best practices and technologies from each other and from the world at large.

The production of the colony far exceeds its needs. Excess production is sold into the market in a multitude of ways. The grain is sold via contracts, where permitted, or by the Canadian Wheat Board, which has a monopoly on the purchase of wheat produced in Canada. Pigs and cows are primarily raised for meat and are slaughtered on site and then sold to wholesalers for further processing and sale to consumers. Garden vegetables are sold to processors or, at the retail level, Hutterites are a common sight at farmers' markets and in some communities they still sell their products door to door.

Hutterites' experience in the agricultural business has created opportunities for them to develop innovative technologies. For example, a colony in Manitoba developed new software. The software was marketed to the other colonies; however, they were under no obligation to purchase this technology if they believed other products in the market were superior.

Expansion – Branching Out

Hutterite communities have traditionally felt that once a colony reaches 130 to 150 members they are at risk of losing the small manageable face-to-face family groups and management inefficiencies begin to surface. Long before these types of problems become acute, the leadership of the colony will have been managing their investments and the delegation of workplace authority so that the colony is prepared for the eventual division and creation of a new colony ('branching out'). Approximately every 15 years or so colonies normally go through a growth cycle that sees the paying off of founding debt, the expansion and modernization of operations and then the saving of money and acquisition of land to branch out (Hostetler, 1974).

When the time for branching out occurs, those with similar work attitudes and complementary ideas will bond to one of two colony preachers who will eventually preside over a split between the existing and new colony. This provides a necessary and healthy outlet for the growing pool of talent and experience in a mature colony that may in some cases be seeing some differences of opinion on how best to run the old colony.

Competitive Advantage – Hutterite Colonies versus Family Farms

Our conclusions about competive advantages are subjective in nature and are gathered solely from our observations of, and experiences with, both Hutterite colonies and family farms. Our parents grew up on family farms and we have spent considerable time visiting the farms and experiencing the work and lifestyles typical there. We have maintained our ties with these farming communities and have sought to expand our understanding of what matters to those communities through our regular visits.

In many rural Canadian conventional farming communities Hutterite colonies are not deemed to be desirable because of their perceived failure to make economic and social contributions to rural communities in which they exist, and a discomfort with the competitive advantages that the colonies have over the traditional family firms, especially with regard to finances and human resources.

Rural people often believe that small towns lose business as the colonies are more self-sufficient than family farms and do not contribute to the economic life to the same extent as farm families. Empirical evidence on this point is hard to come by, as the urbanization of our society and the death of small towns would arguably have proceeded at the same rate in the absence of Hutterite colonies given that the economies of scale in farming are forcing the minimum economic size of farms upward and are displacing the small farm as an economically viable unit. The necessity for increased growth in the size of farms does create competition for available land between colonies and family farms that wish to expand in the same district. This competion does in some cases lead to animosity towards colonies that are ready to branch out and can pay top dollar for whole farms, and thereby make it difficult for family farms to purchase additional land. On the other hand, there certainly are retiring farmers in those communities who have a much more favourable view of how an open marketplace works in their favour when it comes to choosing between potential buyers.

In addition to these economic factors, the Hutterites communal lifestyle minimizes their interaction with their rural neighbours and they do not make contributions to community life. Their belief in pacificism prevents them from participating in local government and other social service clubs and activities. As a result, on a personal level they are not integrated into Canadian society as a whole.

Hutterite colonies have innate human resource advantages, primarily due to the amount of available labour and non-payment of wages. If the average family farm has three to five adults available for farm work, then the average colony can easily have 15 to 20 times more workers. This produces efficiencies that are not easily attained outside of the colony. These efficiencies include: worker specialization and knowledge; flexibility, labour costs, loyalty and unity, and growth potential.

1. *Knowledge*. The colonies have a larger available work force that allows its members to specialize (poultry, hogs, grain, dairy, beef, market gardens, and so on) thereby increasing the depth and breadth of expertise and the amount of energy that can be applied to any one area of a mixed farm operation. However, farmers have a higher level of education, completing high school and often studying an aspect of agriculture at the post-secondary level.
2. *Flexibility*. With a large workforce, manpower can be spread over a wide variety of tasks or all the workers can be focused on one urgent task. For example, during harvest a colony scheduling normal eight-hour shifts can safely sustain 24-hour-a-day harvest operations for a period of weeks until the crop is harvested. This is not sustainable on a family farm where only three or four workers are available and frost and an early snow are a constant threat to a successful harvest.
3. *Labour costs*. Colony members work for the collective good and receive food, clothing and shelter, in addition to a $10 per month allowance for personal purchases. Family farms also traditionally provide the basic necessities of life for their members; however, personal purchases will exceed $10 per month. Additional pressures confront the family farm when farm kids become adults and require a living wage to pursue a desirable lifestyle. Older children working on the farm or individuals hired as employees are routinely paid between $15 and $25 per hour, amounting to at least $30 000 per year per worker. The savings in labour costs could easily run beyond the million dollar year range on an average colony (50+ workers × approx. $30 000 a year = $1.5 million a year). The drastically reduced labour costs and an increased number of workers give the colony substantial advantages over the family farm resulting in increased cash flow and profitability.
4. *Loyalty and unity*. The religious foundation and belief in community

of goods creates a unity of culture that is hard to achieve outside the colony, where individual families and people all have personal values and goals. The unity of purpose and religious education and upbringing reduces the risk of attrition of community members. Furthermore, such attrition has lower economic costs, as the departing member takes little of value when they leave, as all goods are community owned and the expectation is that they would stay. Therefore they take responsibility for their own set-up costs away from the colony.

The loyalty of individual farm family members is more of a moral and loving familial bond which is accepting of the fact that its members are not all focused on the same goals or objectives. Furthermore, as a result children raised on farms do not have stringent social or religious ties that require family farm members to stay on the farm if they have other ambitions or interests. The departure of farm children can result in labour shortages and succession issues. These departures have significant economic costs in lost labour and set-up costs for the departing children (that is, education, housing, transportation) that provide little or no return to the family farming operation.

5. *Expansion.* It is not always possible for the family farm to grow sufficiently in size or productivity to allow all the farm children and their progeny to stay on the farm. The expansion of a family farm to a size where more than one sustainable operation can coexist is a very difficult challenge. As a result, usually only one child will stay on the farm while the rest are compelled to leave farming for other occupations.
6. *Diversification.* The fact that the colony's size allows for different revenue streams insulates them to some extent from downturns and disruptions that can occur to single family farms that find efficiencies by specializing as grain farmers or cattle ranchers. It is no secret what BSE has done to some ranchers and the same thing can happen to a grain farmer who gets hail and grasshoppers, an early frost and then drought in three consecutive years. This kind of luck is hard on both colonies and individual farms, but it is more likely to be survived by the colony if it has a diverse income stream and lower overall per capita operating costs.

In support of the family farm (in spite of its inefficiencies), it has been with us in one form or another since the dawn of agrarian society. There have been many types of communal and family farms throughout the ages. Those on the farm have stayed there because they love what they do and feel a genuine connection to the land and a sense of pride, tradition and community within both their families and agrarian communities. Many farm families feel, however, that this lifestyle is under siege as the increases in farm costs have consistently outstripped farm commodity prices. These increasing costs and stagnant commodity prices have forced farmers to specialize and expand their operations to find efficiencies and economies of scale. This, in turn, has forced the less efficient out of the industry while larger family operations have so far survived.

CONCLUSIONS

In the future – if the Hillview Colony is any indicator – the Hutterite way of life will continue to flourish in the twenty-first century and beyond. The members appear to be content, and thrive in a hardworking and prosperous communal culture. So long as the Hutterite communities can maintain their core values, what we saw of their efficiency, openness to new best practices, vigour and commitment leads us to believe that they will continue to be a part of the North American farming landscape for many years to come.

Having observed both colony and family farm life at first hand, we know there is great dignity and integrity in both lifestyles. All of us urban dwellers are indebted to them for putting food on our tables in such an efficient manner. We hope that both farm cultures will survive into the next millennium.

ACKNOWLEDGEMENTS

The authors would like to acknowledge the insights into their life and hospitality provided us by members of the Hillview Colony, Rosebud, Alberta, with special thanks to their Preacher Jake Hofer and their German Teacher/Garden Boss Joe Hofer and his family. We would also like to acknowledge the insights provided to us on the operation of a family farm by Brian, Gaye, Mitchell and Kalen Boe of Boe Farms Ltd of Dalum, Alberta, Canada.

REFERENCES

Hostetler, John A. (1965), *Hutterite Life*, Scottsdale, AZ, Pittsburgh, PA and Kitchner, ON: Herald Press.

Hostetler, John A. (1974), *Hutterite Society*, Baltimore, MD and London: Johns Hopkins University Press.

Hutterites.org (2005), 'The Hutterian Brethren: Hutterites Living in Community in North America', available at: www.hutterites.org (accessed 20 December 2005).

9. Amish entrepreneurship in the United States*

Léo-Paul Dana

Therefore the Lord God sent him forth . . . to till the ground. (Genesis 3:23)

INTRODUCTION

The Amish People[1] are an offshoot of the Mennonites, a religious group that was established in 1525, in Zurich, Switzerland. Named for Menno Simons, the Mennonites had beliefs which were considered radical at the time; for instance, they believed in the separation of Church and State. These people felt that a religion should involve only voluntary believers, and that no religion should be imposed upon children at birth. Keeping in line with this conviction, they refused to baptize their infants. Instead, individuals could be voluntarily baptized, if and when they felt mature enough to decide for themselves. This religious group was therefore referred to as the Anabaptists.

Anabaptists were persecuted in Europe, because they did not believe in baptism and because they desired separation of Church and State. Religious freedom attracted them to America, and according to Stauffer (1941) the first of these arrived in the United States in 1683. Thus, they left Switzerland, Germany and Alsace Lorraine, for the United States, where a Quaker, William Penn, promised them religious freedom and the federal government offered them land grants.

In 1693, Swiss-born Jakob Ammann felt that the Mennonites were straying from a strictly religious background. He then proceeded to establish a more conservative and disciplined offshoot, which came to be known as the Amish. More so than the Mennonites, the Amish were – and continue to be – careful not to accept innovative technology without considering the effects thereof on their lifestyle, which values asceticism, frugality, simplicity, thrift, work ethic and perhaps most importantly, humility and the family unit. Hostetler (1993) noted that some aspects of being Amish have remained comparatively unchanged for three centuries.

Among the largest concentrations of Amish families is found in Pennsylvania's Lancaster County, which is 946 square miles. It was home to 500 Amish persons in 1900 (Lowry, 1997), and to 25 000 today. Two-thirds of the land in this county is used for agriculture, and this area is said to be the most productive non-irrigated farmland in the United States. Yet farming here involves no highly sophisticated technology. Farms are small and do not benefit from economies of scale. Lee (1984) noted an average farm size of 60 acres.

The objective of this chapter is to give an account of Amish self-employment and entrepreneurship in Lancaster County, Pennsylvania. Focus is on Amish values and the successful small business sector that thrives without modernisation. As stated by Farmer and Richman, 'Prevailing religious beliefs and cultural values . . . have a direct and very significant bearing on the dominant view toward work and achievement' (1965, pp. 156–7).

RELIGION AND ENTERPRISING COMMUNITIES

The impact of religion on economic development has long been a subject of research interest. Classical social theorist, Weber (1904) compared taxation figures in Baden, and reported 4 000 000 marks per 1000 Jews; 954 000 marks per 1000 Protestants; and only 589 000 marks per 1000 Catholics. His thesis argued that while Protestantism stressed the development of economic security, Catholics believed that it was easier for a camel to fit through the eye of a needle than for a wealthy man to go to heaven.

The Weberian thesis and the concept of the Protestant work ethic became highly influential, and this prompted much research. Farmer and Richman, for example, wrote,

> There is a close correlation of countries in terms of how deeply the Calvinist spirit has penetrated their economic and social behavior with real per capita income and level of economic development. Thus, in 1958, all fifteen countries of the world with per capita incomes of over $700 per year were those which had followed the Calvinist ethic extensively; and, with the possible exceptions of France and Belgium, all were quite extensively Protestant in religion. No country where the Calvinist ethic had deeply penetrated was not included in this list of most wealthy countries, while none of the extensively non-Calvinist nations had yet achieved such economic success. (1965, p. 157)

More recently, Klandt found that a Protestant upbringing 'is more likely to lead to independent business activity than a Catholic upbringing' (1987, p. 31).

Every coin has two sides and not all academics agreed with the Weberian school. In response to Weber (1904; 1905), Sombart (1911) examined economic development in Europe, and this was translated as Sombart (1951). In this work, Sombart observed that as Jews moved from southern Europe to northern Europe, the economic centre of Europe shifted with them; he then linked economic development in Europe to Jewish entrepreneurs and argued that they influenced the outward form of modern capitalism. Ex-President of the United States, William Howard Taft wrote about the Jews who 'developed trade, poetry, philosophy, science and literature' (Taft, 1919, p. 7). He also gave examples of how Europeans prospered by means of Jews, who 'were forbidden to hold land. The nobility manufactured the liquor, and they were willing and anxious to have the Jews sell it, who thus, for lack of other occupation, became the innkeepers, the purveyors in the demoralizing liquor business' (Taft, 1919, p. 10). Weber (1922) maintained that Protestantism, by encouraging self-restraint and accumulation of assets, contributed to capitalism. This work was translated by Alexander Morell Henderson and Talcott Parsons, and published as Weber (1947).

Lewis explained,

> 'If a religion lays stress upon material values, upon thrift and productive investment, upon honesty in commercial relations, upon experimentation and risk-bearing . . . it will be helpful to growth, whereas in so far as it is hostile to these things, it tends to inhibit growth. Where Theravada Buddhism is the backbone of social and cultural values . . . it may have a restraining effect on the accumulation of wealth and the rise of an entrepreneurial class. (1955, p. 105).

Yet Guiso et al. (2003) found that Buddhists were in favour of increasing private ownership of business and industry, more so than any other of the groups in their study; the authors also noted that Buddhists were in favour of competition, more so than Christians, Muslims and Hindus, but less than Jews.

Zingales argued, 'Buddhism and Christianity seem most conducive to capitalism, and Islam the least' (2006, p. 228). He elaborated,

> Comparing the average response of different religious denominations we find that, other things being equal, Buddhism seems to promote the best attitudes towards the market system. Christian religions follow . . . Islam appears as the religion least conducive to capitalism. Muslims are very much against competition, against private property and less willing to trade off equality for incentives. (Zingales, 2006, pp. 228–9)

In contrast, Malaysian Prime Minister Abdullah Ahmad Badawi suggested,

> 'Islam preaches a holistic and comprehensive notion of development in this world and for the hereafter. It does not negate the pursuit of material development in this world . . . The teachings of Islam are also eminently suited to development in the modern, knowledge-based economy . . . Besides its emphasis on knowledge, Islam also enjoins a work ethic that equips the individual to excel in economic pursuits. (Badawi, 2006, p. 208)

What impact does religion have on one's decision to be an entrepreneur, and does this affect the nature of entrepreneurship? Fishberg (1911) observed that Jews were concentrated in precarious occupations such as commerce; he elaborated, suggesting that Jews were 'ambitious and persevering, possessing an enormous amount of "push", which he cannot always bring into play while struggling against adverse circumstances' (1911, p. 531). Weber (1930) – in the English translation of his 1920 revision of his earlier (1904; 1905) works – went into detail about social class as a function of religion, and he cited related works including Sombart (1913) and its translation, that is, Sombart (1915). More recently, Rath and Kloosterman elaborated, 'The arrival of Jews from the Iberian Peninsula in the sixteenth century and later from Eastern Europe, and of Roman Catholics from Westphalia throughout the nineteenth century, greatly influenced the Dutch economic landscape as their business acumen enhanced the nation's economic and cultural wealth' (2003, pp. 123–4).

MODERNIZATION, ENTREPRENEURSHIP AND THE AMISH RELIGION

The United States is a pluralistic society in which many minorities retain their respective partial-universes, while sharing a core universe with other Americans. Each coexists in a state of mutual accommodation, tolerance, or at times cooperation. The Amish People, of whom there are about 150 000 nation-wide, have self-imposed a status of social marginality upon themselves, espousing their own community at the exclusion of others, such as to resist modernization; they focus their energy on religion, family and work values leading to successful self-employment in the absence of innovation or modernization.

Levy (1966) described modernization as the ratio of inanimate to animate sources of power. Berger, Berger, and Kellner noted that social scientists often discussed the concept of modernisation interchangeably with that of economic growth and development; they suggested that modernization 'must be seen in close relation to economic growth – more specifically, to the particular growth processes released by recent technology' (1973, p. 8). Yet the Amish have prospered using animate sources of power; they have shown that economic development is possible without modernization. The Amish are an extreme example of a people who value economic development, through a highly disciplined work ethic and a propensity for small business, while excluding from their lives the necessity to modernize. In Amish society, entrepreneurial work is valued as a pleasure which allows individuals to perpetuate religious beliefs. Thus, the Amish view of entrepreneurship looks beyond the maximization of monetary profit. As stated by Penrose, 'The fact that businessmen, though interested in profits, have a variety of other ambitions as well, some of which seem to influence (or distort) their judgment about the "best" way of making money, has often been discussed primarily in connection with the controversial subject of "profit maximization"' (1959, p. 39).

Foster noted the Amish perception that 'factory jobs were both personally unrewarding and economically undependable' (1984, p. 79). Hostetler (1993) and Kraybill (1989) elaborated on Amish culture. Lowry (1997) focused on tobacco farming among the Amish. Lowery and Noble (2000) examined the occupational structure of the largest Amish settlement in Ohio. Stoll (2002) explained why the Amish refuse to use motorised machinery for fieldwork, where it would alter agricultural production that currently uses no pesticides, no herbicides and no genetic modification; given that farm-work is the life of an Amish family, it must embrace rest and pleasure. Based on interviews with over 150 Amish entrepreneurs, Kraybill and Nolt (2004) traced the rise and impact of businesses in Lancaster County, home to the oldest Amish community. Hawley (2005) studied Amish business practices in Missouri, with particular attention given to Amish women in business.

Much has been written about innovation-based entrepreneurship, as pioneered by Schumpeter (1934). There is also significant literature on opportunity-based entrepreneurship, as described by Kirzner (1979). Shapero (1975) was among those who discussed necessity-based entrepreneurship. This paper will now look at religion-inspired humility-based self-employment among the Amish People.

METHODOLOGY

With the methodological mandate to be inductive, naturalistic and sensitive to context, it was necessary for the researcher to be submerged into Amish lifestyle, for an extended period of time, such as to develop closeness in the social sense. This was a challenge because separateness from the world is fundamental to Amish beliefs; a central concern among the Amish is spiritual purity, and isolationism is the means to this. Interaction with other cognitive systems is therefore kept to a minimum, and is generally limited to the economic realm.

While the Amish have a mistrust of outsiders, the Mennonites cater to commercialism and are relatively open to outsiders. Therefore, relationships were established with Mennonite friends of Amish people, in order to be introduced to Amish families. After the author demonstrated genuine interest and respect for Amish values, one Amish family allowed the author to move in, and to participate in milking chores and other activities. Data could then be collecting through participation as well as observation. Thus, ethnographic methods included participant observation, as described by Burgess (1984) and Edgerton and Langess (1974). Triangulation was used for verification, as recommended by Patton (1982; 1987; 1990).

The Amish have their own dialect; although they live in America, the Amish primarily speak *Plaudeutsch*, a dialect from northern Germany. This, however, was not a problem, the researcher being fluent in German. A difficulty arose, however, as the Amish believe that photography is sinful, and they do not approve of audio recording – otherwise very useful in ethnography. The author therefore relied on stenography to record interviews. An assistant took notes simultaneously, and both sets were compared for accuracy.

BELIEFS AND SYMBOLISM

Central to the belief system of Amish society is humility expressed as simplicity – in dress, in worship, and in work. The Amish believe in the development of simple, self-sustaining means to livelihood. They reject all modernization which threatens to erode their traditional way of life. To avoid diluting their beliefs, the Amish have consciously refrained from joining mainstream society. An Amish interviewee explained to the author that he knew he was 'missing out' on some aspects of life, but this was 'worth it, because family life is most important'.

The Amish religion is rooted in strong belief in God and in the community; the people believe that belonging to each other is a prerequisite to understanding the work of God. An elderly Amish man told the author, 'Because we reject infant baptism, each member joins voluntarily and shares responsibly.' All this binds the Amish as a sub-culture, which they call their brotherhood. Interaction with outsiders is kept to a minimum, and is generally limited to the economic realm, for example at a roadside stand or farmers' market.

While the Amish People believe that a community of voluntary believers is the context for life, the fundamental unit of Amish society and of the economy is the family. An Amish woman explained, 'Technology enables individuals to drift apart, while the lack of technology forces individuals to struggle together, thereby encouraging closer ties, and strengthening the family unit.' This explains why, although Mennonites accept motor vehicles, Amish people own neither tractors nor automobiles. The horse-drawn cart is the basic form of transportation.

The horse-drawn vehicles of different Amish families vary according to the specific traditions of local church districts. The box-like style of Amish buggies is symbolic of the lack of pretension in Amish life. The body is either made from wood or fibreglass. Tops are sometimes vinyl. A buggy may take ten days to build, and cost a couple of thousand dollars. Horse-drawn vehicles vary slightly according to specific traditions of local church districts. The typical travelling speed of a buggy is 20 kilometres per hour. Rubber tires are not permitted among the Amish.

The horse in Amish society has several roles. Horses are essential in the provision of transportation. They pull heavy cargoes, and they enable people to travel to and from neighbouring towns. On Amish farms, horses are used to plough fields, to sow seeds and later for harvest. Given that mules have more stamina than do horses, 'mules make better farmers and often both work together', the author was told. Both mules and horses are compatible with Amish lifestyle, avoiding any form of ecological damage. An interviewee explained to the author, 'A tractor, a truck and the like are viewed as polluting to the land with their exhaust, while their weight and their broad tires cause physical damage to the ground; in contrast, animals fertilise the ground.'

Although outsiders may perceive these people as living in the past, the Amish do not consider themselves as static, but rather they view themselves to be successful entrepreneurs in the business of making things and growing food. When asked by the author about the lack of scale economies on Amish farmers, an Amish farmer replied that 'life must be seen in the context of a sense of belonging to a community, such that every member feels needed'.

Central to Amish culture is a highly disciplined work ethic. Idleness is shunned. Discipline and self-determination are admired; therefore, the Amish frown on socialist measures such as unemployment insurance, welfare programs and social security payments. However, Amish capitalism includes altruism, family cohesion and a sense of responsibility to the extended family and to the community. This is exemplified by functions such as barn raisings, which are communal events.

The Amish are generally eager to help one another. One Amish woman explained to the author, 'There is a strong emphasis on service to others.'

The Luneville Sewing Circle, for instance, involves fifteen women who have been meeting regularly since the mid-1950s, for the purpose of sewing diapers, panties and gowns for the poor. As well, they make toys for children.

The Amish wear distinctive clothing, the reason being that standardised dress symbolises humility and loyalty to the community. Keeping in line with the religious ideals of searching for simplicity and humility, both men and women seek a modest appearance. Men and boys alike wear broad-rimmed hats, made of black felt or straw. Among men, beards are required after marriage. Moustaches are shaven, an elderly interviewee explained, 'as these were traditionally worn by soldiers in Germany'. Shirts are of solid colours. Suits are hand-made of dark fabrics. Coats are straight-cut with no lapels. Suit coats and vests have no buttons. Black footwear falls in line with plain broad-fall trousers which are held up by suspenders such as to avoid fitting tightly at the waist. Amish women wear long dresses with long sleeves. These are usually very plain, made of solid-coloured fabrics, with cape and apron. It is the norm for Amish women to have long hair and a prayer head-covering, which is white for married women and black for single girls. During cold weather, a bonnet and shawl are worn. Children do not have styles of their own, but rather both boys and girls are expected to dress, look and act like adults. The author noticed that girls have dolls, but with no faces.

An Amish home must also look humble, unadorned, and painted white. In 1919, Amish leaders agreed that houses should not be connected to electricity, lest this could lead to temptations and hence deterioration of family values. There is no phone in the house, but there is access to one not far away, in case of emergency.

Each house alternates as a church, since the Amish never build churches per se; they believe that each home can serve as a house of God. This is consistent with the cultural importance given to frugality and thrift. No money is spent on a separate church building.

PROPAGATING CULTURAL VALUES

Amish society is very structured, with each individual having an assigned role. It is the duty of a wife to oversee all affairs of the home, including the appearance of the house and garden as well as raising the children and sending them to school, where cultural values are reinforced. Laundry is solely the responsibility of girls and women; daughters learn from their mothers. While field work is the occupation of men, women work alongside men during the harvest. Tobacco, for instance, is harvested in late

August and in early September at which time entire families can be seen in the fields.

Schools are never far from the home, as there are over 100 one-room school-houses scattered across Lancaster County. Every Amish family has access to an Amish school within a four-kilometre distance. Each school typically caters to 20 to 40 Amish children up to the age of 16. Eight grades are taught simultaneously in the one classroom. An Amish school is a place where social skills are developed and sports are practised, but most importantly, Amish schools focus on preparing students to become productive members of Amish society. The teacher is either Amish or Mennonite and stresses a sense of community, humility, simplicity, responsibility and the fear of God. There is minimal reference to science, technology, conspicuous consumption and the military. On some days, students bring pets to school.

Homework is a rare phenomenon as it is understood that the children are kept busy helping their respective families with chores. In fact, preference is given to learning by doing rather than by simply sitting in class. School attendance after the age of 12 is limited to three or four hours per week.

Most of one's education is acquired through a process of watching elders in daily life. Children are therefore taught to respect their elders, to obey them, and to learn from them. From a very young age, Amish children develop a close relationship with their parents. Parents spend almost all of their time with their children, teaching them Amish cultural values. It is not from formal education in school, but rather from their parents that children learn to become self-sufficient in life.

Amish boys normally learn a variety of skills on their father's farm. This typically includes cabinetry, carpentry, furniture-making and masonry. Such skills are helpful when seeking non-farm employment or contractual work to enhance or replace subsistence farming. The author observed a heavy reliance on apprenticeship.

Most importantly for the Amish, each generation transmits cultural values to the next. This includes asceticism, frugality and thrift, virtues which Weber (1904; 1905) linked to entrepreneurial behaviour. Children thus become predisposed towards self-employment, as parents guide them along an almost pre-determined road in life. The young are not encouraged to explore such as to discover themselves, but rather to fit into Amish society, and to feel needed within it. Often, a son learns his trade from his father. Even when a son does not adopt the same profession as his father, it is practical to learn as many manual skills as possible. A son becomes the apprentice of his father at a very young age. Not only does a son learn how to work, but more importantly according to Amish tradition, he is conditioned into accepting the Amish belief that work is healthy and enjoyable. During his spare time, a boy will memorize verses from the Bible, in German and English. This will encourage him to choose humility, simplicity and contentment as a way of life. The same way that sons are close with their fathers, mothers are close with their daughters, teaching them to knit, sew, cook, quilt, garden and perform housekeeping tasks.

If an Amish woman wants to marry an outsider, she must leave the community, unless he joins Amish society. A deterrent to her leaving is that she is unprepared for secular society, while a stumbling block in the attempt to become Amish is the dialect.

AMISH ENTERPRISE

Residents told the author that there are approximately 5000 Amish farms in Lancaster County; these are small with no economies of scale. Long hours are invested in the careful planning of crops; this enables Amish farmers to be among the most productive in the world. The Amish have a deep love for their land, and consequently crop rotation is taken very seriously. Much energy is focused to transforming poor soil into productive farmland. Horses fertilise the fields as they plough and harrow.

People grow what they eat, and they eat much of that which they grow. Common crops include corn, hay, wheat, tobacco, soya beans, barley, potatoes and other vegetables. Menus reflect the season. Food is shared with relatives, friends and the needy around the world. Sometimes, surplus is sold.

Profit is given less importance than is religion and its values. The Amish are aware that larger farms would allow them to further benefit from economies of scale. On the other hand, smaller farms allow families to live closer to one another, and for these people, it is more important to have neighbours nearby than to have a larger farm.

Farmers told the author that a typical Amish farmer of Lancaster County has six horses and 35 dairy cows. They elaborated that whether a farmer owns 50 or 100 acres of land, about 10 acres are devoted to pasture for the almost three dozen cattle. A cow's diet might consist of a blend consisting of 50 per cent corn and 50 per cent hay. At its peak, the average cow produces 10 US gallons of milk per day. Cows are milked twice a day, in the early morning and in the late afternoon. This encourages people to perpetuate their custom of early to bed, early to rise.

Since obtaining electricity from a public utility would be contrary to Amish cultural values, cows are milked either by hand, or by diesel-powered milking machines. Careful attention is paid to maintaining a hygienic environment. Milk and ice-cream made from it are deemed satisfactory for personal consumption. However, the law prohibits the sale of homemade ice-cream produced from unprocessed milk.

By milking their own cows, making their own ice-cream, planting their own fruits and vegetables and slaughtering their own cattle, hogs and poultry, the Amish diet is fairly self-sufficient. Surplus calves, usually male, are sold for their meat. The cash is often spent on flour, sugar and sometimes coffee. While it is the norm for an Amish family to own cattle, sheep are much less common, but nonetheless valued for their wool, as well as their meat.

Farm income is supplemented by a variety of activities, some of them seasonal. This includes making furniture and crafts, which are often sold from the house. Such home-based enterprises allow family members to work together, reinforcing the Amish family unit. It also avoids commuting. On Sundays, no sales are made.

Amish farmers often sell surplus fruits, vegetables, and compost from stands near their homes. Some participate in farmers' markets. Sales peak in the late summer and early autumn. Others offer specific services, and some tend to sell primarily to non-Amish customers.

Carpet-making also peaks in the autumn. When the author asked the reason for this, an elderly Amish woman explained, 'When an Amish girl weds, her mother brings leftover balls of fabric, leftovers from making clothing, and she brings these to a carpet-maker who will weave it. This happens in the fall because couples generally get married in October and November, when farms demand relatively less work.'

Farms tend to remain in the possession of the same family, from one generation to the next, and the Amish generally prefer agriculture over other occupations, as it allows them to work without any threat to the family unit. A problem, however, is that the dramatic population growth among the Amish has resulted in a shortage of agricultural land. There are no longer enough farms for all the young, and long-established farms have been sub-divided so many times that many have become crowded. It was explained to the author that young members of Amish communities have therefore been considering employment in the woodwork trade, cottage industries and farm-related activities.

Hence, although Amish people prefer to work on their family farm, this is no longer an easy option for many. For some years, people moved from Lancaster County to other areas, but it appears that young people today prefer to stay in Lancaster County and work in non-farm activities, rather than move to faraway farmland.

A typical Amish enterprise takes the legal form of a sole proprietorship or else that of a partnership, into which each partner contributes capital, and from which no salaries are paid. These businesses are forms of self-employment. Interviewees told the author that very few Amish firms are incorporated. This minimizes paperwork and reduces tax deductions. The Amish see this as an incentive to make their enterprises profitable by being productive.

Although the US Small Business Administration has programs to help such firms, the Amish do not condone government interaction in the economy, and they refuse to accept government support. Section 310 of the Medicare Section of the American Social Security Act permits the Amish to apply for exemption from self-employment tax.

The author noted a very low failure rate of Amish firms. In addition to their Weberian work ethic and frugality, explanatory variables may include the fact that the Amish are focused and cautious. Reflecting their preference for a family operation, the Amish stay away from mass production. They give much attention to details, resulting in high product quality. Seldom does an Amish enterprise have more than seven employees. Many artisans have more clients than they can provide for. Yet none of the small Amish entrepreneurs interviewed by the author expressed interest in expansion.

Some Amish buggies are exported, but this is done via non-Amish middlemen. Handmade Amish quilts[2] also find their way around the world.

Although the Amish economy is capitalist in its orientation, and despite the fact that the Amish People resent socialist intervention on the part of the government, a voluntary form of socialism exists among the Amish. While they reject *externally* imposed measures, the Amish accept *their own* cultural belief that *each* is responsible for the welfare of others.

CONCLUSION

During the Second World War, Stauffer observed, 'Pennsylvania Dutch folk, especially the women, work hard' (1941, p. 65). A decade later, Williams wrote, 'The Pennsylvania "Dutch" were honest, industrious, intelligent and neat, and so they have remained' (1952, p. 503). Gehman added, 'the Amish – and to a lesser degree their neighbors, the Mennonites and the Brethren, or Dunkers – have managed to resist the encroachments of modern civilization' (1965, p. 227). More recently, Hawley wrote, 'For Amish entrepreneurs, the ultimate entrepreneurial goal is not one of profit viability measured in monetary reward and prestige. Instead, it is one of maintaining cultural separateness and conducting their lives and business in a manner that values humility over pride' (1995, p. 315). Hawley elaborated,

> many Amish businesses are family owned and operated. For them, the concept of 'human resources' hardly goes beyond concerns over family affairs. . .Amish businesses are almost exclusively sole proprietorships, and for those who are not, partnerships between fellow church members are formed. Although many would realize tax and legal benefits by incorporation, such legal manoeuvring continues to be viewed by the Amish as antagonistic to their definition of Amish-ness. (1995, pp. 320–21).

All of the above is still true today. An interviewee explained to the author, 'We keep choosing humility and simplicity as a way of life.'

Changes are occurring nevertheless. Hawley observed, 'Amish entrepreneurs tend to cluster heavily in certain small business ventures. This phenomenon can best be described by order of the *Ordnung*, which requires that the Amish establish only those stores and small businesses that meet the product and service needs of the Amish community' (1995, p. 320). Today, some Amish enterprises cater primarily to customers outside Amish communities. This is due to the fact that there are more Amish people wishing to live in Lancaster County, than there is space for them to have farms. Thus it is no longer possible for all the Amish to rely on farming as a means of livelihood. The population of Lancaster County has been rising, while total farming acreage has been falling. Hence, the Amish of Lancaster County have begun to feel the need for non-farm employment, and this has prompted them to create a variety of new ventures, from micro-enterprises producing preserves to larger firms that produce furniture for export.

Religion is an element of social capital, and Borjas (1992) stated that segregation from a host society helps a community retain this capital. Amish people are participating in the global economy, and the outside world is penetrating Amish territory. Yet increased economic integration does not appear to be bringing a significant departure from traditional values. The Amish continue to exhibit a propensity for entrepreneurial behavior, their society is self-sustaining, with virtually no unemployment, and their membership is growing.

NOTES

* This chapter first appeared as Léo-Paul Dana (2007), 'A Humility-based Enterprising Community: The Amish People in Lancaster County', *Journal of Enterprising Communities: People and Places in the Global Economy*, **1** (2), 142–54. Reproduced with permission.

1. The Amish call themselves 'the Plain People', to distinguish themselves from their host society, which they refer to as 'English', 'fancy people', or 'white folk'.
2. Although this was not a focus of the research leading to this paper, Amish quilts have been well documented; see, for example, Hawley (2005).

REFERENCES

Badawi, Abdullah Ahmad (2006), 'Islam and Development', *Global Agenda 2006*, Davos: World Economic Forum, pp. 208–9.

Berger, Peter L., Brigitte Berger and Hansfried Kellner (1973), *The Homeless Mind: Modernization and Consciousness*, New York: Random House.

Borjas, George J. (1992), 'Ethnic Capital and Intergenerational Mobility', *Quarterly Journal of Economics*, **107**, 123–50.

Burgess, Robert G. (1984), *In the Field: An Introduction to Field Research*, London: George Allen & Unwin.

Edgerton, Robert B. and Lewis L. Langess (1974), *Methods and Rules in the Study of Culture*, San Francisco, CA: Chandler and Sharp.

Farmer, Richard N. and Barry M. Richman (1965), *Comparative Management and Economic Progress*, Homewood, IL: Richard D. Irwin.

Fishberg, Maurice (1911), *The Jews: A Study of Race and Environment*, London: Walter Scott.

Foster, Thomas W. (1984), 'Occupational Differentiation and Change in an Ohio Amish Settlement', *Ohio Journal of Science*, **84** (3), 74–81.

Gehman, Richard (1965), 'Plainest of Pennsylvania's Plain People: Amish Folk', *National Geographic*, **128** (2), 227–53.

Guiso, Luigi, Paola Sapienza and Luigi Zingales (2003), 'People's Opium? Religion and Economic Attitudes', *Journal of Monetary Economics*, **50** (1), 225–82.

Hawley, Jana M. (1995), 'Maintaining Business While Maintaining Boundaries: An Amish Woman's Entrepreneurial Experience', *Entrepreneurship, Innovation, and Change*, **4** (4), 315–28.

Hawley, Jana M. (2005), 'The Commercialization of Old Order Amish Quilts: Enduring and Changing Cultural Meanings', *Clothing & Textiles Research Journal*, **23** (4), 102–14.

Hostetler, John A. (1993), *Amish Society*, Baltimore, MD: Johns Hopkins University Press.

Kirzner, Israel (1979), *Perception, Opportunity and Profit Studies in the Theory of Entrepreneurship*, Chicago, IL: University of Chicago.

Klandt, Heinz (1987), 'Trends in Small Business Start-up in West Germany', in Robert Goffee and Richard Scase (eds), *Entrepreneurship in Europe: The Social Processes*, London: Croom Helm, pp. 26–38.

Kraybill, Donald B. (1989), *Riddles of Amish Culture*, Baltimore, MD: Johns Hopkins University Press.

Kraybill, Donald B. and Stephen M. Nolt (2004), *Amish Enterprise: From Plows to Profits*, Baltimore, MD: Johns Hopkins University Press.

Lee, Douglas (1984), 'The Plain People of Pennsylvania', *National Geographic*, **165** (4), 492–519.

Levy, Marion J. (1966), *Modernization and the Structure of Societies: A Setting for International Affairs*, Princeton, NJ: Princeton University Press.

Lewis, W. Arthur (1955), *The Theory of Economic Growth*, Homewood, IL: Richard D. Irwin.

Lowery, Sean and Allen G. Noble (2000), 'The Changing Occupational Structure of the Amish of the Holmes County, Ohio, Settlement', *The Great Lakes Geographer*, **7** (1), 26–37.

Lowry, Tom (1997), 'The Tobacco Farmers of Lancaster County', *Cigar Aficionado*, 120–29.

Patton, Michael Quinn (1982), 'Qualitative Methods and Approaches: What are They?', in Eileen Kuhns and S.V. Martorana (eds), *Qualitative Methods for Institutional Research*, San Francisco, CA: Jossey-Bass, pp. 3–16.

Patton, Michael Quinn (1987), *How to Use Qualitative Methods in Evaluation*, Newbury Park, CA: Sage.

Patton, Michael Quinn (1990), *Qualitative Evaluation and Research Methods*, Newbury Park, CA: Sage.

Penrose, Edith Tilton (1959), *The Theory of the Growth of the Firm*, Oxford: Basil Blackwell.

Rath, Jan and Robert Kloosterman (2003), 'The Netherlands: A Dutch Treat', in Robert Kloosterman and Jan Rath (eds), *Immigrant Entrepreneurs: Venturing Abroad in the Age of Globalization*, Oxford: Berg, pp. 123–46.

Schumpeter, Joseph Alois (1934), *The Theory of Economic Development: An Inquiry into Profits, Capital, Credit, Interest, and the Business Cycle*, trans. by Redvers Opie, Cambridge, MA: Harvard University Press.

Shapero, Albert (1975), 'The Displaced, Uncomfortable Entrepreneur', *Psychology Today*, **7** (11), 83–9.

Sombart, Werner (1911), *Die Juden und das Wirtschaftsleben*, Leipzig: Duncker und Humblot.

Sombart, Werner (1913), *Der Bourgeois*, Munich and Leipzig: Duncker und Humblot.

Sombart, Werner (1915), *The Quintessence of Capitalism*, trans. by M. Epstein, London: T. Fischer Unwin.

Sombart, Werner (1951), *The Jews and Modern Capitalism*, trans. by M. Epstein, Glencoe, IL: Free Press.

Stauffer, Elmer C. (1941), 'In the Pennsylvania Dutch Country', *National Geographic*, **80** (1), 37–74.

Stoll, Steven (2002), *Larding the Lean Earth: Soil and Society in Nineteenth-Century America*, New York: Hill & Wang.

Taft, William Howard (1919), 'The Progressive World Struggle of the Jews for Civil Equality', *National Geographic*, **36** (1), 1–16.

Weber, Max (1904), 'Die protestantische Ethik und der 'Geist' des Kapitalismus. I. Das Problem', *Archiv für Sozialwissenschaft und Sozialpolitik*, **20** (1), 1–54.

Weber, Max (1905) 'Die protestantische Ethik und der "Geist" des Kapitalismus. II. Die Berufsidee des asketischen Protestantismus', *Archiv für Sozialwissenschaft und Sozialpolitik*, **21** (1), 1–110.

Weber, Max (1922), *Wirtschaft und Gesellschaft*, Tübingen: J.C.B. Mohr.

Weber, Max (1930), *The Protestant Ethic and the Spirit of Capitalism*, trans. Talcott Parsons, New York: Charles Scribner's Sons.

Weber, Max (1947), *The Theory of Social and Economic Organization*, trans. Alexander Morell Henderson and Talcott Parsons, London: Hodge.

Williams, Maynard Owen (1952), 'Pennsylvania Dutch Folk Festival', *National Geographic*, **102** (4), 503–16.

Zingales, Luigi (2006), 'Gods and Mammon', *Global Agenda 2006*, Davos: World Economic Forum, pp. 228–9.

10. Mennonite entrepreneurship in Belize

Carel Roessingh and Karen Smits

INTRODUCTION

While economic integration is expanding over the world, its influence appears to be less remarkable on ethnic communities. Entrepreneurs in ethnic communities tend to remain untouched by most developments in the outside world. Aldrich and Waldinger (1990) believe that an ethnic enterprise is a set of connections and regular patterns of interaction among people who share a common background or migratory experiences. In this chapter we will focus on an Anabaptist group, the Mennonites of Blue Creek in Northern Belize. Because of their common religious belief and shared migration history the entrepreneurs in this community can be described as 'ethnic entrepreneurs'. The Mennonites in Belize can be easily distinguished from their non-Mennonite neighbors by their religion, their appearance (not only their white phenotypic characteristics but also their way of dressing), their language (Low-German) and their way of living. Being born and raised in a Mennonite environment makes the individual part of a strict community, in which almost every aspect of life, from the naming of children, to the use of modern technology, to personal appearance and lifestyle, is regulated (Plasil and Roessingh, 2006).

From its early beginnings the Anabaptist movement enclosed significant differentiations concerning religious principles, ideas and opinions (Urry, 1989). Segregations like the Amish, Brethren, Hutterites and Mennonites derived from this movement and spread out over the world. The Anabaptists live according to their religious beliefs, in communities that are alienated from society. However, as a result of their entrepreneurial activities they are able to remain in business and be part of the economical system of their country. The impact of religion on entrepreneurship is a long debated topic that was first addressed by Weber. In his 1904–05 study *The Protestant Ethic and the Spirit of Capitalism* (2002), Weber introduced a link between socio-economic change and religious belief. He argued that Protestants were in possession of all the conditions that are needed for successful entrepreneurial activities. He intended that the skills needed for running a business are similar to the skills that one needs for practicing a religion: trust, loyalty and a sober lifestyle (Roessingh, 2007). For Anabaptists this lifestyle entails that they do not take processes of modernization or any advanced technology for granted and that they basically focus on religion, family and work (Dana, 2007). These social structures connect people from an ethnic group, and the group members use them either inside or outside the community. Ethnic social structures strengthen the networks of kinship and friendship among a community and can be utilized when someone is looking for a job, a place to live or a contact in an institution of the host society (Aldrich and Waldinger, 1990). As a part of their ideology the Anabaptists prefer an independent position towards institutions, which are controlled by the national or local government of the country in which they live, including also aspects of the way they do business and the way they organize their entrepreneurship.

Aldrich and Waldinger (1990) provide a framework to understand the development of ethnic enterprises by using the concepts of opportunity structures, group characteristics and ethnic strategies. Opportunity structures focus on the market conditions and situations that support products or services, which are not available on the non-ethnic market, but also deal with the degree of access to business opportunities. Ethnic entrepreneurs gain advantage from the set of special characteristics that arises within a community of like-minded spirits sharing the same religious background, because the ones who share their needs are best equipped for the job.

Aldrich and Waldinger (1990) identified two dimensions of group characteristics: predisposing factors and resource mobilization. The first is related to the skills and goals that people put into an opportunity, such as selective migration, culture and aspiration levels. Resource mobilization relies on ethnic social networks, organization capability and government policies. Family members are often providers of financial as well as labor capital and therefore ethnic groups with larger families might reap more benefits than others (ibid.).

The third concept, that of ethnic strategies, is a mixture of opportunity structures and group characteristics, concentrating on the adaptation of ethnic groups and their environment. Ethnic entrepreneurs face a number of challenges in establishing and running their business, like acquiring the education and skills needed to run an organization; recruiting and managing efficient, honest and cheap employees; managing relations; surviving business competition and protecting themselves from political attacks (ibid.). For the recruitment of employees the Mennonites in Belize, for instance, mainly use their social network consisting of family and community members. In this manner the Mennonites often make use of the social capital that is present within the community.

The aim of this chapter is to reveal which relations exist between self-employment, ethnic entrepreneurship and social capital. In the first section we will draw attention to the theoretical concepts of self-employment, entrepreneurship and social capital. The methodology of the research is incorporated in this first paragraph. The second section describes who the Mennonites are and why they immigrated to Belize in the first place. With regard to the case of the enterprise 'Maya Papaya' in the third section we will show how the labor recruitment process works in an Evangelical Mennonite Mission Church (EMMC) Mennonite community in Belize. This chapter ends with a conclusion based on the research findings and the theoretical concepts.

1. SELF-EMPLOYMENT, ENTREPRENEURSHIP AND SOCIAL CAPITAL

The Theoretical Concepts

Roessingh (2007) emphasizes that a similarity can be seen between Weber's argument on the relationship between Christianity and the development of a Calvinistic working ethos, and the entrepreneurial success of religious movements like the Mennonites in Belize. Anderson et al. (2000) and Drakopoulou Dodd and Seaman (1998) also confirm a linkage between religion and entrepreneurship. They demonstrate that religion does not only shape society, but is shaped by society as well. Morrison (2000) declares that there is a significant relationship between entrepreneurship and cultural specificity. She states that the cultural context in which people develop themselves plays an influencing role in shaping and making entrepreneurs and the entrepreneurial behavior that they aspire (Morrison, 2000). Beside the cultural context, Morrison advocates that personality, intuition, society and a certain enterprising spirit are also required to be a successful entrepreneur (Smits, 2006). When talking about an enterprise culture, the concept of self-employment should definitely be included. According to Filion one can describe self-employment as 'a person working for himself or herself, and working basically alone, although possibly interacting with others as part of the work' (2004, p. 311).

Filion (2004) has divided self-employment into two types; involuntary and voluntary self-employment. The first group consists of people who were pushed into creating their own means of income by starting to work for themselves. Typically, this group of people never intended to be self-employed, but due to circumstances were forced to work for themselves. The second type of self-employment, the voluntary one, comprises those who always knew that they did not want to work for a boss and would rather work for themselves. The distinction between voluntary and involuntary self-employment can be compared to the two types of self-employment that Dana (1997) identified: orthodox entrepreneurship and reactive self-employment. In his research Dana took a closer look at the fundamental values of entrepreneurial actors to explain the roots of their decision to opt for entrepreneurship. In his literature review he recognized four spheres of influence with respect to the origins of self-employment in ethno-cultural communities. The factors that influence the decision to become an entrepreneur are first of all a focus on the self, secondly a focus on the ethno-cultural milieu, a third focus on the host society, and finally the fourth sphere is a combination of these factors (Dana, 1997). The conditions that Dana used for describing self-employment within an ethnic enterprise can be related to the Mennonites in Belize.

The first factor centers on the individual, the person as an entrepreneur. In this perspective entrepreneurship is more of a personal quality than it is a profession. One needs certain traits to be able to overcome obstacles that an innovator faces when he exposes his ideas in public (Ripsas, 1998). Ripsas (1998) summarizes some characteristics such as a need for completion, self-confidence/a locus of control, the courage to take risks, personal values and age. Morrison (2000) elaborates that the process of entrepreneurship initiation has its foundation in person and intuition, but also in society and culture. She emphasizes that an enterprising spirit is necessary to be successful. 'The key to initiating the process of entrepreneurship lies within the individual members of society, and the degree to which a spirit of enterprise exists, or can be initiated' (Morrison, 2000, p. 59).

In this respect not only the person but also the culture one lives in has a great influence on entrepreneurship (Smits, 2006). For Morrison (2000) both the culture of a society and the characteristics of the people who live in this society are substantial influences on decisions relating to entrepreneurship. This premises are directly in line with the second factor that Dana (1997) formulated as a sphere of influence for self-employment; the focus on the ethno-cultural milieu. Culture and background can be the variables that not only give people the drive to become a self-employed entrepreneur; they can also push people towards entrepreneurial activities. Cultural beliefs and values can persuade them into entrepreneurial behavior. The third factor that can influence their decision to become an entrepreneur is the focus on the host society. Dana and Dana (2007) are convinced that marginal groups have a sense of separateness from their host society and therefore construct their own adaptive mechanism through entrepreneurship.

As a follow-up, entrepreneurship can lead to social recognition, status and respect. With regard to a combination of the three spheres of influence on entrepreneurship, Dana (1997) concentrates on the resources that ethnic groups can use in their host society to expand their entrepreneurial activities. As ethnic groups have contacts in other societies, knowledge of their products, a different attitude, access to values and so on, their business will be able to enlarge based on their marginality in the host society.

An important aspect of being an entrepreneur who uses self-employment as a means of doing business is the amount of social capital that is present in the community. Social capital is an important source that is obtained from a network of connections that allow persons or organizations to enhance access to needed openings and changes (Ryman, 2004). According to Ryman religious affiliation provides a network of relationships that are likely to generate trust, goodwill and mutual aid. Like-minded individuals in a community gain shared security, solidarity and trust based on their connection with the same religion. To a certain extent, religion is a rich and efficient foundation of social capital because it creates a shared background and common thoughts that bind people. The entrepreneur receives significant advantages from social capital (Ryman, 2004).

The term social capital originates from Bourdieu (1977), who argued that society cannot be divided in terms of economic classes, and instead used the concept of fields. This concept can be explained as a social arena in which people interact in search of advantageous resources. A field is a network of social relations between internally structured positions in terms of power, such as laws, norms and created values. Within this social arena people retain capital that they are able to use as their power. Bourdieu (1977) separated four different kinds of capital: economic capital (that is, land and livestock), cultural capital (that is, education), symbolic capital (that is, traditions) and social capital (that is, relations). Social capital is the network that constitutes one's social power. This network of contacts is based on basic assumptions: shared history, common values, shared beliefs, faith and trust. Kraybill and Nolt (1995) described social capital as cultural resources that include the values, norms, customs and skills coupled with kinship and religious arrangements that are available to empower the work of prospective entrepreneurs. By making use of their social capital entrepreneurs are able to expand their activities with support from their friends, family and community members.

Consequently, one could say that access to social capital and the benefits that accumulate from community bonds will stimulate entrepreneurial activities and success. Also, Yeung (2002) emphasizes that social networks serve as an essential source of finance and capital for entrepreneurs who gain these resources from their social and family ties. This 'network capital' is of great value and the main factor for the expansion of entrepreneurial activities (ibid.). The existence of trust is embedded in relationships, because it increases information and financial flows and thus improves opportunities. Yeung (ibid.) defines trust as some kind of common understanding through which interacting parties in a group are expected to avoid opportunism and to promote welfare among members of the network. He states that trust is a constitutive of social life because disputes and clashes can be resolved through shared understandings (ibid.). Trust improves correlations at all levels and can prevent organizations from acting in an opportunistic manner. As a consequence, trust becomes a surrogate for hierarchical contracts and performs as an alternative control mechanism (ibid.).

Self-employment is a function of social capital because the more people support an entrepreneur in his business the more merits an entrepreneur can obtain. In contrast with business studies that see self-employment as being self-sufficient, we argue that this is too narrow an explanation of the concept. In our opinion self-employment can be put into a broader perspective by explaining the concept in the form of recruitment. What the business analysts seem to overlook is that self-sufficiency sometimes means less independence and more homogeneity. Does self-sufficiency produce independent agents or more closely connected stable networks? In our opinion the latter holds true, since recruiting people from the same 'suit' means building a stable network of employees. Companies tend to hire people that are equal to them; they select their employees not just on skills but also take into account their background, values, attitude and interest. When recruiting new employees an entrepreneur has certain traits in mind, predominantly dependability and trustworthiness (Kraybill and Nolt, 1995). Most business people involve their offspring in their work and new employees are usually members of the immediate family or are related to the same religious ethnic group (ibid.).

Redekop et al. (1995) agree that the economy of the Mennonite society is based on a network of personal relationships. Over the years the Mennonites developed a strong set of values and beliefs that were focused on living in harmony, supporting fellow believers through mutual aid and encouraging members to remain faithful (Ryman, 2004). Elements of social capital such as trust, goodwill and mutual aid contribute to the productive Mennonite lifestyle (ibid.). Also cultural resources such as an energetic work ethic, managerial skills, frugality, strong kinship networks and large stable family units facilitate the Mennonites in expanding their entrepreneurial activities (Kraybill and Nolt, 1995). Mennonites are known for their hard work, their sincere attitude, and their quality goods and services that generate opportunities for broader economic possibilities

(Ryman, 2004). Because market demands have increased and companies enlarged, this has influenced the daily operations of the organizations. Whereas most Mennonite organizations were first built upon the help of family members, along with the growth of the company it became necessary to employ workers from outside the family.

Methodology

The data presented in this chapter are the result of an ethnographic research conducted in a Mennonite community in Belize from February until July 2007. As the Mennonites are an offshoot of the Anabaptists and are known for their entrepreneurial activities in Belize, they will be considered ethnic entrepreneurs. The ethnic identity of the Mennonites can be found in their common religious belief, their basic assumptions on life values and life style, and their shared migration history from Western Europe towards Belize. In his other research among the Mennonites, Roessingh (2007) focused on entrepreneurship and changes in the use of technology within different Mennonite communities.

Compared to other Mennonite settlements in Belize, the community in Blue Creek is the most developed in terms of their use of technology, their social-economic position and management thoughts. Since the intention is to offer an insight into the daily life settings of the Mennonite entrepreneurs, qualitative research methods were used to collect information about the Mennonite companies and the role of self-employment within the community. The advantage of qualitative research is that it aims at an in-depth and interpreted understanding of the participants' social world by learning about the context (Ritchie and Lewis, 2003). The best method to gather information about the daily routine of the Mennonite entrepreneurs is through participant observation, hence by living and participating in their community. Next to participant observation informal conversations and semi-structured interviews were used to collect information on the entrepreneurial activities and self-employment within the community. Before the fieldwork period in Blue Creek, general information was collected and a literature review was written in order to gain a better understanding of the Mennonites and the community itself. This review served as input for a topic list that was created in order to organize the process of data collection in the field. As the research progressed this topic list changed to more specified terms and was extended with extra subjects to investigate.

Interviews were held with entrepreneurs, employees and community members. Most interviews had an informal character and were conducted in the natural environment of the respondent; in the organization, on the field or at the house of the respondent. Near the end of the research some more structured interviews were held in order to fill the gaps or to obtain more detailed information. Most informants were approached after the Sunday service at church, since this is one of the most prominent social events within the community. Other informants were mainly approached after, and as a result of, previous interviews with respondents. This method of sample selection is called snowballing (Ritchie and Lewis, 2003). Informal conversations with community members took place on several occasions, while cooking dinner, cleaning the church, helping out on the farm, visiting, and so on. In the course of the research findings were related to academic literature to be able to gain a deeper analytic perception. In the next paragraph we will explain the Mennonite background and clarify the context of this research.

2. THE MENNONITES AS A COHESIVE GROUP WITHIN THE ANABAPTIST MOVEMENT, AND THEIR ROAD TO BELIZE

The Mennonites are a religious group of people who came to Belize in 1958. They hailed from Mexico and Canada, but a long history lies behind this. The Mennonites originate from the Anabaptist movement of the Protestant Reformation in Europe during the first half of the sixteenth century (Everitt, 1983). This movement has its origin in a 'religious-social rebellion' in sixteenth-century Europe (Redekop, 1989, p. 6). The term 'Anabaptist' stands for 're-baptizer', which means that this religious group believed that adults should be baptized based on their choice to follow Christ. In contrast to the then popular approach that children should be baptized soon after birth, the Anabaptists thought that the basis of faith must be a conscious rational decision. The Anabaptists were convinced that a clear distinction was needed between church and government. Therefore, they rejected the authority of a civil/religious government, demanding to baptize children, swear oaths and join military service, because they felt that the scripture suggested a different approach to a life of faith (Ryman, 2004).

A Catholic priest from a town called Witmarsum in the western part of Friesland in the Netherlands, whose name was Menno Simon (1496–1561), became an important leader of the Anabaptist movement. The Anabaptists first emerged in Switzerland, during a time of important social and religious conflicts all over Europe. From the start there have been many separations within the Anabaptist movement with regard to religious principles, ideas and opinions (Urry, 1989). One of the earliest schisms was the breakaway of the followers of Jacob Ammann (the Amish) from the movement in 1693 (Hostetler, 1993; Kraybill, 1989). Other groups within the Anabaptist movement are the Brethren and the Hutterites. A specific group of Anabaptists around Menno Simons, situated in the Northern part of the Netherlands and Germany, formed a cohesive community and were soon called 'the followers of Menno': the Mennonites.

The Anabaptists distinguished themselves from other movements by their requirement for a separation between religious life and state control, their claim to pacifism and their demand to live in self-controlled communities. The Mennonites, as other Anabaptist groups, are not organized in churches but in congregations or communities (Redekop, 1989). The concept of community (*Gemeinde*) has been and still is very important. The Mennonites distance themselves from certain principles such as worldliness, which means that they believe in 'separation from the world' (Loewen, 1993, p. 17). They aspire to maintain their traditional way of life as much as possible by rejecting influences from the world outside of their communities. Due to this they have little contact with the outside world and are recognized as being focused inward. In their attempt to preserve their traditional way of life the Mennonites have been forced to migrate several times, because they were often seen as antagonists by the ruling churches and governments in the countries they lived in. They first migrated to Poland and Prussia, then to Russia, from where they moved between 1874 and 1880 to Manitoba, Canada (Roessingh, 2007). Once in Canada the Mennonites could still not escape from the country's legislation, so the most traditional Mennonites decided to move further south into the Americas (Loewen, 2006). Via Mexico some Mennonite groups finally relocated in Belize.

Belize, formerly known as British Honduras, is a small country that borders Mexico and Guatemala. The country covers 22,966 square kilometers of the Central American continent and has approximately 300 000 inhabitants (Belizean Government, 2007). Belize is a multi-ethnic society, with the Mestizo and Creole as the largest ethnic groups, and English as its official language. As said, the Mennonites arrived in Belize in 1958. In 2000, of a population of 232,111 in Belize, 4.1 per cent of the inhabitants were Mennonites (Central Statistical Office, 2000).

The ethnic identity of the Mennonites is based on a combination of shared assumptions, life values and life style (Roessingh, 2007). Their religious beliefs are based on the way they interpret and use the Christian religion to fulfill their life (Roessingh and Plasil, 2005). According to Everitt (1983) the Mennonites developed their farming to be an important addition to Belizean agriculture and food production. Nowadays Mennonite entrepreneurs lead the national market when it comes to milk, dairy products and poultry. They often visit shops and supermarkets in the cities to sell their products and some Mennonite companies even export their goods.

The government of Belize accepted the Mennonites because they were known for their agricultural skills. The Mennonites were allowed to stay in order to give an impulse to the agriculture in Belize, which at the time was not functioning, and the Belizean government gave them the space to do this by signing the *Privilegium* (Mol, 2005). In this document the Mennonites' exemption of military duty, their freedom to establish their own schools, the right to have their own social system and the abandoning of swearing the oath were included. Their obligations towards the Belizean government were also described: the Mennonites had to bring in investment money, had to produce for the local market and export, and must pay regular taxes (Higdon, 1997). With this agreement the Belizean government aimed at an improvement of the economical situation of the country.

The Mennonites who bought land in the Orange Walk district, in which Blue Creek and Indian Creek are situated, were members of the Old Colony congregation, a group that originated from a split in Canadian Mennonite settlements in the 1870s and that was known for their traditional way of life. Outsiders used the name Old Colony to refer to 'those people who were loyal to a rigid belief-system and a traditional way of life' (Redekop, 1969, p. 10). This name was also adopted by the members themselves.

Members of the Old Colony church aim to preserve their lifestyle and reject innovations and modern technology (Roessingh and Plasil, 2006). Horse and buggy is still the main use of transportation within Old Colony communities. As the Old Colony Mennonites maintained their traditional values in life and in their agricultural practices, they experienced more problems than other communities in expanding their cultivated acreage (Hillegers, 2005). The group that came down to settle in Spanish Lookout, in the Cayo district, derived from the *Kleine Gemeinde* congregation that was founded in 1874 as a response to the establishment of the Russian Mennonite Church (Loewen, 1993; 2006; Roessingh and Plasil, 2005). Originally this congregation led a traditional life, but the *Kleine Gemeinde* Mennonites became more progressive after their migrations towards Belize. Over the years another Mennonite congregation called the Evangelical Mennonite Mission Church (EMMC) came to Belize. This congregation had its roots in Canada and built its first church in Belize in Blue Creek. The EMMC church is the most progressive congregation within the Belizean Mennonite communities. Services on Sunday, in contrast with the other congregations in Belize, are active, women and men are sitting side by side and the sermons are accompanied by music. During the week several bible study groups are organized in people's houses.

Nowadays there are 12 communities in Belize that are related to the Mennonite religion, not all of which can be divided strictly into this partition because some are related more closely to the Amish offshoot of the religion, and are therefore more traditional, and some congregations are a mixture of the Old Colony and *Kleine Gemeinde* adherents. The communities of Spanish Lookout and Blue Creek can be seen as the most progressive Mennonite communities in Belize because they both have a strong economic position and an intensive economic exchange beyond the boundaries of their community (Roessingh, 2007). In the next paragraph the Maya Papaya case will provide an insight into a Mennonite enterprise and reveal how recruitment is practised within this Mennonite organization.

3. MAYA PAPAYA: NOT MACHINERY BUT HANDS ARE THE MOST IMPORTANT INSTRUMENTS TO CULTIVATE PAPAYAS

Blue Creek: The Community

Blue Creek is located in northwestern Belize, east of the Guatemalan border, south of the Mexican border and near the intersection of the Azul, Bravo and Hondo rivers. This isolated area is part of the Orange Walk district of Belize. Driving from the city of Orange Walk to Blue Creek, you follow an unpaved, bumpy road, passing small Belizean villages called Yo Creek, Trinidad, San Lazaro, August Pine Ridge and San Felipe. After a one-hour drive the hills of Blue Creek appear in sight and once you have crossed a little bridge across the Bravo, the road is paved again. You have now arrived in Blue Creek.

When the Mennonites arrived in Blue Creek in 1958 this area was nothing more than a dense jungle, covered by forests interspersed with swamp savannas with tacky and tough soils (Hillegers, 2005). The Mennonites had to overcome difficulties related to the agro environment and suffered from the malaise caused by the tropical climate that was new to them. They also had to learn how to grow crops in this climate and changed to different products than they were used to cultivating; from oats and wheat in Canada and Mexico to rice, beans and tropical fruits in Belize.

In the first years a shift from traditional towards a more progressive Mennonite lifestyle took place in the community; the frictions about the use of technology became stronger. Some men were convinced that it was impossible to clear the land with steel tires, whereupon they started to use machines with rubber tires. For this reason the more traditional Mennonites left the community and started a new settlement located about 25 kilometers eastwards: Shipyard. Since the uproar in the community kept on going, the EMMC church from Canada sent help in order to structure and organize life in the community. The EMMC is more progressive than the Old Colony and therefore a partition between the two different churches appeared. The EMMC built a new school, church and clinic for the people who had turned away from the Old Colony and peace returned. What once was a dense jungle has been transformed into cultivated hills where crops are grown and cattle are raised. In 1978 the Old Colony partisans had become a minority in the community and most of them left for Bolivia, whereas others joined the *Kleine Gemeinde* church (Kok, 2006).

Nowadays followers of the *Kleine Gemeinde* live in harmony with the EMMC Mennonites in Blue Creek. Both churches have their own school, clinic and shops, but there is no more uproar about the practice of the Mennonite religion. In 2007, the community has about 800 inhabitants and is known as an advanced Mennonite community in the country. The progressive Mennonites distinguish themselves by making use of a more developed economic system of commercial agriculture and agribusiness in their community (Roessingh and Schoonderwoerd, 2005). The organizations in the community do not only produce in order to supply the inhabitants of Blue Creek, but export their products to the local market as well. The Mennonites have created a well-organized network of distribution and transport, and deliver quality products; this way their organizations have become dominant businesses in the country (ibid.). The businesses that are established by Blue Creek Mennonites are all related to agroculture; for example Circle R. is a rice mill, Caribbean Chicken is a chicken slaughterhouse, Valley Ranch Enterprises is a construction company, the Rempels maintain a mechanic shop, practice crop dusting and raise cattle, and Maya Papaya produces papayas. The smaller firms also concentrate on chicken, rice, beans, fruit or cattle. This chapter addresses Maya Papaya and emphasizes to what extent the social capital within the community has had an influence on self-employment and entrepreneurship. We will illustrate how two Mennonite communities work together and exclude outsiders in the recruitment process.

Maya Papaya: The Company

When the Mennonites arrived in Blue Creek, they had no experience with the tropical climate and with producing food in this environment. It took them years of trial and error to adapt to the circumstances in Belize.

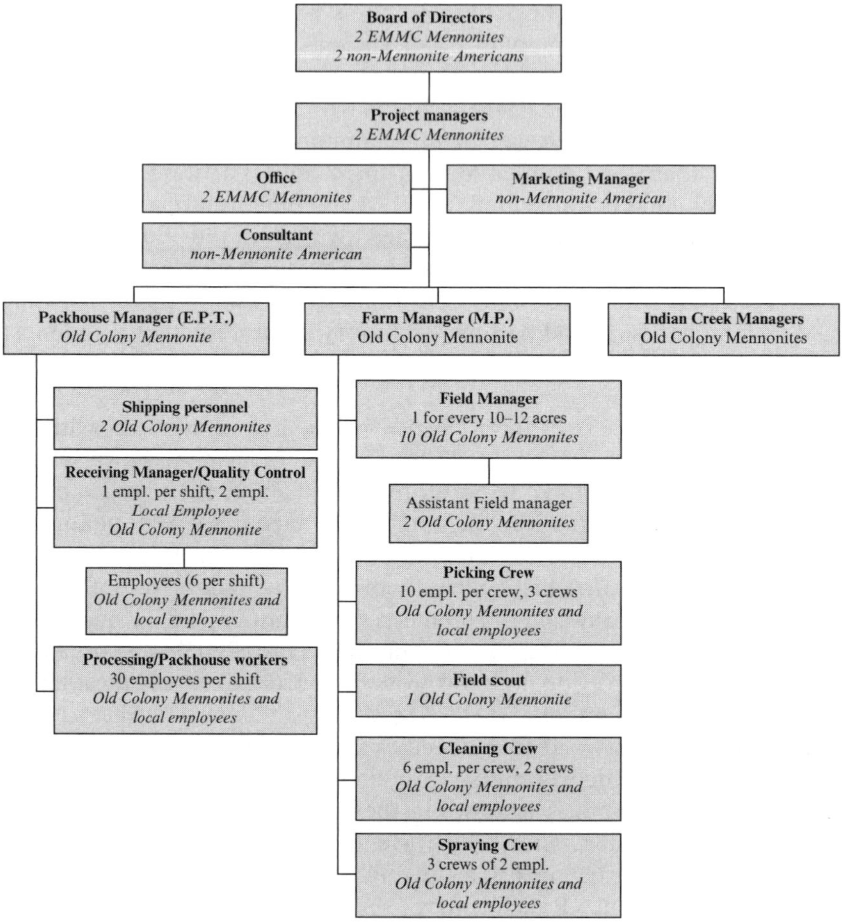

Source: Smits (2006).

Figure 10.1 Organization chart for Maya Papaya

Hard work, perseverance and a strong internal cohesion resulted in the advantages the Mennonites needed to expand as a thriving community. Risks were taken, chances exploited and opportunities developed; the Mennonites expanded business where possible.

Maya Papaya (Figure 10.1) started in 2006 as an initiative of a Canadian Mennonite (Mr Thiessen) who had come over to visit his family, decided to survive the Canadian winters in Blue Creek and built a house in the community. For over four years he and his family have been traveling back and forth between Canada and Belize. During the Canadian winters they live in Blue Creek and when the rainy season in Belize starts, they move back to Canada. In Canada Mr Thiessen runs an asparagus company and through this business he came into contact with two American businessmen (Phil and his son James) who run an asparagus company in Arkansas, USA. Mr Thiessen posed the idea of starting a business in Belize and asked for support. The Americans only wanted to be involved in a company in Belize if Mr Dyck would take part in this business. They had known Mr Dyck for a long time and had discussed several business proposals with him before. At that time, Mr Dyck was involved in a rice business that he had inherited from his father. He owned many acres of land close to Hillbank (further south in the Orange Walk district), which appeared to be fertile soil for papayas. Mr Thiessen and Mr Dyck met via the American businessmen and determined to set up a papaya company, although neither of them had any experience with growing tropical fruit. Beside the fact that the soil seemed to be of the right quality to grow papayas, the investors also anticipated that the closely located Mennonite community Indian Creek could offer labor to work on the papaya fields.

Indian Creek is a sister community of the Old Colony Mennonites in Shipyard. A shortage of land among the farmers in Shipyard resulted in the 1970s in a split in the community, when the younger couples left to find their own property. In Indian Creek they built an Old Colony community according to their traditional religious values and tried to set up a farming system. The farmers tried to live off the land as much as they could by logging trees and planting corn. However, there was little financial capital so most Mennonites from Indian Creek worked in wage labor for other Mennonite communities, in furniture manufacturing, slaughterhouses, feed mills or rice fields.

The Old Colony Mennonites in Indian Creek maintain a traditional way of life; horse and buggy are still used for transportation, women wear long dresses and head covering (white for non-married, black for married women) and men are dressed in overalls with plain colored shirts and wear straw hats. For field work the Old Colony Mennonites use tractors with iron tires, because rubber tires are not allowed. The inhabitants of Indian Creek are focused inward and most of them only speak Low German. Indian Creek is known as a very poor community and according to several respondents the population needs help to survive. Even manufacturing products such as rice or beans is too expensive for this Mennonite group because the purchase of machinery for farming is so costly. Maya Papaya has become an important opportunity for Indian Creek; not machinery but hands are the most important instruments to cultivate papayas.

To start up Maya Papaya the shareholders all invested money and were involved in the strategic decisions about the company. Officially, they constitute the Board of Directors of both Maya Papaya and the asparagus company in Arkansas, but the tasks are divided. Mr Dyck and Mr Thiessen (who still runs an asparagus company in Canada as well) are responsible for the daily operation of Maya Papaya and the Americans are responsible for running the company in Arkansas. When it comes to major decisions such as investment or strategic changes the shareholders get together to discuss these. Both Mrs Thiessen and Mrs Dyck support their husbands by taking care of the administration in the office. Every two weeks the marketing manager (son in law of one of the US shareholders) organizes a conference call, which is used to keep each other informed about both organizations.

Since none of the shareholders had any previous experience in growing papayas, they had to conduct research first. They visited a local papaya company in the north of the country and learned a lot through Mennonites in a community called Little Belize, who had been growing papayas for several years. The men also went to Guatemala to observe similar projects in order to collect as much information as possible. An American consultant was hired to advise the company on the quality of the fruit. He visits the fields in Belize about every two months and teaches the workers how to prevent spots on the fruit and how to produce the best size and shape for the export market. As Mr Dyck states, 'half the taste is in the looks' (interview 17 April 2007). After doing research about growing papayas and setting up a business in Belize the shareholders learned that it would be to their benefit to set up two companies. This way they would be able to profit from the Belizean tax system that contains a law on export processing zones (EPZ). An EPZ is a free trade zone where duty and quotas are reduced and governmental business laws are lowered in favor of new businesses and foreign investments. In general, EPZ areas are the core of intensive manufacturing labor and the import of materials or components and the export of goods form the main industry. With this in mind the shareholders decided to divide the growing and picking of the papayas (Maya Papaya) from the treatment and packaging of the fruits (Eagle Produce Tropics). As a result the company is known in Belize as Maya Papaya and in the United States as Eagle Produce Tropics, because this company actually exports the products. In this chapter we will refer to Maya Papaya for the organization as a whole.

Hillbank is located about 50 kilometers further south of Blue Creek and since the road to this area is not paved it takes over an hour to drive to Maya Papaya. Therefore, Mr Dyck and Mr Thiessen share a little plane (Cessna) with which transport to the plant only takes about 15 minutes. When flying from Blue Creek to Maya Papaya they can see the papaya fields and the buildings that belong to the company from high above. A fence surrounds Eagle Produce Tropics to indicate the EPZ border. From the air they can see that everything is properly organized; fields and buildings are situated perpendicularly in relation to each other. In the fields people are working; spraying the trees, picking fruit or cleaning the ground by taking away leaves. Maya Papaya started in 2007 by exporting two containers of fruit to the United States per week; after the first quarter of the year this amount increased to an average of 10 containers per week and this amount is expected to increase to 25 containers per week by the end of the year. 'The business is growing much faster than we expected, if this growth continues, then we will manage to reach the goal as described in the business plan. I never thought we would make it that far!' (Mr Dyck, interview 17 April 2007).

In March 2007 about nine fields were planted with papaya trees, but more land is being prepared for planting trees. Mr Dyck explained that Maya Papaya does not own all the surrounding acres; other farmers also decided to grow papayas and bought land in this area. One respondent from Blue Creek explained that he decided to quit his rice business because after five years of hard work he only managed to reach breakeven, which was not enough. With the help of others who had bought land in Hillbank he changed to the papaya business and prepared his fields for papayas. The profit will be shared between the owners of the fields and himself.

Maya Papaya is organized to support farmers to grow papayas. The farmers can sell their fruit to the company that will take care of the transportation and export of the papayas. Although Maya Papaya has only existed for over a year, 100 farmers from Indian Creek and Blue Creek have already committed themselves to growing papayas for Maya Papaya. This shows how much trust the farmers have in the company and the papaya business itself. Mrs Dyck explained that the people from Indian Creek were desperate to start up something to earn money with and were happy to seize the opportunity that Maya Papaya offers. The company pays for first expenses so the farmers can start growing papayas and pay back their debts by delivering papayas that meet the company's standards (regarding size and shape).

Within this same period of time the company employed 100 workers, most members of the Indian Creek community. Due to the fact that the company is expanding faster than expected, Mr Dyck had to go to San Felipe to ask locals to work for them. He explained: 'There are no more employees available in Indian Creek, almost everyone is working for us, but we need more workers and we have received phone calls from San Felipe almost every day for the last few months, asking if they can work for us' (interview 28 March 2007).

Two weeks later the production process changed from one shift a day to two 12-hour shifts a day and 30 people from San Felipe started working for Maya Papaya. The shareholders expect they will need more employees soon, because a new packing machine will soon arrive. This machine was invented at Mr Thiessen's asparagus company in Canada and should make it possible to pack five or six containers a day (instead of two, as is the case at the moment). In order to keep the machine running, the company will need double the number of employees in the future. A respondent made clear that it is difficult to find skilled employees:

> Finding a new manager is very hard because no one is well-skilled. We should train someone, but we don't have the time for that, besides no one is available right now. I have once tried to train somebody from San Felipe, but it never worked out, because they don't pick up the game as easily. It costs me too much time. (Interview 4 May 2007)

Employees at Maya Papaya earn on average 30 Belizean dollars (15 USD) a day, managers make 75 Belizean dollars (37 USD) per day. Mr Dyck admits that he would like to pay more to some of his employees, but that this is not possible because it would not be in accordance with the salaries paid in the rest of the country. An entrepreneur from Blue Creek admitted that he sometimes feels guilty for paying his employees just 30 BZD a day, but 'if you pay them more they will see all the money, decide to quit, spend all the money and come back a couple of months later because all the money is gone' (interview 5 April 2007). This respondent assumes that local employees are not reliable when they earn a higher salary. Given that it is not part of their culture, employees do not receive a contract when they start working for Maya Papaya. 'It is very Mennonite to trust each other. My word is what I will do, so if I promise to do something, you can trust me on my word for it' (Mr Dyck, interview 17 April 2007). Although trust and reliability are very important in the Mennonite culture, at the higher levels the company formulates contracts, for example in business deals like they have with a company in the United States that has committed to sell exclusively for Maya Papaya.

In addition to the papaya business Maya Papaya has started with an onion project. The main reasons for this project are investment, protection of the papaya fields and the social aspect. The social aspect is based on the farmers who do not have the skills or the patience to grow papayas. The papaya growing process takes 10 months before a farmer can sell his first fruits and according to Mr Dyck farmers easily give up on this. The onion process is shorter and therefore more interesting for farmers who have the knowledge to cultivate onions. As the farmers have the skills, they will do the work while Maya Papaya will pay for the expenses and put the unions on the market. The company has also initiated this project in order to protect the papaya fields. Besides the fact that onions are a good crop for rotation on a papaya field, Maya Papaya wants to hinder its competitors. A Belizean papaya company is trying to rent property in surrounding villages to farm papayas. Since the competitors only rent the land, they will not protect it from viruses and insects that could also harm closely situated papaya fields from Maya Papaya. Instead, Maya Papaya will buy the land from its owners, and guarantees the farmers that they will be able to work on it for at least 10 years. With this project the company is protecting its papaya fields from destruction by competitors.

Maya Papaya is expanding with respect to projects as well as employees. Whereas the company first only hired people from Indian Creek, currently more and more non-Mennonites are hired. Mrs Dyck elaborated that the shareholders experience difficulties in working with the Mennonites from Indian Creek. She stated that although they share the same background, the EMMC Mennonites are brought up differently, in a fashion that the Old Colony Mennonites would label 'more worldly'. The owners respect the Old Colony religion by, for example, arranging two buses to drive the employees from Indian Creek to Hillbank, one for the men and one for the women. At the shop floor though, everyone is expected to work together. Mr Dyck explained that within the Old Colony, class differences are very important and that this has caused friction between managers before. Class difference is based on family name and has resulted in tension within the work force. For example when two managers had a discussion about an issue, it appeared that one manager found it hard to respect the older, but 'lower class' other manager and therefore did not want to admit that he was wrong. Mr Dyck stated that these issues are based on cultural differences: 'It is human to think that you are better than anyone else, but we have been taught to look beyond that, they [Old Colony Mennonites] haven't' (interview 17 April 2007).

In the beginning Indian Creek Mennonites refused to work with non-Mennonites as well. Maya Papaya does not accept this distinction and has been teaching the employees to cooperate with everyone, regardless of their class or background. Blue Creek Mennonites or English-speaking Mennonites from Indian Creek hold the managerial positions within Maya Papaya. Indian Creek Mennonites and native Belizeans fill lower positions such as picking, cleaning and packing the fruit. Respondents mentioned that in their opinion natives can only perform one task at the time, do not have the skills to take responsibilities or the mindset to work as hard as a Mennonite. Every manager recruits new employees on demand of Mr Dyck. He explains that he asks the managers to hire some more people and whether the new employees should be Mennonites or local Belizeans. This distinction is based on knowledge and reliability; the Indian Creek Mennonites have received less schooling than the native Belizeans but the Mennonites are still entrusted with more responsibilities. Mennonites learn faster and want to work harder, in his experience: 'Mennonites are workaholics, natives have a different attitude. They rather work from 9 to 5 and take no responsibilities' (interview 28 March 2007). Another respondent from Blue Creek emphasized that 'On local workers you always have to keep an eye. . . . You have to be on top of them all the time' (interview 20 April 2007).

In the packaging area some young boys who appear to be no more than 12 years old assist by unfolding carton boxes. Mr Dyck clarified that the company hired a family for this task and the parents took along their kids to help out. Maya Papaya has set the rule not to hire people under the age of 14, but after a talk with the Minister of Education they decided that the Old Colony culture can be taken in consideration regarding this law. 'If they bring their older children to do this job, then these younger ones have to work on the field. I guess this job is less physical than working on the fields' (Mr Dyck, interview 8 May 2007).

Mrs Dyck could tell that the Indian Creek Mennonites have a better life than before they worked for the company. 'I can see the packaging manager growing. Do you see the buttons on his blouse? They fit tight the last few weeks' (informal conversation, 28 March 2007). Due to the fact that the Old Colony Mennonites have a steady income, Mr Dyck noted that their identity is slowly changing towards a worldlier character. Although this is not visible for the outside world yet, he sees the differences in the homes of Indian Creek inhabitants. Mrs Dyck compares the changes with Blue Creek:

> When you look at Blue Creek you don't see any of the girls wearing a head cover these days, things will go the same way in Indian Creek. It just takes time. I hope they don't lose their identity and start to think that they can be someone else, because they can't. (Interview 17 April 2007).

Maya Papaya has had a big impact on the Old Colony Mennonites in Indian Creek. It has been a positive development so far, since they have work opportunities and a solid income. Respondents agreed when we asked about the Mennonite mindset to work from sunrise to sunset and consent on the need to work for themselves. Answers were always related to the way Mennonites have been raised. Some respondents even said that Mennonites are life-long entrepreneurs because it is impossible to take the entrepreneurial frame of mind out of a person.

'I RATHER WORK WITH BROTHERS THAN WITH OTHERS': A CONCLUSION

The aim of this chapter has been to elaborate on the extent to which social capital has an influence on self-employment in relation to entrepreneurship. After a theoretical review we described the context of our research among the Mennonites in Belize and illustrated a case to support the research results. As discussed we have taken into account a different interpretation of the concept of self-employment. Whereas business studies focus on the decision to become an entrepreneur we have expanded the concept by focusing at the recruitment process of entrepreneurs. Exploiting the first definition, Mennonite respondents answered that they want to be self-employed in order to invest money and to be able to do things their own way. As a respondent said in an informal conversation: 'Mennonites want to be free! See, if I want a day off, what the heck, then I take my day off. If I have the chance to do what I want whenever I want, then I rather run my own business and let other people do the work' (interview 9 May 2007). This response is more closely related to Filion's (2004) business perspective on self-employment, who advocates an individual approach. His definition of the concept concentrates on the decision to become an entrepreneur that can be involuntary or voluntary. The Mennonites in this case started Maya Papaya on a voluntary basis. However, this does not imply that they are free in their choice of employees.

Mennonites are involved in a network based on their religion and ethnic background. As part of this network the entrepreneurial Mennonites of Blue Creek are connected to aspects such as loyalty and trust towards the Mennonites of Indian Creek. In our view this is based on what Bourdieu (1977) calls social capital. In this chapter, we take a more collective approach of the concept self-employment. We do not concentrate on the entrepreneur and his decision to start an enterprise, but more on his choice of employees. An essential part of this is the entrepreneur's preference for employees who are part of the same social network, share the same background, values, attitude and interest. Mennonite recruitment is mainly focused on hiring people who share the same basic assumptions. With the case of Maya Papaya we showed how the labor recruitment process is implemented within a Mennonite enterprise in Belize. The first selection of employees centered on people from Indian Creek. Due to the growth of the company the labor pool of Indian Creek appeared not sufficient for Maya Papaya, therefore the entrepreneurs recruited employees beyond their ethnic group; the Mestizo from San Felipe. This is an interesting development because it was not intended in the first place. For the people from Indian Creek, Maya Papaya plays an important role in their social-economic position. The initiative from the Blue Creek Mennonite entrepreneurs gave the Mennonites from Indian Creek the opportunity to invest in their own community. Since the inhabitants gain a stable income they are not as poor as they used to be.

Another aspect of this case is a more general view: whereas the world is in progress and chances on the market become more and more important, this does not immediately reflect on Mennonite communities. Small companies that produce only for their own community do not take part in the world's economic integration. Big companies that extend their products beyond the community on the other hand, do compete on the world market. Maya Papaya is a good example of the latter. The company is expanding and, as a consequence, it is necessary to seek labor and expertise external to the Mennonite society. Nevertheless, the case of Maya Papaya demonstrates that recruitment is first of all based on ethnic background and shared beliefs. Entrepreneurs prefer to have employees from the same 'suit' rather than natives. Trust and loyalty are the main bases for recruitment within Mennonite enterprises.

Departing from a group rather than individual perspective recruitment plays an important role in the realization of self-employment in the case of the Mennonites of the Maya Papaya company, in the sense that recruitment serves as the basis to benefit and strengthen their own religious ethnic group.

Or, as a respondent revealed: 'I rather work with brothers than with others' (informal conversation, 18 April 2007).

REFERENCES

Aldrich, H.E. and R. Waldinger (1990), 'Ethnicity and Entrepreneurship', *Annual Review of Sociology*, **16**, 111–35.

Anderson, A., S. Drakopoulou-Dodd and M. Scott (2000), 'Religion as an Environmental Influence on Enterprise Culture. The Case of Britain in the 1980s', *Journal of Entrepreneurial Behaviour & Research*, **6** (1), 5–20.

Belizean Government (2007), available at: http://www.governmentofbelize.gov.bz/ (accessed 12 September 2007).

Bourdieu, P. (1977), *Outline of a Theory of Practice*, Cambridge: Cambridge University Press.

Central Statistical Office (2000), *Population Census 2000: Major Findings*, Belmopan, Belize: C.S.O. Ministry of Budget Management.

Dana, L.P. (1997), 'The Origins of Self-employment in Ethno-cultural Communities: Distinguishing between Orthodox Entrepreneurship and Reactionary Enterprise', *Revue Canadienne des Sciences de L'Administration*, **14** (1), 52–69.

Dana, L.P. (2007), 'Humility-based Economic Development and Entrepreneurship among the Amish', *Journal of Enterprising Communities: People and Places in the Global Economy*, **1** (2), 142–54.

Dana, L.P. and T. Dana (2007), 'How Do Self-employed Sami People Perceive the Impact of the EU and Globalisation?', *International Journal of Business and Globalisation*, **1** (1), 1–19.

Drakopoulou Dodd, S. and P. Seaman (1998), 'Religion and Enterprise: An Introductory Exploration', *Entrepreneurship: Theory and Practice*, **3** (1), 71–87.

Everitt, J.C. (1983), 'Mennonites in Belize', *Journal of Cultural Geography*, **3** (2), 82–93.

Filion, L.J. (2004), 'Two Types of Self-Employed in Canada', in L.P. Dana, (ed.) *Handbook of Research on International Entrepreneurship*, Cheltenham: Edward Elgar, pp. 308–29.

Hillegers, P. (2005) 'Spanish Lookout Belize. Mennonites in Perspective', MA thesis, Vrije Universiteit Amsterdam.

Hidgon, F.X. (1997) 'Farm Diversification and Specialization: The Adaptation of Mennonite Households in Spanish Lookout, Belize', PhD dissertation, University of Pittsburgh.

Hostetler, J.A. (1993), *Amish Society*, 4th edn, Baltimore, MD: Johns Hopkins University Press.

Kraybill, D.B. (1989), *The Riddle of Amish Culture*, Baltimore, MD: Johns Hopkins University Press.

Kraybill, D.B. and S.M. Nolt (1995), *Amish Enterprise. From Plows to Profits*, Baltimore, MD: Johns Hopkins University Press.

Kok, A. (2006), 'Blue Creek; Belize's Backyard. Developments of Changes of the Health Care in a Mennonite Community', MA thesis, Vrije Universiteit Amsterdam.

Loewen, R. (1993), *Family, Church and Market: A Mennonite community in the Old and New Worlds, 1850–1930*, Urbana, IL: University of Illinois Press.

Loewen, R. (2006), *Diaspora in the Countryside: Two Mennonite Communities and Mid-Twentieth-Century Rural Disjuncture*, Toronto: University of Toronto Press.

Mol, L. (2005), 'Over Working Ladies en General Managers of Household Affairs. Processen van continuiteit en verandering op de arbeidsmarkt voor Mennonietenvrouwen in Spanish Lookout, Belize', Master's thesis, Vrije Universiteit Amsterdam.

Morrison, A. (2000), 'Entrepreneurship: What Triggers It?', *International Journal of Entrepreneurial Behaviour & Research*, **6** (2), 59–71.

Plasil, T. and C. Roessingh (2006), 'Food and Community – The Role of Sharing a Meal Among the Mennonite of Shipyard, Belize', *Belizean Studies*, **28** (1), 42–56.

Redekop, C. (1969), *The Old Colony Mennonites: Dilemas of Ethnic Minority Life*, Baltimore, MD: Johns Hopkins University Press.

Redekop, C. (1989), *Mennonite Society*, Baltimore, MD: Johns Hopkins University Press.

Redekop C., S.C. Ainlay and R. Siemans (1995), *Mennonite Entrepreneurs*, Baltimore, MD: Johns Hopkins University Press.

Ritchie, J. and J. Lewis (2003), *Qualitative Research Practice. A Guide for Social Science Students and Researchers*, London: Sage.

Ripsas, S. (1998), 'Towards an Interdisciplinary Theory of Entrepreneurship', *Small Business Economics*, **10**, 103–15.

Roessingh, C. (2007), 'Mennonite Communities in Belize', *International Journal of Business and Globalisation*, **1** (1), 107–24.

Roessingh, C. and T. Plasil (2005), 'We're Growing Belize. Religious Differentiation and Identity Construction among Mennonite Communities in Belize', paper presented at SSHA conference, Portland.

Roessingh, C. and T. Plasil (2006), 'From Collective Body to Individual Mind: Changes in Leadership and Attitudes in an Old Colony Mennonite Community in Northern Belize', *Journal of Mennonite Studies*, **24**, 57–74.

Roessingh, C. and A. Schoonderwoerd (2005), 'Traditional Farmers or Modern Businessman? Religious Differentiation and Entrepreneurship in a Kleine Gemeinde Community in Belize', *Journal of Developmental Entrepreneurship*, **10** (1), 65–77.

Ryman, J.A. (2004), 'Are You at Peace with God and Your Neighbour? Cultural Resources and Restraints on Mennonite Entrepreneurship', in C.H. Stiles and C.S. Galbraith (eds), *Ethnic Entrepreneurship: Structure and Process. International Research in the Business Disciplines*, vol. 4, Amsterdam: Elsevier, pp. 203–17.

Smits, K. (2006), 'Moving Borders. Power and Entrepreneurship among the Mennonites in Belize', BA thesis, Vrije Universiteit Amsterdam.

Urry, J. (1989), *None but Saints: The Transformation of Mennonite Life in Russia 1789–1889*, Winnipeg: Hyperion Press, Hyperion Press.

Weber, M. (2002), *The Protestant Ethic and the Spirit of Capitalism*, 3rd Roxbury edn, Los Angeles, CA: Roxbury. First published 1904–05.

Yeung, H.W. (2002), 'Entrepreneurship in International Business: An Institutional Perspective', *Asia Pacific Journal of Management*, **19**, 29–61.

11. Collective entrepreneurship in a Mennonite community in Paraguay*

Léo-Paul Dana and Teresa E. Dana[1]

INTRODUCTION

Does enterprise develop the same way amongst all peoples? The convergent perspective was asserted by Farmer and Richman, 'As the general similarity of men everywhere is recognized, and as managerial and technological necessity presses all types of culture toward a common road, nations everywhere become more similar' (1965, p. 400). In contrast, advocates of the divergent position include Hofstede (1980) and Laurent (1983). Subsequently, Huntington (1993; 1996) showed that globalization has neither standardized societies, nor produced a homogeneous world culture. This paper will support the divergent perspective, demonstrating that the nature of collective entrepreneurship among the Mennonites is unlike entrepreneurship in mainstream society.

Farmer and Richman wrote, 'Prevailing religious beliefs and cultural values, in conjunction with parental behavior, child-rearing practices, and the formal system of education in a particular country, usually have a direct and very significant bearing on the dominant view toward work and achievement' (1965, pp. 156–7). This chapter will examine the impact of prevailing religious beliefs on the dominant view toward work and achievement. The focus of this chapter is the Menno Colony of the Chaco, one of the Mennonite communities in Paraguay. It will be illustrated that the values of this religious minority appear to facilitate successful collective entrepreneurship. The Mennonites have prospered here and their activities have created jobs for indigenous people who come from distant places to work for the Mennonites.

MENNONITES

Renshaw described the Mennonites as 'members of a nonconformist church that broke away from Calvin and Zwingli in the sixteenth century' (2002, p. 40). Mennonites adhere to the teachings of the Dutch reformer, Menno Simons. Central to Mennonite doctrine are asceticism, frugality, and thrift along with strict discipline.

They are ideological descendants of a religious movement, which had its origins in the Anabaptist[2] wing of the Protestant Reformation in Western Europe during the early sixteenth century (Dyck, 1967; Redekop, 1989). The Anabaptist movement was founded in Switzerland, in 1525, and the religion began to spread in Germany, and in the Netherlands, as well as in Switzerland. As noted by Roessingh and Schoonderwoerd, 'Hostile reactions from the more established churches to Anabaptist practices, such as adult baptism, non-resistance, their opinion that the church and state should be separated, and their attitude to place themselves outside the political arena, led to persecution. In response to these persecutions, Mennonite groups migrated from Western Europe' (2005, pp. 67–8).

Persecuted in Western Europe, many moved to the Ukraine during the 1700s. The first group of Mennonite immigrants went to the New World in 1683. Others relocated to Canada during the 1800s. Renshaw explained, 'Persecuted in Russia and facing problems with the education board in Canada, they sent expeditions to the Chaco in the 1920s to look for lands that would be suitable for colonization and sufficiently isolated to allow them to practice their religion unmolested by outside interference' (2002, p. 40).

Hecht (1994) studied Mennonites that remained in Canada; based on their relatively low income, compared to other Canadians, he argued that Mennonites did not embrace the Protestant work ethic. *The Protestant Ethic and the Spirit of Capitalism* (Weber, 1930) was based on Weber's (1904; 1905) works that linked asceticism, frugality and thrift to entrepreneurial behaviour. Weber (1922) maintained that Protestantism, by encouraging self-restraint and accumulation of assets, contributed to capitalism. Hecht (1994) showed that the accumulation of assets was not of primary importance to Mennonites in Canada.

Grant and Rosenstock (2006) considered four aspects of Mennonite ethno-religious values: (i) strong work ethic; (ii) self-reliance and entrepreneurship; (iii) family cohesiveness; and (iv) mutual aid. The Menno Colony Cooperative of Paraguay, for instance, was established as a mutual aid organisation. Thiessen elaborated, 'though in religious life Mennonites have asserted the value of community over individualism, in

Figure 11.1 Semi-arid Chaco (photograph by Léo-Paul Dana)

day-to-day practices, most Mennonites are deeply implicated in capitalism's exaltation of the individual' (1998, p. 182).

PARAGUAY

Paraguay, the only land-locked member of Mercosur, is 406 750 square kilometres in area, nestled in between Argentina, Bolivia, and Brazil. A western region of Paraguay is the Chaco, a semi-arid alluvial plain, commonly referred to as Paraguay's Wild West or Green Hell. (See Figure 11.1.)

Paraguay has long been a topic of interest in popular literature (Adams, 1933; Dibble, 1992; Gibson, 1943; Young, 1982). In recent years, this country has also been the subject of academic research (Becker and Suarez, 2001; Pelozo, 2001).

Paraguay's constitution recognizes the unique role that Catholicism plays in this country; the national president is legally required to be Catholic. While Catholicism is the official state religion of Paraguay, other belief systems are tolerated; among these is that of the Mennonites. Although the Mennonites number only about 30 000 people in Paraguay – almost half of whom live in the Chaco – their activities are highly visible in the economy. Yet, with the exception of Hecht's (1975; 1976; 1978; 1988; 1989) there is little literature on this subject.

MENNONITES IN PARAGUAY

Renshaw (2002) traced the origins of the Mennonite communities in Paraguay. 'In 1921 they signed an agreement with the Paraguayan government that allowed them the benefits of the Law of Colonization, freedom from military service, and the right to educate their children in their own Low German dialect' (Renshaw, 2002, pp. 40). (Chaco Indians, in contrast, are educated in Spanish – see Figure 11.2).

The immigrants would be allowed self-rule and German language schools, as well as exemption from military service, in exchange for developing the desolate Chaco, a region of thorn forests and marshes. Renshaw described this region,

> The Chaco, the area of Paraguayan territory that lies to the west of the Paraguay River, constitutes 60 percent of the land surface of Paraguay, but owing to a combination of historical and environmental factors, it has always been the most marginal region of the country . . . most of the population is to be found in the Mennonite Colonies of the Central Chaco. (2002, p. 31)

Renshaw provided an account, 'In 1928 the first settlers from Russia founded the Menno Colony . . . and two years later a second colony, Fernheim, was founded' (2002, p. 41). The Fernheimers had higher levels of education than did the Mennos, and more exposure to urban life. In 1932, they founded the town of Filadelfia, which remains to this day the centre of *Mennonitenkolonie.* In 1937, some Fernheimers left the Chaco and established the Friesland Colony, on the east bank of the Paraguay River; the new colony introduced wheat to Paraguay.

Mennonites from the Soviet Union settled the Neuland Colony in 1947. In 1947 the first group of Mennonite refugees left Germany for Paraguay on the *Volendam.* As stated by Renshaw, 'The Mennonites were essentially subsistence farmers until the mid-1950s, when they began to mechanize their agriculture and develop cash crops' (2002, p. 41).

Loewen suggested that subsistence farming involved 'mutually-dependent gender roles' (1993, p. 93), but the move to a market orientation 'created gender-stratified households' (1993, p. 93). Thus, Grant and Rosenstock (2006) explained that farming became a male-dominated sector.

Renshaw noted, 'Agriculture appears never to have been of as much importance for the Chaco societies as it is for most of the societies of the

Figure 11.2 School for indigenous children (photograph by Léo-Paul Dana)

tropical forest regions of Lowland South America' (2002, p. 89). In his words,

> The Central Chaco is the only region where agriculture is practiced on a commercial scale . . . This population is mainly Indian and Mennonite, in about

> equal proportions . . . On these pastures the Mennonites raise both beef and dairy cattle, and the milk production provides the basis for a flourishing dairy industry . . . The cheese, butter, and milk, which is processed in Filadelfia and Loma Plata, is sold on the national market and is almost the only commercial dairy produce available in Paraguay. (Renshaw, 2002, pp. 40–42)

A MULTICULTURAL CONTEXT

A classic ethnographic study of indigenous life in Paraguay is that by Service and Service (1954). Redekop (1980) wrote about relations between Mennonites and indigenous peoples of the Chaco during the 1970s.

More recently, Renshaw wrote about indigenous people in the Chaco, 'All the Indian communities of the Paraguayan Chaco, with the exception of one or two bands of Ayoreo and Manjuy who managed to remain isolated in the most inaccessible areas of the northern Chaco, are in some sense integrated into the national economy' (2002, p. 63). He described these people as having 'a strong egalitarian ethic, an ethic that predisposes the Indians of the Chaco to view the accumulation of material possessions – beyond a certain, limited level – as a threat to the social order' (Renshaw, 2002, p. 159).

Renshaw described relations between indigenous people and Mennonite settlements, 'Many Indian laborers in the Mennonite Colonies try to associate themselves with a particular patron – a Mennonite who can find work for them whenever they need it, and who in turn is assured of their labor whenever he requires it' (2002, pp. 139–40). He explained, 'The Indians who live in these colonies have generally accepted the religious doctrines of the Mennonite Church, but there is little evidence to suggest they have accepted the Mennonites' economic values' (Renshaw, 2002, p. 165). He suggested that for the Chaco people,

> Commerce is an even more contradictory activity than either agriculture or stock raising, since it implies the deliberate negation of generosity, with market relations taking the place of sharing . . . on the few occasions when individuals have tried to engage in commerce . . . stores have disappeared within a few weeks, since their owners have felt obliged to give credit to their kin and neighbors until the entire stock was used up. (2002, p. 179)

Renshaw proposed another causal variable for the collapse on indigenous enterprises:

> In the Mennonite Colonies credit notes have for years been the standard mode of payment in the . . . edible oil and tannin factories of Loma Plata; they were also reintroduced, despite considerable protest . . . in Filadelfia . . . The

Figure 11.3 Closed (photograph by Léo-Paul Dana)

> credit notes issued by the Fernheim cooperative were redeemable in a well-stocked cooperative store where the prices compared favourably with those of Asunción. One of the impacts of this method of payment . . . was the collapse of many of the small . . . stores' of the indigenous people. (2002, p. 139)

(Figure 11.3 shows a closed shop.)

Renshaw explained,

> in order to understand the economy of the Chaco societies one must look beyond the external constraints that determine the Indians' economic situation and consider the system of values that underlies the economy. This system of values, with its emphasis on equality and personal autonomy, is, I believe, a defining feature of the Indians' sense of ethnic identity. An understanding of the Chaco societies' economic values, especially their conceptions of property . . . also helps shed light on their . . . preference for wage labor over other forms of production . . . .Wage labor is often interpreted as evidence of a distinctly Western or capitalist mode of production. In the Chaco, however, I would argue that it indicates precisely the opposite, since it offers an alternative that allows indigenous societies to maintain their own system of values while providing access to those industrially manufactured goods that are now regarded as necessities. Unlike other forms of production for the market, wage labor offers a relatively quick return on the time and labor invested, and its products . . . can be integrated into the networks of exchange through which the Chaco societies define themselves without seriously challenging their insistence on equality . . . This type of situation is probably common among small-scale, rural societies

Figure 11.4 These cooperative employees are Chaco Indians (photograph by Léo-Paul Dana)

> situated on the periphery of the global economy, societies that maintain their system of values. (2002, p. 180)

(Wage labourers are shown in Figure 11.4.)

COMMUNAL ENTREPRENEURSHIP

A cooperative is an autonomous association of persons who join forces to meet their common needs by means of a jointly owned enterprise. A cooperative may thus be described as a vehicle for collective entrepreneurship where individual skills are integrated into a group and the team's collective capacity to innovate becomes greater than the sum of its parts. Collective entrepreneurship can offer a cooperative the opportunity to tap on individual talents and to harness collective energy.

As discussed by Zeuli and Cropp (2004), cooperatives provide local employment and they tend to have a long-term commitment to remain in the community, providing leadership and development. To be viable, a cooperative must provide benefits to its members, beyond those available in its absence. Hogeland (2004) found that members do not necessarily support a cooperative.

Old Colony Mennonites have traditionally been opposed to two tenets of capitalism, namely the centrality of private property and of self-interest. According to their world view, *Gelassenheit*, people should help their neighbours and share resources. Given this communal ethic, cooperatives can receive a high level of support from Mennonites. Thiessen (1998) observed that the Mennonite work ethic emphasizes collective effort and cooperation, and linked Mennonite business success to the effective integration of religious belief and economic practice.

Peredo and Chrisman (2006) developed the concept of community-based enterprise and argued that this provides a potential strategy for sustainable local development. They maintained 'that in this emerging form of entrepreneurship, typically rooted in community culture, natural and social capital are integral and inseparable from economic considerations, transforming the community into an entrepreneur' (Peredo and Chrisman, 2006, p. 309).

METHODOLOGY

Anthropologists and sociologists have benefited from the Chicago School of qualitative inquiry, ever since the 1920s. In contrast, entrepreneurship research has traditionally been quantitative in nature, with logical-deductive theories fitting into a positivist paradigm. Geertz (1973; 1983) argued that positivism was yielding to a more open-ended perspective, with increasing pluralism. While the post-modern moment was shaped by a refusal to privilege any method or theory (Richardson, 1997), the current seventh movement has been calling for the social sciences to become sites for critical discussions about class, community, globalization, nation-states and race (Denzin and Lincoln, 2003).

For the methodological mandate to be inductive, naturalistic and sensitive to context, it was necessary for the authors of this chapter to be submerged into a Mennonite community, such as to develop closeness in the social sense. Data could then be collected through participation as well as observation. Thus, ethnographic methods included participant observation, as described by Burgess (1984) and Edgerton and Langess (1974).

A total of 128 interviews were conducted in Paraguay, over an extended period during which the authors lived on a Mennonite colony. To be representative of age and gender, structured interviews were administered to a stratified sample; these lasted between 35 and 45 minutes. Semi-structured interviews with opinion leaders lasted up to three hours. To minimize the impact of socially desirable responding (Arnold et al., 1985; Rahim, 1983; and Zerbe and Paulus, 1987), triangulation (Patton, 1982; 1987; 1990) was used. Interviews were transcribed and content analysis (Krippendorff, 1980) was very useful in identifying commonly held beliefs.

OBSERVATIONS

The Paraguayan Chaco, a land of stifling heat and countless poisonous snakes, is home to three Mennonite communities: (i) the Menno Colony, which is the oldest; (ii) the Fernheim Colony, founded in 1930; and (iii) the Neuland Colony, established in 1947 by German Ukrainians. In the Middle Chaco, these communities are thriving on land cleared of scrub.

Interviewees often emphasized to the authors the importance of having a separation of church and state. In the Chaco, the Mennonites are indeed separated from the Paraguayan state. With minimal interference from the Paraguayan government, they maintain their own infrastructure, including their own roads, phone systems, electricity plants, hospitals, banks, traffic police and schools. (They also preserve their language as shown in Figure 11.5.) The Menno Colony has over 1500 windmills, and 2000 kilometres of water pipeline.

Interviewees also emphasized the importance of frugality and industry, and this seems to have led to prosperity in a harsh environment. The economic importance of the Mennonites here far outstrips their numbers. With little concern for poisonous snakes, their farms produce corn, fine quality cotton, dairy products, peanuts and soya beans.

The Menno Colony includes over 1000 dairy farms. Animals eat only from the pastures, with no hormones and no artificial growth-enhancers. They provide half of the country's dairy requirements. Indigenous labourers from the Ayoreo, Lengua and Nivacle groups are often given jobs on Mennonite farms. Amongst themselves, the Mennonites speak their Plattdeutsch dialect of German, but many have learned Spanish and this facilitates dealings with indigenous people (see Figure 11.6).

The administrative and service centre for Mennonite farmers of the Fernheim Colony is Filadelfia, with a population exceeding 3000 people, mostly Mennonites, but also Brazilians and indigenous people from the Ayoreo, Chulupi, and Lengua tribes. Here, one hears Spanish as well as German.

In the Menno Colony, the Sociedad Civil Chortitzer Komitee is responsible for all economic and social affairs. This committee owns all the land of the colony – amounting to more than half a million hectares, mostly used for pasture – and makes areas available to families, as needed. The same committee oversees the colony's 2000 kilometres of road, the

Figure 11.5 Bilingual signage (photograph by Léo-Paul Dana)

Figure 11.6 Fluent in Spanish (photograph by Léo-Paul Dana)

hospital, schools, insurance, and the entrepreneurial cooperative, known as the Sociedad Cooperativa Colonizadora Chortitzer Komitee Ltda.

The Sociedad Cooperativa Colonizadora Chortitzer Komitee Ltda is responsible for agricultural and industrial developments. Whereas cooperatives in mainstream society pay dividends to members, this one was created as a mutual aid organization, as mentioned above. Therefore, unlike other cooperatives, the Chortitzer Komitee decided not to pay dividends to individual members, but instead to contribute to the well-being of the community. Profits have been used to support the hospital, and credit given to those in need. An interviewee suggested that in her opinion, an entity that has a return-on-investment as its goal may oversee environmental or social concerns; in contrast, she explained, a sustainable balance is reached when an economic entity such as a cooperative is dedicated to the social well-being of its members. Her husband elaborated that this was very much compatible with Mennonite cultural values.

The cooperative provides products for consumers, and perhaps more importantly for Mennonite farmers, it provides an outlet and distribution network for their produce. One farmer told the authors that there was a perceived security when it was known that a market was guaranteed for one's goods, 'Instead of looking for markets, we can focus our energy on the work itself'.

Given that Mennonite farmers breed Holstein and Pardo Suizo cattle, milk is in abundance (see Figure 11.7). The Menno Colony accounts for about 300 000 litres of milk per day. Under the banner of its Trebol brand, the cooperative produces a huge range of dairy products, from milk, and chocolate milk, to yogurt, butter and an assortment of cheeses. (Figure 11.8 shows the dairy facility.)

Mennonite farmers also raise Brahman cattle for their meat, and crossbreeding with Angus and Hereford cattle helps attain desired levels of marbling. A farmer explained, 'The Angus is a British breed, with fat between muscular fibrils but not around the muscles'. There are about 300 000 cattle in the Menno Colony, of which roughly a third of the stock is sold each year.

The Sociedad Cooperativa Colonizadora Chortitzer Komitee Ltda built one of the biggest meat packing plants in Paraguay, FrigoChorti. The slaughterhouse is in the middle of the Menno livestock rearing area, thereby avoiding transportation over long distances journeys, which would stress the animals. Six hundred animals are slaughtered a day. (Cattle are transported by trucks as shown in Figure 11.9)

The cooperative's Chorti brand is used for a wide variety of ham, minced meat paddies, and sausages. Much beef is exported to Europe. The cooperative also exports high quality semen, through its Tamyca Centro Genetico. Several interviewees outside the Menno Colony confirmed that the Chortitzer Komitee cooperative is the leading supplier of dairy and meat products in Paraguay.

The international trade of guajak (*Guaiacum officinale*) is controlled, with the requirement of CITES [Convention on International Trade Endangered Species] certification. Verawood (*Bulnesia sarmientoi*) is a substitute that can be freely traded, and the Chortitzer Komitee Cooperative exports this to France where it is used as a base in the production of perfumes.

A recent attempt at establishing tourism involves promoting the Central Chaco as a destination for bird-watchers. In addition, foreigners have

Figure 11.7 *Milk arrivals (photograph by Léo-Paul Dana)*

Figure 11.8 *Dairy processing (photograph by Léo-Paul Dana)*

been willing to pay US$1000 to shoot pigeons. In Filadelfia, Cooperativa Fernheim Ltda, the Fernheim cooperative, owns and operates the 24-room Hotel Florida, which operates in German, English and Spanish.

Mennonite entrepreneurship in Paraguay is not restricted to the Chaco.

Figure 11.9 Cattle transport (photograph by Léo-Paul Dana)

Mennonite Economic Development Associates (MEDA)[3] is comprised of about 60 Mennonite entrepreneurs who established a factory in eastern Paraguay, to produce starch from manioc, a plant with large tubers. The factory buys the manioc from several hundred local farmers. MEDA Paraguay pioneered the commercial development of *stevia*, a Paraguayan plant that is used as a sweetener in diet drinks as far as Japan. Meanwhile, the Chaco chapter of MEDA produces charcoal that is exported to Europe.

An elder interviewee told the authors that the cooperative model was essential to the economic success of the Mennonite communities in Paraguay. In the desolate Chaco, he explained, it would have been hard to survive, let alone succeed, without the values encouraged by their religion, i.e., honesty, mutual help, and solidarity. A cooperative was compatible with these values, and facilitated the road to prosperity. However, as Mennonites prosper in Paraguay, less wealthy indigenous people are blamed for rising crime.

Sitting at his dining room table in Loma Plata, one Mennonite interviewee complained to the authors that 'welfare programmes sustain people in poverty, but it would be wiser to teach them to get out of poverty'. For this reason he praised his religion's emphasis on being self-reliant, on having a strong work ethic. He also mentioned that his people were happy to have control of their own schools, and he expressed discontent at Canadian law that prevented Mennonite control over their schools.

TOWARD FUTURE RESEARCH

The three Mennonite cooperatives in the Chaco appear to be highly successful institutions, acting as growth poles for the region. Theoretically, they could serve as role models. Future research might investigate why Chaco Indian cooperatives have had comparatively little success, despite the fact that 50% of the Indians in the region belong to Mennonite churches.

NOTES

* This chapter is reprinted with permission from *Latin American Business Review*, **8** (4), 2007, 82–96, available at http://www.informaworld.com.

1. The authors thank the late Abram Wiebe-Wiebe of Loma Plata, for his assistance in Paraguay during the data collection phase of this paper. Thanks are also due to the following all of whom provided comments on the first draft of this paper: Werner Franz of the Canadian Mennonite University, in Winnipeg, Manitoba; Alfred Hecht of Wilfred Laurier University, in Waterloo, Ontario; Gerhard H. Penner, administrator of Menno Colony, in the Chaco of Paraguay; and Carel Roessingh of Vrije Universiteit Amsterdam, in the Netherlands. Finally, many thanks to the two reviewers who provided additional insights.
2. For an overview of Anabaptist religions see Kraybill and Bowman (2001).
3. According to Redekop et al. (1995), Mennonite Economic Development Associates is the only Mennonite-related organization that talks about business and church without discomfort.

REFERENCES

Adams, Harriet Chalmers (1933), 'River-encircled Paraguay', *National Geographic*, **63** (4), 385–416.

Arnold, Hugh J., Daniel C. Feldman and Mary Purbhoo (1985), 'The Role of Social Desirability Response Bias in Turnover Research', *Academy of Management Journal*, **28**, 955–66.

Becker, Kip and Marlene de la Cruz Suarez (2001), 'Trade Creation and Trade Diversion for Mercosur', *Journal of Euromarketing*, **10** (2), 67–105.

Burgess, Robert G. (1984), *In the Field: An Introduction to Field Research*, London: George Allen and Unwin.

Denzin, Norman K. and Yvonna S. Lincoln (2003), 'The Discipline and Practice of Qualitative Research', in Norman K. Denzin and Yvonna S. Lincoln (eds), *The Landscape of Qualitative Research: Theories and Issues*, 2nd edn, Thousand Oaks, CA: Sage, pp. 1–45.

Dibble, Sandra (1992), 'Paraguay: Plotting a New Course', *National Geographic*, **182** (2), 88–113.

Dyck, Cornelius J. (1967), *An Introduction to Mennonite History*, Scottdale, AZ: Herald Press.

Edgerton, Robert B. and Lewis L. Langess (1974), *Methods and Rules in the Study of Culture*, San Francisco, CA: Chandler and Sharp.

Farmer, Richard N. and Barry M. Richman (1965), *Comparative Management and Economic Progress*, Homewood, IL: Richard D. Irwin.

Geertz, Clifford (1973), *The Interpretation of Cultures: Selected Essays*, New York: Basic Books.

Geertz, Clifford (1983), *Local Knowledge: Further Essays in Interpretive Anthropology*, New York: Basic Books.

Gibson, Christopher H. (1943), 'Through Paraguay and Southern Matto Grosso', *National Geographic*, **84** (4), 459–88.

Grant, Hugh and Michael Rosenstock (2006), 'Do Mennonites Earn Less than Other Canadians? The Role of Religion in the Determination of Income', *Journal of Mennonite Studies*, **24**, 73–92.

Hecht, Alfred (1975), 'The Agricultural Economy of the Mennonite Settlers in the Chaco Region of Paraguay', *Growth and Change*, **6** (4), 14–20.

Hecht, Alfred (1976), 'The Agricultural Economy of the Mennonite Settlers in Paraguay: Impact of a Road', *Ekistics*, **42** (248), 42–7.

Hecht, Alfred (1978), 'The Geographic Dimensions of the Changing World Economic Order: With Specific Reference to Paraguay', *Die Erde*, **109**, 397–416.

Hecht, Alfred (1988), 'Pioniere im Chaco Südamerikas: Indianer Mennoniten – Paraguayer', *Jahrbuch der Marburger Geographischen Gesellschaft*, pp. 21–4.

Hecht, Alfred (1989), 'Die wirtschaftliche Entwicklung der Mennoniten-Kolonien im Chaco: ein theoretisches Perspektive', *Mennoblatt*, **58** (17), 8–10.

Hecht, Alfred (1994), 'Mennonites and the Canadian Society: A Financial Well-Being Comparison', in Calvin Steiner, Samuel J. Krahn and Victor A. Redekop (eds), *Anabaptist/Mennonite Faith and Economics*, New York: University Press of America, pp. 237–53.

Hofstede, Geert (1980), *Culture's Consequences: International Differences in Work-Related Values*, Beverly Hills, CA: Sage.

Hogeland, Julie A. (2004), 'How Business Culture Drives Economic Behaviour in Coops', *Rural Cooperatives*, January/February, 23–7.

Huntington, Samuel P. (1993), 'The Clash of Civilization', *Foreign Affairs*, **72** (3), 22–49.

Huntington, Samuel P. (1996), *The Clash of Civilization and the Remaking of World Order*, New York: Simon and Schuster.

Kraybill, Donald B. and Carl F. Bowman (2001), *On the Backroad to Heaven: Old Order Hutterites, Mennonites, Amish, and Brethren*, Baltimore, MD: The Johns Hopkins University Press.

Krippendorff, Klaus (1980), *Content Analysis: An Introduction to its Methodology*, Beverly Hills, CA: Sage.

Laurent, André (1983), 'A Cultural Diversity of Western Conceptions of Management', *International Studies of Management and Organization*, **13** (Spring/Summer), 75–96.

Loewen, Royden K. (1993), *Family, Church and Market: A Mennonite Community in the Old and the New Worlds, 1850–1930*, Toronto: University of Toronto Press.

Patton, Michael Quinn (1982), 'Qualitative Methods and Approaches: What are They?', in Eileen Kuhns and S.V. Martorana (eds), *Qualitative Methods for Institutional Research*, San Francisco, CA: Jossey-Bass, pp. 3–16.

Patton, Michael Quinn (1987), *How to Use Qualitative Methods in Evaluation*, Newbury Park, CA: Sage.

Patton, Michael Quinn (1990), *Qualitative Evaluation and Research Methods*, Newbury Park, CA: Sage.
Pelozo, José Aníbal Insfrán (2001), 'Paraguay: Output Growth and Foreign Investment', *Latin American Business Review*, **2** (1–2), 141–59.
Peredo, Ana Maria, and James J. Chrisman (2006), 'Toward a Theory of Community-based Enterprise', *Academy of Management Review*, **31** (2), 302–28.
Rahim, M. Afzalur (1983), 'A Measure of Styles of Handling Interpersonal Conflict', *Academy of Management Journal*, **26**, 368–76.
Redekop, Calvin (1980), *Strangers Become Neighbours: Mennonite and Indigenous Relations in the Paraguayan Chaco*, Scottsdale, AZ: Herald Press.
Redekop, Calvin (1989), *Mennonite Society*, Baltimore, MD: Johns Hopkins University Press.
Redekop, Calvin, Stephen C. Ainlay and Robert Siemens (1995), *Mennonite Entrepreneurs*, Baltimore, MD: Johns Hopkins University Press.
Renshaw, John (2002), *The Indians of the Paraguayan Chaco: Identity & Economy*, Lincoln, NE: University of Nebraska Press.
Richardson, Laurel (1997), *Fields of Play: Constructing an Academic Life*, New Brunswick, NJ: Rutgers University Press.
Roessingh, Carel and Amber Schoonderwoerd (2005), 'Traditional Farmers or Modern Businessmen? Religious Differentiation and Entrepreneurship in a Kleine Gemeinde Mennonite Community in Belize', *Journal of Developmental Entrepreneurship*, **10** (1), 65–77.
Service, Elman Rogers and Helen S. Service (1954), *Tobati: Paraguayan Town*, Chicago, IL: University of Chicago Press.
Thiessen, Janis (1998), 'Mennonite Business and Labour Relations: Friesens Corporation of Altona, Manitoba, 1933–1973', *Journal of Mennonite Studies*, **16**, 181–202.
Weber, Max (1904) 'Die protestantische Ethik und der "Geist" des Kapitalismus. I. Das Problem', *Archiv für Sozialwissenschaft und Sozialpolitik*, **20** (1), 1–54.
Weber, Max (1905) 'Die protestantische Ethik und der "Geist" des Kapitalismus. II. Die Berufsidee des asketischen Protestantismus', *Archiv für Sozialwissenschaft und Sozialpolitik*, **21** (1), 1–110.
Weber, Max (1922), *Wirtschaft und Gesellschaft*, Tübingen: J.C.B. Mohr.
Weber, Max (1930), *The Protestant Ethic and the Spirit of Capitalism*, trans. Talcott Parsons, New York: Charles Scribner's Sons.
Young, Gordon (1982), 'Paraguay: Paradox of South America', *National Geographic*, **162** (2), 240–69.
Zerbe, Wilfred J. and Delroy L. Paulhus (1987), 'Socially Desirable Responding in Organizational Behavior', *Academy of Management Review*, **12** (2), 250–64.
Zeuli, Kimberly A. and Robert Cropp (2004), *Cooperatives: Principles and Practices in the 21st Century*, Madison, WI: University of Wisconsin Center for Cooperatives.

PART III

Islam

12. Islam and entrepreneurship

Wafica Ali Ghoul

INTRODUCTION

The number of Muslims worldwide was last estimated to be 1.6 billion, which represents about one-fifth of the world's population. The number of Muslims who currently live in the Western world (North America and Europe) is growing. There are around 7.5 million Muslims who currently live in the United States, 4 million live in Germany, 6 million in France, 3 million in Canada, and 1.8 million in the United Kingdom (Hassan and Carruthers 2007).

Muslim entrepreneurs around the globe have been increasingly seeking to set up enterprises that are consistent with Shariah law (Islamic principles of living), because they believe that these entities will enable them to achieve their economic goals while respecting and abiding by their religious beliefs.

Feldman (2008) had the following to say about Shariah,

> Shariah represents the idea that all human beings – and all human governments – are subject to justice under the law . . . The word 'Shariah' connotes a connection to the divine, a set of unchanging beliefs and principles that order life in accordance with God's will . . . Shariah is best understood as a kind of higher law, albeit one that includes some specific, worldly command.

Feldman goes on to say that 'a fourfold combination – the Koran, the path of the prophet as captured in the collections of reports, analogical reasoning and consensus – amounted to a basis for a legal system' which is commonly known as Shariah.

A BRIEF OVERVIEW OF ISLAMIC ENTERPRISES

What Are the Features that Distinguish Islamic Enterprises from their Conventional Counterparts?

What follows is a brief overview of the main distinguishing features of Islamic enterprises:

- One of the most distinct features of doing business within the Islamic framework is the prohibition of Riba (the earning or charging of interest); the word 'riba' is Arabic for 'growth', which means that Islam prohibits the growth of one's wealth through lending money to others and charging them interest as a compensation.

  In conventional enterprises the payment of interest is used to compensate lenders for their loss of liquidity, in addition to an inflation premium which makes up for a potential price increase, a default risk premium which is proportional to the credit risk of the borrower, and a maturity risk premium that increases with the life of the loan. Shariah prohibits the payment or receipt of interest because it can lead to an inequitable distribution of wealth, it does not promote productivity, and it can cause the exploitation of the poor and needy, besides the fact that usually there is no risk-sharing in traditional lending.
- Money cannot be traded for money; all transactions should be based on real assets. This is intended to help society through the creation of jobs.
- One cannot sell what one does not own, which presents a problem for hedge funds that use short-sale as one of their main strategies for risk management.
- Speculative activities are forbidden because they are considered to be gambling or *gharar* (which means uncertainty or deceit in Arabic), and they involve taking risks which are intentional, avoidable and significant.
- Another distinct feature is the fact that Islam prohibits any vehicle or tool that promises a fixed rate of return because under Islamic principles all shareholders should be on an equal footing. Islam focuses instead on partnerships and risk-sharing. According to 'Islamic Microfinance: A Business Plan', 'The Islamic conception of abolishment of fixed interest rates does not mean that no remuneration is paid on capital. Profit-making is acceptable in Islamic society as long as these profits are not unrestricted or driven by the activities of a monopoly. Islam deems profit, rather than interest, to be closer to its sense of morality and equity because earning profits inherently involves sharing risks and rewards. Profit-making addresses the Islamic ideals of social justice because both the entrepreneur and the lender bear the risk of the investment.'

What Are the Types of Enterprises which Are Permissible in Islam?

Muslim entrepreneurs are allowed to establish companies, whose activities are *halal* (lawful) not *haram* (unlawful), and thus are not objectionable under Shariah Islamic law. Business activities which are objectionable in Islam are those which involve

- Money-lending and interest payment or receipt, thus conventional banks and insurance companies are haram.
- The production, distribution, and/or profiting from alcohol, pornography, tobacco, gambling, weapons, music, entertainment, processing pork meat or non-halal meat (Ghoul and Karam, 2007).
- Hotels and airlines which serve alcohol on their premises.
- In addition, restrictions are applied to certain financial ratios. Thus the Dow Jones Islamic Market Indices (DJIMI) apply the following:
  '– Total debt divided by trailing 12-month average market capitalization must be less than 33%.
  – The sum of a company's cash and interest-bearing securities divided by the trailing 12-month average market capitalization must be less than 33%.
  – Accounts receivable divided by the trailing 12-month average market capitalization must be less than 33%'(DJIMI website).

Some enterprises have been rather lenient in their application of the Shariah compliance test. They have been taking the liberty to lower the restrictions on non-halal activities, as long as less than 5 per cent of their revenues are derived from such activities, with the condition that any profits from such activities shall be given to Islamic charities. This process is known as 'portfolio purification'. However, this is controversial and a subject of debate.

Typical businesses which generally comply with shariah are those involved in technology, telecommunications, steel companies, engineering, transportation, health care, utilities, construction, as well as real estate.

FACTORS THAT HAVE CONTRIBUTED TO THE RISING INTEREST IN ISLAMIC ENTREPRENEURSHIP

Several factors have been contributing to the recent growing interest in setting up Islamic enterprises. These include:

- The recent surge in oil prices which has created excess liquidity in many parts of the Muslim world.

- The events of 11 September 2001 (9/11) in the USA, which led many Muslims to repatriate their money back home for fear of new Western regulations that resulted in increased scrutiny, combined with a backlash against Muslims around the world, both real and perceived.
- The high population growth rate in Muslim countries, currently estimated to be 1.6 billion Muslims, means that the target audience for Muslim enterprises is significant and growing.
- The recent religious awakening of Muslims and their realization of the importance of compliance with Shariah rules and principles in their business dealings. According to Feldman (2008), 'In the Muslim world, on the other hand, the reputation of Shariah has undergone an extraordinary revival in recent years. A century ago, forward-looking Muslims thought of Shariah as outdated, in need of reform or maybe abandonment. Today, 66 percent of Egyptians, 60 percent of Pakistanis and 54 percent of Jordanians say that Shariah should be the only source of legislation in their countries.'
- High unemployment rates, internal conflicts, wars with neighboring countries, poverty, gender issues, as well as political oppression currently plague most of the Muslim countries. Consequently, the number of Muslims who are choosing to immigrate to the Western world (particularly North America and Europe) has been growing, which necessitates the establishment of Muslim enterprises in Muslim immigrant communities.
- There is an anticipated growth of interest by non-Muslim clients who have been seeking socially responsible and ethical products and services, which would contribute to sustaining the growth of Muslin enterprises (IIR Middle East, 2007).

FACTORS THAT ARE CURRENTLY IMPEDING THE EMERGENCE OF ISLAMIC ENTREPRENEURSHIP

Several factors present hurdles to the healthy growth of the Islamic enterprises, these include the current lack of standardized regulation, an unclear legal framework, different scholars' interpretations of the Shariah, and different levels of strictness.

Divergence Issues in Shariah Interpretation

A major hurdle that currently faces the growth of Islamic enterprises is the fact that the Shariah scholars who belong to different sects of Islam have been issuing divergent interpretations of the teachings of the Holy Koran. This is an issue because it affects the marketability and tradability of Islamic products across the different Muslim countries.

According to Humayon Dar, Managing Director of a London-based Shariah consultancy, the Dar Al Istithmar Insitute, 'There are perhaps 150 [such scholars] worldwide who are involved with Islamic finance but only 20 are internationally recognized' (Tett, 2006).

One might think that with a very small number of recognized Muslim Shariah scholars there would be a convergence of interpretations of Shariah; however the cause of divergence of interpretations is the diversity of personal beliefs of scholars, not to mention diverse Islamic religious sects, regional, and cultural influences. This problem is compounded by the varying degrees of religious strictness among entrepreneurs and clients with whom they are dealing.

Interestingly, Sheikh Usmani argues that 'the interpretations of most aspects of Shariah are never disputed. For example, everyone agrees that interest is not allowed. It is when you address the alternatives to interest that some differences arise' (Wigglesworth, 2007).

Deutsche Bank's Geert Bossuyt, Managing Director, Regional Head of Middle East Structuring, argues that Shariah is inherently open to individual scholars' interpretation; he has reportedly said:

> Shariah itself has inherent flexibility and fewer constraints than is often assumed by the financial services industry. Fundamental research is the key to unlocking this inherent flexibility, thereby allowing this market to grow to its full potential . . . too often, 'innovation' is achieved by pushing the barriers and/or misusing fatwas by taking them out of their context. Innovation ideally should be the result of a well documented and fundamental discussion on Shariah. (MENAFN.COM, 2007)

Corporate Governance and Islamic Enterprises

Islamic enterprises have additional constraints imposed on them besides those dictated by generally expected good corporate governance practices, which conventional enterprises have to abide by. An Islamic enterprise has to operate within the framework of Islamic law known as Shariah, this requires respecting the fundamental values of Islamic Shariah which balance the interests of society and individuals. These values include fairness, non-exploitation of the poor, moral responsibility, accountability, and equity in financial dealings. Not surprisingly, most of the reported development efforts of Islamic governance models have been observed in the financial sector of Islamic business, which is what we focus on next.

A KPMG report (2006) pointed out the lack of a unified Islamic governance model by stating that 'demonstrating compliance with Shariah can be difficult as different institutions have different governance models by which they set, measure, and monitor their compliance. These varying governance models have added a level of operational risk for any Islamic financial institution.'

Two organizations have been spearheading the effort for setting standards for corporate governance at Islamic financial institutions, the IFSB and the AAOIFI. The Islamic Financial Services Board (IFSB) is based in Kuala Lumpur, it began operating in 2003; it is an international organization which has been issuing standards for the effective supervision and regulation of Islamic financial institutions.

The Accounting and Auditing Organization for Islamic Financial Institutions (AAOIFI) is based in Bahrain, it has been working on a set of standards which cover accounting, ethics, and Shariah compliance; it claims that its principles are followed by the majority of Islamic financial institutions.

Islamic corporate governance requires the establishment of operating procedures that guarantee that a Shariah Supervisory Board (SSB) certifies all products, transactions, and services in advance, as well as facilitating the continuous monitoring of the permissibility of existing offerings and practices.

Solé (2007) has defined Shariah non-compliance risk as 'the risk that the terms agreed in a contract do not effectively comply with Islamic jurisprudence and thus are not valid under Islamic law'. This is the risk that Islamic corporate governance practices aim to minimize, through the supervision, guidance, and continuous monitoring by Shariah scholars.

Besides being external auditors, the SSB scholars function as consumer advocates by ensuring that all the transactions conducted by Islamic financial institutions, as well as their products and service offerings are consistent with Shariah law, thus respecting the wishes of the Muslim believers who deal with such enterprises. It is very important that customers have full confidence in the independence, integrity, ability, and credibility of Shariah scholars who certify a product or service as being halal. However, these virtues have been the subject of a lot of debate and controversy lately.

Sheikh Yusuf Talal DeLorenzo, one of the best known Shariah scholars, compared the responsibilities of a Shariah supervisor to those of a financial auditor (DeLorenzo, 2000; emphasis added):

> the functions of a Shariah supervisor may be compared to those of an independent financial auditor, in the sense that regulatory compliance is ensured. Shariah supervisors have both religious and fiduciary responsibilities; there is a need for *impartiality and independence*. In the same way that independent auditors are brought in to review the finances of a business, Shariah Supervisory

> Boards review compliance to Shariah precepts. Independent audits are understood as ways to gain and maintain the trust of investors and consumers. Independent Shariah supervision is the best way to gain and maintain the trust of Muslim investors and consumers.

Additionally, any defects in the products offered should be stated in the SSB report with recommendations for rectifying the defects.

Financing Islamic Enterprises

As with conventional small and medium enterprises, Islamic enterprises have to deal with the difficulty of access to capital, however, there is an additional hurdle which is that when capital is available it has to be compliant with Shariah.

According to Khan (2008) 'the growth and development of many Muslim owned small businesses is constrained as a result of the unavailability of Islamic financial services'. Next we present a simplified discussion of some Islamic finance vehicles commonly used by Islamic enterprises, these are financing vehicles which are considered to be halal substitutes to conventional vehicles

1. *Murabaha: Cost-plus-mark-up financing*. Individual (A) who desires to buy a store for $100 000 approaches an Islamic bank (B), which buys the store, marks it up to $120 000 and sells the store to (A) at cost plus a declared profit for deferred payments.
2. *Ijara: Lease-based products*. Individual (A) needs to use a machine (a productive asset) which costs half a million dollars, bank (B) buys the machine, and rents it out to (A), charging him rental payments, which is Ijara in Arabic. If (A) ends up buying the machine, the contract would be *Ijara-wa-Iqtana*, which means a lease with an option to buy (Iqtana is Arabic for ownership, wa means and).
3. *Bai-Salam: Advance purchase*. This is similar to a Forward or a Futures contract. In Arabic, the word *Bai* means sale, *Salam* is supposed to stand for delivery; it really should be *Tasleem* or handing over of commodities. Assume that merchant (A) wants to have suits manufactured by factory (B), (A) pays (B) in advance, and in return (B) charges (A) a lower price, thus splitting the profits with (B). This contract represents a transaction rather than a loan.
4. *Istisnaa: Progressive financing*. The word *Istisnaa* in Arabic means manufacturing, assume individual (A) wants to build a house, he approaches bank (B) which will pay the builders on behalf of individual (A) as the work progresses. This allows for deferral of payment as well as delivery.

5. *Musharakah: Company or partnership contract*. Two or more persons contribute to the financing as well as the management of the business, in equal or unequal proportions. Musharakah (which means sharing in Arabic), is an equity financing arrangement and partnership where profits are shared according to an agreed ratio, whereas the losses are shared in proportion to the capital/ investment of each partner.
6. *Mudarabah: Investment partnership*. The investor (*Rab al mal* which means provider of capital in Arabic) provides capital to the bank (the *Mudarib*, which means the one who is competing with investor for profit). The bank invests the money in halal activities. Profits are shared on a pre-agreed ratio, whereas losses are born by the investor only. A Mudarabah contract is very similar to a mutual fund because both pool money from many investors and invest it on their behalf, sharing in the profits but not the losses.
7. *Sukuks: Islamic bonds*. The word *Sukuk* is Arabic for a bond, that is, an indenture. Conventional bonds are used to borrow money for financing a project or an asset acquistion, they pay a fixed interest rate to bond holders semi-annually. In Islamic finance, a Sukuk issuance is a method of financing that has to be backed by the project's fixed assets. Sukuks give their owners a proportionate beneficial ownership in the underlying asset. Profits from the project are distributed to owners.

Islamic Enterprises and Risk Exposures

Various types of unique risk exposures plague Muslim economies and need to be managed.

- The prevalence of wars and conflicts in many Muslim countries raises the level of transaction, economic and translation risk exposures and necessitates the development of Shariah-compliant risk management products.
- The economies of many Muslim countries depend heavily on petrodollars; the price of oil has been very volatile, which creates significant risks.
- The phenomenon of the globalization of trade and finance means that most business deals and investments involve multiple countries and currencies.
- A less discussed source of risk exposure is the impact of global warming on agriculture; it is creating additional hazards for farmers' crops world wide.
- After experiencing a boom for at least three years, stock markets in the Middle East are currently in a correction mode, the availability

of risk management devices would attract additional local and foreign investors' interest.

RISK MANAGEMENT AND ISLAMIC SHARIAH

Muslim entrepreneurs are not currently taking serious measures to protect themselves from various risks. Progress is being made mainly in developing instruments that protect against foreign exchange rate fluctuations (profit rate swaps) and stock price volatility (Islamic hedge funds and alternatives to options). However, a concern remains that some Muslim entrepreneurs and their clients will not be comfortable with using them. The Islamic finance industry is being criticized for synthesizing copycats of conventional financial derivative products

Conventional risk management tools, such as derivatives, involve speculation which is equivalent to gambling. The holy Koran prohibits gambling by comparing its cost to its benefit: 'They ask you [O Muhammad] about wine and gambling. Say there is great sin (harm, *'ithm*) in them, and some benefit to mankind. However, their sin (harm, *'ithm*) outweighs their benefits' (2:219).

Kamali (1999) defines *gharar* as follows:

> literally meaning fraud (*al-khid'a*), *gharar* in transactions has often been used in the sense of risk, uncertainty and hazard. In a contract of sale *gharar* often refers to uncertainty and ignorance of one or both of the parties over the substance or attributes of the object of sale, or of doubt over its existence at the time of contract. *Gharar* is, however, a broad concept and may carry different shades of meaning in relationship to different transactions.

El-Gamal (2001) cites Professor Mustafa Al-Zarqa who had the following definition of *gharar*: 'it is the sale of probable items whose existence or characteristics are not certain, due to the risky nature which makes the trade similar to gambling'.

Thus for a contract to be Shariah compliant the object of the trade as well as the price has to be stated, which would eliminate ambiguities that are characteristic of *gharar*.

Examples of Halal Risk Management Tools

Profit-loss sharing account

This is the equivalent of a conventional money market hedge. If a Malaysian company owes a British company a payment of £105 sterling in one year, it can buy £100 today, deposit the pounds in an Islamic bank account, such as a *Mudarabah* account or a *Musharakah* account, such that in one year it can use £105 to cover its liability, and only the amount above £105 is uncovered. Alternatively, if the account falls below £105, then the foreign currency exposure would be limited to the shortage.

Shariah-compliant non-derivative risk management methods

- Invoicing payables and receivables in the same currency, as much as possible.
- Matching the levels of revenues and expenses in a foreign currency.
- Holding similar levels of assets and liabilities in each currency.
- Lagging and leading foreign currency payables payment strategies.
- Portfolio diversification, in terms of financial products, currencies, and projects.

ISLAM AND FEMALE ENTREPRENEURSHIP

Islam does not prohibit or frown upon women being entrepreneurs, in fact, the prophet Muhammad, peace be upon him, was married to a very wealthy and capable woman called Khadijah, peace be upon her, who helped him spread the message of Islam. According to Feldman (2008), there is an 'oversimplified assumption that Muslims want to use Shariah to reverse feminism and control women . . . Large numbers of [Muslim] women support the Islamists in general and the ideal of Shariah in particular.'

CONCLUSION

There are some critics who are of the opinion that by insisting on complying with Shariah law to the letter, some Muslim entrepreneurs might be losing sight of the main objective of Islam, namely, fairness and social equity, as well as protecting the well being (physical and mental health) and providing for a decent living of mankind.

Husain (2007) reports Laldin, chairman of the Shariah advisory committee of HSBC Amanah Malaysia, to have said:

> scholars look at three basic areas when assessing the compliance of products: belief, legalilty and morality . . . products could fairly easily comply with Islamic law but it is more difficult to ascertain whether they comply with the morals of Islam. The price of a product may not be controversial from a legal perspective

but if the product costs more than an equivalent conventional product, it may not fulfill Islam's moral obligations of fairness and social equity.

REFERENCES

DeLorenzo, Yusuf Talal (2000), 'Shari'ah Supervision of Islamic Mutual Funds', 4th Annual Harvard Forum on Islamic Finance 3, 6 April, available at: http://www.djindexes.com/mdsidx/downloads/delorenzo.pdf (accessed 20 July 2009).

Dow Jones Islamic Market Indexes (DJIMI), http://www.djindex.com (accessed 21 July 2009).

El-Gamal, Mahmoud A. (2001), 'An Economic Explication of the Prohibition of Gharar in Classical Islamic Jurisprudence', available at: http://www.ruf.rice.edu/~elgamal (accessed 20 July 2009).

Feldman, Noah (2008), 'The Fall and Rise of the Islamic State', cited at http://www.nytimes.com/2008/03/16/magazine/16Shariah-t.html (accessed 20 July 2009).

Ghoul, Wafica and Karam, Paul (2007) 'MRI and SRI Mutual Funds: A Comparison of Christian, Islamic (Morally Responsible Investing MRI), and Socially Responsible Investing (SRI) Mutual Funds', *Journal of Investing*, (Summer), **16** (2), 96–102.

Hassan, Nevinne and Carruthers, Stuart (2007) 'Canada: Islamic Financial Services: Overview and Prospects for the Canadian Marketplace', *Mondaq Business Briefing*, 11 May.

Husain, Ahmad Sanusi (2007) 'Islamic Scholars Call for 'More Attention to Morals than Law', 27 June, available at: http://islamicfinanceaffairs.wordpress.com/2007/06/28/islamic-scholars-cell-for-%E2%80%98more-attention-to-morals-than-law%E2%80%99 (accessed 21 July 2009).

IIR Middle East (2007), 'Non-Muslims Key to Growth of Islamic Finance', 19 February, available at: http://www.iirme.com/news_details.aspx?newsID=185 (accessed 21 July 2009).

'Islamic Microfinance: A Business Plan', available at: http://faraazm.tripod.com/id31.html (accessed 21 July 2009).

Kamali, M.H (1999), 'Uncertainty and Risk-Taking (*gharar*) in Islamic Law', *Law Journal*, 7 (2).

Khan, Ajaz Ahmed (2008), 'Islamic Microfinance Theory, Policy and Practice', February, available at: http://eng.assaif.org/Publications-Events/Papers-presentations/Microfinance (accessed 21 July 2009).

KPMG (2006), 'Making the Transition From Niche to Mainstream Islamic Banking and Finance: A Snapshot of the Industry and Its Challenges Today', available at: http://www.us.kpmg.com/microsite/FSLibraryDotCom/islamicfinance.aspx (accessed 21 July 2009).

Middle East and North Africa Financial Network (MENAFN.COM) (2007), 'Deutsche Bank Publishes White Paper to Increase Supply of Sharia Compliant Alternative Investments', 30January.

Solé Juan (2007), 'Islamic Banking Makes Headway', IMF Monetary and Capital Markets Department, 19 September, available at: http://www.imf.org/external/pubs/ft/survey/so/2007/RES0919A.htm (accessed 21 July 2009).

Tett, Gillian (2006), 'Banks Seek Islamic Scholars Versed in Finance', *Financial*

Times, 19 May, available at: http://www.us.ft.com/ftgateway/superpage.ft?. . . id=fto05202006141508893 (accessed 20 July 2009).

Wigglesworth, Robin (2007), 'Scholastic Guidance', *IBF*, Shariah section, **11** (September), available at: http://www.cpifinancial.net/v2/Magazine.aspx?v=1&aid=8&cat=IBF&in=11 (accessed 20 July 2009).

13. Xinjiang*

Léo-Paul Dana

INTRODUCTION

This chapter, stemming from field research in China, is about small business in Xinjiang, the country's largest administrative region. Here, the Han-Chinese are a minority, and most people are Muslims. Whereas the Han-Chinese introduced a firm-type economy to Xinjiang, the non-Han sphere of activity is concentrated in the bazaar economy. While the firm-type economy is a means to an end (monetary reward), the bazaar is an end in itself; the bazaar helps the indigenous Uygurs to preserve their cultural identity. Their bazaar is a social and cultural system. Given that these people have a Turkic culture and they speak a Turkic language, this has facilitated trade with bazaar entrepreneurs in the rapidly developing, newly independent republics of central Asia.

A very rich literature has examined the Han-Chinese and their business enterprises, even outside China. Examples include a study of entrepreneurs among Han-Chinese in the State of Mississippi (Loewen, 1971); research on Han-Chinese entrepreneurs in the United States (Light, 1972); a study of self-employment among Han-Chinese in New York (Wong, 1987); a report on Han-Chinese entrepreneurs in Calgary (Ray et al., 1988); a study of Han-Chinese entrepreneurs in Canada (Brenner and Toulouse, 1990); a description of Han-Chinese in Vietnam (Dana, 1994); and an analysis of Han-Chinese entrepreneurs from Hong Kong (Dana, 1995).

In contrast, less is known about non-Han business in China. While the non-Han people are a minority in China, the Han are a minority in Xinjiang.

Xinjiang means 'new frontier' in Chinese. Most of the people here are members of non-Han ethnic minorities, particularly Uygurs, along with Kazakhs and Kirghiz. The Uygurs are Muslims with Indo-European features. They have been here since the times of the Tang Dynasty. The Kazakhs and the Kirghiz are also Muslim, with a Turkic language. In contrast to the Uygurs who have been cultivating the land, the Kazakhs and Kirghiz have retained their traditional nomadic lifestyle, which includes breeding camels and horses, both of these for meat and for milk, as well as for transport. Among the Kazakhs, in Xinjiang, horseback courtship is still practiced, and a suitor must kiss his woman on the gallop.

Recently, a new class of international merchants has been emerging with a pan-Turkic scope. Rather than doing business with Han-Chinese, the Muslims of Xinjiang express a preference to trade with co-religionists from the Turkic republics of the former Soviet Union. While the majority of the world's international trade takes place in the firm-type economy, Uygur traders prefer the bazaar. Definitions are appropriate at this point:

1. The firm-type economy is an economic institution involving a mode of commercial activity such that industry and trade take place primarily within a set of impersonally-defined relationships.
2. The bazaar-type economy is a social and cultural system, a way of life and a general mode of commercial activity such that most of the flow of commerce is fragmented into numerous, disconnected transactions between individuals. The unit of interest is the micro-enterprise and drinking tea may be allocated more attention than would be turn-over or market share.

METHODOLOGY

The research, upon which this essay is based, was conducted using ethnographic methods, in Xinjiang. Open-ended interviews proved most valuable. (These were often over meals; see Figure 13.1).

It was deemed preferable to interview each respondent in the latter's language of preference. The author arrived by train from the Commonwealth of Independent States (CIS) along with a Mandarin-speaking interpreter and a native Uygur translator. A Kirghiz translator was hired on location.[1] Given that many Kazakhs study Arabic, in some cases the author preferred to interview directly in Arabic, rather than to rely on third persons.

As noted by Shenkar (1994), it is notoriously difficult to conduct empirical research in China. Among the methodological difficulties here is the lack of infrastructure. Railway lines by-pass important settlements, such as Turpan (see Figure 13.2).

Furthermore, main highways have disappeared due to the lack of upkeep. Where there are trains, foreigners are supposed to travel by 'Soft-Sleepers' which by-pass smaller towns. These towns are served by 'Hard-Sleepers', tickets for which are controlled by the black market. In order to get a better understanding of Xinjiang and its peoples, the author had to make special arrangements to travel by 'train reserved for local nationals only'.

Figure 13.1 *Mealtime (photograph by Léo-Paul Dana)*

Figure 13.2 *Turpan (photograph by Léo-Paul Dana)*

The purpose of this exploratory study is to stimulate future research. A word of caution, however, is that winter in Xinjiang is harsh and heating is primitive. At the other extreme, summer is stifling, and in Turpan, at 154 meters below sea level (the second lowest depression in the world after the Dead Sea), temperatures can exceed 120 °F. The temperature of the sand in the Taklimakan Desert reaches 150 °F. In between winter and summer are two windy seasons, during which sandstorms are common. Weather changes rapidly, and an old saying states that one wears a fur coat in the morning and changes into a silk shirt at noon.

HISTORICAL BACKGROUND

The Chinese have been making silk for three millennia. Until the year 138 BC, however, the export of silk was prohibited. Then, during a horse-buying mission in Fergana (in today's Uzbekistan, west of Xinjiang), Han-Chinese envoys realized that merchants in central Asia were willing to pay a high price for Chinese silk. Suddenly, the export ban was dropped, and the Silk Road was born.

On two occasions, in 138 BC and in 119 BC, Emperor Wu of the Western Han Dynasty (206 BC to 24 AD) dispatched Zhang Qian to develop relations with central Asia. In this part of the world, trade was not only a means of livelihood, but also a self-expressive art, a game to fathom destiny. As trade increased, the oasis towns of Xinjiang prospered, thanks to the traders whose caravan route took them across the second largest desert in the world, the Taklimakan, the name of which means 'traditional homeland' to the Uygurs. In Mandarin Chinese, in contrast, it is translated as 'the place where those who enter never come out'.

In time, the Chinese became increasingly interested in this non-Han region. Camel caravans crossed the area with silk bound for Europe; going the other way, caravans transported coral, glass, pottery and gold from Europe to China. Whoever controlled the oasis towns could tax the flows of goods across the Taklimakan Desert, thereby controlling the Silk Road, as this web of caravan routes would come to be known. In 60 BC, the Han Dynasty claimed Xinjiang as part of the Chinese Empire.

The Silk Road and the oasis towns of Xinjiang flourished until the seventeenth century. Then, the establishment of sea routes began to divert intercontinental trade. Xinjiang would no longer be in the limelight.

In January 1945, capitalists, in that which is now known as the Xinjiang Autonomous Region of China, declared the independence of the anti-Communist Turkestan Republic (nothing to do with the formerly Soviet Republic of Turkmenistan located further west, and made independent in

1991). To their dismay, Turkestan was absorbed into the People's Republic of China (PRC), which proclaimed its independence on 1 October 1949. Citizens were organized into work teams, and the new China would be divided to include 21 provinces and five autonomous regions.

In 1955, the Xinjiang province was officially renamed the Uygur Autonomous Region. (Locally, however, people still call it Xinjiang.) Its population being 70 per cent Uygur and 90 per cent non-Han at the time, the Beijing government offered incentives for people from other areas of China – primarily Sichuan (China's most populated province) – who accepted to 'colonize' the new frontier. Each year, a quarter of a million Hans immigrate to Xinjiang. The Hans spread Mandarin to this region, but most of them cannot read, write or speak the native language, Uygur. Had the Republic of Turkestan survived, it would have been an island of free enterprise between the PRC and the USSR. Its strategic location might have made it an important ally of the USA during the Cold War. Yet, in the course of human events, this land became Chinese, although its people did not.

PLURALISM

When different people, from different cultures, share activities in a secular mainstream arena, the expression of cultural differences tends to be limited to private life. Often, employment is shared in a common sphere of life, while cuisine, customs, languages and religion are a domestic concern. This may be termed 'melting pot pluralism', and this is descriptive of the situation in the United States. This, however, is not the case in Xinjiang.

When the PRC was proclaimed in 1949, there were only 200 000 Hans in Xinjiang. Incentives to colonize the region attracted many more. Today, there are over a million Hans in Urumqi (formerly Dihua City) alone. Yet they do not integrate with the indigenous people and as a result, there is no melting pot pluralism here.

Urumqi is more than 2000 km from the nearest sea. This makes it, physically, more landlocked than most cities around the world. Yet, in 1992, Beijing declared Urumqi a port, such as to give the same tax incentives as Shanghai and other seaside ports. Although Urumqi is the principal city in this Uygur region, the majority of Urumqi's inhabitants are Han-Chinese. So Urumqi's status as a landlocked port serves primarily Han-Chinese enterprises, including joint ventures with entrepreneurs from Hong Kong.

In Xinjiang, members of different ethnic groups do not share a secular mainstream arena, and there is minimal interaction across cultures. While

Figure 13.3 Arabic script above Chinese (photograph by Léo-Paul Dana)

the Hans speak Mandarin, the non-Han Uygurs speak a Turkic tongue which is written with an Arabic script (see Figure 13.3).

The Uygurs have more in common with their Turkic neighbors of the formerly Soviet, central Asian republics, than with the Han-Chinese. The Uygurs adhere to Islam, which was spread to this region by entrepreneurs traveling the Silk Road. The Uygurs have their own culture and their cuisine reflects the laws of their religion. Perhaps because they are often looked down upon by Han-Chinese, the Uygurs do not generally identify with Chinese nationality, but rather they consider themselves under Chinese occupation.

In February 1997, Chinese leader Deng Xiaoping died at the age of 92, just days after celebrating the new Year of the Ox. World media had been focused on the last days of British rule in Hong Kong, as the PRC prepared to take over the colony on 1 July. Also in the limelight, were China's desires to reunify with Taiwan. Meanwhile, Uygurs in Xinjiang spoke of secession.

DIFFERENT SPHERES OF ENTREPRENEURSHIP

In July 1979, China set up four Special Economic Zones. Next to British Hong Kong: Shenzhen; next to Portuguese Macao: Zuhuai; and next to the Taiwan Strait: Shantou and Xiamen. The opening up of China brought in foreign investment, and new technology helped develop industry. In

1993, the annual conference of the World Assembly of Small and Medium Enterprises was hosted in China's national capital. Yet none of this had much impact on the indigenous people of Xinjiang, who felt linguistically, culturally and geographically removed from Beijing.

In contrast, the demise of the USSR meant little to the average Chinese individual. However, the independence of the five central Asian states, Kazakhstan and the Kyrgyz Republic in particular, had a great symbolic lift for Uygurs, for Kazakhs and for Kirghiz living in Xinjiang. These Turkic-speaking minorities had historical, religious and cultural links with their Turkic-speaking neighbors in the newly formed Commonwealth of Independent States.

For centuries, camels pulled caravans of goods along the Silk Road system, passing through Xinjiang and thereby linking the Orient with the Middle East and with Europe. The Uygur towns, including Turpan, were stopover stations for the camel caravans and travelers would replenish on caravan food, such as raisins, and Turpan became well-known for its pitless variety. Uygur entrepreneurs in Xinjiang have begun to rebuild commercial links between east and west. In Khorghus, formerly a Silk Road town, now on the Kazakhstan side of the Xinjiang–CIS border, a new bazaar is sprawling. Russian soldiers patrolling the CIS border are happy to chug beer from China. Thus, Xinjiang resumed its ancient role of commercial hub, as was the case during the zenith of Silk Road entrepreneurship, centuries ago. Xinjiang is the meeting place of Han and Islamic cultures. Side-by-side are advertisements using Chinese characters next to those in Uygur requiring the Arabic alphabet. A Muslim Uygur sells nan, a flat bread with plov (rice mixed with religiously prepared khalal mutton), along with shashlik (khalal mutton broiled on charcoal). On another street, Han cuisine includes noodles (see Figure 13.4), tofu, dumplings, fried vegetables, white rice and eggs cooked in tea.

Members of different ethnic communities, within Xinjiang, have distinctly different tastes. A particular favorite among the Hui is soup made of flour. In contrast to the Hans who use chopsticks, the Kazakhs in Xinjiang eat with their hands; these people enjoy smoked meat and horse intestines as well as mutton with noodles eaten without utensils. The Kirghiz prefer eating rice mixed with milk, and they exhibit a preference for horse's milk. A popular meal among Uygurs consists of hand-pulled noodles mixed with bits of lamb and vegetables, with strong tea. They enjoy fried sanzi (made from dough), and a variety of steamed foods including buns and dumplings; they also like roasted cubes of mutton on skewers. They eat zhuafan with their fingers and their favorite cake is nang. For the Xibe people, a special meal would include sheep entrails. The Mongolians, the Uygurs and the Xibe drink milk-tea. As for the Kazakhs and the Kirghiz,

Figure 13.4 Noodles (photograph by Léo-Paul Dana)

their favorite drink is fermented horse milk, known in central Asia as koumis, and in China as manaizi.

Members of each ethnic group, in Xinjiang, appear to stick to themselves, and each is physically distinguishable. Rather than wearing Chinese slacks, Uygur women sport colorful dresses or skirts with matching, brightly colored scarves. Among the Uygurs, both men and women wear a colorful head cover. Daggers are fashionable among Uygur, Kazakh, Kirghiz and Mongolian men.

Different groups also select different habitats. Surrounded by the harsh conditions of the Taklimakan Desert, the ancient Uygurs managed to develop a thriving agriculture sector by making use of karez, a highly sophisticated system of underground irrigation channels. For the camel caravans, it was refreshing to stop at an Uygur oasis before continuing for thousands of miles in either direction. The Uygurs continue to cultivate cotton, grapes and melons. Local green grapes are still dried in the traditional manner, producing export-quality pitless raisins. At local markets, such as that in Turpan, donkey carts wait for local loads. Closer to the Kyrgyz Republic, trucks at the Kashgar market represent major international business. The Uygurs are therefore divided; some have opted to urbanize, while many have decided to remain in rural areas, residing in rectangular farmhouses with scuttles on flat roofs. Nomadic Kazakhs, and Kirghiz, in Xinjiang live in felt yurts, which are transported on the backs of camels. In contrast, the Han-Chinese, who are newcomers to Xinjiang,

Figure 13.5 Muslim men in Xinjiang wear head-covering (photograph by Léo-Paul Dana)

usually reside in modern blocks, and these tend to be concentrated in urban centers.

Not only do different groups in Xinjiang eat, dress (see Figure 13.5) and live differently, but most importantly, the Han-Chinese and the non-Han view enterprise from different perspecives. The Han-Chinese, who have come to Xinjiang, are generally those who identified an opportunity for economic advancement. Entrepreneurial spirit among them is focused on the firm-type economy. In contrast, for the indigenous people here, entrepreneurial spirit is centered on the bazaar.

As long as each ethnic group sticks to itself, both types of economy can co-exist. One might expect, however, that some inter-group relations will develop over time. Then the bazaar may become less isolated from the firm-type economy. This may cause changes to business processes, when entrepreneurs no longer feel compelled to follow the ways of their respective traditions.

ENTREPRENEURIAL SPIRIT REBORN

Economic development in Xinjiang was stunted when Silk Road caravans were replaced by other modes of transport. During the twentieth century, cold relations between China and the Soviet Union aggravated the situation, especially between 1971 and 1983 when the Horgas Pass was closed. Since the demise of the USSR, however, the rate of development in Xinjiang has escalated, reflecting new prosperity made possible by growing trade relations between Xinjiang and its three newly independent neighbors, Kazakhstan, the Kyrgyz Republic and Tajikistan.

On 9 June 1992, Beijing approved preferential policies for Xinjiang. The regional government was granted the power to approve foreign investment without reference to Beijing. In addition, Xinjiang was given the power to approve co-operation with its eight neighboring states. Furthermore, each border prefecture in Xinjiang became entitled to set up a border trade company, and barter was encouraged. In 1995, all entrepreneurs in Xinjiang were given the right to freely import, electrical and mechanical products made in the CIS countries. All this prompted an increase in trans-border trade. Then, more trade justified capital expenditures in infrastructure, and in turn encouraged more entrepreneurial activity.

Until the time of World War II, the communications infrastructure in Xinjiang relied essentially on camels, donkeys and horses. From 1949 to 1992, 250 000 telephones were installed in the region. Another 250 000 phones were installed during 1993 alone. In late 1994, a numerical optical cable linked Xian with Urumqi.

The region's first railway was built in 1962, with other lines opened in 1984, 1990, 1992, and 1994. During the spring of 1992, a new train service linked Xinjiang and the newly independent Republic of Kazakhstan. The establishment of Xinjiang Airline Company, in 1985, contributed to the airport at Urumqi becoming one of the four largest in the PRC. Flights now link Xinjiang with Europe and North America as well as with other cities of Asia.

Up until 1993, foreigners in the PRC were not allowed to use local currency. Instead, they were required to use Foreign Exchange Certificates (FEC), a regulation which complicated otherwise simple transactions. Foreigners are now permitted to use the same currency as the locals.

Improvements in infrastructure, coupled with gradual liberalization since 1979, have facilitated entrepreneurship, and this has helped the region's economy to grow impressively. Unpublished government sources in Beijing claim that GNP for this region grew at an average rate of 11.2 per cent during the fifteen year period from 1979 to 1994. Similar statistics suggest that gross production in Xinjiang exceeded 63 billion yuan in 1994, an increase of 10.9 percent over 1993, with growth in the service sector leading at about 15 percent during the mid-1990s. Xinjiang's international trade reaches US$1 billion annually. Over 500 foreign firms are in business in this region, of which more than 400 are involved in joint ventures.

UYGUR ENTREPRENEURSHIP

In contrast to the Han-Chinese entrepreneurs, who are often industrialists, Uygur entrepreneurs generally focus their efforts in one of two activities: many Uygurs are farmers selling produce to the bazaar; others are traders in the bazaar economy.

Since ancient times, the Uygurs have been able to farm successfully, despite desert conditions. This has been possible thanks to their discovery of karez wells, which are underground shafts sunk along mountain slopes and converted to form a network of subterranean canals, used as irrigation ditches.

In addition, Xinjiang built about 500 water reservoirs, with a total storage capacity of approximately six billion cubic meters. Today, this region of 1.6 million square kilometers includes almost four million hectares of arable land, more than any other province or region of China.

Xinjiang has long been famous for its quality and abundance of fruit, and unpublished sources at the agricultural ministry claim that the per capita fruit share is 112 kg, which is 2 times higher than that of the world average. Local fruit include apricots (especially near Kuqa), figs (from Artush), musk melons (near Qishan), perfume pears (from Kurle), watermelons (from Qapqal), and the famous seedless white grapes which are dried in traditional towers, to produce clear raisins.

Other than fruit, beets, cotton, maize and wheat are the dominant crops here. Unofficial figures, provided to the author by the agricultural ministry, report that during the mid-1990s, Xinjiang's annual grain output exceeded six million tons, while beet harvests approached three million tons and cotton, almost one million tons. Also, vast prairies have made it possible for the Uygurs to develop high quality livestock, including large-tail sheep, milk-beef cattle, Baicheng chickens and large Turpan donkeys. Annual meat production in Xinjiang has been about ½ million tons.

Turpan has long been a market town for Uygur farmers. In the markets here, merchants buy and sell foodstuffs, clothing, saddlebags and home-made knives among other things. Much of the food which is on display, including dried apricots, raisins, almonds and walnuts, is classified as caravan food. This is the food that the merchants of the Silk Road once stocked up on, in the same markets.

Kashgar is also a major town on the Silk Road. Here, one finds so much Arabic influence that it is easy to forget that one is in China. Alongside barbers and food vendors in the bazaar, traders sell camels near donkeys pulling carts piled high with cargo. The Sunday bazaar, in Kashgar, may be the largest in central Asia. Each Sunday attracts 100 000 individuals who buy and sell in this bazaar with tents and stalls that easily cover a

Figure 13.6 Spices (photograph by Léo-Paul Dana)

square mile. Among the merchandise are spices (see Figure 13.6), clothing, electronic goods, knives, wood, chickens, sheep, horses, camels and even small birds, which are kept as musical pets, in wooden cages.

Several vendors sell fast food called *girde nan*, i.e., circular bread sprinkled with sesame seeds and served warm. At Hotan, yet another node of the Silk Road, horses are more important than camels, as horse oil is used for medicinal purposes – specifically to mend bones. As is normally the case in a bazaar economy, the market is segmented according to producers. (This is quite a contrast with the firm-type economy in which segmentation refers to consumers.) An important sector of the market in Hotan is reserved for curbside doctors and dentists. Here, dentures are prepared next to carts hitched to donkeys waiting for freight. Perhaps the most striking bazaar is at the Horgas Pass, to the south-west of Bortala. Like other towns of the Silk Road, the settlement was impoverished when caravans stopped passing through it. In 1971, all international activity was banned here, as the border with the USSR was closed. The local inhabitants had no electricity, no running water, and no trade.

Life finally improved in 1983, when the border was re-opened, and trade indeed has grown rapidly. According to information obtained by the author during an interview in Almaty, the capital of Kazakhstan until recently, entrepreneurs carried 20 million kilos of goods across this border in 1984; the same official projected that trade would surpass 500 million kilos in 1998. Dana (1997) elaborates on entrepreneurship in Kazakhstan.

A unique feature along the border of China and Kazakhstan is 'The Bazaar for Entrepreneurs from Both Sides'. This market has two entrances, one in Xinjiang and the other in Kazakhstan. Uygur entrepreneurs from Xinjiang bring beer, vodka, sugar, candies, clothing, leather goods, sporting apparel, toys, housewares, tools, cigarettes and jewelry, all of which they sell to the buyers from Kazakhstan, including Kazakhs and Russians, most of whom arrive by bus.

All persons who enter the market from the Kazakhstan gateway pay admission, in American dollars. Entry costs $3 per couple. Once inside, people can buy Chinese renminbi that can be used to buy merchandise, which is normally stuffed into the shopping bags that the buyers bring with them. Excess baggage will travel by truck; waiting outside the gate is a long row of empty trucks with Kazakh plates. At the end of the day, the Uygur vehicles are empty, and the vendors have money in their pockets, in their bags and even in their stockings.

Although the bazaar is not simply a means to monetary reward, it is producing wealth among the Uygurs. More importantly, it allows Uygur traders to socialize among others sharing similar cultural values. The flow of commerce is still fragmented into numerous disconnected transactions between individuals – just as it was generations ago. This allows the sharing of cigarettes over tea; of greatest significance, from an economic perspective, it helps to spread risks.

TOWARD THE FUTURE

In September 1991, *The Economist* suggested that central Asia could fall to Islamic fundamentalism. In 1998, there were over 22 000 mosques in Xinjiang – one per 400 worshippers. Fundamentalism, however, is not on the agenda, as the Muslims here are Sunni and not extreme in their religious views. Instead, much effort is being focused on enterprise.

Economic development in Xinjiang has escalated, as Han-Chinese entrepreneurs prosper in the firm-type economy, and indigenous Muslim Uygurs thrive in agriculture and/or trade in the bazaar. In specific, pan-Turkic trade is on the rise, between Uygur entrepreneurs in Xinjiang and other Muslims in republics to the west.

Of course, the independence of the formerly Soviet republics in central Asia sparked the rekindling of cultural, religious and business links between entrepreneurs in these republics and with their Turkic cousins in Xinjiang. Their common cultural, linguistic and religious background also facilitated pan-Turkic business.

Interestingly, watching neighboring Kazakhstan and the Kyrgyz Republic as they begin to prosper since independence, many Uygurs are wondering whether their own enterprises might fare better in an independent Xinjiang, free from regulations imposed by China. In 1993, anti-Chinese violence broke out in Xinjiang, but the Han-Chinese police quickly crushed this. Officially, all of China has only one time zone, which is the same as that of Beijing. All of China respects this; however, Uygurs function according to an unofficial time zone. Uygur entrepreneurs, in Xinjiang, are more concerned with conducting business with Kazakhstan and the Kyrgyz Republic, than with pleasing politicians in China's capital; although the Han-Chinese in Xinjiang respect Beijing time, most Uygurs set their watches two hours behind the official time of China. This presumably facilitates pan-Turkic trade between Uygurs and entrepreneurs in Kazakhstan and in the Kyrgyz Republic; more importantly, it is a highly symbolic gesture.

CONCLUSION

This chapter has provided an ethnographic account of the bazaar economy, as operated by indigenous entrepreneurs in western China. This institution contrasts sharply with the firm-type economy of the Han-Chinese.

The study found that while the firm-type economy is a means to monetary gain, the bazaar is an end in itself, as it helps the Uygurs preserve their traditions. The Uygur entrepreneurs of the bazaar are more concerned with social relations and less focused on the maximization of profits; nevertheless, their bazaar is an institution that gives rise to considerable profitability. Whereas traditional economic theory assumes that the decision-maker of the firm-type economy is rational, this research reveals that in the bazaar, focus is on personal relations. In contrast to the firm-type economy where segmentation refers to market, in the bazaar context, segmentation refers to the clustering of producers. In the bazaar, competition is not limited to sellers; competition takes place between the buyer and the seller who negotiate prices.

The growth of firms among Han-Chinese entrepreneurs in Xinjiang is often related to advances in technology and to government incentives. Among the Uygurs, growth is a function of personal relations.

> It matters not if a cat is black or white. As long as it catches mice, it is a good cat. (Deng Xiaoping, 1904 [1997])

NOTES

* This article originally appeared as 'Small Business in Xinjjang' in the *Asian Journal of Business & Information Systems*, **3** (1), Summer 1998, 123–35. Reproduced with permission.

1. The author would like to express special gratitude to the three armed bodyguards whose presence was also much appreciated, especially after dark.

REFERENCES

Brenner, G. and J.-M. Toulouse (1990), 'Business Creation Among the Chinese Immigrants in Montreal', *Journal of Small Business & Entrepreneurship*, **7** (3), 38–44.

Dana, L.-P. (1994), 'A Marxist Mini-Dragon? Entrepreneurship in Today's Vietnam', *Journal of Small Business Management*, **32** (2), 95–102.

Dana, L.-P. (1995), 'Enterprising Culture in Hong Kong', *Journal of Enterprising Culture*, **3** (4), 497–510.

Dana, L.-P. (1997), 'Change, Entrepreneurship and Innovation in the Republic of Kazakhstan', *Entrepreneurship, Innovation, and Change*, **6** (2), 167–74.

Light, I. (1972), *Ethnic Enterprise in America*, Berkeley and Los Angeles, CA: University of California Press.

Loewen, J. 1971, *The Mississippi Chinese: Between Black and White*, Cambridge, MA: Harvard University Press.

Ray, D.M., A. Momijan, W.E. McMullan and S. Ko (1988), 'Comparison of Immigrant Armenian Entrepreneurs in Los Angeles and Immigrant Chinese Entrepreneurs in Calgary', Calgary, University of Calgary Faculty of Management Research Papers.

Shenkar, O. (1994), 'The People's Republic of China: Raising the Bamboo Screen Through International Management Research', *International Studies of Management and Organization*, **24** (1–2), 9–34.

Wong, B. (1987), 'The Role of Ethnicity in Enclave Entrepreneurs: A Study of the Chinese Garment Factory in New York City', *Human Organization*, **16** (2), 120–30.

14. Muslim entrepreneurs in France

Hadj Nekka and Alain Fayolle

INTRODUCTION

The purpose of this study was to highlight some of the specific aspects of small and medium-sized enterprises (SMEs) created by foreign entrepreneurs. In France, research into this subject is still in its infancy and the field is relatively new, even though the numbers of such firms are expected to increase in the coming years. For the research, a small number of in-depth cases, all SMEs in the Nord-Pas region of Calais, France, were studied empirically. The preliminary results presented here are concerned with the characteristics of the entrepreneurs and how they manage their firms. A typology is proposed and will eventually be tested on a larger sample.

Research into venture creators of foreign origin is still in its infancy, and the field is relatively new in France.[1] One of the main reasons for this is probably the fact that these firms currently represent only a small percentage of the general population, although their numbers are expected to grow in the coming years. The empirical research we propose here will therefore provide some much needed additional information. The study examines the conditions in which these firms emerge within their geographical and cultural environment, and the different management methods used. It is an approach that opens up some interesting prospects in the field of management science, and one we hope will enable us to explore a number of avenues, including culture as a key element in explaining success or failure, the role of the environment, and the predictability of the firm's development path or the methods it uses to survive. The research described here is exploratory in nature, and is based on seven case studies of SMEs in the Nord-Pas region of Calais, France.

1. ENTREPRENEURSHIP AND SMALL BUSINESS MANAGEMENT

Researchers have been studying entrepreneurship for more than 15 years, and much of their work has focused on entrepreneurial behaviour. Their findings tend to support the premise that entrepreneurs are created, not born (Fayolle, 2003; 2004). Indeed, most people, regardless of their origins, profiles or experience, seem able to become entrepreneurs. Nevertheless, entrepreneurship is a complex and multidimensional act,[2] even with regard to business owners' behaviour (Marchesnay, 1998). For the time being, research into venture creators' behaviours and motivating factors can only be descriptive in nature (Bruyat, 1993). Attempts at theory development are questionable due to the presence of prejudices and preconceived notions, while problems with definitions have weakened research methodologies and made it impossible to compare results. Proposals to reposition the concept of entrepreneur in a broader context have also helped to keep research at the exploratory level. At the same time, research into entrepreneurial traits has revealed a broad range of characteristics and some considerable differences between the qualities expected in theory and the qualities actually observed empirically. All these elements together have tended to direct the research thrust more towards entrepreneurial typologies and away from the idea of a model entrepreneur. The typologies complement one another, however, and can be combined to explain the actions taken in small firms according to the style employed by their entrepreneurs.[3]

The notion of entrepreneurship still divides researchers. On one side of the fence are those who believe the concept applies to new venture creations only, while on the other side are those who think it also includes creative processes leading to functional improvements in existing businesses.

The current expansion of entrepreneurship research coincides with a well-expressed social need. The issues at stake are major, and include reducing the mortality rate of new ventures by introducing appropriate support processes along with customized, effective financial assistance programmes. Management researchers must also innovate in terms of their pedagogy too, since small business management systems and management tools have not yet been invented. The research described here is designed to throw new light on a specific group of venture creators. Such an approach is of considerable pedagogical interest, and has implications for management. The population of creators studied for the research encompasses the different and occasionally complementary notions of employer, entrepreneur and manager. The notion of employer reflects a certain level of individual emancipation, in that it gives legitimacy to the individual's connection with the adoptive society. The notion of entrepreneur encompasses the desire to innovate and create, along with a sense of freedom, independence and autonomy. Lastly, the notion of manager refers to responsibility, rationality and maturity.

Our discussion of the literature review has been divided into three sections dealing respectively with entrepreneurs, venture creators and small business management.

1.1 Entrepreneurs

It is not our intention here to present the entire body of economic theory in order to give meaning to the notion of entrepreneur. Instead, we will concentrate on the contribution of Schumpeter, who is by far the most explicit author in terms of establishing the economic function of entrepreneurs (Casson, 1991). Schumpeter believes the function of entrepreneurs is to innovate or create new combinations.[4] It is therefore reasonable to postulate that intrapreneurs and entrepreneurs share numerous psychological traits. They differ from managers in that they need freedom, prefer projects rather than power, are able to tolerate moderate risk, and view failure and mistakes as necessary elements of learning (Roberts, 1980). In an environment that is becoming increasingly complex, all firms, regardless of their status, must be able to adapt through organizational innovation. The notion of 'persistent entrepreneur' is clearly useful here. A persistent entrepreneur does not stop at creating just one firm, but continues throughout his or her career (Verstraete, 1998). Thus, a creator could lose his or her entrepreneurial quality by focusing too much on management (Stevenson, 1998), or maintain it by applying new solutions to improve the firm's operations (Labourdette, 1992) or seeking out new opportunities (Miles and Snow, 1978). According to Davidsson (1989), entrepreneurs are people who recognize the value of an idea and exploit it, regardless of whether or not they invest their own money in the venture.

1.2 Venture Creators: A Profile

According to Bonnet (1998), research in France suggests that venture creators are often job seekers. In fact, employees and labourers account for more than half of all venture creators. There is ample evidence to show that the creator's profile, including his or her initial training, will determine the sector in which the firm operates. Venture creators whose main focus is development[5] account for approximately 20 per cent of the total, while those whose main focus is insertion account for the remaining 80 per cent (Gouzien and Turquet, 1994).

Virtually all successful venture creators have specific motivators and qualities, but there is no single typical psychological profile (Papin, 1997). This does not mean, however, that profile variables should be ignored. The model developed by Covin and Slevin (1991) shows that the creator's basic education, professional experience, subsequent training, intellectual aptitudes and temperament all shape his or her entrepreneurial behaviour, which in turn determines the firm's behaviour. The creator's profile can even be described as fundamental, in that the behaviour of the individual and the behaviour of the firm are inseparable at the start-up stage. As the firm develops, other players are brought in and the creator must change his or her behaviour to avoid conflict. The firm's behaviour will be analysed using internal, external, organizational and strategic variables, and it is this process that will determine performance. It has to be said that the processes leading up to the discovery of an opportunity are complex and are largely conditioned by unconscious phenomena and the psychological profile of the people concerned.

Empirical research to establish a causal link between the creator's profile, the creator's behaviour and the firm's performance appears to support this approach. Capiez (1999) has contributed two findings of considerable interest. First, he suggests that the creator's training, qualifications and temperament will determine his or her entrepreneurial behaviour (and hence the behaviour of the firm), characterized by a tendency to make more use of technology as the environment becomes more complex. Performance is associated with this behaviour. Second, Capiez (1999) states that firm behaviour based on extended cooperation with influential players from the environment and a form of organization in which information is used for forecasting purposes will improve the firm's performance in terms of both profitability and market share.

Given the nature of the population studied, we feel it would be useful to apply some of the typologies developed by sociologists. Weber (1988), for example, distinguishes between two small business leadership categories, namely, entrepreneurs, defined as innovative people inhabited by a capitalist mindset and an entrepreneurial culture, and owner-managers, who are more focused on asset management and income production. The former are in the minority, while the latter, who are often conservative, authoritarian and creatures of habit, represent the majority of small business owners and are present in large numbers in all types of professional groups.

Despite the obvious interest of this first classification, however, we finally chose the typology devised by Marchesnay (1998), which appears to be better suited to our needs. Marchesnay believes the entrepreneurial profile can be based on two elements of legitimacy, namely, territory and competition. Accordingly, he proposes a four-component typology of *isolated*, *professional*, *nomad* and *enterprising* entrepreneurs. *Isolated* entrepreneurs exhibit reactive, defensive behaviour, focused on survival, with very little local support. *Professional* entrepreneurs are more connected to their environment. They want their firms to survive over time, so they can retain their power and be financially independent. They adopt a paternalistic style, seek income-producing situations and protect their firms by maintaining close contacts with others. *Nomads* are guided by a managerial logic dominated by a need for efficiency, and are not as interested in local connections. If the economy demanded it, they would relocate without a second thought. Lastly, *enterprising* entrepreneurs maintain close ties with their local environment for emotional or cognitive reasons, but unlike the others, they have a need to compete.

We believe this typology deserves to be reviewed, among other things to take into account the concept of fatality as addressed by the psychologists.

Venture creation is more a process of building social contacts between a range of players than an obstacle course (Mustar, 1997). This is particularly true of innovative firms and firms with strong development potential. Empirical research so far has confirmed the idea that it is possible to confuse the problems specific to venture creation and those encountered in any other innovative process (Mustar, 1994).

1.3 Small Business Management

Small business management can be divided into management methods and management style.

1.3.1 Management methods

Small firms need management models that are consistent with two of their distinctive competencies, flexibility and interactivity. There are two managerial orientations that are dependent on the characteristics of the environment. The first orientation focuses on the ability to adjust of firms that have, through their interactions, developed reciprocal benefits, while the second involves firms developing or surviving by revolving around large corporations. Given these two orientations, the first thing to do is to study players that are relatively stable in the environment. The emergent strategic vision is a vital element in the firm's ability to compete, and the entrepreneur plays a key role in overseeing the economic reliability of projects while remaining connected to the environment. If problems arise, membership of social clubs may be the only way of developing relationship networks, but business owners are naturally prudent and do not trust easily (Frémicourt, 1998). The premise is simple, namely, that an economically integrated project facilitates the social integration of the firm's leader. This is clearly illustrated by the case of innovative firms (Mustar, 1997).

1.3.2 Management style

This aspect is increasingly important in a context where the business owner's rational thought is no longer as powerful as was previously claimed (Laroche and Nioche, 1994). As their firms develop, business owners must have an overview of the problems and be able to identify factors of change in order to build their strategies. To do this, they must be both leaders and managers.[6] Management style refers to the way they manage their employees and the types of contacts they maintain with the firm's partners. It is extremely important, especially in organizations wishing to develop teamwork or project-based organization.[7] The business owner must make sure the firm's standards are broad enough not to hinder the expression of personal style and narrow enough not to allow for too many individual approaches that are impossible to manage (Le Saget, 1992).

Style may be a source of contradiction that damages the social climate and has a negative impact on the quality of skills management within the organization. There are two contradictory behaviours here (Beaucourt, 1996). The first behaviour involves highlighting attempts at skill development when they are strategic assets for the firm, or denying them when they generate routine behaviours or rigid approaches. The second involves objecting to any form of organizational change. Unfortunately, current research suggests that this latter behaviour is almost natural in organizational development (Koenig, 1999).

In reality, management styles are not always stable, and it is quite possible that business owners will shift from one style to another. To situate extreme cases, the emphasis will be placed on fluctuations between participation and exclusion of employees, making it impossible to reconcile all the issues at the same time. Beaucourt (1996) believes it is possible to provide a response to the goals of cooperation and creativity, which are both complementary and competitive. She suggests the introduction of adjustment procedures requiring permanent management of the meanings produced by collective action.

2. CREATION AND MANAGEMENT OF SMALL FIRMS BY ENTREPRENEURS OF MAGHREBIAN ORIGIN

This second section begins by setting out the methodology used for the research, including the selection of firms in the Calais Nord-Pas region. It then presents our findings and proposes a typology of the managerial behaviours observed. We have tried to establish links between business owner profiles, values and management practices.

2.1 Methodology

This section describes the research territory and the data collection and processing method.

2.1.1 Research territory

In small firms, it is very difficult to distinguish between the firm and its owner. The links between the organization and its environment are coordinated and managed directly by the owner. At the same time, the small firm as a transaction space (Julien and Marchesnay, 1988) forms an excellent basis for studying inter-organizational links.

We selected the seven sample firms through personal contacts.[8] The Calais Nord-Pas region was chosen for its venture creation support structures (Lifooghe, 1995; Paris, 1993). Such structures are only effective if they are able to address the needs of everyone concerned, regardless of origin. Clearly, support should continue after venture creation. Indeed, some authors believe it is only then that the real problems begin (Sammut, 1998). Given the importance of the insertion logic in the venture creation process, the work of Plumly and Oliver (1987) on the influence of individual fatalism concerning the job search is clearly relevant. They believe fatalistic individuals expend less energy on the job search and are less likely to take the initiative, on the basis that opportunities are rare and in any case the link between individual effort and reward is very weak. The authors therefore conclude that these people need advice, encouragement and incentive. Other authors also believe venture creation incentives involve financial assistance, infrastructure availability and training and advisory support (Albert et al., 1994; Duchéneaut and the Euro PME Research Centre, 1995).

2.1.2 Data collection and processing

We began with an in-depth interview with the owners of the sample firms, during which we proposed areas for discussion (the venture creation process and type of management) and then left the owners to talk about those subjects as they wished. The interviewer asked questions where necessary, to obtain clarification, refocus the discussion or reformulate a statement. The goal was always the same, namely, to identify the path taken by the venture creator and the type of management he or she practised. This initial interview was followed by a second, semi-directed interview to look in more detail at the two areas. All the interviews were recorded and transcribed, and the transcriptions were then subjected to a content analysis. The information was processed without a formal analysis grid, so that the key concepts, their foundations and their links could emerge freely.

2.2 Exploratory Research Findings

The research findings will be presented in three parts, the first dealing with the business owners' profiles, the second with their management methods and the third with their position in the typologies proposed by Marchesnay (1998) and Miles and Snow (1978).

2.2.1 Venture creators' profiles

The venture creators in our sample were motivated mainly by an insertion logic, but sometimes by an entrepreneurial logic that was apparent, although not strongly, in the subjects' remarks, in a discourse focused mainly on the state of the labour market and their labour relations experience as employees. Their perception was generally positive, since they felt they had needed a trigger to propel them into venture creation. The sole female venture creator in the sample was the exception. She emphasized the suitability of her temperament and skills for venture creation. Three values appeared to underlie the subjects' choice of venture creation, namely, freedom, independence and a favourable social status. The creators' training and prior experience determined their choice of sector. Only two of the sample mentioned economic timeliness as a third variable. Social origin was not a key factor, either in triggering venture creation or in selecting the sector. As Table 14.1 shows, and as suggested in the findings cited by Bonnet (1998), the profiles of the venture creators in our sample are similar to the general trend and there do not appear to be any elements that are specific to ethnic origin.

Similarly, our findings do not contradict those obtained from studies of individual cases, which showed that individuals may be forced into entrepreneurship by their inability to accept authority and organizational rules (Kets De Vries, 1998).

2.2.2 Management methods

The role played by family members in the sample firms is important. The venture creation adventure begins individually, but soon becomes a family affair. The family element emerges upstream, as the venture creators seek funding, and during the start-up phase, when family members are recruited to work for the new company.[9] It appears to have a significant impact on the firm's fate, at least in cases where the venture creators finance their firms through personal and family assets.

Success factors include technical skill, product quality, flexibility and the ability to react to market needs. A small structure that is more flexible and easily adaptable to market needs is considered important. The firm's image is also important – its reputation among its customers, its ability to

Table 14.1 Profile of the seven venture creators

Firm's characteristics	E1	E2	E3	E4	E5	E6	E7
Sector	Hydraulic, pneumatic	Sales promotion	Pipes and boilers	Computing	Sheet metal and painting	Abrasive processing	Metallurgy
Workforce	25	25	98	60	40	6	10
Date of creation	1986	1993	1990	1983	1984	1993	1996
Type of creation	Individual	Individual	Group, individual takeover	Alone with help from spouse	Takeover	Alone with help from brother	Individual
Date of arrival in France	1954	Born in France	1962	Born in France	1960	1968	1962
Age of creator	50	38	45	43	44	47	54
Gender of creator	Male	Female	Male	Male	Male	Male	Male
Religion	Belief in Moslem principles	Islam	Belief in basic Moslem principles	Completely indifferent	Completely indifferent	Belief in basic Moslem principles	Islam
Level of education	University technical diploma	Licence	Bachelor's degree	Higher technician's licence	Higher technician's licence	Higher technician's licence	None
Type of training	Mechanical	Biochemistry	Boiler techniques	Hosiery and spinning	Technical	Mechanical	None
Management education	No	Yes	Yes	No	No	Yes	No
Social origin	Son of a labourer	Daughter of a labourer	Son of a miner	Son of a labourer	Son of a labourer	Son of a labourer	None

meet deadlines and its compliance with signed contracts. All this appears to be directed outwards, to such a point that subjects rarely mentioned the quality of internal relationships and communications. These findings are similar to those obtained by Bamberger (1980).

The human factor appears to be more present in industrial firms and less present in service firms. The creator's ethnic origin can sometimes be an asset for the firm in terms of human resources management. For example, one of the subjects whose firm had a large workforce said the best way for him to communicate with and motivate his staff was to attend workshops. He said that, as a foreigner, he needed to work hard to succeed and was admired, respected and supported by his employees, who saw him as an example of success. To overcome the communication difficulties arising from intercultural differences, the subject said he relied on simplicity, honesty and mutual respect.

The managerial problems mentioned by subjects included competition, which was an unavoidable factor in the region, and the aggressive attitude of the large department stores, which was a permanent threat. They also mentioned cash flow problems and administrative difficulties, including accounting and the shortage of qualified employees. Other problems included difficulties in meeting delivery deadlines, signing contracts and entering into agreements. Problems due to the economic environment were highly controversial, however, and most of our subjects felt the real problem was lack of prospective thinking.

As far as development is concerned, the subjects mentioned the need to find managers so that they themselves would be free to spend their time on the broader aspects of innovation. They were also interested in developing human resources management and communication. Balancing the firm's functions was a managerial priority. An increase in turnover does not always reflect good management, however (Molina, 1990). Organizational, social and strategic innovation is also essential. Some of the subjects said they were looking for partners to develop new products and enter new markets, and in this respect it was important for them to have internationalization strategies. Generally speaking, the subjects did not have the same perception of development. Some were not interested in achieving development or growth in order to maintain their authority, whereas others regarded development as an indicator of capital building, efficiency or productivity.

The elements identified above are fairly general in nature, and there is nothing in particular that could be attributed specifically to the presence of a Magrhebian business owner. The individual obstacles to entrepreneurship identified by Mehling (1991) in a study of SMEs in Africa, namely the desire for immediate profit, a lack of technical training and a shortage of managers, were not observed in our sample firms.

Table 14.2 Types of entrepreneurs in the sample

Sociological focus	Focus of activity		
	Defensive	Prospective	Analytical
'Isolated'		E7	
'Professional'			
'Nomadic'	E4 E6	E3	
'Entrepreneurial'	E2	E1	E5

2.2.3 Typology of Maghrebian entrepreneurs

Given the lack of literature in France on immigrant entrepreneurs, we would have liked to use our data to construct an original typology. However, because of the sample's small spread in terms of size and especially age, we felt it would be more appropriate to use an existing typology. We selected two entrepreneurial typologies: the former from Marchesnay (1998), primarily for its territorial aspect and the latter from Miles and Snow (1978) for its competitive dimension. The results of our analysis can be seen in Table 14.2.

Table 14.2 shows six types of entrepreneurial profiles:

1. *Isolated-prospective.* These people were unhappy as employees, and see venture creation as a challenge. They select broader markets and are prepared to seize every opportunity. They would like to enter the Algerian market, but remain faithful to their original region. Everyday management is difficult for them.
2. *Defensive-nomadic.* They opt for venture creation as a means of achieving insertion, but select a sector in which they identify an opportunity. In their opinion, the firm's success depends on its ability to meet the expectations of its customers and on its commercial qualities. The problems they encounter are the same as those faced by most growing firms, including competition and the challenge of managing a growing organization. The initial host environment serves as a starting point for other initiatives, some of which may involve foreign markets. These entrepreneurs are able to adapt well to local and cultural specifics and prefer to delegate management tasks.
3. *Defensive-entrepreneurial.* They have wanted to launch their own business since childhood, and eventually do so in a field in which they are skilled. In their opinion, success means being a good manager and conveying an image that outside partners find reassuring. They need

to control everything and to be admired. They focus exclusively on their own specialty field, even when they know it is risky. They believe their ethnic origin is a considerable asset for their firms.

4. *Prospective-nomadic.* The new business enables them to obtain professional acceptance and develop their skills. They attribute their business success to their managerial skills and ability to earn territorial legitimacy. They believe their ethnic origin makes things harder for them, but think this can be overcome by proving their worth. They enjoy power and seize every opportunity available to them, including an economically and socially favourable environment.
5. *Prospective-entrepreneurial.* They are motivated by a belief that their ethnic origin would make it difficult for them to have successful careers as employees. They need salary progression to achieve their sole objective, which is to master their trade and obtain experience. They believe they can compete on merit. The main problems they face are the lack of qualified labour and dysfunctional logistics. They are well connected inside their community and are willing to seek out the skills they need both inside and outside the firm. They prefer to concentrate on the entrepreneurial aspects of business, delegating managerial tasks to managers. They are demanding of themselves and the people around them, and believe their status will open doors for them in the community.
6. *Analytic-entrepreneurial.* Because of their experience, they are able to buy out firms in difficulty. They believe the firm's ultimate success depends entirely on their own skills. They need to control everything and maintain a good relationship with the environment. They feel they are part of their community. The problem for them is to work in a sector that is not economically profitable. Although buying a company is a delicate operation, the change gives them new motivation. This appears to be confirmed by the fact that mortality rates among firms created from scratch is higher than for buyouts, and also by the fact that these entrepreneurs select sectors in which they have already worked (Bonneau, 1997).

All business owners need to accept the dialectic and ambiguity in their firm's operations if they are to avoid undue anxiety. Researchers have been working for more than a decade on tools to help them with this (Lagadec, 1996). Lagadec uses the term 'mutation' to describe the evolution of the business owner's function: 'In the past, they had to be able to know and apply existing models, even though those models were totally unsuited to their non-standard systems; now, however, they need to be prospective thinkers and be willing to take responsibility' (free translation). In other words, business leaders must be creators and visionaries who have their feet firmly on the ground (Daigne, 1995).

CONCLUSION

In this research we examined the venture creation and management process in firms launched by Maghrebian entrepreneurs. The first lesson to be drawn from our findings is that anyone can become involved in entrepreneurship, anywhere in the world, and especially outside their community of origin, as Shapero has shown. And second, entrepreneurship involves the community as a whole, even though venture creation is first and foremost an individual act (Mehling, 1991).

The study shows that the motivations and characteristics of Maghrebian entrepreneurs are no different from those of other entrepreneurs. On the other hand, the family plays a different role in the management of Maghrebian firms than in firms created by French entrepreneurs. Further research is required on this point.

It would be useful to continue the research using a larger sample of firms, to examine both the ethnic element and some more general factors. There is no shortage of possibilities here. Business development is divided into three phases, namely, creation, survival and disappearance. The creation phase is covered by entrepreneurship theory, the survival phase by adaptation theory and the disappearance phase by failure theory (Desreumaux, 1994). Entrepreneurship will always be relevant in a context of change where more entrepreneurs are needed in firms (Tarondeau et al., 1994). A preliminary typology of Maghrebian entrepreneurs, such as that proposed here, will serve as a starting point for future research. As Filion (1997) points out, a typology can be used to establish the value system and intentions of the person concerned, and to explain how that person makes decisions, devises strategic orientations and develops a visionary process.

NOTES

1. Unlike other countries, which have extensive bodies of research into ethnic entrepreneurship.
2. Although the work of Kets de Vries and Stevenson throws new light on who entrepreneurs are and the similarities between some of their behaviours.
3. For example, M. Marchesnay (1998) tried to combine the well-known work of Smith and Miles and Snow.
4. He identifies five types of innovation, namely the introduction of a new product, an improvement to the quality of an existing product, the introduction of a new produc-

tion process, the opening of a new market, and the identification of a new source of raw material supplies or semi-finished goods.
5. The authors refer to entrepreneurial logic.
6. Some venture creators are well aware of the need to build a team in order to carry out these two roles successfully.
7. A young firm is a project of itself.
8. The authorities do not have statistics on this particular population of venture creators.
9. Five of the subjects said family members held important positions in their firms.

REFERENCES

Albert, P., A. Fayolle and S. Marion (1994), 'L'évolution des systèmes d'appui à la création d'entreprises', *Revue Française de Gestion*, **100**, November–December, 100–112.

Bamberger, I. (1980), 'Situations et comportements stratégiques des petites et moyennes entreprises', *Direction et Gestion* (4), 21–30.

Beaucourt, C. (1996), 'La dimension symbolique des configurations organisationnelles', *Revue Française de Gestion*, **101**, January–February, 121–31.

Bonneau, J. (1997), 'Les repreneurs d'entreprises', *Problèmes économiques* (2531), 15–18.

Bonnet, J. (1998), 'Le renouvellement du tissu productif à travers la création d'entreprises en France', *Revue Internationale P.M.E.*, **11** (1), 9–40.

Bruyat, C. (1993), 'Création d'entreprise: contribution épistémologique et modélisation', doctoral thesis in management science, Ecole Supérieure des Affaires, Université Pierre Mendès France, Grenoble, France.

Capiez, A. (1999), 'Formation et contribution du créateur d'entreprise au développement économique', in *Dimensions économiques et managériales du capital humain*, Angers: Presses Universitaires d'Angers.

Casson, M. (1991), *L'entrepreneur*, Paris: Economica.

Covin, J. and D. Slevin (1991), 'A Conceptual Model of Entrepreneurship as Firm Behavior', *Entrepreneurship Theory and Practice*, **16** (1), 7–25.

Daigne, J.-F. (1995), *Ré-ingénierie et reprise d'entreprises*, Paris: Economica.

Davidsson, P. (1989), 'Continued Entrepreneurship and Small Business Growth', PhD dissertation, Stockholm School of Economics.

Desreumaux, A. (1994), 'Théories de l'évolution de l'entreprise: bilan et perspectives', *Cahier de Recherche*, **94** (4), IAE de Lille.

Duchéneaut, B. and the Euro PME Research Centre (1995), *Enquête sur les PME françaises*, Paris: Maxima.

Fayolle, A. (2003), *Le métier de créateur d'entreprise*, Paris: Les Editions d'Organisation.

Fayolle, A. (2004), *Entrepreneuriat. Apprendre à Entreprendre*, Paris: Dunod, collection Gestion Sup.

Filion, L.J. (1997), 'Le champ de l'entrepreneuriat: historique, évolution, tendances', *Revue internationale P.M.E.*, **10** (2), 129–72.

Frémicourt, E. (1998), 'Former les dirigeants de PME', *Revue Personnel*, (389), 43–7.

Gouzien, A. and P. Turquet (1994), 'Chômeurs créateurs d'entreprises: logique entrepreneuriale ou logique d'insertion?', paper presented at the conference 'Sciences de Gestion et Problémes d'emploi', Lille, 22–23 September.

Julien, P.-A. and M. Marchesnay (1988), *La petite entreprise: principes d'économie et de gestion*, Paris: Vuibert.
Kets De Vries, M.F.R. (1998), 'Un rebelle créatif', in Sue Birley and Daniel Muzyka (eds), *L'art d'entreprendre*, Les Echos Editions, Paris: Village Mondial, pp. 20–23.
Koenig, G. (1999), 'Les ressources au principe de la stratégie', in G. Koenig, *Nouvelles théories pour gérer l'entreprise du XXIè siècle*, Paris: Economica, pp. 199–239.
Labourdette, A (1992), *Théories des Organisations*, Paris: PUF.
Lagadec, P. (1996), 'Un nouveau champ de responsabilité pour les dirigeants', *Revue Française de Gestion*, **108**, March–April–May, 100–109.
Laroche, H. and J.-P. Nioche (1994), 'L'approche cognitive de la stratégie d'entreprise', *Revue Française de Gestion*, **99**, June–July–August, 64–78.
Le Saget, M. (1992), *Le manager intuitif: une nouvelle force*, Paris: Dunod.
Liefooghe, C. (1995), 'Services aux entreprises et developpement local: l'exemple du valenciennois', *Journées de l'IFRESI*, 260–65
Marchesnay, M. (1998), 'Confiances et logiques entrepreneuriales', in *Economies et Sociétés*, *Sciences de gestion*, série S.G., (8–9), 99–117.
Mehling, J. (1991), 'Doit-on et peut-on promouvoir les PME en Afrique?', *Gestion 2000*, **2**, April–May, 93–106.
Miles, R.E. and C.C. Snow (1978), *Organizational Strategy, Structure, and Preocess*, New York: McGraw-Hill Book Co.
Molina, N. (1990), 'Problèmes posés à une PME par sa croissance', *Revue Direction et Gestion*, (124–125), 81–8.
Mustar, P. (1994), 'La politique d'innovation en France: le colbertisme entamé', in F. Sachwald (ed.), *Les nouvelles dimensions de l'internationalisation*, Paris: Institut français des relations internationales, Masson.
Mustar, P. (1997), 'Recherche, innovation et création d'entreprise', *Encyclopédie de gestion*, Paris: Economica.
Papin, R. (1997), 'Création d'entreprise', *Encyclopédie de gestion*, Paris: Economica.
Paris, D. (1993), *La mutation inachevée, mutation économique et changement spatial dans le Nord-Pas-de-Calais*, Paris: l'Harmattan.
Plumly, L.W. and J.E. Oliver (1987), 'The Locus of Control Attribute and the Job Search Process', *Psychological Reports*, **61**, 907–10.
Roberts, E.B. (1980), 'New Venture for Corporate Growth', *Havard Business Review*, **58** (4), 134–42.
Sammut, S. (1998), 'Comment aider les petites entreprises jeunes', *Revue Française de Gestion*, November–December, 28–41
Stevenson, H.H. (1998), 'Les six dimensions de l'entrepreneur', in Sue Birley and Daniel Muzyka (eds), *L'art d'entreprendre*, Les Echos Editions, Paris: Village Mondial, pp. 23–7.
Verstraete, T. (1998), 'Le créateur s'inscrivant dans une logique entrepreneuriale: apporteur de valeur ou organisateur?', in J.-P. Bréchet and P. Mévellec (eds), *Marketing, Stratégie et Organisation*, Actes des XIVémes journéls nationales des IAE, Vol. 4, Nantes: Presses académique de l'ouest, pp. 667–90.
Weber, H. (1988), 'Cultures patronales et types d'entreprises: esquisse d'une typologie du patronat', *Sociologie du Travail*, (4), 545–66.

PART IV

Minorities in a Host Society

15. On entrepreneurship among Druze

Sibylle Heilbrunn and Khaled Abu Asbeh

INTRODUCTION

The Druze living in Israel are a minority within a minority. They are part of a religious community located primarily in Lebanon, Israel and Syria including about 1.3 million people altogether. Druze women doing business are a minority within the Druze minority within the Palestinian minority within the Jewish majority in the state of Israel. As such, Druze women doing business are special. This chapter attempts to add to the understanding of these women entrepreneurs.

The purpose of this study is to add to the understanding of Druze women entrepreneurs belonging to a minority within a minority within the Israeli society. More specifically we intend to explore the work–family conflict as experienced by women entrepreneurs belonging to such a minority. As a gender minority Druze women are facing the work–family conflict and as a national minority they face deficiencies of infrastructure and government assistance. The success stories reveal that product and/or service innovativeness are a critical factor for developing an outstanding business.

Historical Background and Religion

The Druze religion is rooted within Ismailism founded as a religious-philosophical movement by Fatimid Caliphate in Egypt during the tenth century (Aridi, 2002). One of the first prophets of the newly founded community was Al Darazi, thus the name 'Druze'. Following persecutions the Druze left Egypt and settled in an area which is located where Syria, Lebanon and Israel meet nowadays. Later many moved on to more northern parts, especially Mount Lebanon and the Houran region in Syria (Ben-Dor, 1995). The Druze religion is based on 'Epistles of Wisdom' which was written by five propagators between the years 1017 and 1043 (Firro, 2005). It is an interpretation of Judaism, Christianity and Islam stressing that the Creation describes Adam as the first believer. Mentors and prophets from all three religions such as Jethro and Moses, John the Baptist and Jesus of Nazareth, Salman the Persian and Mohammed are believed to be reincarnations of the monotheistic idea. The Egyptian Akhenaton, Greek philosophers such as Socrates, Plato and Aristotle, and Alexander the Great are considered to be of influence on the Druze religion (Aridi, 2002). In addition to monotheism the Druze faith is characterized by hidden layers of meaning, transmigration of souls and reincarnation (Ben-Dor, 1995). The secrecy of the Druze religion is based upon the belief of reincarnation. When the religion was revealed anybody could join and all living today are a reincarnation of someone who was living then. Thus, the Druze do not accept newcomers and are not missionizing (Aridi, 2002). The religion is secret, thus religious books and documents can be read only by the 'knowers' (*ukkal*) from whom are expected moral and pious conduct. The 'ignorants' (*juhhal*), the largely secular majority of the Druze, are not allowed access to secret holy books and documents, and are expected to accept the religion via tradition passed throughout the generations (Aridi, 2002; Ben-Dor, 1995). The *juhhal* constitute about 80 per cent of the Druze population whereas the *ukkal* are about 20 per cent. Druze women are highly evaluated and spiritually wise, and are preferred over men as *ukkal*. The rights of Druze women are almost equal to those of the Druze men.

Druze in Israel

In Israel there are about 118 000 Druze including the ones living in the Golan Heights. Their native language is Arabic and they are Arabs by culture and social tradition (Kaufman, 2004). In Israel they live in 20 villages and cities situated in the north of the country. The Carmel City – including Daliyat el Carmel and Ussafiya – constitutes the largest Druze center in Israel with a population of 24,700. The Druze in Israel share identity with the Druze community in other countries, a fact that distinguishes them as a minority within the Arab Muslim majority which itself is a minority in Israel (Kaufman, 2004).

During the last three decades the Druze society underwent processes of social and economic change. Due to historic concerns for security the Druze villages and towns till today are located in mountain areas. But land is scarce in these areas and not especially fertile and, with the growing population, agriculture could no longer provide a living. In addition with growing influences of modernization there was a dramatic shift away from agriculture as the main occupation. Thus while in the 1950s nearly 90 per cent of the Druze were working in agriculture, in the 1990s the rate dropped to about 10 per cent (Merkovitch, 2005). The military skills of the Druze have their roots in a long history of persecution by neighbors and authorities. Since the mid-1950s the Druze have been drafted into the Israeli army and, although there is controversy as to the circumstances leading to the draft, it is a fact (Ben-Dor, 1995), and as such sets the Druze apart from the Palestinian Arabs living in Israel. Thus, when agriculture was no longer providing sufficient income, the military skills of the Druze men provided occupational opportunities for many and the Druze men serve in large numbers in the army, the police, the border police and prison services (Ben-Dor, 1995).

But since the Druze comprise a minority within a minority in the state of Israel, they face barriers to entering the dominant labor market. A report prepared for the Ministry of Industry, Trade and Labor in 2003 focuses on the following issues when describing the occupational profile of the Druze in Israel: low level of formal education, lack of occupational opportunities for academics, lack of occupational opportunities for women in particular, existence of an ethnically split labor market excluding the Druze from the dominant mainstream, and cultural barriers (Nadiv and Shelach, 2003).

As had been mentioned before, the Druze believe that women play a very central role in society in general, and in the family in particular. Today this role is changing since the women increasingly study and work outside their homes thus crystallizing a novel role including home, family and occupational career (Abu-Asbeh, 2008). It is important, though, to mention that the more traditional and religiously oriented Druze women continue to focus on their life around the home and the family, thus on this issue there are gaps within the Druze society in Israel which can explain the findings of Levi and Lotan (2007).

Following Levi and Lotan (2007) the educational profile of Druze women has changed dramatically during recent years and is now characterized by polarity. Whereas at all educational levels the Druze women rate considerably lower than the Jewish women, at the level of professional and academic education the percentage of Druze women is higher than that of their Jewish counterparts. As a result, the labor market participation of these women is similar to that of the Jewish ones.

Since the Druze are a minority within a minority in Israel, it is not surprising that their rate of self-employment is significantly higher than that of the Jewish majority, who do not have to deal with similar barriers in the labor market. Thus, following Nadiv and Shelach (2003), the rate of self-employed Druze men is about 20 per cent versus 11 per cent of the Jewish men and the rate of self-employed Druze women is 12 per cent versus 6 per cent of the Jewish women. Most of the Druze businesses owned by women are in the field of trade.

THEORETICAL FRAMEWORK

The Minority Issue

Minority entrepreneurship is defined as business ownership by any individual who is not of the majority population (Richtermeyer, 2002). The Palestinian Arabs are a national minority within the state of Israel. As such they suffer from discrimination in the economic, social and political sphere (Khattab, 2002). The Druze, belonging culturally and ethnically to the Arab population, can be defined as a religious minority within the Arab minority and as such they share a set of connections and regular patterns of interaction among people with a common religious background (Waldinger et al. 1990). A number of studies show that, due to the fact that the Druze are drafted into military service, they are a 'preferred' minority versus the Arab Palestinian population and, due to governmental engagement, occupational opportunities have increased in Druze villages and cities more so than in Arab Palestinian ones (Khattab, 2002, Levin-Epstein and Semyonov, 1992; Sofer et al., 1995). Druze women are a gender minority. Thus, Druze women entrepreneurs are a minority within a minority within a minority. Minority entrepreneurs face several barriers when starting a business, such as low levels of education, lack of capital, limited markets, low earnings of clientele, low financial returns on investment, and so on.

Female entrepreneurs do not only contribute to employment creation and economic development via their increasing number, but also add to the diversity of entrepreneurial processes (Verheul and Thurik, 2001). Sa'ar (2007) states that the very fact of being self-employed improves women's status and self-evaluation versus their families and environments. But many factors prevent women from opening a business (Erdem, 2004) and a number of studies deal with gender specific difficulties of women entrepreneurs (Constant, 2004; Greene, et al., 2003; Heilbrunn, 2004; Loscocco et al., 1991; Mirchandandi, 1999). One of the major gender specific difficulties of women entrepreneurs concerns the traditional work–family conflict.

Work–Family Conflict

In spite of the female revolution of the last century which has led to significant changes in the socio-economic and cultural status of women in many societies, women still are responsible for a larger share of the family and home responsibilities (Hoffman, 2003). Thus women are under constant pressure attempting to balance home and work responsibilities (Parise,

2002), leaving work in order to work at home and leaving home in order to go to work (Simon et al., 2004). Thus, although career chances of women have changed, the typical family role has not and domestic commitments remain the responsibility of women (Winn, 2004; 2005).

Following Schindehutte et al. (2003), women entrepreneurs value the ability to pursue career goals with family obligations in addition to the rather prominent reasons of male as well as female entrepreneurs to start a business, such as the need for achievement and autonomy. They attempt to balance economic goals, such as profit and growth, and non-economic goals such as personal fulfillment and helping others (Brush, 1992). Previous research suggests that women and men share similar motivations in business ownership but that women have an additional motivation to find paid work that is more compatible with family responsibilities.

Huang et al. (2004) found that work–family conflict is positively correlated with demands of the business as well as with the demands of the family. The latter also depends on the number and ages of dependent children. Thus, the role of business women as entrepreneurs can hardly be combined with typical female role expectations. Das (1999) reports that one of the main problems of women entrepreneurs is to deal with the tension between career opportunity and private personal life. In addition, several studies have found that conflicts between home and family demands constrain business growth (McKay, 2001; Stoner et al., 1990). Shelton (2006) found that work–family conflicts have a negative influence on the well-being of the entrepreneur which then impacts the venture performance.

THE STUDY

The purpose of the study was to investigate characteristics of Druze women entrepreneurs and to add to the understanding of the entrepreneurial processes ongoing within this special group. Furthermore we wanted to explore the extent to which these women experience the classical work–family conflict characterizing women entrepreneurs in general.

Method

Twenty-one Druze women entrepreneurs answered a questionnaire including closed and open questions administered by students during 2006 in their own language. The women were chosen on the basis of personal acquaintance by the students and thus this is not a representative sample of Druze women entrepreneurs. Closed questions concerned demographic

Table 15.1 Descriptive data on age and number of children

	N	Mean	Std. Dev	Min.	Max.
Age	21	40.47	8.9	26	57
Number of Children	21	3.95	1.2	2	7

Table 15.2 Descriptive statistics of the evaluation of husband and family support

	N	Mean	Std. Dev	Min.	Max.
Husband's Support	21	3.1	0.79	1	4
Family's support	21	4.0	0.89	2	5

issues, information about the business such as age, number of employees, location and type of business. We also asked the women to rank the support they received from their husbands and families on a scale from 1 (very low) to 5 (very high). Open questions in the questionnaire concerned difficulties at start up, subjective evaluation of success of the business, and dealing with the home–family conflict. In addition the authors conducted telephone interviews with four Druze women entrepreneurs whose businesses have been published in local newspapers. One 'success story' of a Druze business woman was investigated via an in-depth interview.

Findings

Nineteen out of the 21 women are married and two of them are widowed. Table 15.1 presents the demographic characteristics of the women entrepreneurs in terms of age and number of children.

Table 15.2 presents the descriptive data on the issues of support of the husband and the family during setting up the business.

The data show that the family's support ranks slightly higher that the support the women receive from their husbands, which is probably due to the fact that husbands tend to work whereas the extended family provides assistance to the women especially with childcare.

The average age of the businesses is 5 years (Std. Deviation = 2.59). All of the businesses are located in the village/town where the women live; five of them are home-located businesses. Table 15.3 shows the distribution of types of businesses.

Table 15.3 shows that most of the businesses are in the field of trade and shops. Four of the women entrepreneurs had businesses concerned

Table 15.3 Distribution of types of businesses

Type of business	Frequency	Percentage
Trade and shops	15	71.4
Personnel services	4	19.0
Professional services	2	9.5
Total	21	100.0

Table 15.4 Summary of open questions

Question	Content of answers	No of times item mentioned*
1. Difficulties at start up	Lack of support from authorities	16
	Finding an adequate location for an adequate price	10
	Recruiting capital	12
Total		38
2. Work–family conflict	Problem because although family members help, I feel that I neglect the household and the children and can't keep up with standards	17
	Big problem because the husband is basically against my business	1
	No problem since family members (mother and older children) help	4
Total		22
3. Evaluation of success	The business adds to the family income and I feel very successful	9
	The business is a great success financially wise	3
	The business is not very successful	9
Total		21

Note: * The sum of answers may add to more than 21 because the women mentioned more than one possibility.

with personal services such as cosmetics, hairdressers, and so on (all of them home-located) and two were professional businesses, a lawyer (home located) and a graphic studio.

Table 15.4 summarizes the answers of the women to the open questions

Table 15.4 shows that lack of support by the authorities constitute a major difficulty for the Druze women. More than half of the women had difficulties in recruiting capital and in finding an adequate location for a reasonable price. The data also reveal that although most women receive help from family members, they perceive the work–family conflict as a major problem. One of the women reported that her husband is entirely against her being self-employed and only about 20 per cent of the women do not have any problems with the role conflict. As to success evaluation, the data reveal that about half of the women perceive their business as a success, most of them being satisfied with the fact that they add to the family income. Nine out of 21 think that their business is not very successful.

Four telephone interviews were conducted with Druze women whose businesses have been published in local newspapers and on the Internet: a flower shop, a handicraft workshop for processing, adapting and design of jewelry, house wares and picture frames, a school for professional hairdressing and makeup, and a coffee shop specializing in pancakes and wafers. Table 15.5 summarizes the results of the telephone interviews.

The main and common issue of these four businesses owned by Druze women entrepreneurs concerns the innovativeness of their product/service. Three of the four businesses have been successful over time and have developed since start-up in terms of number of clients and products. Thus, the flower shop, for example, is now selling flower arrangements in combination with presents, providing flower arrangements for family celebrations and marketing actively events such as Valentine's Day. The coffee shop presents an example for a business based upon a rather unusual product. Belgium wafers and pancakes are certainly not within the culinary mainstream of the local population. The very specialty and high quality of the products as well as the special atmosphere in the coffee shop are the clue to success. The school for professional hairdressing and makeup enables Druze and Arab women to learn a profession in their own language and within the context of their own culture. As such it is innovative and provides an opportunity for these women to acquire a profession. The fact that women from Jordan are coming to Israel in order to join the courses demonstrates its innovativeness and its locating a market niche.

Case Study: 'Grandma Jamila'

'Savta (Grandma) Jamila's Soaps' is a one-woman industry. She is a 69-year-old Druze widow from Peki'in who married at 16 and was the mother of three at 21. (Today she is the mother of five and grandmother to 15 grandchildren.) This situation forced her to find employment, so she became one of the first Druze women to work outside the home, as

Table 15.5 Summary of telephone interviews

	Motivation to open the business	Innovativeness of product/ service	General remarks
Flower shop	To realize my dream and to be economically successful and independent	Flower arrangements as presents for holidays and family celebrations are a rather recent development in the market.	Opened 7 years ago, clientele constantly growing, central location, well managed
Handicraft workshop	To do what I am best at and to have a second career	High-standard art products for average household with reasonable prices	Opened 3 month ago, based upon high professional expertise of the owner
School for professional hairdressing and makeup	Communicate the craft to others and provide them with a profession	Increasing awareness of beauty care of women	Started as a studio for cosmetics, developed into a school 15 years ago, students come also from neighbor countries such as Jordan
Coffee shop	To do what I am best at and to have a career	Non-conventional bakery products very special to the local population	Started to prepare the products for family and friends, then decided to open the coffee shop, competitive advantage due to products and atmosphere

opposed to the accepted Druze norms. Jamila has not attended school, but inherited knowledge of medicinal herbs from her mother. In her spare time she began creating blends of medicinal soaps.

Jamila started making soap from olive oil 50 years ago, based on a secret mixture of herbs. Legend has it that Jamila's soaps help cure skin diseases, sores and other injuries. Although it is not a medicinal soap, the myth has been alive for many years. Lately, Jamila's sons have joined the business and are carrying on her legacy.

The beginning was not easy. She gave out her first bars of soap to relatives and neighbors for free, and to the many tourists who came to visit the holy places in her village. At first she was assisted by her husband and eldest son.

Jamila started selling her soap to shops about 15 years ago, after she had received a lot of feedback from people regarding the soap's effectiveness. She began to take part in fairs and festivals in order to market her product. The most effective means of publicity was the many tourists who came to the village, among them the *Yediot Aharonot* reporter Shelly Sieglizer, who published an article about the endeavor. In addition, her social network and that of her family – one son lives in Holland and markets her soap there – has been a great help with the product. The main way is still by word of mouth.

The products are not marketed abroad under Israeli identification, so as to allow them to enter Arab markets as well. Nowadays, the soap is also sold in Europe, recognized mainly through the tourists who have been to Israel. In Israel the product can be purchased through the factory, the shop in Peki'in, Super-Pharm outlets and other shops.

Recently, the manufacturing facilities of the natural soaps have moved to the Tefen Industrial Park, employs over 40 workers (in addition to the five who work in the Peki'in shop), and exports to 22 countries around the world. Almost all employees are women, mainly due to Jamila's guiding principle of helping poor women and thus granting them some degree of independence.

At first Jamila worked very hard, despite the support from her husband and son. The combination of work and home was almost impossible, so she got very little rest. Today she employs a woman to take care of her home. Jamila no longer works in the manufacturing process, but mainly receives visitors and tourists and tells her unique story. Her sons are now in charge of the endeavor.

The soap is sold with a small pamphlet, in which Jamila's vision is outlined, alongside the special qualities of the soap and how to use it. The soap is sold for 21–25 NIS in Israel, and for a much higher price in overseas markets.

DISCUSSION AND CONCLUSION

Druze women are a minority within a minority within a minority. The women investigated in this study are all older than 40 years, are married and most of them have more than four children. Their businesses are located in the villages /cities where they live and some of them are home located. When analysing the entire data gathered by various tools in this study, the following processes emerge.

As a gender minority Druze women are facing the work–family conflict. But the data reveal that while they do receive support from husband and family (see Table 15.2), they still perceive their situation as problematic since many of them feel that they neglect the household and the children, and cannot keep up with the accepted standards (see Table 15.4). Thus, following Das (1999) we can state that for Druze women it is a problem to deal with the tension between career opportunity and private personal life. The Druze business women belong to a national minority within the state of Israel. As often found in studies on minority entrepreneurship, also in our study most of the businesses are in trade (see Table 15.3). The difficulties reported by the women account for the fact that the Arab minority suffers from economic discrimination and government support is limited (Khattab, 2002). Thus, it is not surprising that the women reported difficulties due to infrastructure deficiencies (see Table 15.4).

Only the fact that all of the businesses investigated in this study are located within the village or city where the women live can be related to the aspect of the Druze being a religious minority within the Palestinian Arab minority in Israel. More research is needed in order to investigate this issue, especially since the Druze are a 'preferred minority' and have more trade contacts with the Jewish majority than the Arab Palestinian minority. The businesses which were published in local newspapers and on the national Internet are all situated in Carmel City which is the largest Druze center in Israel and which attracts many tourists. The success stories reveal that product and/or service innovativeness are critical and make the difference. All five cases represent excellent product development, innovative ideas and novel market niches. Only 'Grandma Jamila' managed to expand her business to international markets and that – no doubt – was due to her large family network. She represents an outstanding example of a Druze business woman succeeding as a woman within a religious minority belonging to a national minority in Israel.

Much further research is needed on this subject, especially since the sample of women investigated here is small and probably does not represent the Druze businesses in Israel.

REFERENCES

Abu-Asbeh, K. (2008), 'External and Internal Barriers met by Arab Adults in the High-Technology Labor Market. Research Report', The Center for Jewish – Arab Economic Development (R.A.), Tel Aviv.

Aridi, N. (2002), 'The Druze in Israel', *Focus on Israel*, Israeli Ministry of Foreign Affaires, 23 December.

Ben-Dor, G. (1995), 'The Druze Minority in Israel in the mid-1990s' Jerusalem', *Letter of Lasting Interest*, no. 315, 1 June.

Brush, C. (1992), 'Research on Women Business Owners: Past Trends a New Perspective and Future Directions', *Entrepreneurship Theory and Practice*, **16** (4), 5–30.

Constant, A. (2004), 'Immigrant versus Native Businesswomen: Proclivity and Performance', Discussion Paper No. 1234, Institute for the Study of Labor (IZA).

Das, M. (1999), 'Work–Family Conflicts of Indian Women Entrepreneurs: A Preliminary Report', *New England Journal of Entrepreneurship*, **2** (2), 39–52.

Erdem, S. (2004), 'Women Entrepreneurs in Transition Economies: Main Obstacles and Recommended Solutions', Turkish Manas University Conference in Economics, available at: http://www.manas.kg/pdf/economickonferans/articles/15.pdf (accessed 15 May 2008).

Firro, K.M. (2005), 'Duze *maqamat* (Shrines) in Israel: From Ancient to Newly-Invented Tradition', *British Journal of Middle Eastern Studies*, **32** (2), 217–39.

Greene, P.G., M.M. Hart, E.J. Gatewood, C.G. Brush and N.M. Carter (2003), 'Women Entrepreneurs: Moving Front and Center – An Overview of Research and Theory', available at: www.usasbe.org/knowledge/whitepapers/greene2003.pdf (accessed 16 May 2008).

Heilbrunn, S. (2004), 'On the Impact of Gender upon Difficulties Faced by Entrepreneurs', *International Journal of Entrepreneurship and Innovation*, **5** (3), 159–67.

Hoffman, K.J. (2003), 'From the Kitchen to the Office: Issues and Impact Women experience in Balancing Work and Home Responsibilities', PhD thesis, San Francisco University, Faculty of Saybrook.

Huang, Y., L. Hammer, M. Neal and N. Perrin (2004), 'The Relationship between Work-to-family Conflict and Family-to-work Conflict: A Longitudinal Study', *Journal of Family and Economic Issues*, **25**, 79–100.

Kaufman, I. (2004), 'Ethnic Affirmation or Ethnic Manipulation: The Case of the Druze in Israel', *Nationalism and Ethnic Politics*, **9**, 53–82

Khattab, N. (2002), 'Ethnicity and Female Labour Market Participation: A New Look at the Palestinian Enclave in Israel', *Work, Employment and Society*, **16**, 91–110.

Levi, S. and A. Lotan (2007), 'Data on the Druze in the Labor Market', research report prepared for the Knesset, Centre for Research and Information, The Knesset.

Levin-Epstein, N. and M. Semyonov (1992), 'Modernization and Subordination: Arab Women in the Israeli Labor Force', *European Sociological Review*, **8** (1), 39–51.

Loscocco, A.K., J. Robinson, R.H. Hall and J.K. Allen (1991), 'Gender and Small Business Success: An Inquiry into Women's Relative Disadvantage', *Social Forces*, **79** (1), 65–85.

McKay, R. (2001), 'Women Entrepreneurs: Moving beyond Family and Flexibility', *International Journal of Entrepreneurial Behavior & Research*, **7** (4), 148–65.

Merkovitch, H. (2005), 'Adequate Representation of the Arab Population in Public Services', report prepared for the Commissionership of State Service, p. 2 (in Hebrew).

Mirchandandi, K. (1999), 'Feminist Insight on Gendered Work: New Directions in Research on Women and Entrepreneurship', *Gender, Work and Organization*, **6** (4), 224–35.

Nadiv, R. and S. Shelach (2003), 'Profile of Self-employed and Occupational Characteristics 1970–2001', report prepared for the Ministry of Industry, Trade and Labor, Jerusalem (in Hebrew).

Parise, P.A. (2002), 'Gender Education and Life Cycle Stage: The Relationship to Work and Family Conflict', PhD thesis, Wayne Huizenga Graduate School.

Richtermeyer, G. (2001), 'Minority Entrepreneurs: A Review of the Current Literature. Outreach and Extension', University of Missouri, Lincoln University, USA.

Sa'ar, A. (2007), 'A Business of Your Own', a report prepared for the National Insurance Institute, Research & Planning Administration, Jerusalem.

Schindehutte, M., M. Morris and C. Brennan (2003), 'Entrepreneurs and Motherhood: Impacts on their Children in South Africa and the United States', *Journal of Small Business Management*, **4** (1), 94–108.

Shelton, L.M. (2006), 'Female Entrepreneurs, Work–Family Conflict and Venture Performance', *Journal of Small Business Management*, **44** (2), 285–98.

Simon, M., A. Kummerling and M. Hasselohm (2004), 'Work and Home Conflict in European Nursing Profession', *International Journal of Occupational and Environmental Health*, **10**, 384–91

Sofer, M., I. Schnell, I. Drori and A. Atrash (1995),'Entrepreneurship and Industrialization in the Israeli Arab Society', Ra'nana, Beit Berl: The Institute for Israeli Arab Studies (in Hebrew).

Stoner, C.R., R.I. Hartman and R. Arora (1990), 'Work/Family Conflict: A Study of Women in Management', *Journal of Applied Business Research*, **7** (1), 67–74.

Verheul, I. and A.R. Thurik (2001), 'Start-up Capital: Does Gender Matter?', *Small Business Economics*, **16**, 329–45.

Waldinger, R., H. Aldrich and R. Wards (1990), *Ethnic Entrepreneurs: Immigrant Business in Industrial Societies*, Sage Publications.

Winn, J. (2005), 'Women Entrepreneurs: Can We Remove the Barriers?', *International Entrepreneurship and Management Journal*, **11**, 381–97.

Winn, J. (2004), 'Entrepreneurship: Not an Easy Path to Top Management for Women', *Women in Management Review*, **19** (3), 143–53.

16. Home of Sephardi middlemen*

Léo-Paul Dana and Teresa E. Dana

INTRODUCTION

The Kingdom of Morocco, Maghreb el Aqsa (literally: land farthest west) covers the western extreme of North Africa, separated from Spain by the Strait of Gibraltar. A rich history has made Morocco fairly heterogeneous.

The Indigenous people here are Berbers. Shor and Shor (1955, p. 188) wrote, 'Some tribesmen in the High Atlas accept Islam but not Koranic law'. Hunt explained,

> They have occupied the rugged mountains since before the Muslim Arabs swept in from the east in the 8th century. The Berbers adopted Islam as they had previously taken to Christianity, but it was not a total embrace. Their religion combines Islamic and older tribal beliefs. (Hunt, 1980, p. 119)

Racially, the Berbers have mixed with other groups, and the distinguishing feature of the Berbers is language. Their language has three dialects: Tamazight, Tarifit, and Tashlhiyt.

As explained by Tayler (2005, p. 79), 'Though dominated by Arabs for centuries, Berbers make up a majority in Morocco'. Authorities have claimed that Berbers are 'disturbing national unity' (Crawford, 2002, p. 62). Venema and Mguild wrote,

> Arabs also regularly use stereotypes. With reference to the Middle Atlas Berbers, one informant said: 'they live as savages in tents near caves and forests'. They are nomads who use boots and plastic for clothing. They don't speak or read Arabic . . . (Venema and Mguild, 2003, p. 35)

Crawford (2002, p. 53) asserted, 'Morocco's Imazighen (Berbers) are often ignored in current academic literature'. This chapter gives an overview of ethnic groups in Morocco and their respective spheres of economic activity.

METHODOLOGY

With the mandate to be inductive and contextually sensitive, methodology for this exploratory study involved ethnographic fieldwork in Morocco, using qualitative methods. An emic research design was deemed most appropriate, in order to understand the underlying structures of culture from within. It was helpful to observe and interview simultaneously. Photography was heavily relied upon. As discussed by Patton (1982; 1987), social integration was a prerequisite to obtaining meaningful responses.

HISTORICAL BACKGROUND

The oldest inhabitants of this region are the Berbers, and they were joined by Jews over 2000 years ago. The region was invaded by Phoenicians, Romans, Byzantines and Arabs, but the Ottomans never occupied Morocco. Therefore Morocco today is quite different from its neighbours who were exposed to Ottoman rule. Fogg wrote,

> In the latter part of the seventh century A.D., the first Arab invaders reached the western plains of Morocco. They were aristocratic family, high literary culture, and full of proselytising zeal, and were the first cause of the important addition of Islamic culture to the partly Christian but mainly animistic and naturistic people who then inhabited N. Morocco. Being few in number, however, the former modified the social structure and the race of the N. Morocco Berbers in only a negligible way. (Fogg, 1940, p. 85)

Fogg elaborated:

> The Arabs who came as a result of the eleventh-century invasion of North Africa were in different case, however. They were unlettered nomadic Bedawin, who arrived in very large numbers, impelled principally by the purely economic considerations of finding new pasturage and new camping-grounds. Being nomadic pastoralists, they were ill-adapted to dislodging the mountain Berbers, who, largely on account of their physical environment, led a sedentary type of existence which was utterly opposed to that of the Bedawin. (Fogg, 1940, p. 85)

There was, therefore, little interaction between these ethnic groups, each of which had its own settlements (see Figure 16.1) and respective economy.

Judeo-Berber symbiosis was widespread. However, to escape legal discrimination on the basis of religion, numerous Berber tribes converted to Islam. Yet many Jews and Judaized Berbers resisted conversion and retained their cultural values along with related behavioural

Figure 16.1 Berber settlement

predispositions. Autonomous Judaized Berber tribes existed in Morocco, until the twelfth century.

A Muslim kingdom was established, consisting of invading Arabs as well as Indigenous Berbers and a substantial Jewish community which was particularly involved in the realm of commerce. Each ethnic group remained within its cultural boundaries, allowing themselves to maintain their respective traditions. Over time, different business activities became associated with particular cultural groups. Morocco reached its zenith between the twelfth and fifteenth centuries, at which time its empire stretched across the Strait of Gibraltar into Europe, and also as far east as today's Tunisia.

European influence arrived in Morocco during the sixteenth century when the Portuguese built a settlement at Mogador. In 1764, Sultan Sidi Mohammed Ben Abdellah (literally: Son of the Servant of God) decided to build a city on the site of Mogador. He then commissioned Nicolas-Théodore Cornut, an architect from Avignon, to draw the municipal plans. The new town was called Essaouira, literally meaning 'the well designed'. Seeking that his settlement be blessed, the sultan engraved the words Barakat Mohammed (blessing of Mohammed – prophet of Islam) on the city walls. Seeking prosperity for his subjects, the sultan invited Jews to immigrate to his new city and to start new enterprises. Many came and initiated trade with England.

Essaouira became known as the dividing town, with Chiadma Arabs living in blazing heat to the north, and Hahas Berbers fighting blizzards in the Atlas Mountains to the south. Essaouira itself prospered as the port of Timbuctoo (Mali), wherefrom camels brought gold, ivory, ostrich feathers, and salt, along with treasures from Black Africa. Until the twelfth century, half of the population in Essaouira was comprised of Christians and Jews.

Although neighbouring Algeria and Tunisia were both invaded by the Ottomans, Morocco remained an independent kingdom for over a millennium. While Europe began to industrialize, Morocco's independence allowed for its bazaar economy to remain static. The situation changed in 1912, when France and Spain claimed protectorates in Morocco. The ancient kingdom was then divided, and the port of Tangiers (Tanja in Berber and Arabic, Tanger in French and Tánger in Spanish), was declared an international city. Each sector had its own administration and respective currency.

The strategy of France was to divide and rule. In 1928, a French official wrote, 'We must utilise to our advantage the old dictum "divide and rule". The presence of a Berber race is a useful instrument for counteracting the Arab race' (Halstead, 1967, p. 72). Ben Kaddour elaborated, 'To strengthen the so-called "Berber race", the French introduced on 16 May, 1930, the Berber Dahir that legalised the customary courts in Berber areas . . . On the economic level, tribal notables were given land and were transformed into feudal landlords, while on the political level, these tribal chiefs were appointed as caids' (Ben Kaddour, 1973, p. 260).

Some Berber families became prosperous. Among the wealthy, it was common to acquire domestic help, sometimes from Mali. Descendants of dark-skinned Mali servants still live in Morocco and work for Berber families (see Figure 16.2).

In 1953, Sultan Sidi Mohammed bin Youssef was exiled. He returned to Morocco in 1955. In 1956, Morocco regained its independence and Sultan Sidi Mohammed bin Youssef became King Mohammed V.[1] Ben Kaddour (1973, p. 261) observed, 'When Morocco became independent in 1956, 70% of the population, including 80–85% of the Berbers were living in rural areas'. Coram (1973, p. 269) wrote about the Berbers, 'favoured by the colonial regime, they were denied identity as a group . . . after independence'. In fact, only a handful of caids survived the transfer of power (Hart, 1973).

In February 1961, Hassan II succeeded Mohammed V. In September 1969, a military regime overthrew the monarchy in Libya. On Saturday, 10 July 1971, officers tried to topple Hassan II.

In 1976, the Western Sahara (up to that time a Spanish territory known as Spanish West Africa) was divided between Morocco and Mauritania. In 1979, Mauritania pulled out, allowing Morocco to annex the balance of this territory. Thus, Morocco today is the merger of several previously separate political entities.

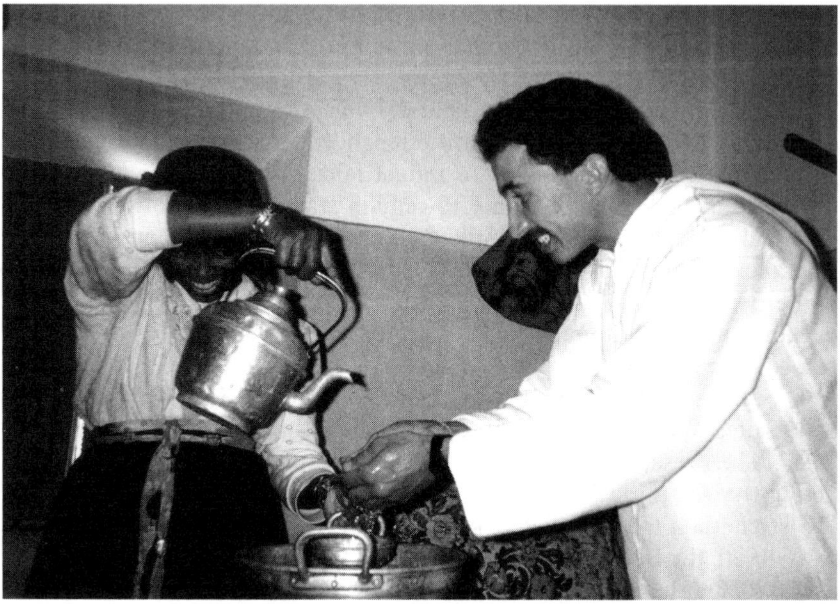

Figure 16.2 Servant pouring water for Berber master

A single currency (the dirham) and a uniform system of administration was implemented such as to erode the economic barriers between zones. Perhaps because Morocco was occupied for only a short period, Westernisation did not take deep roots here, and to this day, important demographic and cultural differences remain within Morocco.

Morocco's ethnic diversity has contributed to a contrasting and exciting mixture of Arab, Berber, African, Islamic and European influences. In Tangiers, people still speak Spanish (see Figure 16.3), and in many instances, Ladino (Judaeo-Spanish). In Casablanca (see Figure 16.4), French is common. In the Atlas Mountains, Berber dialects prevail. In September 2003, the government allowed for the first time, the teaching of the Berber language in over 10 per cent of the schools in Morocco.

PLURALISM AND CLUSTERING

There are different models of pluralism. Melting pot pluralism involves a multicultural society, the members of which interact in a shared, secular mainstream arena, reserving the expression of cultural differences to private life; this is the case in the USA. At the other extreme is structural

Figure 16.3 *Gran Teatro Cervantes, Tangiers*

pluralism involving different communities, each with distinct lifestyles; separate institutions reduce the need to share a core universe.

Structural pluralism in Morocco allowed for each ethno-cultural community to retain its respective language and cultural values. Islamic tradition required that non-Muslims be treated as second-class citizens; nevertheless, a symbiotic relationship flourished between Jews and Muslims, and each was given special neighbourhoods in which to reside and to set up enterprises. This, in turn, formalized economic specialization along ethnic lines. Whereas Islam frowns upon the concept of interest, for example, Jews often served as bankers financing new venture creation and other business activity. Some items were sold only by Jews while others were sold only by Muslims. Silversmiths were invariably Muslim, while goldsmiths were Jewish. Jews were also very active in the spice trade, and they specialized in the socio-economic function of distribution. Merchandise was often purchased on credit, thereby requiring a relationship of trust between supplier and peddler. Many Jews were peddlers, or suppliers to other vendors, inland. They served as Barthian middlemen, as suggested in Figure 16.5.

According to Waterbury (1972), Casablanca was a fishing port with a population of 12 000 at the time of the establishment of the French protectorate in 1912. Under French rule, European entrepreneurs opened factories, producing glass, soap, textiles, trucks and wines. Jewish merchants, for example, enjoyed a virtual monopoly of maritime trade until WWII.

Figure 16.4 Hotel Trans-Atlantique, Casablanca

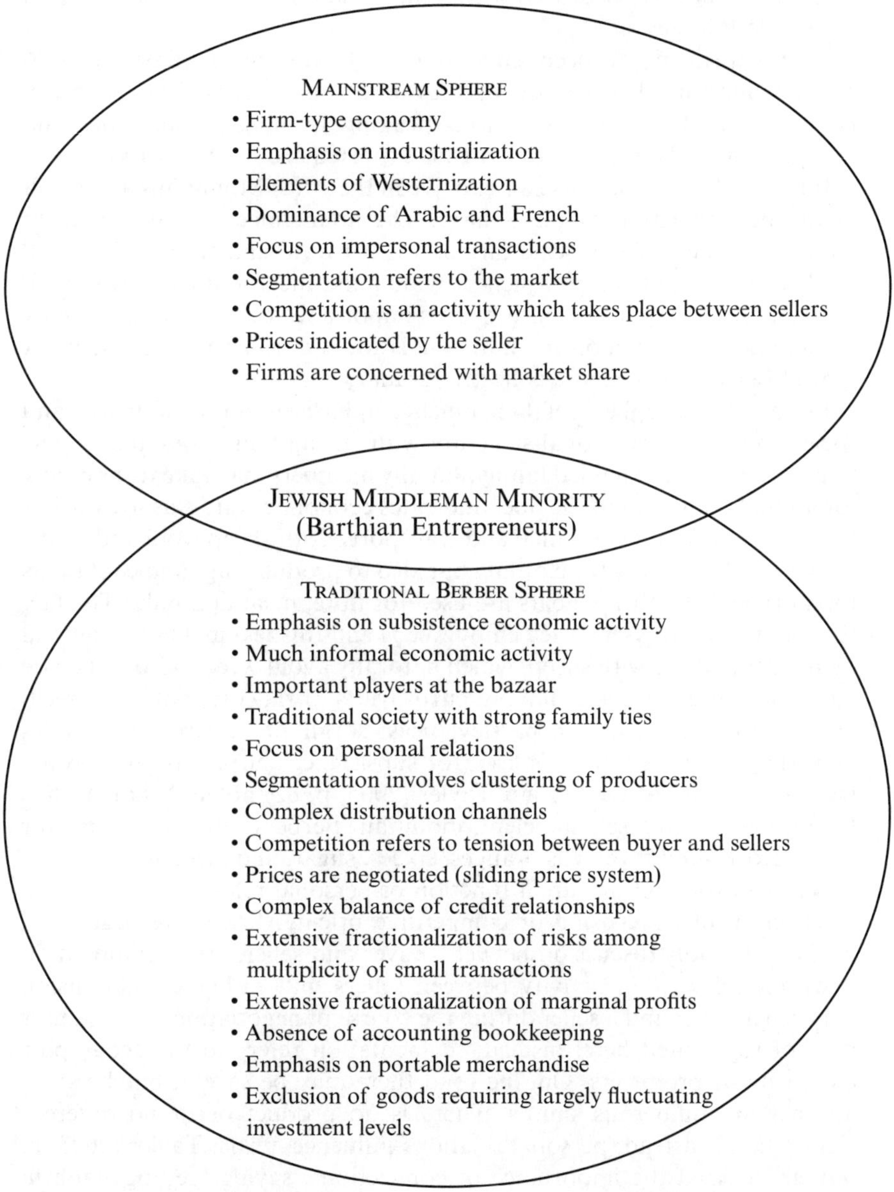

Figure 16.5 Spheres of values in Morocco

Until independence, Morocco was home to half a million Europeans and to over 250 000 Jews.

In the north of Morocco, sub-tropical Mediterranean climate is tempered by maritime breezes, and ample rainfall allows agriculture to thrive. Here, one finds numerous Arabic-speaking farming communities and orange groves, the produce of which is exported around the world.

It is said that the Berbers came to live in the Atlas Mountains as a result of the desertification of the Sahara. The abundance of water in these mountains allows small-scale farmers to cultivate and to care for small herds of goats and sheep, which provide milk, meat and cash. Although the economy is capitalist, culture gives importance to the extended family home, and it is common for individuals to lend a hand when useful. A typical Berber village has a collective granary.

In the Berber sphere of life, much emphasis is on subsistence, and society retains a traditional structure with strong family ties and importance given to the extended family. Family members may take turns caring for animals. The size of the flock indicates economic status, as livestock is the source of food, wool, hide and transport. Both sheep wool and camel wool is used, not only for clothing but also to produce rugs and containers for storage. Like sheep, goats are used for fibre, meat and milk. The fact that goats are browsers (they enjoy weeds and thistles) makes this animal highly compatible with sheep, which naturally avoid weeds. Crops include almonds, barley, beans, cannabis, citrus fruits, cork, corn, dates, flaxseed, grapes, mint, oats, olives, parsley, peas, sorghum, tobacco, vegetables and wheat. Some produce is used for subsistence; surplus is given away, traded, and sold at the bazaar. Tayler (2005, p. 82) noted, 'Though they take pride in being self-sufficient, mountain Berbers rely on markets for such hard-to-find staples as oranges, spices, sugar, and medicines'.

Business transactions are a function of personal relations, rather than a reflection of advertising or competitive pricing. Prices are negotiated during a friendly discussion between buyer and seller. Here, competition does not refer to an activity between sellers, but rather to the tension between a buyer and a seller during the course of negotiations. Consumers are not segmented here; instead, segmentation refers to the geographic clustering of producers. On one road there may be several butchers; on another are numerous smiths. There is no product or brand differentiation here. Instead, personal relations influence a sale. Tayler (2005, p. 90) emphasized the importance of connections, saying 'getting a job in Morocco, for Berbers and Arabs alike, frequently depends not on talent but on connections'.

> We are brothers; but when we do accounts, we are enemies. (Berber proverb quoted in Waterbury, 1972, p. 48)

Language perpetuates ethnic identity and occupational clustering in Morocco. In the eastern province of Azilal, farmers speak Tashlhiyt, and shepherds speak Tamazight. The son of a shepherd usually becomes a shepherd, and, because of linguistic preference, he often marries the daughter(s) of a shepherd family. A farmer's son usually becomes a farmer and marries into a farming family. Camels are often used to plough fields. At the edge of the Sahara Desert (see Figure 16.6), camels are traded at periodic camel markets.

SPHERES OF ECONOMIC ACTIVITY

Barth (1963) viewed entrepreneurship as an activity involving the relationship of persons and institutions in different ethnic communities; Barth (1967) elaborated on how entrepreneurs are the social agents of change, active in the transformation of a community. Morocco is one such country wherein entrepreneurial behaviour may be said to follow Barth's pattern. French traders are primarily found in urban centres and they participate in the formal firm-type sector of the economy. Much Indigenous enterprise takes place in the subsistence and informal sectors. Also important is the bazaar economy. One often sees overflowing jars containing a pink mixture against magic or a green mixture against magic and a blue mixture against the evil eye.

Subsistence economic activity refers to that which is consumed internally rather than sold (Cole and Fayissa, 1991; Dana, 2005). There is no external exchange; no business transaction takes place. Wealth is created, but nothing is sold for profit; that which is created is consumed or saved for personal use. Internal subsistence activity includes subsistence agriculture, involving no market transaction external to the producer. While internal economic activity exists, as an activity of choice, even amid the most advanced and industrialised backdrop (Dana, 1995), for some people in Morocco, this is the only strategy for survival.

Informal economic activity involves undeclared activity that can take the form of an impromptu stall or itinerant vending. For discussions of entrepreneurship in the informal sector, see de Soto (1989), Morris and Pitt (1995), Peattie (1987), Portes et al. (1989), Rosser et al. (2000), Sanders (1987) and Tokman (1978). Waterbury noted, 'in 1960, there were 41.4 commerçants per 1 000 inhabitants in Casablanca. This does not include unlicensed tradesmen and marchands ambulants who must easily outnumber the licensed tradesmen' (Waterbury, 1973, p. 244)

In the informal sector, the law is often bent, but authorities generally tolerate the sector. A relevant discussion from Dana (1992) is presented

Figure 16.6 Camels at the edge of the Sahara desert

concisely by Chamard and Christie (1996). Johnson et al. (1998) discuss discretion in the sector.

In contrast, the bazaar is home to more structured entrepreneurship.

> Before protectorate times, the site of a market showed little or nothing to indicate its character as a market; but when the Spaniards established their interventor posts and the French their Affaires Indigènes bureaux at tribal market sites, a natural result was that permanent shops began to be built all along the four edges of the market site itself. (Hart, 1973, p. 35)

Figure 16.7 At the bazaar

To this day, prices in the bazaar are not indicated (see Figure 16.7) but rather they are negotiated; the sliding price system of the bazaar results in the primary competitive stress being between buyer and seller (Parsons and Smelzer, 1956). The lack of information results in an imperfect market and with few exceptions, such as basic food staples, retail prices are not indicated; rather, these are determined by negotiations. Rosen wrote, 'Lacking detailed knowledge of the quality of particular goods, their purchase price by the dealer, and the consequent worth of various items presented for the bargainer's consideration, it is often the case that for certain major goods a man chooses the seller to deal with rather than the goods as such.' (Rosen, 1973, p. 160)

The customer tests price levels informally, before bargaining begins. It may be the buyer who proposes a price, which is eventually raised. As discussed by Geertz, the 'relatively high percentage of wholesale transactions (i.e., transactions in which goods are bought with the express intention to resell them) means that in most cases both buyer and seller are professional traders and the contest is one between experts.' (Geertz, 1963, p. 33)

Unlike Western relationship marketing, which is customer-centred (Evans and Laskin, 1994; Zineldin, 1998), the focus in the bazaar is on the relationship itself. Once a mutually satisfactory transaction has taken place, the establishment of a long-term relationship (Webster, 1992)

Figure 16.8 The purchase is secondary to the event

makes future purchases more pleasurable, and profitable. A buyer (see Figure 16.8) looks forward to chatting again with vendors. As Hart (1973, p. 34) noted, 'Market day is for social intercourse as well as trade'.

There are many bazaars in Morocco; producers are clustered, creating an illusion of competition. The grand bazaar of Fès is described by de Perigny (1917). Very noticeable in Fès, is the cluster of tanners (see Figure 16.9) soaking sheep hides in tannic acid.

Marrakech (see Figure 16.10) likewise has an important grand bazaar. The city's central square, Djemea el Fna, is also known as the 'assembly place of the nobodies' (Zwingle, 1996, p. 106). On a random day in the big square, there may be 50 orange juice sellers side-by-side. Water vendors wearing similar brass aprons carry water in identical goatskin bags. From the square, the bazaar spreads into the alleys where turbaned merchants conduct business. Sitting at a café, drinking the best mint tea around, an onlooker can view the square as it transforms itself over the course of the day. At dawn, stall and shop owners begin to open their places of business. They receive merchandise delivered on horse-drawn carts. One wholesaler supplies oranges to numerous orange juice vendor stalls.

As the sun rises, jugglers, magicians, acrobats and storytellers start their acts. The heat of the day begins to burn, but the music of the snake charmers echoes loudly. Caution must be taken when a show begins, as

Figure 16.9 *Tanner in Fès*

the charmer has tactics to make tourists pay dearly for the show. Sellers of cigarettes and film, as well as thieves and hustlers, mingle their way through the thick crowds of locals and tourists alike. An artisan works red-hot iron, while servants carry dough to the public ovens known as farran. Not far away, a Berber pharmacist sells gazelle skulls (for good luck) and kohl stone which is used as mascara. There are also products believed to combat evil eye and other evil spirits.

The souqs of Marrakech shimmer with intense colours and emanate smells of sweat and spices. There are scents of bay leaf, cinnamon, cumin, fresh mint, ginger, leather, musk, paprika, potter's clay, saffron, sandalwood, thyme, and vervain. Sounds include crying crows and braying donkeys along with traditional music. A call to prayer is heard behind the metalsmith's hammering. Louder than the bells of the water peddler are the screams of vendors whose high-pressure sales tactics are constantly used to lure tourists into buying silver and gold (usually plated) and amber (usually plastic) items.

A MIDDLEMAN MINORITY

In a study of entrepreneurs in the USA, Loewen (1971) found that in some neighbourhoods inhabited by Afro-Americans, residents lacked the capital to open up shops. Yet mainstream (white) merchants were reluctant to remain in business in such areas of towns. Loewen observed

Figure 16.10 Marrakech

that Chinese shop-keepers emerged as the brokers between the economic sphere of white people, and that of local Afro-Americans. Thus, these Chinese entrepreneurs came to mediate boundary transfers. Bonacich (1973) coined the term 'middleman minority' to refer to such an ethno-cultural group which acts on culturally-influenced economic niches. Kim (1981) described Koreans in New York City as a middleman minority.

In Morocco, different communities retained their respective cultural traditions for many centuries. When the French introduced industrialisation to North Africa, they were reluctant to deal directly with the population at large. Favret (1973, p. 323) described the Jews 'as middlemen between European producers and Algerian markets'. Waterbury wrote about the situation in Morocco, 'The French were all the more solicitous toward the Swasa and Jews in that the only other Indigenous group attempting to carve a niche for itself in the commercial and industrial establishment of Casablanca was the Fassi (people from Fes) bourgeoisie, and it was distinctly hostile toward the French' (Waterbury, 1973, p. 241).

Thus, Jews served as intermediaries, and Jewish entrepreneurs served as a bridge between the firm-type sector introduced by the French, and traditional activity in the bazaar economy, as depicted in Figure 16.5. Waterbury (1972, p. 45) wrote, 'Jews at Tangier . . . controlled most of the wholesale businesses in foodstuffs'. Waterbury (1973, p. 242) also noted, 'For years, four or five Jewish families had controlled tea imports and wholesaling in Morocco'. Dunn (1973, p. 95) observed, 'As almost everywhere else in Morocco, most of them found their professional niche as merchants, jewellery makers or cobblers'. Hart (1973) also mentioned them making jewellery. Why were they often concentrated in the realm of business? Adam explained, 'the Jews were tradesmen (and artisans . . .) because they were denied the right to own land; where this was granted (in certain valleys of the High Atlas, for instance among the Ait Bougmez) Jews became farmers' (Adam, 1973, p. 329).

However, Jewish farmers were relatively few in Morocco, and being Jewish was almost synonymous with being self-employed (see Figure 16.11). Adam (1973, p. 329) explained, 'It is true that neighbouring tribes are inclined to call men from the trading tribes "Jews"'.

While the French used Jewish entrepreneurs as middlemen, Berbers also preferred to deal with Jewish middlemen. Rosen explained, 'when there were numerous Jewish merchants in Sefrou, Berbers clearly preferred dealing with them because the Jews were socially non-competitive, linked in a clearly symbiotic relationship with the Muslims, and interested mainly in straightforward economic relationship with the Berbers' (Rosen, 1973, p. 161).

As summarized in Figure 16.5, the mediation of boundary transfers became an economic specialisation of the Jews. In this capacity, Jewish entrepreneurs were social agents of change, in the Barthian sense, as they introduced the features of the firm-type economy, along with technology and industrialisation. Emancipated Jews left the mellah communities and moved to the nouvelles villes (literally: new towns), modern areas built by the French.

European settlement in Morocco was clustered along the coastline, and in Casablanca, for example, the architecture still reflects a strong European presence. European entrepreneurs introduced industrialization and a Western-style firm-type economy to these areas. The Jews served as middlemen, and when Tangiers was an international zone, its streets were lined with hundreds of duty-free shops.

During the French rule of Morocco, the French authorities preferred to deal with Jews than with Muslims, and consequently used them as a middleman minority. After independence, the Jews continued to serve as a middleman minority between the Western-style modern sphere and the traditional bazaar economy of the Indigenous people. This facilitated the exchange of goods and ideas. In recent years, however, demographics have

Figure 16.11 Catering to ethnic enclave

Figure 16.12 Multicultural society

been changing and thousands of Jewish entrepreneurs have gone to seek opportunities elsewhere.

CONCLUSION

In this pluralistic society (see Figure 16.12), ethnicity has greatly influenced occupational clustering, and economic specialization has traditionally taken place along cultural lines. Urbanized Berbers are pushing for rights in mainstream society. Meanwhile, those in the Atlas mountains 'eke out a living' (Tayler, 2005, p. 79) as self-employed farmers, carrying on a 5000 year old culture.

'Family businesses are common; they provide a cushion against poverty for those who learn a trade as children, then live in the family home as adults' (Zwingle, 1996, p. 108).

Given the increased need for cash, 'Women plow the fields and raise the children while their men increasingly toil in the cities' (Tayler, 2005, p. 89). In addition, Moroccans working abroad send sizable amounts of their income home, as gifts and in the form of investments.

Geertz wrote, 'the distinction – partly cultural, partly linguistic, partly social, partly a kind of ethnopolitical myth, a traditional, almost instinctive way of perceiving group differences – between "Arab" and "Berber" remains an important, elusive factor in Moroccan national life' (Geertz, 1973, p. 302). Over three decades later, this is still true.

> The king talked of a multiple Moroccan identity, which was taken to mean Arab, Berber, French and Jewish. – Morocco's Brave New King. (*The Economist*, 30 October 1999, pp. 47–8.)

ACKNOWLEDGEMENT

The authors thank the three reviewers who supplied substantial suggestions on an earlier version of this paper.

NOTES

* This chapter originally appeared in a refereed journal as follows: L.-P. Dana, and T.E. Dana (2008), 'Ethnicity and Entrepreneurship in Morocco: A photo-ethnographic Study', *International Journal of Business and Globalisation*, **2** (3), 209–26. Reproduced with permission and available at: http://www.inderscience.com/browse/index.php?journal ID=245.

1. A monarch in Morocco is simultaneously the chérif, the religious émir of the Muslims, and the *khalif.* It is an Islamic tradition that a leader exercises religious influence as well as executive, legislative and judicial powers.

REFERENCES

Adam, A. (1973), 'Berber Migrants in Casablanca', in E. Gellner and C.A. Micaud (eds), *Arabs and Berbers: From Tribe to Nation in North Africa*, London: Gerald Duckworth, pp. 325–43.

Barth, F. (1963), *The Role of the Entrepreneur and Social Change in Northern Norway*, Norwegian Universities Press: Bergen.

Barth, F. (1967), 'On the Study of Social Change', *American Anthropologist*, **69** (6), 661–9.

Ben Kaddour, A. (1973), 'The Neo-Makhan and the Berbers', in E. Gellner and C. Micaud (eds), *Arabs and Berbers: From Tribe to Nation in North Africa*, London: Gerald Duckworth, pp. 259–67.

Bonacich, E. (1973), 'A Theory of Middleman Minorities', *American Sociological Review*, **38** (5), 583–94.

Chamard, J. and M. Christie (1996), 'Entrepreneurship Education Programs: A Change in Paradigm is Needed', *Entrepreneurship, Innovation, and Change*, **5** (3), 217–26.

Cole, W.E. and B. Fayissa (1991), 'Urban Subsistence Labor Force: Towards a

Policy-oriented and Empirically Accessible Taxonomy', *World Development*, **19** (7), 779–89.
Coram, A. (1973), 'Note on the Role of the Berbers in the Early Days of Moroccan Independence', in E. Gellner and C. Micaud (eds), *Arabs and Berbers: From Tribe to Nation in North Africa*, London: Gerald Duckworth, 269–76.
Crawford, D. (2002), 'Morocco's Invisible Imazighen', *Journal of North African Studies*, **7** (1), 53–70.
Dana, L.P. (1992), 'Entrepreneurship, Innovation and Change in Developing Countries', *Entrepreneurship, Innovation and Change*, **1** (2), 231–42.
Dana, L.P. (1995), 'Entrepreneurship in a Remote Sub-arctic Community: Nome, Alaska', *Entrepreneurship: Theory and Practice*, **20** (1), 55–72. Reprinted in N. Krueger (ed.) (2002), *Entrepreneurship: Critical Perspectives on Business and Management*, London: Routledge, vol. 4, pp. 255–75.
Dana, L.P. (2005), *When Economies Change Hands*, Binghamton, NY: International Business Press.
De Perigny, M. (1917), *Au Maroc: Fès la capitale du Nord*, Paris: Pierre Roger.
De Soto, H. (1989), *The Other Path: The Invisible Revolution in the Third World*, New York: Harper and Row.
Dunn, R.E. (1973), 'Berber Imperialism: The Ait Atta Expansion in Southeast Morocco', in E. Gellner and C. Micaud (eds), *Arabs and Berbers: From Tribe to Nation in North Africa*, London: Gerald Duckworth, pp. 85–108.
Evans, J.R. and Laskin, R.L. (1994), 'The Relationship Marketing Process: A Conceptualization and Application', *Industrial Marketing Management*, **23** (5), 432–52.
Favret, J. (1973), 'Traditionalism through Ultra-modernism', in E. Gellner and C. Micaud (eds), *Arabs and Berbers: From Tribe to Nation in North Africa*, London: Gerald Duckworth, pp. 307–24.
Fogg, W. (1940), 'Villages, Tribal Markets, and Towns: Some Considerations Concerning Urban Development in the Spanish and International Zones of Morocco', *The Sociological Review*, **32**, 85–107.
Geertz, C. (1963), *Peddlers and Princes: Social Development and Economic Change in Two Indonesian Towns*, Chicago, IL: University of Chicago Press.
Geertz, C. (1973), *The Interpretation of Cultures*, New York: Basic Books.
Halstead, J.P. (1967), *Rebirth of a Nation: The Origins and Rise of Moroccan Nationalism (1912–1944)*, Cambridge, MA: Harvard University Press.
Hart, D.M. (1973), 'The Tribe in Modern Morocco: Two Case Studies', E. Gellner and C. Micaud (eds), *Arabs and Berbers: From Tribe to Nation in North Africa*, London: Gerald Duckworth, pp. 25–58.
Hunt, C. (1980), 'Berber Brides Fair', *National Geographic*, **157** (1), 118–29.
Johnson, S., D. Kaufmann and P. Zoido-Lobaton (1998), 'Regulatory Discretion and the Unofficial Economy', *American Economic Review*, **88** (2), 387–92.
Kim, I. (1981), *The New Urban Immigrants*, Princeton, NJ: Princeton University Press.
Loewen, J.W. (1971), *The Mississippi Chinese: Between Black and White*, Cambridge, MA: Harvard University Press.
Morris, M.H. and L.F. Pitt (1995), 'Informal Sector Activity as Entrepreneurship: Insights from a South African Township', *Journal of Small Business Management*, **33** (1), 78–86.

Parsons, T. and N. Smelzer (1956), *Economy and Society*, Glencoe, IL: Free Press.

Patton, M.Q. (1982), 'Qualitative Methods and Approaches: what are they?', in E. Kuhns, and S.V. Martorana (eds), *Qualitative Methods for Institutional Research*, San Francisco, CA: Jossey-Bass, pp. 3–16.

Patton, M.Q. (1987), *How to Use Qualitative Methods in Evaluation*, Newbury Park, CA: Sage.

Peattie, L. (1987), 'An Idea in Good Currency and How it Grew: The Informal Sector', *World Development*, **15** (7), 851–60.

Portes, A., M. Castells and L.A. Benton (eds) (1989), *The Informal Economy: Studies in Advanced and Less Developed Countries*, Baltimore, MD: Johns Hopkins University Press.

Rosen, L. (1973), 'The Social and Conceptual Framework of Arab-Berber Relations in Central Morocco', in E. Gellner and C. Micaud (eds), *Arabs and Berbers: From Tribe to Nation in North Africa*, London: Gerald Duckworth, pp. 155–73.

Rosser, Jr, J.B., M. Rosser and E. Ahmed (2000), 'Income inequality and the informal economy in transition economies', *Journal of Comparative Economics*, **28**, 156–71.

Sanders, R. (1987), 'Toward a geography of informal activity', *Socio-Economic Planning Sciences*, **24** (4), 229–37.

Shor, J. and F. Shor (1955), 'From Sea to Sahara in French Morocco', *National Geographic*, **107** (2), 147–88.

Tayler, J. (2005), 'Among the Berbers: A Journey through Morocco's High Atlas Mountains', *National Geographic*, **207** (1), 78–97.

Tokman, V.E. (1978), 'Competition between the Informal Sectors in Retailing: The Case of Santiago', *World Development*, **6** (9), 1187–98.

Venema, B. and A. Mguild (2003), 'Access to Land and Berber Ethnicity in the Middle Atlas, Morocco', *Middle Eastern Studies*, **39** (4), 35–53.

Waterbury, J. (1972), *North for the Trade: The Life and Times of a Berber Merchant*, Berkeley, CA: University of California Press.

Waterbury, J. (1973), 'Tribalism. Trade and Politics: The Transformation of the Swasa of Morocco', in E. Gellner and C. Micaud (eds), *Arabs and Berbers: From Tribe to Nation in North Africa*, London: Gerald Duckworth, pp. 231–58.

Webster, F.E. (1992), 'The Changing Role of Marketing in the Corporation', *Journal of Marketing*, **53**, 1–17.

Zineldin, M.A. (1998), 'Towards an Ecological Collaborative Relationship Management', *European Journal of Marketing*, **32** (11–12), 1138–64.

Zwingle, E. (1996), 'Morocco: North Africa's timeless mosaic', *National Geographic*, **190** (4), 98–125.

17. Ashkenazi middlemen in the agricultural sector in Europe*

Léo-Paul Dana

INTRODUCTION

Based on oral testimonies of retired entrepreneurs and verified by means of triangulation, this chapter gives an account of the livestock distribution system which prevailed in Alsace until the Second World War. In this region of traditional rivalry between French and Germans, the sector was dominated by family enterprises speaking *Jédich-Daitch*, serving as a middleman minority, and dealing between French-speakers and German-speakers, who did not trade with one another.

The agro-marketing sector in Alsace developed in a manner distinctly different from its counterparts elsewhere. In Australia, Canada, New Zealand, the United Kingdom and the United States, livestock auctions have long existed, and farmers have been dealing directly at these markets. In contrast, the distribution of livestock in this multicultural region of France relied primarily on networks of middlemen known in local dialect as *Päjmes Händler* and in French as *marchands de bestiaux* – merchants of livestock. This was the case until the mid-twentieth century, when co-operatives started to become major players.

Entrepreneurs who remember working in this industry are few and aging. Most of the relevant documents were destroyed during the Second World War. It is timely, therefore, to research this sector, while the last of its players are still alive. Based on first-hand accounts, the purpose of this chapter is to provide for future generations, information about the activities of formerly essential small enterprises in the food sector, which once provided an essential service, now replaced by new distribution channels.

A retired farmer interviewed by the author expressed his view:

> Many ambulant merchants came to our village. I remember the coffee merchant, and the man who used to come to sharpen knives and scissors. One peddler would bring us dishware and pottery, and another fellow used to bring us brushes, but the livestock merchants were the most memorable. It was always exciting when they came. They were very important for us, because they

> bought our surplus animals that cost too much to feed and more importantly, they brought us horses when ours died and we needed transport. We could not imagine life without livestock merchants.

RELATED RESEARCH

Several studies, published in the nineteenth century, describe the rise of the rural merchant class in France. These include Benoit (1889), Cahun (1886), Levy (1862), Stenne (1877) and Weill (1870). In Alsace, a multicultural region consisting of Catholics, Protestants and Jews, the rural merchant class was comprised of Jewish entrepreneurs, many of whom were itinerant merchants, and these people dominated the trade of livestock.

According to Levy (1862), Jewish leaders of the nineteenth century preached that an education at a technical school would lead to a better future than commerce. Yet most of the Jews of Alsace continued to earn their livelihood as merchants, acting as intermediaries between Catholics and Protestants.

Reuss (1898) focused on the occupational clustering of the Jews in nineteenth century Alsace. During times of peace, Alsatian Jews thrived, trading a wide assortment of merchandise, precious metals and livestock, especially cattle. During wartime, these traders prospered by selling horses to the military; horses were needed for transport, and horsemeat was relished by the soldiers. In addition, troops bought horse-feed from Jewish merchants. Those known as *Pfühändler* bought grain and sold flour; the *Nahloshändler* peddled general goods. Some specialized in sharpening knives and scissors; others served as *prête-noms*, lending money on behalf of Catholic clergymen, who were not supposed to charge direct interest to other Catholics. Marx (1975) discussed the role of Jewish financiers in Alsace.

From the above literature it appears that Catholics disliked buying from Protestants and vice versa. Yet everybody bought from the Jews, and these were the middlemen. A similar scenario is described by Loewen (1971), who found Chinese entrepreneurs were the middlemen between Afro-Americans and whites in Mississippi.

Bonacich (1973) pioneered a middleman minority theory. This was built upon by Aldrich, Jones and McEvoy (1984), Bonacich (1987), Marger (1990), Min and Jaret (1985), and Zenner (1991).

Like the entrepreneurs described by Barth (1963; 1967), the merchants of Alsace were also agents of change. Barthian literature views entrepreneurship as an activity involving the relationship of persons and institutions in different ethnic communities. Barth (1963) placed great emphasis on the existence of different spheres of values, and central to his discussion is the concept of the entrepreneur as being an essential broker, mediating boundary transfers in this situation of contacts between cultures. Given that farms in Alsace were dispersed and that farmers seldom travelled beyond their church, residents relied on the Jewish merchants to bring them innovations from the city, for example, the first musical recording, the first electrical appliance, the first disposable shaver, the first radio, and so on.

Central to the success of the Jewish middlemen in Alsace were their networks, as is the case in much modern-day entrepreneurship (Aldrich, 1989; Aldrich et al., 1984; Aldrich et al., 1987; Aldrich and Zimmer, 1986; Bonacich et al., 1977; Boubakri, 1999; Brenner and Toulouse, 1999; Dhaliwala, 1998; Dubini and Aldrich, 1991; Dyer and Ross, 2000; Iyer and Shapiro, 1999; Jagd, 2005; Koniordos, 2005; Light, 1972; Miles et al., 2005; Peterson and Roquebert, 1993; Ram, 1994; Ray et al., 1988; Shenker, 1994; Waldinger, 1988; and Wong, 1987). The literature explains that minority entrepreneurs can benefit greatly from the social capital of an ethnic network, including co-ethnic suppliers, markets, employees, as well as finance and information.

Juteau and Paré (1996) and Lee (1999) found co-ethnic suppliers were prevalent among Jewish entrepreneurs in Canada and in the United States, respectively. Lee (1999) noted that this provided access to lower wholesale costs, which could translate to lower retail costs and enhanced competitiveness. For the livestock merchants of Alsace, however, co-ethnic suppliers were not an option, as Jews did not breed animals. Nor could they limit themselves to a co-ethnic market.

The merchants of Alsace often operated their micro-enterprises without paid employees, depending instead on unpaid family labour. Much current literature likewise indicates a reliance, by ethnic minority entrepreneurs, on unpaid family members (for example, Juteau and Paré, 1996; Wong and Ng, 1998). Butler and Greene (1997) pointed out that this led to a stereotype of exploitation. In the case of the Alsatian livestock merchants, according to respondents and their families, unpaid labour did not involve exploitation, but rather a very valuable apprenticeship. Thus, sons and nephews learned the trade from their fathers and uncles, who served as role models and mentors.

These merchants also relied heavily on family for financing. In addition, members of the ethnic community also provided finance when needed. This was similar to the credit networks described by Iyer and Shapiro (1999) and by Juteau and Paré (1996) in their studies of Jewish entrepreneurs in the United States and in Canada respectively. Mechanisms to provide financing to co-ethnics are quite widespread, as discussed by Basu

(1998), Bates (1997), Boubakri (1999), Gold (1992), Laguerre (1998), Lee (1999), Peterson and Roquebert (1993), Phizacklea and Ram (1996), Shin and Han (1990), Saxenian (1999) and Yoon (1995).

In addition, the Jewish merchants of Alsace relied on their ethnic network for information and advice. Such practice is commonly referred to by the literature, including Basu (1998); Dadzie and Cho (1989); Marger and Hoffman (1992); Peterson (1995); Saxenian (1999); and Yoon (1995). Iyer and Shapiro (1999), and Juteau and Paré (1996), refer to information networks of Jewish entrepreneurs in the United States and Canada respectively. In Alsace, *Schmüsser* were individuals who provided information, for a fee.

The social network of the merchants of Alsace also included a feature seemingly absent in the literature. Travel was intrinsic to their livelihood and during business trips these frequent travellers would pray, and eat, with co-religionists, and sleep at their homes. The religious duty of allowing animals to rest on the Sabbath (from sunset on Friday until dusk on Saturday) made it impossible to travel with livestock during this time of rest. Therefore, business trips were often extended due to religious obligations, and considerable time was spent with the families of other merchants. During this time, matchmaking was a common occurrence, as the son of a merchant fancied the daughter of another. The co-religionists shared the same language, holidays, belief system and dietary restrictions. All this, in turn, reinforced social networking among this ethnic minority.

Writing about entrepreneurs in twenty-first century Europe, Sternberg and Lückgen (2005) emphasized the difficulty of small firms to obtain financing in Germany. This is not a new phenomenon. During the nineteenth century, credit institutions were reluctant to give loans to small farmers in Germany. Therefore, some farmers leased cattle from Jewish entrepreneurs. Others bought cattle on credit from Jewish merchants.

HISTORICAL BACKGROUND

Raphaël (1980) discussed the factors that led Jews to become merchants in Alsace. These people were once active farmers in Europe. Over time, however, a number of factors led them to abandon their farms and their vineyards. Their religion prevented them from working on Saturday, and the Church forbade them labouring in their fields on Sundays. The Church also banned them from giving employment to Christians. In addition, experience taught the Jews that, in times of religious persecutions, it was more convenient to have moveable assets, such as gold, cattle and later diamonds, than to own immovables.

During the thirteenth century, Jews began abandoning agriculture, at an alarming rate. Rabbi Meir ben Baruch of Rothenburg, an influential German spiritual leader of the times, described as a calamity the fact that Jews were leaving the land in order to pursue commercial profits. By the fourteenth century, Jews no longer had a choice; under the Saxon civil code, *Meissener Rechtsbuch*, Jews were banned from owning land. Yet, in Alsace, this did not lead to urbanization, because Jews were not allowed to live in the cities.

Alsace remained part of the Holy German Empire until being acquired in 1648, by the Kingdom of France. At the time, the French army was facing a shortage of horses, and a lack of animal feed for the horses it had. The Jews of Alsace, with their experience in commerce, efficiently supplied the French with horses and with animal feed. The French offered protection to these people who supplied their army, and this led to a mass immigration of Jews from central Europe, to Alsace. Whereas the Jewish population in Alsace had consisted of 525 families in 1689, according to the census of 1784, the province was home to 3910 families that year, amounting to 19 624 people. Still forbidden to own land, deprived of entry into universities, excluded from the guilds and not allowed to reside in cities, these people tended to be travelling merchants, linking the urban and rural economies. In September 1791, Jews were permitted to reside in the cities of Alsace, and this helped them expand their commercial networks.

In 1870, the Germans took back Alsace from France, and the Kaiser built large and ornate synagogues for the Jews (see Figure 17.1 and 17.2). This ensured the continued growth of commerce in Alsace.

'*Nix tse handle*?' the fathers used to scream, as their sons would wobble along the main road of each village. In Alsatian dialect, this meant, 'Anything for sale?' The peddlers would stock up with second-hand wares before departing to sell them in the next town. The fathers and elder brothers would carry their loads on backs. This included utensils, candles and soap, as well as animal hides, laces, string and used clothing. Wealthier merchants used man-powered pushcarts. The exceptions were those known as *Esseljéde* (donkey-Jews), as they would travel from one village to another with a donkey-drawn cart; they traded kitchenware and other household items, accepting rags and beehives as payment. Livestock merchants constituted a class of their own. Some had a horse-drawn wagon on which two calves could be transported.

At the end of the nineteenth century, Jews had a monopoly in cattle dealing in areas of Baden, Bavaria, Hanover, Rhineland and Westphalia. Until the First World War, most independent cattle dealers in Germany (including Alsace) were Jewish.

Figure 17.1 The synagogue in Benfield was enlarged in 1876

THE LIVESTOCK SECTOR

Livestock breeders, having responsibilities linked to their land and to their animals, could not easily spend time away from their farms, in order to sell their animals to butchers. It was highly inconvenient for the farmers to displace themselves to urban areas, searching for buyers to purchase livestock. Jews, not being tied to the land, identified a highly lucrative opportunity, buying live animals from families in rural areas, and providing urban butchers with livestock. The Jews of Alsace soon came to dominate this trade, constantly travelling between supply and demand. They managed the link between the rural and urban economies, providing cash for farmers and a source of meat for consumers. In addition, they spread information as required. If one farmer needed a bull, temporarily, for breeding purposes, a livestock merchant could source this need.

For farmers who wished to raise cattle, but not necessarily breed them, Alain Levy provided calves, with a promise to buy them back for their meat. For those who wished to buy calves but lacked cash, the livestock merchant provided short-term credit.

Figure 17.2 The synagogue in Ingwiller was enlarged in 1891 and renovated in 1903

'We could provide credit,' explained an interviewee, 'because we learned to spend little, in order to have some cash left over – frugality.'

Another respondent elaborated,

> On a work day, we left home at dawn, and all we ate all day was some cheese and some bread, or potatoes, perhaps with boiled eggs. In the fall or in winter we sometimes had a few nuts. We drank water from public fountains. At times, we had a little beer, but we reserved wine for special occasions. Only after a successful deal would we splurge on coffee and some *eau-de-vie*. Of course, on Friday nights we dressed up and celebrated the Sabbath with a special meal, very labour-intensive in its preparation, stuffed stomach for example. The rest of the time, we were thrifty.

Weber (1904–05), in his culturalist theory, also referred to frugality, thrift and the willingness to defer gratification.

The livestock merchants of Alsace were eager to fulfil various needs of consumers, and prospered from the opportunities they identified.

However, their culture did *not* consider commerce to be a socially desirable occupation. A retired merchant explained to the author, 'Our rabbis were telling us to learn trades, for example at the *Ecole des Arts et Métiers de Strasbourg.* I think it is Psalm 128, if I recall correctly, at my age, that teaches us something like this: When you subsist from the labour of your hands, then you shall be happy and satisfied.'

Another respondent explained,

> Social reform allowed us to enter mainstream society, but we perceived there to be excessive risk in attempting an activity completely unknown to us. Why take an unnecessary risk? For us, entrepreneurship was the only means to eliminate risk. It was our expertise to travel across the countryside and to buy livestock, and that is what we did best.

For longer expeditions, merchants invariably departed in the early morning. Grandmothers and mothers blessed the travellers and wives often joined their husbands for the first few steps, reciting together prayers for a safe return. Although calves often rode in carts, larger animals walked behind, attached by means of a rope.

The traders did not travel randomly. Rather, their itineraries were carefully planned within networks of like-minded people who would host them. Until the twentieth century, there were 145 Jewish communities in the Bas-Rhin department of Alsace, and another 58 in the Haut-Rhin department to the south. By travelling within this network of communities, it was possible for the travellers to observe their day of rest on Saturday, and to acquire food prepared according to religious laws. In December, friends and relatives prepared a winter specialty – potato pancakes fried in oil, and known in *Jédich-Daitch* as *latkes.* In the spring, during the festival of Passover, unleavened bread was readily available. The wives of peddlers in one village were very welcoming of the peddlers from another. The hospitality was reciprocated, as the husbands of the hosts would be accommodated by the families of the visitors, in their respective hometowns. Their success as entrepreneurs, and their survival as a linguistic and religious minority, depended on the social cohesion within this regional ethnic network.

Farmers interviewed by the author explained that as youngsters they would feel uncomfortable when they heard the merchants talking in a foreign language amongst themselves.

> Although ours was a relatively large farm, whenever we had more than twelve cattle, we would sell the surplus. During negotiations to purchase cattle from my father, the buyers would discuss the price amongst themselves, speaking in *Jédich-Daitch.* We never knew what they were saying, but we assumed that they

were planning a strategy to pay us a lower price. In any case, we seldom rejected an offer, because we did not have the resources to search for another buyer. Rarely would more than one or two teams of livestock merchants approach us, since they appeared to have charted the territory in such a way as to avoid excessive competition.

Another interviewee expressed his feeling,

The Jews were very knowledgeable and well-organised. The value of dairy cattle was related to their capacity to produce milk. In the case of *Navelbehejmess* (an animal sold for meat), the price was a function of its weight.[1] The value of beasts of burden reflected their ability to perform work. In addition, prices reflected the time of year.[2] I used to milk the cows, and I was amazed how the livestock merchants could figure out, with great accuracy, the milk producing capacity of a cow. In addition, these expert buyers would guess, apparently quite accurately, the weight of an animal. So we were happy to make a sale, but the fact that they spoke a different language made us nervous, because they could understand everything we said, but they could also say things which we could not understand.

Livestock merchants told the author their side of the story. 'We used *Jédich-Daitch* among us because that is what we spoke best. When asking my father or brother whether he agreed on my weight estimate of a given animal, it would have felt very awkward to do so in French or German, both of these being foreign languages for us.'

Youngsters played a very active role in the family business. As preschool children, they would play beside the cows, in the stable. When they got slightly older, they took pride in sweeping the stable. School-age boys, referred to as *die Jénglich,* were responsible for milking the cows, before having breakfast, which often consisted of soup. After eating, the lads would chop hay and beets for the animals. After school, children would participate in short-haul animal deliveries, to the neighbouring village, for instance.

During school holidays, boys as young as 10 years old became involved in longer deliveries, taking livestock to the market. An interviewee reminisced being an adolescent, 'To get to the market on time, it was necessary for us to rise before dawn and as a reward we were sometimes treated to sausages! Other times we ate bread moistened with beer.'

In his biography, Weill (1870) recalled being the companion and apprentice of his father, an established livestock merchant. While the father rode on horseback, the son would walk alongside, leading one or two cows. By the age of 14, noted Alexandre Weill, teenagers were considered mature adults, responsible for their own purchases and sales. According to this biography, a merchant of the nineteenth century did not interfere with the transactions of a 14-year-old son. In contrast, interviews conducted by the author indicate that merchants of the twentieth century felt it necessary to give advice to their sons.

The merchants would visit up to eight villages in a day, looking to negotiate transactions. Some Jews did not themselves deal with livestock, but served as brokers, or informers who simply sold information which would lead to transactions. These entrepreneurs were called *Schmüsser*, and their commission was referred to as *Sassergeld.* Operating informally, these individuals mingled with the villagers, identified needs and opportunities and then waited by the side of a road, knowing that livestock merchants would be passing by eventually. The *Schmüsser* then sold their information to livestock merchants. (The word they used for this activity was *vermassere*, literally meaning 'to inform'.) In order to reduce time spent away from their own villages, the transient merchants preferred to pay for this market research, rather than to conduct this time-consuming task themselves. The *Schmüsser* thus formed an integral part of the business network.

Also integral to the social capital of livestock merchants were the *Unterbieter.*[3] Livestock merchants would send these people ahead of themselves, to offer farmers low prices, in order to give the impression that market values were depressed. When the actual merchant followed, his offer appeared relatively high, making the seller feel good about his sale to the highest bidder.

Beyond the ethnic boundary of cultural resources, a network of buyers and sellers also developed. When a merchant had more animals than he had the capacity to take care of, he often looked beyond his ethnic resources, to a larger network encompassing local farmers with whom friendships had been developed.

> From time to time, I had a temporary surplus of cattle. Although I needed to board them somewhere, I could not look to other merchants for assistance, because if I had an excess of animals and not enough space, chances were that they were in the identical situation. So, it was very useful to have an arrangement to board livestock on the property of a farmer.

In many cases, farmers and merchants developed friendships and conducted business together on a regular basis. Butchers also liked having a regular supplier of quality animals, and so livestock merchants often had regular buyers. These were known as *Kaunem* (possibly from the German verb *kaufen* meaning 'to buy' or the Hebrew *kaunim* meaning 'purchasers'.

A retired merchant recalled,

> I had twenty regular clients, each of whom I visited five or six times a year. I also had a butcher who was a regular buyer and over time, we developed an intense trust. He knew it was good to buy from me, and I knew I could sell to him, so it reduced any risk of uncertainty. You see, the average turnover rate was 15 days, from the instant we bought a cow until the moment we sold it. No merchant wanted to hold an animal longer than that, because it represented tied-up capital, and expenses, as the animal needed to eat and it took up place.

Another merchant elaborated,

> In the old days, there was also the risk of an animal catching tuberculosis. During my career, as a livestock merchant, I saw at least twenty calves die unexpectedly, before I had a chance to find a buyer for veal. If I knew a butcher who would buy regularly from me, I might have been able to sell the calves before they got sick. A sick animal could be sold to the candle factory, but we would not sell it for food. So, it was good to have one or more regular buyers.

Cattle were also traded at the bi-weekly livestock market which took place, in the town of Saverne, on every second Thursday (except on Jewish holidays, such as *Rosh Hashanah*, *Yom Kippur* and the *Fête des Cabanes*). Information flow was relatively less imperfect here, compared to those conducted on a farm, because buyers and sellers had a large variety of animals and prices to compare. According to documents at the town hall of Saverne, most transactions that took place at the local livestock market took place between Jewish merchants and did not involve farmers or butchers.

One merchant explained to the author,

> When dealing with meat-cattle, our margins were slim and after transportation and other expenses not much profit remained! The market of Saverne was fabulous because, there, we could buy and sell an animal, all on the same day, without travelling with it long distances. Sometimes, I found a seller and a buyer and I introduced them to each other. They would pay me a commission for making possible a transfer and I did not even take possession of the animal. In this way, the market allowed me to earn money as a commission agent, rather than being an actual merchant.

Some market transactions were more complex than were others, requiring legal documentation. Saverne merchant Jacob Kahn, for instance, sold a pregnant cow to a resident of the Pfalsburg area with the agreement that eight days after its birth the calf would be returned to the vendor. It was also possible to sell a cow with a promise that the seller would be entitled to a supply of milk.

A more common, yet detailed, transaction was the *Anschlag*. This was a sale of an animal, which led to a sharing of profits (or losses) at the time of resale.

Some sales were paid cash, while others were on instalment, at times without interest. As well, some transactions involved barter. When Théodore Lévy, a merchant based in Marmoutier, sold two horses to Antoni Hiegel, a farmer from Dimbsthal, the former accepted a blind horse, as a trade-in, in partial payment.

In some cases, the merchants would try to enhance the appearance of an animal, before bringing it to the market. For this, they hired the service of professionals outside their ethnic network. A village-smith was paid to sharpen the horns of an animal. Tails were sometimes trimmed, teeth were cleaned, and in the case of horses, white eyebrows were plucked. A well-fed and good-looking animal could yield a handsome profit, especially when sold with a guarantee. The standard guarantee, *landesübliche Währschaft* lasted for six weeks. When dealing with merchants who had established good reputations, farmers were willing to pay a premium for a healthy animal with a guarantee.

Constantly travelling, assisted by their vast networks rich with ethnic resources, the livestock merchants of Alsace were aware of prevailing prices in different areas, and this allowed them to identify opportunities for arbitrage. These Jews could read and write using the Hebrew alphabet (from right to left), as well as the Latin one, from left to right. They spoke *Jédich-Daitch* among themselves and Yiddish with Jews from Switzerland. With local farmers, they spoke Alsatian dialect, to which they referred as *Galeres-Daitch*. The merchants also mastered French and German, which they used in mainstream society. The daughters of wealthy Jews frequently studied in Lorraine, and girls from poor backgrounds often spent some time working as maids of richer Jews, in Paris. Thus, even women learned to speak French. Knowledge of several languages, coupled with human relations skills, enhanced their ability to negotiate. Business skills were developed from a very young age, as children watched their fathers doing transactions. Commerce was a way of life, and attempting another occupation would have been perceived as being an unnecessary risk. A network of livestock merchants, across the region, facilitated the dissemination of knowledge and availability of finance among co-religionists. In the event of bankruptcy, an individual was given assistance by other merchants. All of these factors predisposed Jews to follow the role of their fathers and to take over the family business, from one generation to the next.

THE SECTOR TRANSFORMED

The Second World War witnessed the disappearance of Jews from many communities across Alsace. Without the elaborate network which had existed earlier, the livestock sector would never be the same again. Farmers realized that the function formerly performed by the livestock merchants needed to be done by new entities. Co-operatives arose to fulfil this need.

Yet the nature of the sector changed as the small-scale family farm declined in importance. Rather than own one horse and a couple of cows, as did the typical family farm of the early twentieth century, a modern farmer may have 150 animals or none at all. Nowadays, fewer farmers raise animals, and it is less common for a farmer to have just a few dairy cattle. No longer are Alsatian farmers generalists, owning a few animals, and planting some crops (usually beets, potatoes, cabbage, and wheat) to feed themselves and their animals. The trend has been to specialize in large-scale production of beets or tobacco or grapes.

No longer do young boys wake up early to mix beets and bran for their fathers' cattle. Large-scale feeders provide the animals with corn. No longer does a farmer need to get a breeding-bull for a few days. Artificial insemination has become the norm. Breeding stock are bought and sold by means of ads in newspapers such as *L'Est agricole et viticole.*

The last livestock market of Saverne took place in June 1973, survived by large ones outside Alsace, namely those in Dijon and Nancy. Urban butcheries nowadays buy directly from farmers and the marketing of livestock for butchering is done via co-operatives.

No longer does each village have its own slaughtering facilities. The slaughterhouses of Mützig and Wasselone are among the many that closed down. Large-scale slaughterhouses have replaced the traditional smaller ones that were scattered across the region. Outside Strasbourg, the only slaughterhouse which remains in the Bas Rhin Department of France (northern Alsace) is in the municipality of Haguenau. Animals from farms as far as Valff are processed in large plants located in Strasbourg. The only local slaughtering would be the undeclared slaughter of non-registered calves (the birth of which has not been registered) for personal consumption.

No longer do livestock merchants roam the countryside of Alsace walking animals from one village to another. Trucks and trains transport livestock, and meat is exported by air. 'It is all different now, and not necessarily for the better,' exclaimed one interviewee. 'Now, we are living in the era of mad cow disease!'

ACKNOWLEDGEMENTS

The author expresses sincere thanks to Edna Bonacich (Professor of Sociology and Ethnic Studies, University of California), Jerome Katz

(Coleman Foundation Endowed Chair in Entrepreneurship, Saint Louis University), and Morton Weinfeld (Professor of Sociology, McGill University) who reviewed this chapter and provided constructive feedback on its first draft. In addition, deep gratitude is due to the many individuals who agreed to recount their experiences as merchants in Alsace, and also to those who introduced the author to retired entrepreneurs who once worked in the sector. Special thanks to the following, whose assistance was extraordinary: Monsieur Rolff Baer, owner of Nouveau Marché, in Molsheim; Monsieur and Mme. Gilbert and Brett Blum, retailers in Hochfelden; Monsieur Jean Bowman, retired livestock merchant, in Mützig; Monsieur Norpère Cahn, retired livestock merchant, in Mützig, and his spouse, Mme. Norpère Cahn; Monsieur Olivier Cahn, financial consultant, in Strasbourg; Monsieur Roger Cahn, cloth retailer in Westhoffen; Monsieur Rav Cerf, retired entrepreneur in Brumath; Monsieur Léon Kahn, retired entrepreneur in Obernai; Monsieur Roger Levy, retired livestock merchant, in Scherviller, and his spouse, Mme Jeanine Levy; Monsieur and Mme. Paul Metzger, butchers in Brumath; Mme. Marguerite Meyer, of Place des Fines Herbes, in Obernai (widow and sister-in-law of livestock merchants); Monsieur le Professeur Freddy Raphael, in Strasbourg; and Monsieur Rav Strauss, real estate agent in Benfeld. Librarians at the Université Louis Pasteur and at the Université Robert Schuman were most helpful in the search for rare books.

NOTES

* This chapter originally appeared as 'A Historical Study of the Traditional Livestock Merchants of Alsace', *British Food Journal*, **108** (7), 2006, 586–98. Reproduced with permission.

1. A carcass is roughly 45 per cent the weight of a live cow. A live dairy cow weighs in the vicinity of 500 kilogrammes.
2. The price of livestock underwent seasonal fluctuations. In the fall, prices were depressed, reflecting the fact that animals needed shelter during the winter, and space was limited. In March, the same animal would be worth much more, because space was less of a constraint, and there was less of a perceived need to sell.
3. This slang term is derived from the verb *unterbieten*, which means to beat somebody's offer.

REFERENCES

Aldrich, Howard E. (1989), 'Networking among Women Entrepreneurs,' in Oliver Hagan, Carol Rivchun and Donald L. Sexton (eds), *Women-Owned Businesses*, New York: Praeger, pp. 103–132.

Aldrich, Howard E. and Catherine Zimmer (1986), 'Entrepreneurship Through

Social Networks,' in Donald L. Sexton and Raymond W. Smilor (eds), *The Art and Science of Entrepreneurship*, Cambridge, MA: Ballinger, pp. 3–24.

Aldrich, Howard E., Trevor P. Jones and David McEvoy (1984), 'Ethnic Advantage and Minority Business Development', in Robin Ward and Richard Jenkins (eds), *Ethnic Communities in Business: Strategies for Economic Survival*, Cambridge: Cambridge University Press.

Aldrich, Howard E., Ben Rosen and William Woodward (1987), 'The Impact of Social Networks on Business Foundings and Profit in a Longitudinal Study', *Frontiers of Entrepreneurship Research*, Wellesley, MA: Babson College, pp. 154–168.

Barth, Frederik (1963), *The Role of the Entrepreneur and Social Change in Northern Norway*, Bergen: Norwegian Universities Press.

Barth, Frederik (1967), 'On the Study of Social Change', *American Anthropologist*, **69** (6), 661–9.

Basu, Anuradha (1998), 'An Exploration of Entrepreneurial Activity among Asian Small Businesses in Britain', *Small Business Economics* **10** (4), 313–26.

Bates, Timothy (1997), 'Financing Small Business Creation: The Case of Chinese and Korean Immigrant Entrepreneurs', *Journal of Business Venturing* **12** (2), 109–24.

Benoit, A. (1889), 'Les Israélites en Alsace sous le Directoire et le Consulat,' *La Revue Nouvelle d'Alsace-Lorraine*, **8**, (April).

Bonacich, Edna (1973), 'A Theory of Middleman Minorities,' *American Sociological Review*, **38** (5), 583–94.

Bonacich, Edna (1987), '"Making It", in America: A Social Evolution of the Ethics of Immigrant Entrepreneurship', *Social Perspectives*, **30**, 446–66.

Bonacich, Edna, Ivan Light and Charles Choy Wong (1977), 'Koreans in Business', *Society*, **14**, pp. 54–9.

Boubakri, Hassen (1999), 'Les entrepreneurs migrants d'Europe', *Culture & Conflits, Sociologie Politique de l'International*, Spring–Summer, 69–88.

Brenner, Gabrielle A. and Jean-Marie Toulouse (1990), 'Business Creation among the Chinese Immigrants in Montreal', *Journal of Small Business and Entrepreneurship*, **7** (4), 38–44.

Butler, John Sibley and Patricia Gene Greene (1997), 'Ethnic Entrepreneurship: The Continuous Rebirth of American Enterprise', in Donald L. Sexton and Raymond W. Smilor (eds), *Entrepreneurship* 2000, Chicago, IL: Upstart, pp. 267–89.

Cahun, Léon (1886), *La Vie Juive*, Paris: De Brunhoff et Cie.

Dadzie, Kofie Q. and Youngil Cho (1989), 'Determinants of Minority Business Formation and Survival: An Empirical Assessment', *Journal of Small Business Management*, **27** (3), 56–61.

Dhaliwala, Spinder (1998), 'Silent Contributors: Asian Female Entrepreneurs and Women in Business', *Women's Studies International Forum*, **21** (5), 463–74.

Dubini, Paola and Howard E. Aldrich (1991), 'Personal and Extended Networks are Central to the Entrepreneurship Process', *Journal of Business Venturing*, **6** (5), 305–13.

Dyer, Linda M. and Christopher A. Ross (2000), 'Ethnic Enterprises and Their Clientele', *Journal of Small Business Management*, **39** (2), 48–66.

Gold, Steven J. (1992), 'The Employment Potential of Refugee Entrepreneurship: Soviet Jews and Vietnamese in California', *Policy Studies Review*, **11** (2), 176–85.

Iyer, Gopalkrishnan R. and Jon M. Shapiro (1999), 'Ethnic Entrepreneurial and Marketing Systems: Implications for the Global Economy', *Journal of International Marketing*, **7** (4), 83–110.

Jagd, Søren (2005), 'The "Network Ethic" and the New Spirit of Capitalism in French Sociology of Capitalism', in Sokratis M. Koniordos (ed.), *Networks, Trust and Social Capital: Theoretical and Empirical Investigations from Europe*, Aldershot: Ashgate, pp. 47–69.

Juteau, Danielle and Sylvie Paré (1996), 'L'entrepreneurship ethnique', *Interfaces*, **17** (1), 18–28.

Koniordos, Sokratis M. (2005), 'Informal Support Networks in the Making of Small Independent Businesses Beyond "Strong" and "Weak" Ties?', in Sokratis M. Koniordos (ed.), *Networks, Trust and Social Capital: Theoretical and Empirical Investigations from Europe*, Aldershot: Ashgate, pp. 167–203.

Levy, Isaac (1862), *Isaïe ou le Travail*, Paris.

Laguerre, Michel S. (1998), 'Rotating Credit Associations and the Diasporic Economy', *Journal of Developmental Entrepreneurship*, **3** (1), 23–34.

Lee, Jennifer (1999), 'Retail Niche Domination among African-American, Jewish and Korean Entrepreneurs', *American Behavioral Scientist*, **42** (9), 1398–417.

Light, Ivan (1972), *Ethnic Enterprise in America*, Berkeley and Los Angeles, CA: University of California.

Loewen, James W. (1971), *The Mississippi Chinese: Between Black and White*, Cambridge, MA: Harvard University Press.

Marger, Martin N. (1990), 'East Indians in Small Business: Middleman Minority or Ethnic Enclave', *New Community*, **16** (4), 551–9.

Marger, Martin N. and Constance A. Hoffman (1992), 'Ethnic Enterprise in Ontario: Immigrant Participation in the Small Business Sector', *International Migration Review*, **26**, 968–81.

Marx, Roland (1975), 'Les Juifs et l'usure en Alsace', *Saisons d'Alsace*, **55–6**, 62–7.

Miles, Raymond E., Grant Miles and Charles C. Snow (2005), *Collaborative Entrepreneurship: How Communities of Networked Firms Innovate to Create Economic Wealth*, Stanford, CA: Stanford University Press.

Min, Pyong Gap and Charles Jaret (1985), 'Ethnic Business Success: The Case of Korean Small Business in Atlanta', *Sociology and Social Research*, **69** (3), 412–35.

Peterson, Mark F. (1995), 'Leading Cuban-American Entrepreneurs: The Process of Developing Motives, Abilities and Resources', *Human Relations*, **48** (10), 1193–215.

Peterson, Mark F. and Jaime Roquebert (1993), 'Success Patterns of Cuban-American Enterprises: Implications for Entrepreneurial Communities', *Human Relations*, **46** (8), 921–37.

Phizacklea, Annie and Monder Ram (1996), 'Being Your Own Boss: Ethnic Minority Entrepreneurs in Comparative Perspective', *Work, Employment & Society*, **10** (2), 319–39.

Ram, Monder (1994), 'Unraveling Social Networks in Ethnic Minority Firms', *International Small Business Journal*, **12** (3), 42–53.

Raphaël, Freddy (1980), 'Les Juifs de la campagne alsacienne: les marchands de bestiaux,' *Revue des Sciences Sociales de la France de l'Est*, **9**, 220–45.

Ray, Denis M., Asley Momijan, W. Ed McMullan and Sylvia Ko (1988), 'Comparison of Immigrant Armenian Entrepreneurs in Los Angeles and

Immigrant Chinese Entrepreneurs in Calgary', Calgary, University of Calgary Faculty of Management Research Papers.
Reuss, Rodolphe (1898), *L'Alsace au 17e Siècle: au point de vue géographique, historique, administratif, économique, social, intellectuel et religieux*, Paris: E. Bouillon.
Saxenian, AnnaLee (1999), *Silicon Valley's New Immigrant Entrepreneurs*, San Francisco, CA: Public Policy Institute of California.
Shenker, Oded (1994), 'The People's Republic of China: Raising the Bamboo Screen through International Management Research', *International Studies of Management and Organization*, **24** (1–2), 9–34.
Shin, Eui-Hang and Shin-Kap Han (1990), 'Korean Immigrant Small Businesses in Chicago: An Analysis of the Resource Mobilization Process', *Amerasia*, **16** (1), 39–60.
Stenne, G. (1877), *La Dime*, Paris.
Sternberg, Rolf and Ingo Lückgen (2005), *Global Entrepreneurship Monitor (GEM). Länderbericht Deutschland 2004.* Cologne: Wirtschafts-und Sozialgeographisches Institut, Universität zu Köln.
Waldinger, Richard (1988), 'The Ethnic Division of Labor Transformed: Native Minorities and New Immigrants in Post-industrial New York', *New Community*, **14** (3), 318–32.
Weber, Max (1904–05), 'Die Protestantische Ethik und der Geist des Kapitalismus', *Archiv fur Sozialwissenschaft und Sozialpolitik* (20–21); revised 1930, *The Protestant Ethic and the Spirit of Capitalism*, trans. Talcott Parsons, London: G. Allen and Unwin.
Weill, Alexandre (1870), *Ma Jeunesse*, Paris: Dentu.
Wong, Bernard (1987), 'The Role of Ethnicity in Enclave Entrepreneurs: A Study of the Chinese Garment Factory in New York City', *Human Organization*, **46** (2), 120–31.
Wong, Lloyd L. and Michele Ng (1998), 'Chinese Immigrant Entrepreneurs in Vancouver: A Case Study of Ethnic Business Development', *Canadian Ethnic Studies*, **30** (1), 64–85.
Yoon, In-Jin (1995), 'The Growth of Korean Immigrant Entrepreneurship in Chicago', *Ethnic and Racial Studies*, **18** (2), 315–35.
Zenner, Walter P. (1991), *Minorities in the Middle: A Cross Cultural Analysis*, Albany, NY: State University of New York Press.

18. The Jewish sub-economy of Montreal*

Morton Weinfeld

INTRODUCTION

Jews in Montreal have been very visible in the business realm of Montreal, Canada, owning factories and retail outlets as well as service firms. In 1913, for example, Ida Steinberg created a grocery store that led to the introduction of the supermarket concept in Quebec. Sam Steinberg (see Figure 18.1) and his brothers expanded the family business into the largest chain of supermarkets (see Figure 18.2) in the province. This chapter shall discuss the Jewish sub-economy in Montreal.

The study of ethnic economies in general and ethnic enclaves in particular, particular those in North America or Europe, has relied on case studies of groups which are often foreign born, of racial minority origin, subject to ongoing forms of overt and systemic discrimination, and economically disadvantaged. (Light and Gold, 2000; Portes and Bach, 1985; Stiles and Galbraith, 2004; Waldinger, 1996, Waldinger et al., 1990). As a result Jews as an entire group today fall outside this purview. Rather, attention on Jewish economic behavior has focused on their proclivity towards entrepreneurship, as 'middlemen minorities' participating in the wider economy historically in the diaspora and recently in urban centers. (Bonacich, 1973). Of course, historians also noted the unique concentrations of immigrant Jews in the Lower East Side of Manhattan, and other cities in the American northeast, in the early twentieth century. But the assumption is that as Jews – like other older immigrant minorities – are increasingly native born and more socio-economically successful, they will lose any economic specificity as they blend into the mainstream economy. As Portes writes: 'The institutional completeness of immigrant enclaves is short-lived, seldom lasting longer than one or two generations' (1995, p. 28).

The purpose of this chapter is to challenge that view, through a study of the economic activity of Canadian Jews, primarily in Montreal but in Toronto as well. This is a group which is mainly non-immigrant, white,

Figure 18.1 Mr Sam Steinberg (photograph by Léo-Paul Dana)

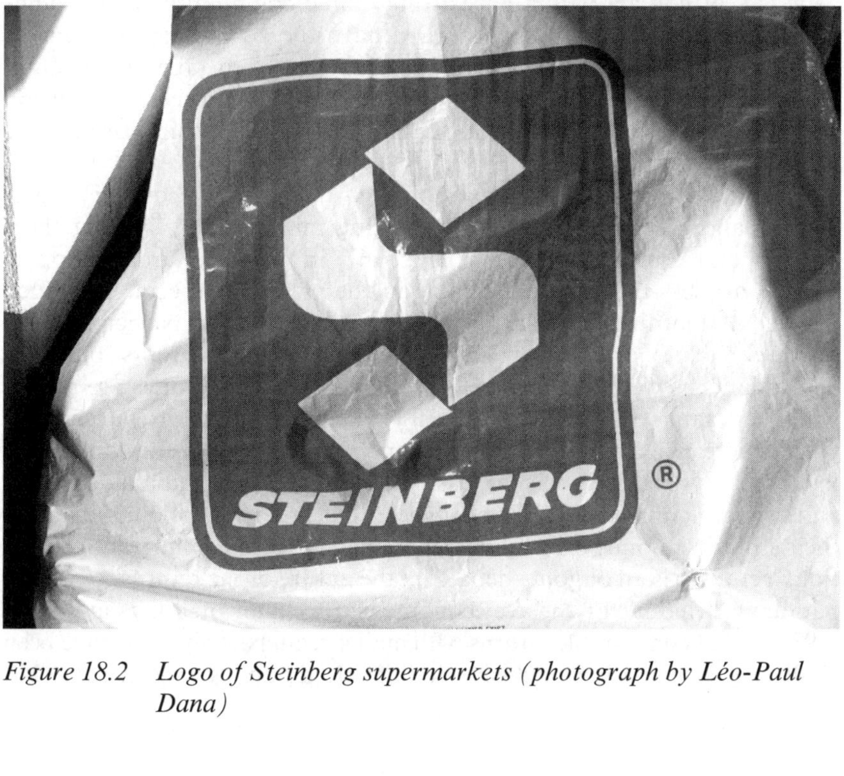

Figure 18.2 Logo of Steinberg supermarkets (photograph by Léo-Paul Dana)

and economically successful compared to other Canadians. Yet I shall argue that what I call a Jewish sub-economy exists in those cities, and participation in it by Jews defies conventional explanation. It may be that the social and cultural capital available to Jews even as they move past the immigrant generation and into higher socio-economic strata continues to provide some benefits, whether economic or social-psychological.

Some analysts may persist in seeing a modern economy as a single, complex system obeying market rules in which all individuals participate as rational economic maximizers. Of course victimized minorities have never been able to participate in this mythic economic reality. As argued by critiques of neo-classical economics, there are 'dual' or 'split' labor markets in which minorities, as well as other workers, are relegated to non-competitive, low-paying jobs in depressed economic sectors (Bonacich, 1972; Cain, 1976). This has been a social structural explanation for the turn to self-employment among many victimized groups, to escape external victimization (for example, Bean and Spencr, 1999)

A second type of economic victimization may result unintentionally from the voluntary actions of minority groups, who limit their economic activities and relations to members of their own groups. Immigrants arriving in reasonably open societies may seek initial employment through networks of contact within an existing ethnic community. Thus voluntary ethnic economic segregation may have the advantage of linguistic familiarity, genial work atmospheres, absence of 'red tape', recognition of the employee's cultural or religious needs, and a perceived greater job security, all reinforced by ties of origin, family relationships, or sense of communal obligation.

Nevertheless, the consequences of such 'voluntary' economic segregation can be seen as negative, penalizing minorities by locking them into an 'ethnic mobility trap' (Wiley, 1967) in which rewards or opportunities are less than those available in the mainstream economy. Such behavior, accordingly, inevitably produces less than full participation in post-industrial society and penalizes not only the immigrants, but their descendants as well (Porter, 1975). Immigrant social histories are replete with such data (Howe, 1976). Sowell (1975) and Nelli (1967) argue that what is here called an ethnic sub-economy is an asset only for immigrants in ethnically stratified societies, easing the processes of initial adaptation and economic integration. They suggest that minorities should abandon their ethnic economic base following the passing of the immigrant generation. Yet there is an ongoing debate on the nature of the returns to participation in the ethnic or enclave economy; early claims by Portes and Bach (1985) about comparable returns with mainstream participation have been challenged by varied inconclusive findings (Light and Karageorgis, 1994).

Indeed, there is significant variation in findings depending on the group, the city, the industry, and gender (Li, 1994; Logan and Alba, 1999)

Some minority groups tend to be disproportionately represented as entrepreneurs or as self-employed. These groups eventually achieve for themselves or their children a certain measure of relative economic success, notwithstanding the fact that at given points in their occupational careers, many of them struggle near or at the poverty line. Light (1979) has reviewed three sets of theoretical explanations for the high degree of self-employment among Jews, Asians, and other minorities: (1) the cultural theory of entrepreneurship, in which the cultural values or social institutions of an ethnic heritage are seen as functional for successful enterprise; (2) middlemen minority theories, which emphasize the solidarity of sojourning minorities linked to a homeland; and (3) the disadvantage theory, which sees the trend to self-employment as a rational response to various forms of discrimination in the labor market.

All three approaches, comprising both culture and social structure, have been used to explain Jewish economic and business success and occupational mobility, in various societies (Eitzen, 1971; Glazer, 1958; Rosen, 1959; Slater, 1969; Strodtbeck, 1958). This chapter will not adjudicate among these approaches. It should be noted that this earlier literature focused on Jewish achievement within the broader mainstream educational and economic systems and is tangential to the central concern of this chapter.

Self-employment, often in small business, has often been linked with the spread of ethnic economic enclaves. But the rise of a new middle class of educated independent professionals complicates the meaning of self-employment. Middle-class professionals who set up their own offices are exhibiting a form of entrepreneurial activity, but a far cry from the traditional business form. The self-employed small business entrepreneur usually needed hard work, savings, business acumen, and pluck; the self-employed professional relies in theory on educational achievement and recognized credentials. We now realize that both sets of self-employed also rely on networks comprising strong and weak ties, possibly embedded in ethno-specific contexts and communities (Granovetter, 1995).

This trend among the self-employed has been accompanied by growth in high-status salaried occupations, whether as managers in large firms or as professionals in public or quasi-public bureaucracies. Such occupations bring greater rewards in prestige and income than do many self-employed occupations, and have become increasingly popular among Jews, Asian minorities, and other historic middlemen groups. Thus, a label such as middleman minority may be descriptively misleading about the scope of 'ethnic' economic activity, ignoring the increasing occupational diversity found within minority groups. For example, Bonacich (1973) describes the high concentration of Jewish retailers in Stamford, Connecticut, in the 1930s as evidence of the Jewish tendency to middlemen minority status even within a modern industrial setting. Yet at the same time there were large numbers of working-class Jews in nearby New York, as well as a growing number of salaried Jewish professionals. Today it is the growth of the professional class that represents the newer form of diversity, again far removed from the middleman minority model.

Many analyses of the economic conditions of minorities contain fragmentary evidence, usually ethnographic, of the presence and use of economic networks operating within a given group. This study represents a beginning effort to systematically and quantitatively explicate the concept of what I call the ethnic sub-economy for an atypical group, using the case of Jews in Montreal.

THE ETHNIC SUB-ECONOMY

I define an 'ethnic sub-economy' as a network of diverse economic relationships which may link employees, employers, lenders, consumers, wholesalers, suppliers, professionals and clients of a specific ethnic group or minority. I prefer the term sub-economy as it usually denotes a smaller scale than a comprehensive mainstream economy. As I use the term, it ranges far beyond simple entrepreneurial notions, or the boundedness of geographic enclaves. The image is one of a parallel economy, but the precise size and configuration of the economic roles may vary. It need not be limited to one class, or one economic sector or niche, or to one spatial area in a given urban setting.

An ethnic sub-economy may exist regardless of the conditions of immigration of the group, attitude to the homeland, and degrees of hostility facing the group. The size and shape of an ethnic sub-economy may be measured by tracing the relative frequency of economic transactions ethnic members have within their own group. The ethnic sub-economy may include its own markets for labor, capital, goods, services, and information, which may parallel those existing in the 'mainstream' economy. Whether economic advantage or penalty accrues to participants in the sub-economy must be established empirically. An ethnic sub-economy may have a greater working-class or greater middle-class dimension. Indeed, like the mainstream economy, its social class composition and industrial base may change over time. Whereas the middleman minority, by definition, fulfils intermediary economic functions, linking ethnic groups or economic sectors through mainly entrepreneurial activity, the ethnic sub-economy might be conceived as a potential total economy in miniature, much like the enclave economy but without the requirement of residential proximity (Portes and Bach, 1985).

Earlier studies suggested the existence of ethnically based economic markets in Montreal and Toronto. Ethnic groups in Toronto report that they rent or buy housing predominantly from persons of the same ethnic origin (Weinfeld, 1977). A detailed study of rental housing in Montreal identified ethnic networks which operated in various neighborhoods to promote exchanges of labor and information and to influence landlord tenant relationships (Krohn et al., 1977). One study of the business elite in Quebec noted the marked tendency for large firms owned by Jews to recruit primarily Jewish persons for senior management positions (Sales, 1979, p. 136). Another study of Montreal's Italians – an overwhelmingly immigrant group at the time – found them to be likely to work for or with other Italians (Boissevain, 1970, p. 21).

This study presents and analyses data concerning the economic behavior of a random sample of Jewish household heads in Montreal. The objective is to attempt to establish the degree to which a Jewish sub-economy existed in the late 1970s, and to begin an initial examination of some of its features. The analysis is focused within the Jewish group and is not concerned with relative Jewish over- or under-representation in certain economic classes or sectors. Rather, the aim is to identify the pattern of intra-group economic behavior, and address the following questions: (1) What are the dimensions of the Jewish sub-economy in Montreal? (2) To what extent is this an 'immigrant' phenomenon, that is, does it persist beyond the immigrant generation? (3) To what extent is participation in the Jewish sub-economy in Montreal associated with disadvantage, such as a perception of anti-Semitism, or with positive factors such as a 'preference' for dealing with Jews or religio-cultural affinity, which might channel interactions to other Jews? (4) To what extent is participation in the Jewish sub-economy associated with either economic benefits or losses for the participants?

METHODS AND SAMPLE

The data were collected from a survey of 657 Jewish household heads in Montreal. The sample was generated by creating a 'master list' of Jewish households in Montreal and sampling randomly within the list. The master list eventually included an estimated 85 per cent to 90 per cent of all Jewish households in Montreal. A questionnaire containing 332 questions was administered to each subject in the form of one-hour interviews.

Table 18.1 presents the broad occupational and income distributions for the sample. The variance is substantial, particularly as regards the

Table 18.1 Occupational and income distribution of Jewish households in Montreal

Census occupational categories	Current/last/usual		
	Occupation %		Family income %
Managers and administrators	43.0	Less than $10000	26.0
Professional and technical	12.3	10000–19999	24.9
Clerical	13.2	20000–29999	16.4
Sales	11.4	30000–49999	19.4
Service	1.8	50000+	13.3
Skilled Labour	7.9		–
Other	10.2		100.0
Not reported	–		
	100.0		

distribution by family income. But on balance the sample scored higher than any other Montreal groups on these measures, using census data a comparison. In addition, 37 per cent of the respondents were self-employed; 29.6 per cent were college graduates (bachelor, masters, doctorate, or professional degree).

SIZE AND SHAPE OF THE JEWISH SUB-ECONOMY

Three questions about respondents' 'company, institution, or organization' were available from the survey questionnaire to ascertain the degree of individual participation in the Jewish sub-economy. Respondents were asked about the ethnic origin of the majority of their clients/customers, the executive or management of their organization and of their work associates. The distributions for these questions are presented in Table 18.2.

We see that 24.4 per cent indicated that Jews comprised the majority of the customers or clients of his firm or organization. In addition, 69.8 per cent of the respondents indicated that the 'majority of the executive management' was Jewish. (This latter figure includes those who were self-employed, either in business or the free professions. In fact, 33 per cent of the sample worked for other Jews.) In other words, only 30.2 per cent of the sample were employed by Jewish firms or organizations.

Finally, 35 per cent of the respondents indicated that 'all or most' of their

Table 18.2 Ethnic background of majority of . . .

	I. Clients/ customers* %	II. Executive/ management (includes self-employed) %	III. Business associates . . .	%
English Canadian	20.0	13.8	None are Jewish	6.2
French Canadian	21.6	6.5	Few are Jewish	20.3
Jewish	24.4	69.8	Some are Jewish	38.5
Other Combination	34.4	9.9	Most are Jewish	23.5
	100.0	100.0	All are Jewish	11.5
	N = 536	N = 550		100.0 N = 548

Note: *Excludes respondents indicating 'don't know' or 'not applicable'.

associates (partners, suppliers, employees, employers, customers/clients, colleagues, and so on) were Jews. Only 6.2 per cent indicated they had no business association or contacts with Jews. Bearing in mind that Jews represented only 4 per cent of the metropolitan Montreal population, this is a very high degree of concentration. Researchers have attempted more recently to estimate the size of 'ethnic ownership economies'. In American cities, combining formal and informal sectors, Light and Gold (2000) have estimated that 20 per cent of the average minority group worked in ethnic ownership economies. These would, of course, vary by group and by city, but the levels found in these studies seem lower than those in our Montreal sample.

Studies of immigrant life and histories of Jewish economic integration suggest that firms operating in an ethnic sub-economy would be smaller than those operating in the large-scale mainstream economy. The respondents were divided into two groups: those whose firm/organization employed fewer than 50 employees (64 per cent) and those which employed 50 or more (36 per cent). Of the former, 38.9 per cent identified all or most of their business associates as Jews, compared to 25.2 per cent of the latter (large firms). While those involved in smaller enterprises were, therefore, more likely to be participants in the ethnic sub-economy, we still find that significant numbers of those in large enterprises were also participants.

PARTICIPATION IN THE JEWISH SUB-ECONOMY AND LENGTH OF RESIDENCE IN MONTREAL

Participation in any ethnic sub-economy, according to prevailing views, should be more typical of immigrants than of native-born members of an ethnic group, and of more recent immigrants compared to those who arrived earlier. Much of the theory and research on these areas is logically embedded within a framework of the sociology of migration, or of the economic activity of immigrants and minorities (Light and Bonacich, 1991; Portes, 1995). This view would be based not only on a hypothesized pattern of cultural/linguistic preferences, but on the supposition that majority group hostility, and thus exclusion from full economic participation, might be greater for (more recent) immigrants.

Table 18.3 presents the trend on generational participation in the Montreal Jewish sub-economy. Generation is measured as foreign-born (first generation), those native-born, but with both parents foreign-born (second generation), and those with at least one parent native-born (third generation or above. We find no evidence that, as might be expected, lower levels of participation in the Jewish sub-economy are associated with generation in North America, For example, for the third generation, 28.3 per cent still have primarily Jewish customers/clients, 60.6 per cent work for themselves or other Jews, and 28.4 per cent indicate that all or most of their business associates are Jewish.

A similar finding arises in comparing Jewish immigrants resident in Canada for different periods of time. The foreign-born respondents are divided into three roughly equal groups: those in Canada for fewer than 25 years, those resident for 25–44 years, and those in Canada for 45 or more years. There is no evidence of any decrease in participation in the Jewish sub-economy moving, from the 'greeners' (more recent immigrants) to the old-timers.

The data suggest that in no way can the Jewish sub-economy in Montreal be considered a phenomenon of (recently arrived) immigrants.

ANTI-SEMITISM, RELIGIOSITY, AND PARTICIPATION IN THE JEWISH SUB-ECONOMY

Participation in the Montreal Jewish sub-economy is not particularly prevalent among (more recent) immigrants. An alternate determinant of participation might be the perception of anti-Semitism. Those respondents who believe that non Jews are basically anti-Semitic might seek to avoid any economic consequences of this anti-Semitism (note: all that is required

Table 18.3 Length of residence in North America by participation (per cent) in the ethnic sub-economy

	Indicators of participation for all respondents									
	Ethnic background of majority of						Among my business associates . . . are Jews			
	Customers clients			Executive management			None or few	Some	Most of all	
Generation	Jewish	Non-Jewish		Jewish	Non-Jewish					
First	19.8	50.2	(N = 263)	69.2	30.8	(N = 276)	32.7	33.5	33.8	(N = 260)
Second	29.3	70.7	(N = 174)	75.6	24.4	(N = 180)	21.5	38.2	40.4	(N = 186)
Third+	28.3	71.7	(N = 97)	60.6	39.4	(N = 94)	19.6	52.0	28.4	(N = 102)
Years in Canada	For foreign born respondents									
less than 25	21.5	78.5	(N = 94)	54.8	45.2	(N = 98)	44.6	27.3	28.2	(N = 95)
25–44	24.3	75.7	(N = 80)	77.1	22.9	(N = 86)	20.6	38.9	30.5	(N = 78)
45+	23.0	77.0	(N = 89)	74.6	25.4	(N = 92)	18.2	36.4	45.5	(N = 87)

Note: Chi-square significant at $p < 0.05$. The readers will note that in those cases of significant differences in the generational patterns, the direction of the differences in no case conforms to the assimilationist expectation, that of decreasing levels of participation in the Jewish sub-economy with higher length of residence in North America.

is a perception of anti-Semitism, rather than a first-hand encounter with it or other objective evidence of its existence). Alternatively, more frequent participants might come to believe, perhaps as a rationale for their behavior, in the prevalence of higher levels of anti-Semitism.

The data in Table 18.4 suggest that there are no significant differences in participation between those respondents perceiving more anti-Semitism, as measured by an index of perceived anti-Semitism. For example, of those who perceive little anti-Semitism, 21.8 per cent have Jews as a majority of customers, 68.1 per cent work for themselves or other Jews; the corresponding percentages for those perceiving much anti-Semitism are 26.6 per cent and 70.9 per cent. Thus fear of anti-Semitism does not seem to be systematically associated with participation in the Jewish sub-economy.

An alternative voluntaristic factor associated with participation might be religiosity. As Howe (1976) has described, some of the early twentieth-century immigrant workers in the needle trade in New York enjoyed the relative freedom to observe the Sabbath and holidays as a result of working for a Jewish employer. Moreover, the demands of a Jewish community for religious products or services (kosher food, Hebrew teachers, and so on) would create employment and business opportunities for religious Jews. Such an explanation would correspond to the 'special consumer demands' theory of ethnic enterprise for Asian or European immigrants (Light, 1972, p. 11–15). Thus, we might expect participation in the Jewish sub-economy to be greater for more religious Jews.

Table 18.4B presents data that indicate no difference between more or less religious Jews – as measured by an index of religiosity – in their participation in the Jewish sub-economy. Among the least religious third of the respondents, there are 32.5 per cent with all or most of their business associates Jews, 66 per cent self-employed or working for other Jews, and 28.1 per cent with primarily Jewish customers. The percentages for the most religious third do not differ significantly. Clearly, the Jewish sub-economy survives due to factors other than the greater religiosity of its participants.

Apart from a religious motivation, Jews may simply prefer to have economic dealings with other Jews due perhaps to custom, language (Yiddish or Hebrew) similarities, or similar cultural sensibilities. Respondents were asked to indicate degrees of (dis)agreement with the statement: 'I prefer doing business with an establishment that I know is owned by Jews.' Those with greater agreement might be expected to be greater participants.

The data in Table 18.4C indicate that Jews agreeing with this statement are indeed more likely to have a majority of Jewish customers or clients, and to indicate that all or most of their business associates are Jews. There is no significant difference in proportions self-employed or working for

Table 18.4 Properties of respondents of selected characteristics (per cent) by nature of participation in Jewish sub-economy

	Indicators of participation									
	Customers/clients majority			Executive management			Among my business associates . . . are Jews			
	Jews	Non-Jews		Jews	Non-Jews		None or few	Some	Most or all	
A. Perceived Anti-Semitism										
Low	21.8	78.2	(N = 252)	68.1	31.9	(N = 270)	28.5	39.4	32.1	(N = 274)
High	26.6	73.4	(N = 244)	70.9	29.1	(N = 247)	24.0	37.4	38.6	(N = 276)
B. Religiosity										
Low	28.1	71.9	(N = 167)	66.7	33.3	(N = 171)	23.3	44.2	32.5	(N = 172)
Medium	20.9	79.1	(N = 177)	66.8	33.2	(N = 190)	28.7	36.2	35.1	(N = 188)
High	24.1	75.9	(N = 170)	76.0	24.0	(N = 175)	27.4	35.4	37.1	(N = 175)
45+	23.0	77.0		74.6	25.4		18.2	36.4	45.5	
C. Prefer doing business with Jews										
Disagree strongly or somewhat	19.2	80.8	(N = 329)	67.7	32.3	(N = 365)	28.5	43.7	27.7	(N = 375)
Agree strongly or somewhat	35.6	64.4	(N = 160)	73.9	26.1	(N = 165)	21.6	27.2	51.2	(N = 145)*

Note: *Chi-square significant at $p < 0.05$.

other Jews. Thus, we have here some evidence (for two out of three indicators) that respondents' explicit preferences are associated with participation in the Jewish sub-economy. This is not surprising. Yet the minority tendencies are also quite striking. For example, of those Jews who do not prefer doing business with other Jews, we still find 19.2 per cent with primarily Jewish customers and 27.7 per cent with Jews as most or all of their business associates.

COSTS AND BENEFITS OF THE JEWISH SUB-ECONOMY

Are participants in the Jewish sub-economy, whether ethnic employers or co-ethnic employees, economically better or worse off when compared to Jews active in the mainstream economy?

Three measures of economic performance are analysed: occupation, intra-generational mobility, and income. Occupation is measured by the Blishen score, an index of socio-economic status computed for various occupations using Canadian census data (Blishen, 1971). Intra-generational mobility is measured as the difference in occupational scores between respondents' first full-time job in Canada and their present (or last, usual) job. Income is measured by total annual income.

Table 18.5 presents the data in tabular form. Looking at all three indicators of socio-economic achievement and all three measures of participation in the Jewish sub-economy, we find a consistent pattern (nine chi-squares) of no significant difference in economic achievement between those respondents with greater and those with lesser degrees of participation in the ethnic sub-economy. We find no evidence of either economic costs or economic benefits associated with participation in the Jewish sub-economy.

Correlation and regression analyses (not presented here) were used to isolate the independent effects of participation in the Jewish sub-economy on economic achievement. The sample was divided into foreign-born and native-born respondents on the assumption that different processes might be at work for these two groups. The zero-order correlations confirmed the cross-tabular findings for both foreign- and native-born. (Participation in the Jewish sub-economy was measured by the proportion of respondent's business associates who are Jewish [Table 18.2, section III]. The correlations were .07, .04, and .01 with occupation, mobility, and income for foreign born, and were .10, .05 and .03 for the native-born. None of these is substantial in magnitude or significant statistically.)

A regression analysis controlled for the effects of age, sex, years in

Table 18.5 Eccentric achievement and economic segregation (per cent)

	Business associates who are Jews			Ethnic origin of majority of clients/customers		Ethnic origin of majority of executive management	
	None or few	Some	All or most	Non-Jewish	Jewish	Non-Jewish	Jewish
Occupation							
High	43.2	47.0	51.4	45.3	49.2	46.8	45.7
Low	56.8	53.0	48.6	54.7	50.8	53.8	54.3
	100.0	100.0	100.0	100.0	100.0	100.0	100.0
	(N = 132)	(N = 197)	(N = 173)	(N = 384)	(N = 128)	(N = 160)	(N = 372)
Intra-generational mobility							
High	45.5	46.4	45.0	47.8	34.4	40.0	47.2
Low	54.5	53.6	55.0	52.2	65.6	60.0	52.8
	100.0	100.0	100.0	100.0	100.0	100.0	100.0
	(N = 132)	(N = 196)	(N = 173)	(N = 383)	(N = 128)	(N = 160)	(N = 372)
Income							
High $20 000+	50.0	63.2	52.5	52.9	52.7	57.2	50.2
Low $20 000	50.0	36.8	47.5	47.1	47.3	42.8	49.8
	100.0	100.0	100.0	100.0	100.0	100.0	100.0
	(N = 121)	(N = 171)	(N = 160)	(N = 338)	(N = 112)	(N = 145)	(N = 313)

Canada (for the foreign-born), and education of the respondents for the same three dependent measures: occupation, mobility, and income. In the income equations, spouse's labor force status (employed or unemployed) and respondent's occupation were also included as variables. Interaction effects of economic segregation and both years in Canada and education were estimated as well.

In none of the six equations (three each for native- and foreign-born) does the standardized beta for the effect of segregation on economic achievement attain statistical significance. The same is true for interaction effects. Those variables which are significant and which explain the major part of the variance in occupation, mobility, and income are sex, age and education of respondents. In no equation does economic segregation (entered last) explain more than 0.1 per cent of the variance. The major finding would seem to be that reported economic segregation plays an insignificant role in the economic achievement of our respondents.

DISCUSSION

It seems that a large number of Jews in Montreal participate, in varying degrees, in this communal economic system. The measures used in this study have been conservative. For example, respondents who answered that the 'majority' of their customers were Jews were identified as participants; those with a large minority of Jewish customers (30 per cent, 40 per cent) were excluded in the analytical categories. (Remember again that Jews represented at that time only 4 per cent of the population of Metropolitan Montreal.) We might estimate that between one-quarter and one-third of the respondents were almost exclusively economically active within the Jewish sub-economy.

To be sure, anyone with direct or indirect familiarity with North American urban life is aware of the existence of ethnic residential and commercial concentrations. In Canadian cities, Jews, even though a middle-class suburban group, have been the most residentially concentrated identifiable minority group (Balakrishnan and Hou, 1999). This concentration reflects voluntaristic patterns, and may also shed light on the persisting preferences for in-group economic activity. It is likely that the factors which promote residential concentrations for Canadian-born and middle-class Jews are similar to those promoting participation in the Jewish sub-economy.

Participation in the Jewish sub-economy of Montreal cannot be explained by the factor of immigration, by perception of anti-Semitism, or by religious correlates. Respondents who 'prefer' dealing with other Jews are slightly more likely to participate. Yet, there are more participants in the Jewish sub-economy who do not prefer business dealings with Jews than there are those who do. Finally, there seem to be neither economic costs nor benefits associated with participation. Though it was not examined, it seems likely that a (mis)perception about relative economic payoff cannot explain the participation either. Stated differently, participation in the Jewish sub-economy is distributed randomly over occupational and income groupings.

The question remains: why do many Jews in Montreal concentrate their economic activity among other Jews? In fact the existence of a Jewish sub-economy in Canada is not unique to Montreal. Reitz found similar patterns in Toronto in the late 1970s. Unlike other minority groups, successful Jews did not abandon Jewish neighborhoods; they recreated middle- and upper-middle-class Jewish neighborhoods in the suburbs. Jews had distinctive occupational patterns, similar to those noted by Rosenberg for Canada in 1931. Reitz found that

> Jewish men are . . . 8 times more likely than other men to work in textile products. They are also 6 times more likely to be physicians, 7.9 times more likely to be lawyers, and 3.5 times more likely to be university teachers. Jewish women are three or four times more likely than other women to work in sales, particularly real estate. Jewish women are also concentrated as social workers (2.7 times more likely), in commercial and fine art (2.3 times) and as lawyers and social scientists. (1990, p. 165)

Reitz also found that Jews in Toronto had higher ethnic economic concentrations compared to other groups, and – as in Montreal – that these levels were just as high for third-generation Jews as for immigrants. In most cases, these proportions were even higher than for immigrant Jews.

The Jewish sub-economy is diverse, includes many different sections. One section, more extensive than that found among other minority groups, consists of all the Jewish communal organizations – synagogues, schools, social, advocacy, and cultural organizations – which employ staff and provide services. These represent a kind of public sector of the Jewish economy. A second consists of businesses which provide special 'Jewish' services for Jews. The Montreal and Toronto Jewish business directories for the year 2000 listed scores of kosher bakeries, butchers, fish markets, caterers, and supermarkets, as well as, Judaica gift stores and bookstores. Toronto has 36 kosher restaurants or delis – including two Second Cups!

A third is the section where the business networks are Jewish but the products made or sold are not. The rag trade is the historic example. A Montreal Jewish telephone directory called the 'Blue Book' listed in its 1998 edition 3000 companies and organizations. These included, for example, 20 computer consultants, 27 photographers, 87 accountants or accounting firms – and the lists are not exhaustive. But the message is clear. The stated purpose of the Blue Book is to help Montreal Jews find Jewish companies that can supply them with the products or the services they need.

Since the Canadian Jewish sub-economy has persisted past the immigrant generation and into the middle class, it consists of more than Jewish shops clustered along Bathurst Street in Toronto or in the Snowdon area of Montreal. The phenomenon has become more upscale. Jewish lawyers, physicians, dentists, and accountants are often in partnerships or share offices with other Jewish professionals, and will often have more Jewish clients than would be likely by chance. Obviously this is facilitated by having a critical mass of Jews in the area.

There is no research on possible differences in the ways Canadian Jews in the professions or business conduct themselves, with colleagues, clients or patients. But consider the following cases taken from Toronto and Montreal, based from qualitative research conducted in 2000 on the nature of Canadian Jewish life (Weinfeld, 2001, pp. 101–2). These shed light on the kinds of subtle psycho-cultural dynamics at work which may sustain Jewish economic networks:

1. A Jewish businessman involved in a high-tech service industry, who has worked for and had dealings with both Jewish and non-Jewish businesses – mainly the former – distinguishes between his personal comfort and business relations. He admits that he feels more comfortable with Jews. He can relate better to them and they to him, particularly in the social interactions that accompany business meetings. They are the majority of his business associates. But that does not translate into 'dollars and cents. I would not be swayed if a person was a Jew, I want to get the best price no matter'. Moreover, he has never experienced any direct anti-Semitism. He actually prefers to deal with non-Jews when it comes to prompt payment of bills. And within the Jewish fold, ethnic stereotypes are alive and well. 'The Israelis and Moroccans are the worst, they're slow and will try to kill you.' He claims despite his comfort levels with Jews he much prefers to deal with (non-Jewish) Lebanese, who 'keep their word'. So, whatever comfort level drew him to prefer working with Jews, it does not extend to uniform business judgments in favor of all types of Jews.
2. A successful Jewish lawyer with a prominent 'Jewish' firm feels Jewishness intrudes in several ways. He claims that Jews are drawn to law historically because of the affinity with the legalistic nature of

the Talmud. (Easy to assert, harder to prove.) There is a distinctive culture in Jewish law firms. For example, in a 'WASP' law firm, he says, there will be a lock on the liquor cabinet; in his law firm they lock the supply of cookies. According to this lawyer, 'WASP' firms have more decorum; in Jewish firms there is more outspokenness, 'more yelling'. There are also subcultural differences by region. He believes that Jewish lawyers in Quebec yell more, while those in Ontario will try to 'out-WASP the WASPs': moreover, he feels that Jewish clients prefer Jewish lawyers. On the one hand, they would feel more comfortable confiding in them; on the other, it would be easier to 'give them shit'.

3. A doctor who works in a 'Jewish' hospital – one founded originally under Jewish auspices – insists that he chose medicine in no way because he is Jewish. Still he recalls that the Jews in his medical class certainly tended to socialize together. The atmosphere in this hospital is close-knit and friendly, and 'when things happen in Israel, people in the hospital want to fly off'. And what of the medicine itself? He observes no obvious difference in the medical practice of Jewish physicians versus non-Jews – though Jewish patients, in his view, tend to be more demanding.

There is likely an effect of referral networks at work here. Jewish doctors, lawyers, or accountants for example, might be more likely to refer patients or clients to other Jewish professionals whom they already know. But despite these various sorts of subjective rationalizations, the objective fact remains. Jews in business and the professions, especially in Toronto and Montreal, interact very disproportionately with other Jews.

The question remains: why does the Jewish sub-economy persist into second and third generations? Immigrants may pass on to second and third generations established economic networks, which are no worse than any other new ones. Inertia may maintain them. The phenomenon may reveal weaknesses in the impersonal, universalistic assumptions of neoclassical economics. One subject for systematic investigation might be the role of the extended family in minority groups as a mediating agent in contemporary economic activity which could, of course, solidify the tie to the ethnic sub-economy.

Several lines of research suggest themselves. Comparative research might establish the generalizability of the findings about the Jewish sub-economy through quantitative studies of Jews and other non-immigrant, middle class minority groups in a number of different urban settings. Perhaps Jews, especially in Canadian cities like Montreal and Toronto, are special cases. Certain environments may be more or less conductive to the existence of ethnic economic systems. Replicating studies in Montreal and Toronto in the twenty-first century would indicate if the earlier trends are fading.

It is worth noting that language does not play a role in the Jewish sub-economies of Montreal or Toronto, where English (and French for Sephardic Jews) are the common languages of work. This contrasts with other ethnic economies/enclaves such as Chinatowns or the Latino areas of Miami or Los Angeles, where linguistic specificity persists into the second generation. In the early twentieth century Yiddish was a distinctive language spoken by the masses Jewish immigrants used it in the workplace, notably the garment industry, but no longer. It is only within a distinctive Hasidic sub-economy within the Jewish sub-economy, that one can find Yiddish still being used as a language of commerce.

Another line of research might lead to investigation is a political economy of minority groups. Some minority groups, certainly the Jews, are characterized by a wide array of political and social institutions and formal organizations. Groups vary in their 'institutional completeness', or the degree to which needs of members may be met through institutions and resources indigenous to the group, such as welfare organizations, churches, newspapers, social and cultural clubs, and so on (Breton, 1964). In the Jewish case, the degree of institutional completeness and the proliferation of local, regional, and national organizations constitutes a complex polity (Elazar, 1976).

Minority groups differ in the degree to which they may be organized as a polity. The 'ethnic' sub-economy may be considered as the economic analogue to the ethnic polity

A more complete elaboration of the workings of a Jewish sub-economy would include treatments of both 'public' and 'private' sectors. The public sector of the sub-economy would be sustained through the pattern of philanthropic contributions or fee for services used to support welfare institutions, churches, and other cultural, social, or political institutions (these revenues could also include government grants). The funds would be used in part to employ communal public servants. Some portion might also be reallocated to other, perhaps more needy, members of the group. In the Jewish case, the public sector of the Jewish sub-economy is immense.

For example, Elazar has estimated for the 1970s a total Jewish communal budget of $2 billion in the United States (1976, p. 293–313). Canadian Jewish communal expenditures are at least as robust (see Weinfeld, 2001, ch. 6). Using standard economic measures, it might be possible to obtain from survey data, or in other ways, quantitative estimates of the size of an ethnic sub-economy, including both public and private sectors. One might compute average and total revenues for participants, as well as other economic indicators, such as rates of return, productivity, economic growth, and so on. It may well be that the high levels of participation found in Montreal, and in Toronto, reflect the unusually extensive array of Jewish communal institutions, which employ a fair number of Jews in those cities.

In any event, the evidence from Montreal and Toronto presented here suggests that substantial Jewish sub-economies within native-born and middle-class groups exist, and they are hard to explain. Subtle factors like inherited networks, cultural or even primordial preferences, as well as employment via political/communal structures, may play a role. If such patterns are found for other similar groups, it suggests that ethnic economies are rooted in more than economic disadvantage and/or immigrant status.

NOTE

* This article originally appeared in the *International Journal of Business and Globalisation*, **1** (1), 2007, 34–50. DOI: 10.1504/IJBG.2007.013718. Reprinted with permission.

REFERENCES

Balakrishnan, T. R, and Feng Hou (1999), 'Residential Patterns in Cities', Shiva Halli and Leo Driedger (eds), *Immigrant Canada: Demographic, Economic, and Social Challenges*, Toronto: University of Toronto Press, pp. 116–47.

Bean F. amd Spener, D. (1999), 'Self Employment Concentration and Earnings among Mexican Immigrants in the United States', *Social Forces*, **77**, 1021–47.

Blishen, Bernard (1971), 'A Socio-Economic Index for Occupation in Canada', in B. Blishen, F. Jones, K. Naegele and J. Porter (eds), *Canadian Society*, Toronto: Macmillan, pp. 395–508.

Boissevain, Jeremy (1970), *The Italians of Montreal*, A Study for the Royal Commission on Bilingualism and Biculturalism, Ottawa: Information Canada.

Bonacich, Edna (1972), 'A Theory of Ethnic Antagonism: The Split Labor market', *American Sociological Review*, **37**, 547–59.

Bonacich, Edna (1973), 'A Theory of Middleman Minorities', *American Sociological Review*, **38**, 583–94.

Breton Raymond (1964), Institutional Completeness of Ethnic Communities and the personal Relations of Immigrants', *American Journal of Sociology*, **70**, 193–205.

Cain Glen (1976), 'The Challenge of Segmented labor Market theory to Orthodox Theory: A Survey', *Journal of Economic Literature*, **14**, 1214–57.

Eitzen, Stanley D. (1971), 'Two Minorities: the Jews of Poland and the Chinese of the Philippines', in Niorman Yetman and C. Holy Steele (eds), *Majority and Minority*, Boston, MA: Allyn and Bacon, pp. 112–38.

Elazar, Daniel J. (1976), *Community and Polity: the Organizational Dynamics of American Jewry*, Philadelphia, PA: Jewish Publication Society.
Glazer, Nathan (1958), 'The American Jews and the Attainment of Middle Class Rank: Some Trends and Explanations', in M. Sklare (ed.), *The Jews*, New York: Free Press, pp. 128–46.
Granovetter, M. (1995), 'The Economic Sociology of Firms and Entrepreneurs', in Alejandro Portes (ed.), *The Economic Sociology of Immigration: Essays on Networks, Ethnicity, and Entrepreneurship*, New York: Russell Sage, ch. 4.
Howe, Irving (1976), *World of Our Fathers*, New York: Basic Books.
Krohn, Roger, Berkely Fleming and Marilyn Manzer (1977), *The Other Economy: The Internal Logic of Local Rental Housing*, Toronto: Peter Martin.
Li, Peter (1994), 'Self Employment and its economic return for visible minorities in Canada', D.M. Saunders (ed.), *New Approaches to Employee Management 2 Discrimination in Employment*, Stanford, CA: JAI Press, pp. 181–99.
Light, Ivan (1972), *Ethnic Enterprise in America*, Berkeley, CA: University of California Press.
Light, Ivan (1979), 'Disadvantaged Minorites in Self-Employment', *International Journal of Comparative Sociology*, **20**, 31–45.
Light, Ivan and Edna Bonacich (1991), *Immigrant Entrepreneurs*, Los Angeles, CA: University of California Press.
Light, Ivan and Steven Gold (2000), *Ethnic Economies*, San Diego, CA: Academic Press.
Light, I. and and S. Karageogis (1994), 'The Ethnic Economy', in N. Smelser and R. Swedberg (eds), *The Handbook of Economic Sociology*, New York: Russell Sage, ch. 26.
Logan, J. and R. Alba (1999), Minority Niches and immigrant Enclaves in New York and Los Angeles: Trends and Ian pacts', in F.D. Bean and S. Bell-Rose (eds), *Immigration and Opportunity*, New York: Russell Sage, pp. 172–93.
Nelli, Humbert (1967), Italians in Urban America: A Study of Ethnic Adjustment', *International Migration Review*, **1**, 38–55.
Porter, John (1975), 'Ethnic Pluralism in Canadian Perspective', Nathan Glazer and Daniel Moynihan (eds), *Ethnicity*, Cambridge, MA: Harvard University Press.
Portes, Alejandro (1995), *The Economic Sociology of Immigration*, New York: Russell Sage.
Portes Alejandro and Robert Bach (1985), *Latin Journey*, Los Angeles, CA: University of California Press,
Reitz, Jeffrey (1990), 'Ethnic Concentrations in Labor markets and their Implications for Ethnic Inequality', in R. Breton, W. Isajiw, W. Kalbach and J. Reitz (eds), *Ethnic Identity and Equality: Varieties of Experience in a Canadian City*, Toronto: University of Toronto Press, pp. 135–95.
Rosen Bernard (1959), 'Race Ethnicity and the Achievement Syndrome', *American Sociological Review*, **24**, 47–60.
Sales, Arnaud (1979), *La Bourgeoisie Industrielle au Quebec*, Montreal: Les Presses de l'universite de Montreal.
Slater, Miriam (1969), 'My Son the Doctor: Aspects of Mobility Among American Jews', *American Sociological Review*, **34**, 359–73.
Sowell, Thomas (1975), *Race and Economics*, New York: David McKay.
Stiles, Curt and and Craig Galbraith (eds) (2004), *Ethnic Entrepreneurship: Structure and Process*, Oxford: Elsevier.

Strodtbeck, Fred (1958), 'Family Interaction, Values, and Achievement', in M. Sklare (ed.), *The Jews*, New York: Free Press, pp. 147–68.
Waldinger, Roger (1996), *Still the Promised City: African Americans and New Immigrants in Post-industrial New York*, Cambridge, MA: Harvard University Press.
Waldinger, R.H. Aldrich and R. Ward (eds) (1990), *Ethnic Entrepreneurs*, Newbury Park, CA: Sage.
Weinfeld, Morton (1977), 'Determinants of Ethnic Identification of Slavs, Jews, and Italians in Toronto', PhD Thesis, Harvard University.
Weinfeld, Morton (2001), *Like Everyone Else But Different: The Paradoxical Success of Canadian Jews*, Toronto: McClelland and Stewart.
Wiley, Norbert (1967), 'The Ethnic Mobility Trap and Stratification Theory', *Social Problems*, **15**, 147–59.

19. A case history of a successful Hindu entrepreneur in the United Kingdom

Shiv Chaudhry and Dave Crick

INTRODUCTION

A number of profiles exist in respect of 'successful' entrepreneurs; although interestingly, it might be argued that a limited number exist in respect of those from ethnic minority communities. This is somewhat surprising given the realization that large ethnic minority populations are prevalent in certain countries and their propensity to engage, in some cases very successfully, in self-employment is widely known (Aldrich et al., 1989; Basu, 1998; 1999; Bates, 1999; Bates and Dunham, 1993; Borooah and Hart, 1999; Ram et al., 2000; McEvoy et al., 1982; Nowikowski, 1984). Consequently, a need exists to profile certain leading entrepreneurs from ethnic minority backgrounds to serve as role models for future businessmen and women from ethnic communities.

In addressing this gap in the literature, this chapter considers one case history drawn from a larger investigation that profiled entrepreneurs from the Asian (originating from the Indian subcontinent) community in the UK. Entrepreneurs from this community were chosen due to their propensity to engage in entrepreneurial activities vis-à-vis other communities (Ward, 1991). For the larger investigation ten case histories were undertaken, but this chapter discusses one of these in-depth to serve as a learning vehicle for future entrepreneurs from the Asian community in the UK.

BACKGROUND LITERATURE

A body of literature exists on the business practices of ethnic minority-owned firms; arguably however, findings have concentrated on small anonymous studies involving firms that are not readily identifiable by potential entrepreneurs and some are generalized and dated in nature

(Chaudhry and Crick, 2004a). Historically, in respect of motives for engaging in entrepreneurial activities, existing literature suggests that positive features include the potential for earnings advantage; upward social mobility; and investment in family futures. On the negative side, however, long hours, hard work and the risk of failure have been identified in previous studies (Aldrich and Waldinger, 1990; Bachkaniwala et al., 2003; Barrett et al., 2002; Bates, 1989; Light, 1972; Min, 1987; Portes and Zhou, 1992; Sanders and Nee, 1996; Waldinger, 1986; Ward, 1987).

Various theories have been proposed to account for ethnic entrepreneurship (see, for example, Yoon, 1991 for a more detailed explanation). First, the 'theory of middleman minorities' considers ethnic enterprise arising out of an orientation towards the country of origin and hostility from a native population. Firms will depend to some extent on white suppliers and serve minority customers. Furthermore, production will tend towards vertical integration, with a particular reliance upon ethnic finance sources and family labour (Bonacich, 1973; 1987). Second, 'Ethnic enclave theory' views ethnic enterprise as a self-generating process. Here, ethnic enterprise acts as a training system for new entrepreneurs through employment in existing enterprises, generating network linkages and an evolving cadre of ethnic business institutions. The ethnic enclave can support local institutions, generates a basis for informal communication of market opportunity, and provides community role models (Aldrich et al., 1989; Waldinger, 1989). Third, 'Reactive cultural theory' suggests that ethnic entrepreneurship is an adaptation to historic and racialized labour market discrimination; immigrants are forced to adopt marginal niches in the economy, using mechanisms such as ethnic sources of rotating credit. This provides a means of upward social mobility (Light, 1972; Nowikowski, 1984).

In terms of previous UK studies, results suggest that members of ethnic and non-ethnic minority backgrounds tend to move into self-employment because of the need for 'independence' and 'autonomy' (Blackburn, 1993; Storey, 1994). Nevertheless, in the case of ethnic minority-owned firms, issues have been identified that arguably require specific initiatives in order to assist them (Ram and Smallbone, 2003; Ram et al., 2000; 2002). First, specific issues with discrimination, racism and unequal gender relations have been highlighted (Ram, 1992; Ram and Sparrow, 1993). Debate on the financing of ethnic minority-owned businesses (Deakins et al., 1992; Jones et al., 1992) has questioned whether problems are business-related (Curran and Blackburn, 1993), or race-related (Deakins et al., 1995).

The issue of networks, utilization of cultural resources and markets served have been widely discussed in previous literature. Chaudhry and Crick (2004a) argued that such practices have historically been typified as the 'Asian Way' of undertaking business. For example, Werbner (1990) suggests that 'social networks' are a major influence on success for ethnic minority enterprises. It has been suggested that performance is affected by the ability to utilize internal cultural resources, such as family labour and specialist knowledge, to be able to satisfy the requirements of their own ethnic community (Jones et al., 1993; Mitter, 1986; Ram et al., 2001; Werbner, 1984). Even so, these practices, while arguably beneficial for some firms, have been questioned in terms of exploitative practices and in respect of limiting the performance of some businesses. For example, Ram and Hillin (1994) suggest that the unwillingness or inability of ethnic minority entrepreneurs to attract custom from outside the local ethnic community is a key constraint on business viability in the long term. Moreover, sustainability, and perhaps growth, must be viewed by the entrepreneurs' ability to 'break-out' and tap into 'majority' markets. As such, previous studies in the UK show that no agreement exists in respect of any single theory fully explaining ethnic minority-owned firms' behaviour.

Chaudhry and Crick (2004a; 2004b) suggest that the ethnicity literature has become somewhat dated and Asian-owned firms have been found to exhibit various types of behaviour. Their study involving interviews with academics, business advisors and firms in various sectors suggested that some entrepreneurial behaviour met the stereotypical image portrayed in much of the literature, while other practices made it difficult to differentiate Asian-owned firms from those in the 'mainstream' community. They argue that it is wrong to stereotype Asian-owned firms and behaviour is a function of a number of issues that includes among others: characteristics of the entrepreneur including attitudes to risk and business experience, industry sector, family and network influences, generational issues, and resources at their disposal. Indeed, Chaudhry and Crick (2004a; 2004b) argue that as the Asian population has integrated into the mainstream community over time, best aspects of both communities' practices have been adopted forming an 'Anglo-Asian Way' of undertaking business. They assert that this integration has influenced a cultural change in employment whereby some (although certainly not all) younger members of the Asian community are showing more interest in entering professions rather than working hard and taking risks in entrepreneurial practices like earlier generations.

In taking the argument of Stanfield II (1998) further, since many theories within the social sciences have largely been developed within a 'white' context, it cannot be assumed *a priori* that they are fully appropriate for addressing issues concerning race and ethnicity. Indeed, some community practices have been seen to be different in previous studies while more recent work (for example, Chaudhry and Crick, 2004a; 2004b) suggest that as integration between communities increases, entrepreneurial practices are changing making certain literature outdated. The chapter contributes to the growing body of literature involving ethnic minority-owned firms and presents a case history of a 'successful' entrepreneur in the UK from the Asian community. Specifically, it addresses the need to profile 'successful' entrepreneurs from ethnic minority communities to identify issues of importance in their respective cases and serve as examples for future entrepreneurs from particular community groups.

METHOD

Although the problem of locating and facilitating access to Asian firms is widely known (Krcmar, 1987; Pardesi, 1992; Patel, 1989; Rafiq, 1988), in the course of the larger study from which this chapter is drawn, interviews were undertaken with 10 'leading' Asian entrepreneurs in the UK. Initially, an interview was undertaken with Sir G.K. Noon, an Asian entrepreneur who had prior association with the researchers (Chaudhry and Crick, 2004c) and his name was used to facilitate access to others on the Asian Eye report of the top 100 wealthiest Asian business people in the UK. The number of entrepreneurs that were interviewed was based on time and cost considerations and selected case histories have been published elsewhere (for example, Chaudhry and Crick, 2004d).

The relatively small number of interviewees permitted the researchers to check for systematic patterns of response as a means of validating the data, as well as searching for idiosyncrasies requiring further examination and interpretation (for example, each provided their own story about how success was achieved). All but one of the interviews was tape-recorded and transcribed (one entrepreneur preferred not to be taped). Both authors were present at all but one of the interviews (a postponement meant that one researcher had other commitments during the rescheduled appointment). Interviews with the entrepreneurs were transcribed and systematically checked by the authors for patterns in the data. The interviewees subsequently checked case histories.

A semi-structured qualitative approach was considered appropriate (King, 1994). This enabled key topic areas to be covered but in a way that allowed entrepreneurs to tell their own particular account of the way in which events materialized and a rationale to account for them. This enabled the researchers to address process-based issues concerning why events happened and how they unfolded over time (Denzin and Lincoln, 1998). It was recognized that interviews with the entrepreneurs themselves did not constitute case study research and therefore interview data was compared (where possible) with trade data, newspaper articles and the like to support the validity of the findings.

MR NARESH PATEL: A CASE STUDY

Naresh Patel was born in 1942 in Kenya, East Africa. His wealthy father was a partner in a portfolio of businesses located in Kenya. However, in 1954, due to problems experienced within the partnership, Naresh Patel's father terminated his ties with the businesses and left with very little money. As Naresh Patel explains,

> at the time I was about twelve years old and my father had problems with his partners and he walked out with very little. He had eight children to support and because he was a retail businessman he had to start all over again from a small shop. As I was the eldest of the children a great deal of my time was spent helping my father in his shop so that the family could be financially maintained.

However, from a young age, Naresh had a keen interest in photography and was told by an acquaintance that it was possible to study photography in England. Consequently, Naresh visited the local British Council and acquired the relevant information. Initially, Naresh's father was not enthused by the idea, given that Naresh was the eldest in the family and within the Asian family context had certain responsibilities on his shoulders. His father was also aware of children of other families who had gone overseas to study, never to return. As Naresh comments,

> I had to promise my father that I would come back. All he could manage at the time was to borrow enough money to buy me a one-way ticket. I told him not to worry because I had been told that people can work and earn money alongside studying in the UK, and so I would be able to buy the return ticket.

So, Naresh came to the UK in 1960. He soon realized that the only job opportunities available to him at the time were either off-loading goods or stacking shelves for supermarkets or washing dishes in restaurants. Subsequently, alongside washing dishes in a restaurant in Golders Green, London, Naresh studied photography at the London School of Printing and Graphic Arts. As luck would have it during the course of his studies, Naresh came across a manager from Agfa who offered him the possibility of gaining experience of working in a photographic laboratory. Naresh agreed and in the three/four years that followed, Naresh worked in Johnson's Laboratory alongside studying photography.

In the mid-1960s, Naresh returned to Kenya with aspirations of running his own colour photography laboratory,

> because of the knowledge acquired from my studies and the experience gained by working for Johnson's, I felt that the time was right for me to start a colour photograph laboratory in Kenya. Colour photographs were quite a new thing in Kenya at the time and the couple of laboratories, which were operating, provided a very bad service. For example, they were sending some of the negatives to England for processing; imagine how long the customers had to wait for their photographs. In order to buy the necessary equipment to start colour processing, I again had to ask my father to lend me about 5000 shillings (about £250), which he did. I had to work day and night. During the day I used to go and collect the films from the shops, at night I was processing them and the next morning I would deliver the finished product back to the shops. My customers were very satisfied with the quality of the photographs and the efficient service I was providing. On the back of the success of this, I was able to buy better premises and sometime later my two brothers, having completed their studies, were able to join me in the business.

Within five years, the Colorama business became a well-known name to visitors in Kenya, Uganda and Tanzania with the advertising slogan, 'Tourists – see your pictures before you leave the country, you may never come back!' He chose the name Colorama for the following reasons: 'Color' because all photographic material supplied to Kenya at the time came from Kodak USA and therefore, the American spelling was adopted. 'Rama' because whilst on a trip to India, Naresh stopped over in Genoa, Italy and wanted to purchase some postcards of Rome, and realized that Italians referred to it as Roma, a word he instantly liked. He decided to adapt the word 'Roma' to 'Rama' on the advice of his father because it was the name of one of the Hindu gods.

In the early 1970s, whilst attending a photography-related exhibition in England, Naresh met by chance a number of Asian pharmacists (who were originally from East Africa). During casual conversations, they told Naresh that the service he was providing in East Africa could be replicated in England.

> I saw that there was a lot of potential here in England, because I met a lot of chemists at that time and many of them were originally from Kenya. They told me that the tourists in London were experiencing the same problems as those in Nairobi because the major film processors like Boots and Dixons were taking 7 to 10 days to process the films. So, I thought why not start here and if anything goes wrong I could always go back to my business in Kenya.

A couple of years later, Naresh was informed by one of his network of friends that a souvenir shop was up for sale in Greenwich, London. So, in 1974, Naresh bought the premises. With the help of one of his brothers (the other remained in Kenya to look after the business there), sister and brother-in-law, he was able to convert the basement of the building into a film-processing unit whilst keeping the ground floor for retail sales of photographic films and related products. However, Naresh soon realized that the premises were too small for the level of business he was aspiring towards. Therefore, within a short space of time, Naresh sold the Greenwich shop and bought a larger one in Norbury, South London.

> Within a year we firmly established ourselves with Norbury as our base. But it was not just the bigger premises, it was mainly due to the increase in our manpower, all my family members: my wife, brother's wife, my sisters and cousins. It was important at the time just to have family members working in the business because we could not afford to pay salaries. I remember quite clearly that we used to collect films to process from pharmacies all over London via the London Underground because we did not have the vans to do it. Also, the equipment/machinery I needed to process the films was bought on credit from suppliers based in Epsom. The only reason I was able to get the equipment on credit was that they were the suppliers to my business in Kenya.

Although the business expanded quite rapidly, Naresh is quick to point out that it was not easy, especially in the early days.

> We used to literally go shop-to-shop looking for business (customers). I would go into a shop and ask to see the pharmacist himself and tell him about the colour processing service we could provide. A significant number would listen attentively and after a little time give me orders. However, there were quite a few who would just tell me to go away! So, we (Naresh, his brother and brother-in-law) would go together in a car and if the pharmacist said no to one of us, then the other would go into the shop and try to persuade him and if he said no to him then the third one of us would go and try. Eventually, we found that in the end the majority of the pharmacists were prepared to at least listen. Once they agreed to listen, then I would give them a run down of the service. I would give details of the efficiency of the service; show them samples of the quality of the finished photographs and so on. In most cases, they were convinced and so our business took off.

A major account that Naresh obtained in the first year of his UK operation was that of the department store, Selfridges.

> I went to Selfridges and observed that there were so many people coming into the store with their films and asking what the delivery time was, and they were told a week to 10 days, so they (customers) went away. So, I thought I would speak to the manager. I told him what I had seen but he did not believe me. I persevered and managed to persuade him to come with me to the retail floor and see for himself. He was amazed that I was right. So I said why don't you

> give me the business and I can guarantee to bring back the processed films the next day and that way you won't lose all these customers. He agreed and that's how I got my first major contract.

Hence, the Selfridges contract and the large number of independent retail pharmacies formed a significant customer base for Naresh from which to expand,

> so at that stage we were providing a 24-hour service and after a few years we started an overnight service, then we started a 7-hour service: collecting in the morning and delivering back in the evening. To keep up with the volume of business coming in, we soon realized that we needed more space and so we moved to a much larger laboratory in the Elephant and Castle area of London, which is our current laboratory. We just literally kept taking on more customers (independent pharmacies) including a lot of Jewish customers. This was, I think, primarily due to the fact that they realized that we were providing a very good service and they were therefore willing to support us and give us their custom. Within a few years, we had almost 250 staff working at the Elephant and Castle laboratory. Over time we ended up collecting and delivering the films to over 2000 pharmacies. In addition to the Elephant and Castle laboratory, we now have one in Manchester which services the north of England and Scotland.

Eventually, through his accumulated knowledge, experience and contacts in the industry, Naresh started selling his own film under the Colorama brand and opening Colorama retail outlets, which today total around 40, where consumers can now have their films back within one hour.

In the early 1980s, based on the realization that he had built up an effective distribution channel, Naresh and his brothers recognized their next opportunity.

> We thought, after a while, that we were going to these 2000 shops every single day to collect and deliver films. So, why can't we start something else with it (film) which would be useful to the pharmacist, and that was medicines, and so we formed another company called Colorama Pharmaceuticals with a friend, Arun Patel. Colorama Pharmaceuticals is a wholesale company that supplies all pharmacy-related products to the chemists on a next day delivery basis. This idea took off in a really big way, and the fact that we were having to visit the shops anyway for our film business meant that extra costs incurred for this additional business were minimal.

With the film-processing and pharmaceutical distribution businesses running well, Naresh decided to fuel the expansion of his company by diversifying into a different market.

> I happened to think at the time that we were doing as much as we could on the photographic side of things. You see, in order to get more market share we

> needed to take-over some of our rivals, and we did go that way, we took over a couple of companies. But we always felt that photography is an area where tremendous changes would come in due to technology etc., and that would over time require a tremendous amount of investment. So, we just thought that we should look into other fields as well and we thought of the food business because everybody needs food of course.

Accordingly, Naresh and his brother Mahesh joined up with an old friend of theirs from Kenya, namely Jitu Patel, who was working for a large organization as a chartered accountant. Jitu had aspirations of wanting to run a business and through the course of his work, he came across an old food company that was up for sale.

> He said that the company was not making good money because the management was not right. The actual owners were semi-retired and lived overseas. So, he approached them and consequently Jitu and my family bought the company and re-named it Europa Foods. At that time they had about 13 shops but with hard work and the hiring of a competent team we expanded to the extent that we now have around 60 shops following a takeover of the Cullens Group in 1997.

When quizzed about what factors have in the main contributed towards his successes in business, Naresh highlights the importance of the family unity (particularly his brothers) and cultural network, a competent management team, hard work, sincerity, religious beliefs, luck and the courage to take some amount of risk which he partly attributes to his business upbringing in East Africa.

With respect to his business in East Africa, Naresh explains,

> my younger brother stayed over there to run the business. But because our businesses were rapidly expanding here (England) we asked him (younger brother) to join us, which he did. For a time we left the East African businesses in the hands of managers. Then just a few years back it became too difficult to handle, so we sold our African operations to a local competitor.

As to the future of the businesses, Naresh comments,

> we are now narrowing the field, we are happy with what we have. A lot of people ask us why we are not going into Europe and other places, but we believe that the best business is that which one can directly control. Once you lose that control then the business suffers. So we are happy as long as we can maintain what we have.

Up to the present day Naresh Patel and his brothers continue to 'maintain' their businesses very well, and at the time of the interview, the family had accepted an offer by Tesco Plc to buy their well-established Europa Foods business.

DISCUSSION

The case history of Mr Naresh Patel provides an example to demonstrate the key issues pertaining to the background of a 'successful' Asian entrepreneur (as evidenced by his place in the Asian Eye's 'rich list' report), that is, contributing to existing literature that has tended to discuss small anonymous firms (Chaudhry and Crick, 2004, 2004c; 2004d). However, from the outset, it could be argued that a number of issues arise from the study that could equally be applied to entrepreneurs from various communities, for example, hard work, luck, opportunity recognition, risk taking and so on (Chaudhry and Crick, 2004a; 2004b). Furthermore, Mr Patel exhibited similar characteristics (at varying stages of his life) to a number of other Asian entrepreneurs that have not reached the same level of 'success'. Examples include: discrimination in the labour market, serving cultural niches, networking, and making use of cultural resources (Aldrich et al., 1989; Bates and Dunham, 1993; Nowikowski, 1984; Ram et al., 2000; Werbner, 1984). A major issue that differentiates Mr Patel from earlier work is that his 'success' can largely be attributed to him 'breaking out' of serving a cultural niche, professionalizing his business and addressing the needs of the 'mainstream' market (Ram and Hillin, 1994). Future entrepreneurs from the Asian community (and perhaps other ethnic minority communities) should note this as a learning point from the case study.

Interestingly, the case history of Mr Patel suggests that the reaction to fortuitous events and not just management skills plus hard work can influence business performance. This observation is to some extent contrary to certain strategic planning literature (refer to many management texts); however, management of serendipitous events is arguably difficult for business schools to teach. Nevertheless, successful entrepreneurs like Mr Patel appear to be able to manage luck and serendipitous events. For example, he put himself in a position, via networks and the like, to maximize the chances of identifying opportunities and, moreover, to take risks so that less lucrative ventures are offset by the gains from more successful activities. Mr Patel has maintained his core business and searched for opportunities that are applied to this; however, diversified opportunities have also been identified. In doing so, he has attempted to 'professionalize' his business in order to run a portfolio of operations.

Opportunity recognition and exploitation for entrepreneurs from various ethnic communities can take a whole host of forms, but will be influenced by different environmental forces at given points in time. Some of these will be termed as serendipitous and the way one entrepreneur reacts to the same chance event is likely to be different from another. This makes the teaching of entrepreneurship at business schools difficult, but not impossible. Indeed, current and future entrepreneurs need to be able to access case histories such as the one presented in this chapter in order to provide a learning vehicle that contributes to their future educational and business success.

REFERENCES

Aldrich, H. and R. Waldinger (1990), 'Ethnicity and Entrepreneurship', *Annual Review of Sociology*, **16**, 111–35.

Aldrich, H., C. Zimmer and D. McEvoy (1989), 'Continuities in the Study of Ecological Succession: Asian Businesses in Three English Cities', *Social Forces*, **67**, 920–44.

Bachkaniwala, D., M. Wright and M. Ram (2003), 'Succession in South Asian Family Businesses in the U.K.', *International Small Business Journal*, **19** (4), 15–27.

Barrett, G., T. Jones, D. McEvoy and C. McGoldrick (2002), 'The Economic Embeddedness of Immigrant Enterprise in Britain', *International Journal of Entrepreneurial Behaviour & Research*, **8** (1), 11–31.

Basu, A. (1998), 'An Exploration of Entrepreneurial Activity Among Asian Small Businesses in Britain', *Small Business Economics*, **10** (4), 313–26.

Basu, A. (1999), 'Determinants of South Asian Entrepreneurial Growth in Britain: A Multivariate Analysis', *Small Business Economics*, **13** (1), 57–70.

Bates, T. (1989), 'The Changing Nature of Minority Business: A Comparative Analysis of Asian, Non-Minority, and Black-Owned Businesses', *The Review of Black Political Economy*, **18**, 25–42.

Bates, T. (1999), 'Existing Self-Employment: An Analysis of Asian Immigrant-Owned Small Businesses', *Small Business Economics*, **13** (3), 171–83.

Bates, T. and C. Dunham (1993), 'Asian American Success in Self-Employment', *Economic Development Quarterly*, **7**, 199–214.

Blackburn, R. (1993), 'Ethnic Minority Business in Britain: The Experience of Different Business Owners', paper presented at the Helsinki School of Economics.

Bonacich, E. (1973), 'A Theory of Middleman Minorities', *American Sociological Review*, **38**, 583–94.

Bonacich, E. (1987), '"Making it" in America: A Social Evolution of the Ethics of Immigrant Entrepreneurship', *Sociological Perspectives*, **30**, 446–66.

Borooah, V.K. and M. Hart (1999), 'Factors Affecting Self-Employment Among Indian and Black Caribbean Men in Britain', *Small Business Economics*, **13** (2), 111–29.

Chaudhry, S. and D. Crick (2004a), report to the Birmingham Chamber of Commerce, 'An Exploratory Study into the "Asian Way" of Undertaking Business', University of Central England Business School.

Chaudhry, S. and D. Crick (2004b), 'An Exploratory Investigation into the Asian Way of Undertaking Entrepreneurial Practices in the UK', paper presented at the McGill Conference on International Entrepreneurship, Montreal, September.

Chaudhry, S. and D. Crick (2004c), 'A Case History of a "Successful" Asian Entrepreneur in the U.K: Sir G. K. Noon', *International Journal of Management Cases*, **7** (1), 5–12.

Chaudhry, S. and D. Crick (2004d), 'Understanding Practices at the Marketing/Entrepreneurship Interface: A Case Study of Mr Kirit Pathak', *Qualitative Market Research: An International Journal*, **7**, 183–93.

Curran, J. and R. Blackburn (1993), *Ethnic Enterprise and the High Street Bank*, Kingston Business School Report.

Deakins, D., J.G. Hussain and M. Ram (1992), *The Finance of Ethnic Minority Small Businesses*, Birmingham: University of Central England.

Deakins, D., M. Majmudar and A. Paddison (1995), *Ethnic Minority Enterprise in the West of Scotland*, Paisley: University of Paisley.

Denzin, N.S. and Y.S. Lincoln (1998), 'Introduction: Entering the Field of Qualitative Research', in N.S. Denzin and Y.S. Lincoln (eds), *The Landscape of Qualitative Research: Theories and Issues*, London: Sage Publications.

Jones, T., D. McEvoy and J. Barratt (1992), 'Raising Capital for the Ethnic Minority Small Business', in A. Hughes and D. Storey (eds), *Financing the Small Firm*, London: Routledge.

Jones, T., D. McEvoy and J. Barratt (1993), 'Labour Intensive Practices in the Ethnic Minority Firm', in J. Atkinson and D. Storey (eds), *Employment, the Small Firm and the Labour Market*, London: Routledge.

King, N. (1994), 'The Qualitative Research Interview', in C. Cassell and G. Symon (eds), *Qualitative Methods in Organizational Research: A Practical Guide*, London: Sage Publications.

Krcmar, K.M. (1987), 'Minority Enterprise in the Clothing Industry: An Analysis of Asian Jeans Manufacturers in Birmingham', unpublished PhD, Aston University.

Light, I. (1972), *Ethnic Enterprise in America: Business and Welfare Among Chinese, Japanese and Blacks*, Berkeley, CA: University of California.

McEvoy, D., T. Jones, J. Cator and H. Aldrich (1982), *Asian Immigrant Business in British Cities*, British Association for Advancement in Science, Section E No. 75, London.

Min, P.G. (1987), 'Factors Contributing to Ethnic Business: A Comprehensive Synthesis', *International Journal of Comparative Sociology*, **28**, 173–93.

Mitter, S. (1986), 'Industrial Restructuring and Manufacturing Homework: Immigrant Women in the UK Clothing Industry', *Capital and Class*, **27**, 37–80.

Nowikowski, S.E. (1984), 'Snakes and Ladders: Asians in Britain', in R. Ward and R. Jenkins (eds), *Ethnic Communities in Britain*, Cambridge: Cambridge University Press.

Pardesi, U. (1992), 'Marketing in Indigenous and Asian Small Firms in the West Midlands', unpublished PhD, Aston University.

Patel, S. (1989), 'The Nature and Dynamics of Asian Retailing in Britain', unpublished PhD, Open University.

Portes, A. and M. Zhou (1992), 'Gaining the Upper Hand: Economic Mobility Among Immigrant and Domestic Minorities', *Ethnic and Racial Studies*, **15**, 491–522.

Rafiq, M. (1988), 'Asian Businesses in Bradford, West Yorkshire', unpublished PhD, University of Bradford.

Ram, M. (1992), 'Coping with Racism: Asian Employers in the Inner City', *Work Employment and Society*, **6** (4), 601–18.

Ram, M. and G. Hillin (1994), 'Achieving "Break-Out": Developing Mainstream Ethnic Minority Businesses', *Small Business and Enterprise Development*, **1** (2), 15–21.

Ram, M. and D. Smallbone (2003), 'Policies to Support Ethnic Minority Enterprise: the English Experience', *Entrepreneurship & Regional Development*, **15** (2), 151–66.

Ram, M. and J. Sparrow (1993), 'Minority Firms, Racism and Economic Development', *Local Economy*, **8** (3), 117–29.

Ram, M., S. Marlow and D. Patton (2001), 'Managing the Locals: Employee Relations in South Asian Restaurants', *Entrepreneurship & Regional Development*, **13** (3), 229–45.

Ram, M., B. Sanghera, T. Abbas and G. Barlow (2000), 'Training and Ethnic Minority Firms: The Case of the Independent Restaurant Sector', *Education & Training*, **42** (4/5), 334–41.

Ram, M., D. Smallbone and D. Deakins (2002), *Ethnic Minority Businesses in the U.K.: Access to Finance and Business Support*, London: British Bankers Association.

Sanders, J. and V. Nee (1996), 'Immigrant Self-Employment: The Family as Social Capital and the Value of Human Capital', *American Sociological Review*, **61**, 231–49.

Stanfield II, J.H. (1998), 'Ethnic Modelling in Qualitative Research', in N.S. Denzin and Y.S. Lincoln (eds), *The Landscape of Qualitative Research: Theories and Issues*, London: Sage Publications.

Storey, D.J. (1994), *Understanding the Small Business Sector*, London: Routledge.

Waldinger, R. (1986), *Through the Eye of a Needle: Immigrants and Enterprise in New York's Garment Trades*, New York: New York University Press.

Waldinger, R. (1989), 'Structural Opportunity or Ethnic Advantage? Immigrant Business Development in New York', *International Migration Review*, **23**, 48–72.

Ward, R. (1987), 'Resistance, Accommodation and Advantage: Strategic Development in Ethnic Business', in G. Lee and R. Loveridge (eds), *The Manufacture of Disadvantage*, Milton Keynes: Open University Press, pp. 159–75.

Ward, R. (1991), 'Economic Development and Ethnic Business', in, J. Curran and R.A. Blackburn (eds), *Paths of Enterprise*, London: Routledge.

Werbner, P., (1984), 'Business on Trust: Pakistani Entrepreneurship in the Manchester Garment Trade', in R. Ward and R. Jenkins (eds), *Ethnic Communities in Business*, Cambridge: Cambridge University Press, pp. 166–88.

Werbner, P. (1990), 'Renewing an Industrial Past: British Pakistani Entrepreneurship in Manchester', *Migration*, **8**, 7–41.

Yoon, I.J. (1991), 'The Changing Significance of Ethnic and Class Resources in Immigrant Businesses: The Case of Korean Immigrant Businesses in Chicago', *International Migration Review*, **25**, 303–31.

PART V

Comparative Studies

20. A critical investigation of the Protestant ethic on a divided island*

Godfrey Baldacchino and Léo-Paul Dana

INTRODUCTION: BASIC COMPARISONS AND CONTRASTS ON A DIVIDED ISLAND

The world is full of islands; but only very rarely are islands divided between different jurisdictions: it is as if to prove that geographic boundedness is naturally meant to be run as a single administrative unit. In fact, there are currently only 11 cases of islands where bounded geography must share political fragmentation amongst two or three sovereign state jurisdictions. They include Borneo, Sebatik Island (off Borneo), Cuba (if one counts Guantánamo Bay as a distinct, though anomalous, jurisdiction), Cyprus, Usedom/Uznam, Hispaniola, Ireland, New Guinea, Timor, Isla Grande de Tierra del Fuego and Saint-Martin/Sint Maarten (Royle, 2001, pp. 150–51). These islands offer interesting and rare opportunities to undertake comparative analysis of salient features, when many other intervening variables can be plausibly considered to be held constant. Relevant examples of such a methodology are Dana (1995b) and Diamond (2005), who undertake an insightful critique of differential environmental policy and its effects on Hispaniola, comparing and contrasting the policies of governments on Haiti with those of the adjoining Dominican Republic.

The island of St Martin (comprised of Dutch Sint Maarten and French Saint Martin) is the smallest of these island mavericks, and has been formally partitioned since 1648: the world's smallest land mass ever to be shared by two separate governments, each of which operates in a shifting, often tense, sub-national relationship with a much larger, remote and ultimately benign European state. Dutch Sint Maarten is, since 1954, a component of a now disintegrating five-island Netherlands Antilles, itself a partner in the Kingdom of the Netherlands, whereas French Saint Martin is a municipality and sub-prefecture (along with seven other islands) of

Table 20.1 Basic data for Dutch Sint Maarten and French Saint Martin

Dutch Sint Maarten	French Saint Martin
Population (1997): 38 876	Population (1999): 29 888
Live Births (1997): 610	Live Births (1999): 745
Deaths (1997): 101	Deaths (1999): 103
Marriages (1997): 329	Marriages (1999): 124
Main language spoken: English	Main language spoken: French
Official language: Dutch	Official language: French
Main trading currency: US$	Main trading currency: €
Official currency: Dutch Antilles Guilder (NAF)	Official currency: €
Capital: Philipsburg	Capital: Marigot
Chief Trading Country: USA	Chief Trading Country: France

Source: http://www.internationalspecialreports.com/archives/00/stmaarten/7.html.

Guadeloupe, which has been, since 1946, a fully-fledged *département d'outre mer* of France (see Table 20.1).

Yet these different jurisdictional structures deflect from the fact that the inhabitants of 'S'Maat'n' are one people. They speak a dialect of English which is little different from that spoken on nearby Anguilla, Saba and Sint Eustatius. They also share many surnames such as Arnell, Baly, Carty, Fleming and Gumbs. The common use of English, and the ties of families and friendships make for one community of islands. Direct-dial telephones make for easy and effective communication (Kersell, 1993).

INFLUENCES OF THE PROTESTANT ETHIC

> American business sometimes thinks that . . . it is dangerous to have the government in business. In France . . . business wants government intervention in the business sector for the purpose of keeping potential danger out. (Dana, 1988a, p. 126)

When Max Weber postulated his Protestant Ethic thesis, one of his basic aims was to overturn the Marxist claim that it was the economic infrastructure which not just inspired but moulded people's social consciousness (Weber, 1905/1956). In contrast, Weber argued that economic history has various examples of how, in sharp contrast, it was practice and belief that inspired economic behaviour. The Protestantism sweeping across most of Northern Europe, with its extolling of virtue arising from

Figure 20.1 *Separated only by a road-sign (photograph by Léo-Paul Dana)*

business success and profit maximization, helped to legitimate capitalism. Moreover, it led to an interesting split in European cultures which today still pervades many areas of religious, social and economic life. Thus, while primarily Catholic countries in Europe – like Belgium, France, Italy or Spain – protect workers from being fired, the primarily Protestant nations of Scandinavia and the Netherlands have weak job protection laws (e.g. *The Economist*, 2005).

Of course, it would be nothing less than a caricature to explain European labour law differences as arising simply from a religious practice that may hardly resonate today in a largely secularised Europe. Moreover, isolating any 'Protestant Ethic' effect is difficult, since each country would have its own cultural and historical baggage, raft of legislation, specific labour retention programmes, plus the decisions of political elites and implementation record of bureaucrats. Yet St Martin provides as close a 'controlled experiment' as possible to singling out the differential attitude of France and the Netherlands to entrepreneurship, business promotion and the role of the state in facilitating employment and business development.

Over the past century, each of the two groups on St Martin has been exposed to a different set of conditions, each corresponding to one of two general models. The burgers of Dutch Sint Maarten have been exposed to a fairly lax and liberal approach by their government in their attempt to reduce state regulation and encourage small business start-ups. Across the tenuous and fairly porous border (see Figure 20.1), the *citoyens* of French Saint Martin have been exposed to a policy of fairly heavy regulation. This has resulted in significant differences in the environment for small business and entrepreneurship. In this study, a causal relationship is identified.

Following an analysis for external validity, findings support the hypothesis that heavy business regulation hinders entrepreneurship while a limited environmental approach facilitates entrepreneurial behaviour.

A couple of qualifiers are in order here. First, we are not ascribing a direct and simple uni-causal relationship between religious beliefs and business practices and cultures. Religious practice in both France and the Netherlands, as in other European countries, is much reduced today and many are those who are formally or functionally unaffiliated to any church. However, the pro-business culture of the Netherlands was already very strong when the Seven Provinces eventually built an international empire based on trade; yet it found a natural ally in the precepts of the protestant religion, which regarded business success as an indicator of goodness and possibly eternal salvation. (Moreover, the Dutch exported Catholicism – and not Dutch Reformed Protestantism – to the Dutch Antilles, since they felt that they should not share the same religion as their wards.) Meanwhile, as the prototype 'nation state', France has maintained a strong and protectionist role for its government as a national champion, a mediatory role that has also been historically fulfilled in parallel by the Catholic Church. Thus, in both these countries, religion is both a cause and an effect of behavioural patterns that may themselves have historical, political or economic antecedents. Second, the role of the state in relation to business practice in these two countries need not be the same role that the state plays in other areas of public life. Indeed, in Northern Europe, there is a high sense of government penetration in private lives (as in a highly protective and comprehensive social system). Citizens are generally disposed to accept high taxes to guarantee a strong welfare state.

METHODOLOGY

Due to the lack of reliable secondary sources in rapidly developing nations, on-site investigation and verification is often required. Consequently, this study involved three data collection techniques, undertaken mainly by one of the co-authors (Dana): (1) preliminary research involving secondary sources, particularly articles and validated internet sources; (2) information search by telephone; and (3) field research based on interviews with government officials, Chamber of Commerce representatives and entrepreneurs from both Dutch Sint Maarten and French Saint Martin. An ethnographic approach was used with triangulation techniques in order to verify information with independent sources. The paper is also based on previous research published by one of the authors (Dana, 1990).

In Philipsburg, capital of Dutch Sint Maarten, the Sint Maarten Department of Business Licenses and the Chamber of Commerce and Industry of the Dutch Windward Islands were most helpful. Given that French Saint Martin is a sub-prefecture of Guadeloupe, an official from the regional government in Basse-Terre, Guadeloupe, was also interviewed extensively on several occasions. Interviews in Dutch Sint Maarten were conducted in English. Those in French Saint Martin and Guadeloupe were conducted in French and subsequently translated by the co-author (Dana).

The CIA *World FactBook* estimates a GDP (gross domestic product) per capita (corrected for purchasing power parity) for the Netherlands Antilles as a whole of US$11,400 in 2003; the equivalent figure for the whole of Guadeloupe is US$7900 (CIA, 2005). Unfortunately, reliable and updated GDP figures for both Dutch Sint Maarten and French Saint Martin have not been forthcoming. This, in itself, is a reflection of the much tighter policy of centralization in the French state, which makes island specific data harder to obtain, in contrast to more internal autonomy within the Dutch system. Such comparative quantifiable data would have been helpful for the sake of comparison. This qualitative, exploratory study, using soft concepts and measures, can therefore hopefully only serve as a basis for more definitive and empirical research.

MODELS

Karl Polanyi (1944) long ago identified the different logic of states and markets: the purpose of state policy is to influence, control or regulate what would otherwise not always be free and unencumbered market transactions since individual or organized actors may abuse, or be abused by, those in dominant positions. This is all the more likely in small jurisdictions where the competitive element is naturally restricted because of small size and difficulty of market access by external players; in such situations, commercial operations tend easily towards natural monopolies (e.g. Armstrong et al., 1993).

Espoused before Polanyi, and going back to Adam Smith, is the idea that markets are themselves institutions: 'Like public agencies, markets exist only within a certain organizational framework, and variation in that framework can profoundly affect their operation' (Hall, 1986, pp. 11–12). Thus public policy is one instrument available to governments to affect the operation of markets.

One can identify two broad models, or extreme positions, to which government policies with respect to markets belong:

Table 20.2 The research design for this study

	Contextual variables	Intervening variable
French Saint Martin	Common to both	Government policy with respect to business practice (Regulation for Protection)
Dutch Sint Maarten	Common to both	Common to both government policy with respect to business practice (Protection from Regulation)

Model I Regulation for Protection: Rules are established to protect existing businesses and consumers at large, even if some hinder entrepreneurial behaviour. There may be high entry costs, exasperating bureaucratic procedures, complex and numerous compliance regulations (including hygiene, occupational safety, building standards, high levels of corporate taxation and minimum wages for staff).

Model II Protection from Regulation: A policy of minimal intervention and minimal regulation allows entrepreneurs to dedicate more resources to their enterprises, protecting them from the burden of excessive paperwork requirements and the constraints of heavy regulations, but in turn resulting in larger attrition and turnover rates of firms.

This chapter contrasts both models, and evaluates their results in a setting where other independent variables can be plausibly considered to have been kept constant over a substantial period. French Saint Martin is used as the control group where entrepreneurs operate in a Model I policy context. The treatment group, that is DFM, is protected from regulation by a Model II policy where the local state ensures a proper tax climate and positive stimulation of economic conditions with minimal regulation.

Keeping other variables constant (such as geography, history, culture, insularity, climate, soil fertility, vegetation, elevation and population density), facilitated by a very fluid border between Dutch Sint Maarten and French Saint Martin, government policy with respect to business practice, restricted to its respective jurisdiction, is the key variable analysed in the framework of two examined theoretical models (see Table 20.2).

Peterson and Peterson (1981) found that government paperwork requirements are a burden on managerial time of owner-managers. Thus, a reduction of such time-consuming regulation may be said to promote a more entrepreneurial environment. Is this argument borne out by the evidence? A comparison of the control group and the treatment group reveals countless new ventures and a thriving entrepreneurial environment under Model II policy in Sint Maarten, in contrast to much less economic activity in Saint Martin under Model I policy. Therefore, this study suggests that, while keeping other variables constant, limiting government intervention to ensuring a proper tax climate and positive stimulation of economic conditions, that which Peterson and Ainslie (1988) describe as a limited environmental approach (a Model II approach), does yield an environment more conducive to entrepreneurship.

THE ENVIRONMENT FOR ENTREPRENEURSHIP

> The rich and the famous of the world honeymoon on Anguilla, winter in their mansions on French Saint Martin, shop and gamble away their wealth on Dutch Sint Maarten. (Kersell, 1993, p. 1)

Nafziger (1971) was among the many to note the shift of emphasis in economic development theory, away from the growth of financial capital to human capital, inclusive of entrepreneurs engaging in entrepreneurial activity. Among the environmental factors that powerfully condition the ease and scope of entrepreneurial activity, are government, laws, regulations and procedures (Staley and Morse, 1971). Government policy, in turn, reflects attitude. Attitude, according to Kunkel (1965), may be defined as persistent, general orientation, a state of readiness, exerting a directive or dynamic influence.

A government may perceive entrepreneurship as: (i) having a high social value worthwhile of being encouraged; or (ii) an unnecessary or neutral activity which does not require specific policy; or (iii) an activity undertaken by actors who are not bona fide and whose motives are suspect. Policy would then tend towards being a reflection of such an attitude; and a government may decide to intervene (through regulations, paperwork requirements, subsidies or trade agreements) or not to intervene, such that its values affect economic development.

It was Weber's (1905/1956) thesis that first proposed a causal link between entrepreneurship and cultural values such as frugality, deferred gratification and asceticism. Thus, culture came to be the explanatory variable, which resulted in entrepreneurship being more prevalent among some cultures than among others. Considerable empirical research confirmed that some groups were somehow culturally predisposed to engage in entrepreneurial activity, while other cultures tended to refrain from new venture creation.

Hofstede (1980) demonstrated how people's attitudes towards work are culturally influenced. Boissevain and Grotenberg (1987), Jenkins (1984), Min and Jaret (1985), Reeves and Ward (1984), Shapero (1984), Shapero and Sokol (1982), and Ward (1987), among others, noted that some cultures value entrepreneurship more than do others. Depending on whether a government values entrepreneurship or not, public policy may increase or decrease the attractiveness of entrepreneurial opportunity.

Although Schumpeter (1934) suggested that entrepreneurship results in an improved standard of living for a society, governments around the world have historically given little if any support to entrepreneurs, especially those involved in small- and medium-sized operations. Entrepreneurial behaviour was often limited to those locations whose citizens held values predisposing them to engage in such activity. No effort was made to increase entrepreneurship; on the contrary, up to the late 1970s, many nations preferred instead to encourage mergers of existing firms into larger units (Strinati, 1982). Scase (1980) noted that the trend was to evolve away from small independent businesses, as governments believed instead that a measure to facilitate economic growth would be to encourage a close partnership between existing large firms in the private sector and state agencies.

More recently, the trend has been reversed; and the state has started to recognize the usefulness of entrepreneurs, a healthy small business sector, and an environment fostering entrepreneurship and conducive to small business. As demonstrated by Rainnie and Scott (1986), entrepreneurship has become increasingly recognized as a means of improving output and, as discussed by Scase and Goffee (1987), public policy has largely shifted from discouraging to encouraging independent business. Particularly among more industrialized nations, entrepreneurship has been recognized as being in the national interest, making important contributions to industrialized expansion and job creation. Examples include Australia (Dana, 1988b), France (Pache, 1996), Britain (Gibb, 1986–87), the Netherlands (Bijmolt and Zwart, 1994; Boissevain and Grotenbreg, 1987), New Zealand (Ghosh and Taylor, 1995), Northern Ireland (Hisrich, 1988; Jenkins, 1984), Norway (Weaver, Berkowitz and Davies, 1998), Japan (Morita and Oliga, 1991), Sweden (Johannison, 1987), and the United States (Dana, 1995a). Interest in entrepreneurship has also been on the rise in island economies, including Malta (Briguglio, 1998); Papua New Guinea (Ojuka-Onedo, 1996); and Samoa (Fairbairn, 1988).

TWO BUSINESS ENVIRONMENTS, ONE ISLAND

To many Europeans and North Americans, the island of St Martin means baking in the sun on the miles of pristine white sand. For social scientists, the island is an ideal yet under-explored setting for research where one side can serve as the control group for an experiment while the other side can serve as the treatment group.

To American Navy buffs, the Dutch West Indies of the Lesser Antilles are significant, because it was there, in the Caribbean Sea, that the flag of a US warship received its first foreign salute, on 16 November 1776. To cruise ship passengers, the Netherlands Antilles are of particular interest because of duty-free bargains specifically in Dutch Sint Maarten.

French Saint Martin comprises 21 square miles; its official capital is Marigot on the island, but the administrative centre is Basse-Terre, on the island of Guadeloupe. Saint Martin's president is that of France. Complete autonomy from France is not envisioned, and self-determination appears to be locked with a process of deeper integration with the *metropole.*

Dutch Sint Maarten embraces just 16 square miles; its capital is Philipsburg. The government has a Netherlands Antilles constitution. Sint Maarten, as part of the Netherlands Antilles, has been self-governing since 1954; the Netherlands Antilles has equal political status with the Netherlands, as does Aruba since 1986, in the union known as the Kingdom of the Netherlands.

The most striking difference between the two sectors of the island is that, whereas French Saint Martin is largely rural and agricultural, Dutch Sint Maarten has a thriving business community with a sophisticated entrepreneurial activity.

Over three decades ago, the assistant editor of *National Geographic*, James Cerruti, reported that 'Sint Maarten alone . . . has achieved full employment. Indeed Sint Maarten also employs about a thousand workers from French Saint Martin and British Anguilla' (1970, p. 142). Today, Sint Maarten also provides jobs to numerous workers from the Dominican Republic and elsewhere. Sint Maarten has maintained prolonged economic prosperity at a time when some of its Caribbean neighbours are battling economic malaise.

Control Group: Saint Martin under Model I Policy

The French side of the island, French Saint Martin, seems to have inherited an abundance of regulations from its mother country. French Saint Martin is a sub-prefecture of Guadeloupe, which in turn is an overseas department of France. In contrast to Dutch Sint Maarten, which is largely self-governing, Saint Martin sends two elected senators to the senate in France. Legislative reform tends to be slow, with decision-makers being physically far from the area they govern and not necessarily always aware and sensitive to local needs and their pressing nature. Rules are made in France, but must be obeyed in French Saint Martin. Some prices, as well as wages, are regulated. A new venture in French Saint Martin must include local participation. In contrast to Dutch Sint Maarten where local participation in a new venture is not a legal requirement, such regulation in French Saint Martin may deter business start-ups and foreign investment by entrepreneurs from abroad.

With reference to foreigners visiting or doing business in French Saint Martin, regulations stipulate that, for stays of 21 days or more, proof of departure (such as an aeroplane ticket) is required, as well as proof of citizenship which must be in the form of a valid passport. To enter Dutch Sint Maarten, an expired passport or any other proof of citizenship is sufficient. This procedure, or lack of, has not changed much since the widespread tightening of security since 9/11. What makes this difference in regulation redundant is that there is no physical barrier, nor border checkpoints between French Saint Martin and Dutch Sint Maarten. Yet the French legal system prevails in the French half of the island, fraught with more prohibitions than allowances, and few business incentives.

Model I policy in French Saint Martin also reinforces some Gallic business practices: whereas the presence of a lawyer at contract negotiations is regarded as a practical procedure in the US or in Dutch Sint Maarten, it is interpreted as a lack of trust in French Saint Martin, where personal loyalty comes before business considerations. One prefers to do business with a friend in French Saint Martin rather than seek the most efficient working relationship.

Treatment Group: Dutch Sint Maarten under Model II Policy

Model II policy in Dutch Sint Maarten has resulted in considerably less regulation there than in the contiguous French Saint Martin. Therefore, form is less important an element in doing business than efficiency and pragmatism. According to their French neighbours, business needs the state to keep any dangers at bay; in contrast, the Dutch Sint Maarten attitude is that it might be dangerous to have the state involved too much in business. Government is viewed in the Dutch Sint Maarten largely as a facilitator, and not, as in French Saint Martin, as primarily a regulator.

An environment of low restriction levels is attractive to entrepreneurs. In Dutch Sint Maarten, minimal government intervention has helped maintain and cultivate an entrepreneurial spirit. Starting a firm is very easy. A citizen by birth or bearing Dutch nationality does not even require a licence to do business. Incorporation can be done by a lawyer specifically appointed to pass deeds. Only two founders are required; only 20% of the authorized capital must be subscribed for at the time of incorporation; if shares thus issued are registered, only 10% of their par value needs to be paid up. There is no restriction on nationality or residence of shareholders, managing directors or members of the board. The cumulative result is that Dutch Sint Maarten has a very healthy and growing small-business sector as entrepreneurs create new ventures. This provides numerous jobs, explaining why unemployment in Sint Maarten has been nil during recent years, especially impressive in the Caribbean where other islands were suffering economic malaise during a prolonged recession.

Dutch Sint Maarten has no exchange control on currencies imported or exported. Bank accounts may be opened in any currency, or even in troy ounces of gold. The Bank Van De Nederlandse Antillen has been in business since 1928; the ABN Algemene Bank Nederlandse NV since 1919. Other banks include Barclays Bank PLC (Banco Barclays Antiliano NV), Chase Manhattan, Citco Bank Antilles, Nederlandse Credietbank, the Bank of Nova Scotia and the Windward Islands Bank.

The Netherlands Antilles government is actively helping perpetuate an entrepreneurial spirit through specific new venture programmes, in addition to maintaining low taxes and no import duties. Programmes include tax holidays and benefits such as no withholding tax on dividends or interest paid by a Netherlands Antilles corporation. Specifically, qualifying new investments get exemptions from all taxes on profits for ten years, as well as exemption from property tax. New industries involving at least NAF 50000 (US$28000) are exempt from profit tax, as well as income tax on proceeds from an enterprise, and onproceeds from distribution of profits (Öostindie and Klinkers, 2003, *passim*).

To prevent double taxation, the Netherlands Antilles has concluded tax treaties with the US, the UK, Denmark, Norway and the Netherlands. Through establishing subsidiaries in Netherlands, a company in Sint Maarten may also benefit from tax treaties with Austria, Belgium, Canada, the Czech Republic, Finland, France, Germany, Hungary, Indonesia, Ireland, Israel, Italy, Luxembourg, Malawi, Malta, Singapore, Slovakia, South Africa, Spain, Japan, Surinam, Sweden, Switzerland and Thailand. In some cases, the government will grant monopoly status to protect a new industry. The government is also willing to finance certain entrepreneurial initiatives. The result of all the above is numerous businesses in a healthy economy with market competition.

To boost the tourism industry and to facilitate international business, Dutch Sint Maarten opened its Juliana International airport (SXM) in 1950. Today its 2000-metre runway accommodates daily flights overseas, to 24 destinations in the Caribbean, US and Europe (www.pjiae.com/destinations.html). In 1999, 1.6 million passengers used SXM and there were 78 daily schedule and charter flights (www.internationalspecialreports.com/archives/00/stmaarten/7a.html). Airlines serving Dutch Sint Maarten include ALM, Air France, Air Guadeloupe, Air St. Barthelemy, American Airlines, KLM, Leeward Island Air Transport (LIAT), and Windward Island Airways. Until their demise, both Eastern Airlines and Pan Am served Dutch Sint Maarten. In contrast, Espérance Airport (SFG) on the French side is tiny and deserted. It provides services for small planes and inter-island flights.

To further enhance tourism, five casinos have been opened in Dutch Sint Maarten. To gain more appeal with Americans, the government has pegged its currency to the US dollar, eliminating fluctuations. To facilitate trade, Dutch Sint Maarten uses the same currency as the islands of Bonaire, Curacao, Saba and Sint Eustatius.

The absence of customs formalities makes Dutch Sint Maarten a veritable free port, making the island a trans-shipping centre for business trading with other Caribbean islands. Furthermore, the high import duties of neighbouring islands are often reduced for freight arriving via Dutch Sint Maarten, and the result has been the creation of numerous import/export operations.

ANALYSIS

Dutch Sint Maartin, according to McElroy (2003, p. 236), is the world's most heavily penetrated tourism location, located in the world's most heavily penetrated tourist region. It has a thriving business community with relatively sophisticated entrepreneurial activity. In contrast, French Saint Martin is more laid back, largely rural and agricultural. Correlation of policy model with economic activity suggests a causal relationship. Internal validity is established in the case of this French Saint Martin/Dutch Sint Maarten, Model I/Model II study. Co-variation between the presumed cause and effect has been demonstrated; there is temporal precedence of the cause; and there is no apparent alternative interpretation for the cause and effect relation. Internal validity is established, as Model II policy among the treatment group has yielded an environment more conducive to entrepreneurship than possible under Model I policy in the control group. While the control group suffers from unemployment, the treatment group cannot satisfy the demand for employees; furthermore, the control group is largely rural and agricultural while the treatment group is mostly involved in service industries.

CONCLUSION

'The Netherlands is ranked as the 24th country for the ease of doing business there; France, the 44th' (World Bank, 2005, p. 3). The online business directory for Dutch Sint Maarten/French Saint Martin lists 61 business operations, all being service oriented: 18 operate from French Saint Martin; 42 operate from Dutch Sint Maarten; and one operates from both (www.StMaarten.org).

Two models of state-market relations have been examined: that of French Saint Martin where regulation is meant for protection, and that of the treatment group, Dutch Sint Maarten, where the government is more actively supportive of new ventures, along with minimal regulation. In contrast to the situation within the control group, the treatment (Model II policy) has maintained a healthy, growing, private business sector in Dutch Sint Maarten. The citizens of French Saint Martin may feel that their economy is lagging behind, and that the private sector is somewhat stifled: the unemployment rate in the whole prefecture of Guadeloupe was 26.1 per cent in 2000 (Eurisles, 2002, p. 75) and 35 per cent of all employees were employed in the public service (ibid., p. 40). Unemployment in Dutch Sint Maarten was reported as 12.9 per cent in 2000 and the public sector's contribution to GDP was just 11 per cent. Meanwhile, rather than encourage economic advancement, French Saint Martin levies a tax on personal assets. So it is no wonder that many from the French Saint Martin go to Dutch Sint Maarten to work, legally or otherwise. The Dutch Sint Maarten's Department of Business Licenses is aware of such practices, but tolerates them as its economy is growing so rapidly its own local labour force cannot keep up with demand.

This is not meant to paint too rosy a picture about Dutch Sint Maarten. In the 1990s, investigations were started following allegations of connections between the Dutch Sint Maarten government and the Italian Mafia. In 1993, the Dutch government directly intervened on Dutch Sint Maarten and temporarily took over the government, an extreme measure felt necessary because of alleged corruption and government malpractices. Moreover, the state's investments in public infra-structure – including schools, roads, health and utilities – lag behind population growth. One particular (French) observer does not mince his words: '[Dutch] Sint Maarten . . . [a territory] with disaster written all over it, with its mafia barons, gambling racket, and crowds in access of one million tourists a year channeled through a large international airport' (Doumenge, 1998, p. 341).

S'Maat'ners live on the same tiny island, and share a common heritage. Their ancestors were both imported from the slave-exporting territories of West Africa in the sixteenth century. So it may be 'The Protestant Ethic', and its legacy, that is the main differentiator between the two halves. Model II policy has made entrepreneurial ideology prevalent in Dutch Sint Maarten but less so in French Saint Martin where Model I type policy prevails. The people in the control group are visibly more preoccupied with *joie de vivre* than with making money. Moreover, apart from the 'pull' factors of public policy, there may be differential 'push' factors also at play: a weaker benefit system for the unemployed in Dutch Sint Maarten may act to incentivise the resort even more to entrepreneurship, while a more generous welfare system makes the opportunity cost of starting one's own business less of an enticing prospect in French Saint Martin.

Some entrepreneurial spirit may be filtering across the border by osmosis: the infrastructure and regulatory environment of French Saint Martin under Model I-type policy is such that its entrepreneurs may find it more attractive to emigrate (to a Model II environment) than to operate their business in a location which hinders entrepreneurial activity. Indeed, following a referendum in 2003, the citizens of French Saint Martin have voted overwhelmingly in favour of adopting more locale-specific, and more liberal, tax and immigration policies. French Saint Martin is now effectively almost a separate *territoire d'outre mer* (TOM): the practices of its Dutch neighbour are partly to blame for this (Mrgudovic, 2005, p. 80).

ACKNOWLEDGEMENTS

Our thanks to Andrew Blackadder, Te'o I. J. Fairbairn, Coen P.A. Heijes, Billy MacKinnon and Gert Oostindie for critical and useful insights on earlier drafts.

NOTE

* This chapter was originally published as follows: 'The Impact of Public Policy on Entrepreneurship: A Critical Investigation of the Protestant Ethic on a Divided Island Jurisdiction', *Journal of Small Business and Entrepreneurship*, **19** (4), 2006, 419–30. Reproduced with permission.

REFERENCES

Armstrong, H., G. Johnes, J. Johnes and A. Macbean (1993), 'The Role of Transport Costs as a Determinant of Price Level Differentials between the Isle of Man and the United Kingdom, 1989', *World Development*, **21** (2), 311–18.

Bijmolt, T.H.A. and P.S. Zwart (1994), 'The Impact of Internal Factors on the

Export Success of Dutch Small and Medium-Sized Firms', *Journal of Small Business Management*, **32** (2), 69–83.
Boissevain, J. and H. Grotenberg (1987), 'Ethnic Enterprise in the Netherlands: The Surinamese of Amsterdam', in R. Goffee and R. Scase (eds), *Entrepreneurship in Europe: The Social Process*, London: Croom Helm, pp. 105–30.
Briguglio, L. (1998), 'Surviving the Competition: Small Business in Malta', in G. Baldacchino and R. Greenwood (eds), *Competing Strategies of Economic Development for Small Islands*, Charlottetown, PEI: Institute of Island Studies, University of Prince Edward Island, pp. 119–33.
Central Intelligence Agency (CIA) (2005), *World FactBook 2005*, Washington, DC: Central Intelligence Agency. Also available at: www.cia.gov/cia/publications/factbook/ (accessed 5 May 2006).
Cerruti, J. (1970), 'The Netherlands Antilles', *National Geographic*, **137** (January), 115–46.
Dana, L.P. (1988a), 'Current Research', in Rein Peterson and Kimble Ainslie (eds), *Understanding Entrepreneurship*, Dubuque, IA: Kendall/Hunt, p. 126.
Dana, L.P. (1988b), 'The Spirit of Entrepreneurship and the Commonwealth Government of Australia', *Journal of Small Business Management*, **26** (1), 63–5.
Dana, L.P. (1990), 'Saint Martin/Sint Maarten: A Case Study of the Effects of Culture on Economic Development', *Journal of Small Business Management*, **28** (4), 91–8.
Dana, L.P. (1995a), 'Entrepreneurship in a Remote Sub-Arctic Community: Nome, Alaska', *Entrepreneurship Theory and Practice*, **20** (1), 57–72.
Dana, L.P. (1995b), 'Public Policy and Entrepreneurship in the Caribbean', *Journal of Private Enterprise*, **10** (2), 119–41.
Diamond, J. (2005), *Collapse: How Societies Choose to Fail or Succeed*, London: Penguin.
Doumenge, F. (1998), 'Considerations for Small Island Development Today', in G. Baldacchino and R. Greenwood (eds), *Competing Strategies of Socio-Economic Development for Small Islands*, Charlottetown, PEI: Institute of Island Studies, University of Prince Edward Island, pp. 337–46.
Eurisles (2002), *Off the Coast of Europe: European Construction and the Problem of the Islands*, Eurisles on the Initiative of the Islands Commission of CPMR.
Fairbairn, T'eo I.J. (1988), *Island Entrepreneurs: Problems and Performance in the South Pacific*, Honolulu, HI: East West Center.
Ghosh, B.C. and D.B. Taylor (1995), 'Marketing Practices', *Journal of Small Business and Entrepreneurship*, **12** (3), 40–49.
Gibb, A.A. (1986–87), 'Education for Enterprise Training for Small Business Initiative: Some Contrasts', *Journal of Small Business and Entrepreneurship*, **4** (1), 42–8.
Hall, P. (1986), *Governing the Economy: The Politics of State Intervention in Britain and France*, Cambridge: Polity Press.
Hisrich, R.D. (1988), 'The Entrepreneur in Northern Ireland', *Journal of Small Business Management*, **26** (3), 32–9.
Hofstede, G. (1980), *Culture's Consequences: International Differences in Work-Related Values*, Beverly Hills, CA: Sage.
Jenkins, R. (1984), 'Ethnicity and the Rise of Capitalism in Ulster', in Robin Ward and Richard Jenkins (eds), *Ethnic Communities in Business: Strategies for Economic Survival*, Cambridge: Cambridge University Press, pp. 57–72.

Johannison, B. (1987), 'Towards a Theory of Local Entrepreneurship', in R.G. Wyckham, L.N. Meredith and G.R. Bushe (eds), *The Spirit of Entrepreneurship*, Vancouver: Simon Fraser University, pp. 1–14.

Kersell, J.E. (1993), 'Mini-Remnants of Three Empires: Governing West Indian Dependencies', Waterloo, ON: University of Waterloo, available at: ww.arts.uwaterloo.ca/PSCI/kersell/mn_rmn.htm (accessed 5 May 2006).

Kunkel, J.H. (1965), 'Values and Behaviour in Economic Development', *Economic Development and Cultural Change*, **8** (2), 257–77.

McElroy, J.L. (2003), 'Tourism Development in Small Islands across the World', *Geografiska Annaler*, **85B** (4), 231–42.

Min, P.G. and C. Jaret (1985), 'Ethnic Business Success: The Case of Korean Small Business in Atlanta', *Sociology and Social Research*, **69** (3), 412–35.

Morita, K. and J.C. Oliga (1991), 'Collective Global Entrepreneurship: A Critical View of the Japanese Case', in J.C. Oliga and T.B. Kim (eds), *Proceedings of the ENDEC World Conference on Entrepreneurship and Innovative Change*, Singapore: Nanyang Technological University–Peat Marwick Entrepreneurship Development Centre, pp. 450–51.

Mrgudovic, N. (2005), 'The French Overseas Territories in Change', in D. Killingray and D. Taylor (eds), *The United Kingdom Overseas Territories: Past, Present and Future*, Occasional Paper No. 3, London: Overseas Service Pensioners' Association in collaboration with the Institute of Commonwealth Studies, pp. 65–86.

Nafziger, E.W. (1971), 'Indian Entrepreneurship: A Survey', in Peter Kilby (ed.), *Entrepreneurship and Economic Development*, New York: Free Press, pp. 287–316.

Ojuka-Onedo, A.E. (1996), 'Interventionist Policy in Enterprise Development Using the Rural Poor in Agrarian Developing Countries', *Entrepreneurship, Innovation and Change*, **5** (3), 263–65.

Öostindie, G. and I. Klinkers (2003), *Decolonizing the Caribbean. Dutch Policies in a Comparative Perspective*, Amsterdam: Amsterdam University Press.

Pache, G. (1996), 'The Small Producer in the French Food Distribution Channel', *Journal of Small Business Management*, **34** (2), 84–8.

Peterson, R. and Ainslie (1988), *Understanding Entrepreneurship*, Dubuque, IA: Kendall/Hunt.

Peterson, R. and M. Peterson (1981), *The Impact of Economic Regulation and Paperwork*, Regulation Reference Working Paper Series, Ottawa: Economic Council of Canada.

Polanyi, K. (1944), *The Great Transformation: The Political and Economic Origins of Our Time*, New York: Farrar and Rinehart.

Rainnie, A. and M. Scott (1986), 'Individual Relations in the Small Firm', in J. Curan, J. Stanworth and D. Watkins (eds), *The Survival of the Small Firm*, Aldershot: Gower.

Reeves, F. and R. Ward (1984), 'West Indian Business in Britain', in R. Ward and R. Jenkins (eds), *Ethnic Communities in Business*, Cambridge: Cambridge University Press, pp. 125–48.

Royle, Stephen A. (2001), *A Geography of Islands*, New York: Routledge.

Scase, R. (1980), *The State in Western Europe*, London: Croom Helm.

Scase, R. and R. Goffee (1987), *The Real World of the Small Business Owner*, London: Croom Helm.

Schmpeter, J.A. (1934), *Theorie der Wirtschaftlichen Entwicklung*, Munich and Leipzig: Duncker und Humblot.

Shapero, A. (1984), 'The Entrepreneurial Event', in C.A. Kent (ed.), *The Environment for Entrepreneurship*, Lexington, MA: D.C. Heath, pp. 21–40.

Shapero, A. and L. Sokol (1982), 'The Social Dimensions of Entrepreneurship', in C.A. Kent, D.L. Sexton and K.H. Vesper (eds), *Encyclopedia of Entrepreneurship*, Englewood Cliffs, NJ: Prentice Hall, pp. 72–90.

Staley, E. and R. Morse (1971), 'Developing Entrepreneurship: Elements for a Program', in P. Kilby (ed.), *Entrepreneurship and Economic Development*, New York: Free Press, pp. 357–84.

Strinati, D. (1982), *Capitalism, the State and Industrial Relations*, London: Croom Helm.

The Economist (2005), 'Choose Your Poison', Charlemagne, London, Economist Intelligence Unit (1 October), 50.

Ward, R. (1987), 'Ethnic Entrepreneurs in Britain and Europe', in R. Scase and R. Goffee (eds), *Entrepreneurship in Europe*, London: Croom Helm, pp. 83–104.

Weaver, K.M., D. Berkowitz and L. Davies (1998), 'Increasing the Efficiency of National Export Promotion Programs', *Journal of Small Business Management*, **36** (4), 1–11.

Weber, M. (1956), *The Protestant Ethic and the Spirit of Capitalism (1905)*, trans. by Talcott Parsons, New York: Scribner and Sons.

World Bank (2005), *Doing Business Report: An Overview*, Washington, DC: World Bank, available at: www.doingbusiness.org/documents/2006_overview.pdf (accessed 5 May 2006).

21. Italian Catholics of Lancashire and the Jewish community of Yorkshire

Claudio Vignali, Neil Robinson and Gianpaolo Vignali

INTRODUCTION

Glazer and Moynihan (1963) compared Jews with Italian Catholics in New York. The objective of this chapter is to compare these two groups in England, with a focus on their entrepreneurship.

The war of the roses is a play on words. In recent UK history the red rose was a symbol of Lancashire whilst the white rose was a symbol of Yorkshire, two of the most famous shires in the UK. They were the homes of two distinct royal families that always fought for power. The whites were linked with peaceful activities whilst the reds were aggressive in their approach. We have linked this historical fact to the two immigrant communities that have made the UK their homes. The Italians who live in Lancashire started as entrepreneurs but did not have the sense of commitment to the community as did the Jewish community that settled in Yorkshire. They were more committed to the future and invested heavily in both their entrepreneurial skills and their local environment. *The lesson to be learned is that social responsibility is necessary if a true integration is required.*

ENTREPRENEURSHIP IN THE UK JEWISH COMMUNITY

It is not exactly clear when the first Jewish communities settled in England, although it is generally assumed that the earliest Jewish commune would have been created during the Middle Ages, perhaps during 1066. This would have developed as an advancement of the Jewish colonies already living in Northern France. It is estimated that the Jewish population in

England at this time would have been around 5000 (Elazar, 1999). From the late tenth century Jewish communities experienced much discrimination with legislation in place to hinder and prevent Jews from amassing personal wealth and to prevent business ownership. In the late twelfth century King Edward I prevented Jews from living in England and banished them, resulting in a mass exodus from England to Europe (Evans, 2000).

Whilst a comparatively small number of Jews stayed in England, life was often harsh and uncomfortable, with discrimination and reprisal attacks being routine. Jewish worship or communal gatherings were frowned upon and stamped out, often resulting in death and destruction.

This kind of state-sponsored religious hatred was commonplace, right up until the mid-seventeenth century, with Jews being perceived and often caricatured as evil and uncaring. In the mid-1650s the Lord Protector (Oliver Cromwell) allowed the Jews to return from mainland Europe to England, after listening to an impassioned speech on the merit of allowing the Jews to return to England, by Manassah Ben Israel, a Rabbi from The Netherlands.

The persecution of Jewish communities throughout Europe during the early to mid-sixteenth and seventeenth centuries played a key part in creating mass migration across Europe. Indeed the mass persecution of Jewish communities is documented extensively throughout Europe's history. This has created Jewish enclaves of displaced refugees, seeking security and safety from persecution, and from this we see the creation of Jewish communities, traditionally living in slum conditions within large cities.

Despite their ethics for hard work and reputable family life, the Jewish communities often lacked basic citizenship, which was awarded to the general populace, and often faced discrimination in day-to-day life. As early as 1753 an offer to grant the Jewish communities basic rights and citizenship by Parliament was shelved. It was nearly 100 years later, when in 1858 it was decided to award Jewish communities the same rights as the common man (Evans 2000). Ironically this lack of representation did not deter Jewish families from advancing their ambitions, and history has shown that many Jews have progressed to positions of great power and wealth, with little or no assistance from the state.

It is against this backdrop that we find large Jewish communities inhabiting urban locations, which have themselves acted as community focal points and in some cases perpetuated the myth and stereotypes about differing religious groupings. This cultural ghettoization is often reinforced by cultural practices, dress and customs, which are integral to the religious beliefs of many minority groupings. This scenario has been played out extensively within the Italian, Irish and Polish communities who have settled in the North of England. Similar practices to these have been reinforced by the Jewish communities throughout England, who are often located close to industrial urban locations as business interests often necessitate the need to access key markets. Indeed, many of the Jewish faith have settled in the North of England in areas such as Manchester, Liverpool and, more notably, Leeds, which plays host to a rich array of cultural diversity and ethnic history.

The Jewish community of Leeds has lived there from the early to mid-eighteenth century. On the whole the community were primarily of Russian extraction fleeing persecution from Tsarist pogroms and anti-Jewish sentiment, and made their homes in Leeds and the surrounding North West. Leeds during the late eighteenth and early nineteenth century saw many industrial marvels, including the creation of the Leeds to Liverpool canal and the railway networks, all of which created good infrastructure provision and aided local commerce (Williams, 1987). At around this time Leeds began to experience an expansion in a number of retail business concerns, including the growth of the clothing industries (Chapman, 1999). This saw many Jewish immigrants setting up businesses as tailors and apparel manufacturers.

The Jewish community of Leeds has played a major part in the creation of wealth and prosperity of the region. In the mid-1850s Michael Marks a Russian immigrant found employment with a local Leeds employer called 'Barran', which employed Jewish refuges. In 1884 Marks made the acquaintance of Isaac Dewhurst, who had a number of properties and warehouses in the Leeds area and decided to enter into a mutually beneficial arrangement, whereby Marks would purchase products from Dewhurst and in turn sell them for profit in the surrounding locality of Leeds.

This business arrangement soon proved to be very beneficial to both parties and it was not long before retail outlets were set up in the open markets of Leeds, Castleford and Wakefield. It was during this period that Marks came up with the idea of the 'one penny market stall', which he experimented with on the six-day covered markets of Yorkshire and Lancashire. This proved to be very successful and saw Marks increase his retail strength and customer loyalty base. Towards the end of the eighteenth century Marks required additional capital to facilitate expansion and looked towards locating a business partner, this he found in Tom Spencer a friend of Isaac Dewhurst. The partnership was an immediate success and led to the creation of a number of related stores in Manchester, Birmingham and Sheffield. Today Marks & Spencer is represented globally and employs thousands of people worldwide (see Table 21.1).

The Jewish community in the Yorkshire area has grown dramatically, and outside London and Manchester is a dominant force in the

Table 21.1 Marks & Spencer

Business type	Number of stores in UK	Number of customers served in UK per week	Size (square feet)	Largest UK store	Group turnover £	Overseas links
Clothing, food, homeware and financial services	375	10 million	12.5 million	Marble Arch (London, UK)	8 000 million	55 stores managed under franchise in 28 territories mostly in Europe, the Middle East, Asia and the Far East. M&S also own the US supermarket group, Kings Super Markets

Source: Marks & Spencer.

commercial area. Various family groupings have created internationally acclaimed commercial empires. The Silver family was a major developer of the paint industry. It has no longer an influence in the silver paint and lacquer company, as it is now part of the internationally known Kalon group.

Retrospectively speaking, the Kalon group was established following the Second World War in 1947 as the Silver Paint and Lacquer Company, after spotting a market opening for the production and sales of paint-related products. This business opportunity came at a time when Britain was experiencing much post-Second World War austerity and at a time when the home furnishings and paint market had yet to realize its full potential. From its original sites in Birstall and Morley the group increased output, continually adding to its product range and expanding its business market to encompass the growing DIY decorative paints market, as well as the ever-expanding lacquers market. Growth continued throughout the

1950s and 1960s, facilitated in part by the home building boom under the Macmillan and successive post-war governments.

The Silver Paint and Lacquer Company, now part of internationally renowned Kalon Group PLC, manufactures and distributes a multitude of paints, decorating-related products and building-related chemicals throughout the UK, Northern Europe and the former Soviet Union. The huge growth of the business is in part due to the foresight shown by its early predecessor, the Silver Paint and Lacquer Company, which was instrumental in developing a number of key brands within the UK market, many of which are still marketed and have proven successful. These include the Leyland, Johnstone's and Deval brand names. Looking to the future, the Kalon Group plans to further establish itself as a key market player, with opportunities within Europe, all of which would not have been possible without the foresight and entrepreneurial stance taken by the Silver Paint and Lacquer Company nearly half a century earlier.

In addition to the aforementioned paints group, Yorkshire has been home to other successful businesses and entrepreneurial families. This includes the Ziff family, a major UK retailer in the shoe industry and the owner of Stylo Barretts, as well being a major shareholder in Town Centre Securities. Stylo PLC is a retail and property group which has been quoted on the London Stock Exchange from the early 1940s. Its retail wing encompasses a number of footwear brands which are represented on the UK high streets. These include Barratts stores (shoe related), Priceless Facia (discount footwear) and, in 2003, control of the Shellys footwear chain. In parallel to this, the group also has a growing property portfolio with net assets of over £50 million (www.barratts.co.uk) The Bradford-based footwear enterprise has seen many changes over the last 65 years including the introduction of new manufacturing techniques and product modification, all of which ensure that Stylo Barratts continues to offer good value and choice to its customers, a retail ethic which is close to its Yorkshire roots.

Other well-known families from this locality include Morrisons, the major UK food retailer. The Morrisons story is a wonderful example of what can be achieved when the entrepreneurial spirit is distilled and bottled. The Morrisons group was founded in 1899 by William Morrison, a purveyor of food-related products based in Bradford, West Yorkshire, and it was during this time that William recognized his potential for combining his small-scale retail outlet, which consisted of farm and dairy products. William's ambition and drive acted as the catalyst for his business venture, and from these humble beginning the shape of a retail giant was drawn.

Through much hard work and common belief the Morrison family have built the business from a collective of small market stalls to a stock

BOX 21.1 KEY DATES

- 1899: William Morrison, establishes the company (father of present Chairman Ken Morrison).
- 1958: The first town centre shop is opened.
- 1960s: Opening of the first Morrisons supermarket in Bradford
- 1967: Morrisons becomes a public company
- 2000: Ken Morrison was awarded a knighthood in the 2000 New Year's Honours List, for services to food retailing
- 2001: Morrisons joins the FTSE 100 (top 100 listed shares) for the first time

Source: Adapted from www.morereasons.co.uk/history.html.

exchange listed company. Key to its business success is its belief in good value and quality, for its customers. This operational philosophy has seen the organization grow greatly during the mid to late 1990s and shares commonalities in origin with another Yorkshire success story, this being Marks & Spencer.

Today the retail giant has an eclectic product portfolio, specialising in a multitude of both food and non-food related products, which are sold under the Morrisons retail umbrella and has seen the group expand its size to more than 500 stores nationwide.

The Jewish entrepreneurship community in Yorkshire is far too extensive to elaborate on, but it is the driving force in the local community giving the local economy employment and helping to develop cultural and educational links. They sponsor university professorships and endow the local universities with economic support.

THE ENTREPRENEURS IN THE UK ITALIAN COMMUNITY

It is not clear when the Italian community entered the UK. Some historical texts indicate that it was in the renaissance and I do not either confirm or reject this idea. It is clear that after the First World War when the Italians were on the British side fighting the Austro-Hungarian Empire, many emigrated to Greater Manchester and settled in the Castle Field area of the city.

BOX 21.2 MORRISON GROUP INFORMATION

- Morrisons group size = 500 stores +.
- Morrisons is the UK's fourth largest supermarket chain.
- Over 10 million customers shop with Morrison and Safeway each week.
- 145 000 employees work for Morrisons (stores, factories, distribution centres and head office).
- Annual turnover = £14 billion.
- 310 sites have petrol filling stations.
- 310 stores have customer cafés.
- Morrisons share in the UK's grocery market is more than 15 per cent.
- Morrisons owns Safeway supermarkets.

Source: Adapted from www.morereasons.co.uk/history.html.

The Italians were artisans, they were expert tailors, cooks, and worked well in textiles. They settled in Lancashire and brought their skills with them. Unlike other immigrant communities they always had the intention to return home, so their sense of community spirit was limited. They believed in hard work but saved their money and returned the capital to their local communities in Italy.

After the Second World War there was a larger influx of Italian labour into Lancashire. This new immigrant group was similar in ideology to the first group. However, due to the economic famine they had experienced in the Second World War they were more prepared to invest their earnings into the system. Families like the Vignalis of Parma created the Vignali Meat Company, which was later bought by Trust House Forte, they being part of the first wave of Italian immigrants and developers of the world famous hotel group; the Costas who created Costa coffee, the now famous coffee house retailers owned by Interbrew; and, finally, the Neapolitans who developed Pizza Express.

In general however the majority of these entrepreneurs developed small family-run Italian restaurants, which are still evident throughout Lancashire and the whole of the UK.

It is important to understand not only how the Italian entrepreneurs came to prominence in the UK but also how they operate. Given the choice, Italians would prefer to do business with even a superficial acquaintance rather than a complete stranger. Since familiarity is so important in Italian business culture, it is important that a relationship is built straight from the beginning with their clients.

In Italian business culture, punctuality is not as much of a priority. As a visitor, however, it is usually a good policy to arrive on time. Be prepared to wait 15–45 minutes before your Italian counterpart appears or lets you into his or her office.

In Northern Italy business hours for small businesses, shops and public offices are usually 8.30 a.m. to 12.30 p.m. and 3.30 p.m. to 6.30 p.m., Monday to Friday. Also, a lot of businesses are open on Saturday mornings. Larger companies, more commonly related to how companies work in the UK, usually work from 8.30 /9.00 a.m. until 6.00/6.30 p.m. with an hour or so for lunch. This lunch break will be significantly longer when eating out at a restaurant with guests.

In central and southern Italy, business hours are from 8.30 a.m. to 12.45 p.m. then 4.30 p.m. or 5.00 p.m. to 7.30 p.m. or 8.00 p.m., Monday to Friday, and 8.30 a.m. to 12.45 p.m. on Saturday. The southern business pace is usually less intense.

In many cities, such as Rome, there is a long break lasting as long as two hours, from 1.30 p.m. to 3.30 p.m. Business is often discussed during this break, over lunch. Generally, the best times to plan appointments are between 10.00 a.m. and 11.00 a.m., and after 3.00 p.m. Be aware of summer vacation periods. Most firms are closed in August. If you write for an appointment in mid-July, you may not receive a satisfactory reply until September.

Many Italian public holidays follow those of continental Europe but are usually different from the UK. It is worth checking while planning a trip that a public holiday does not fall in the middle of it, as the company and whole region may close down that day. In the UK a structured holiday and work system operates which takes some account of religious festivals such as Easter and Christmas, with a number of public holidays being bestowed upon the population. Many service sector businesses often open fully throughout this period and make the most of the additional financial equity in circulation. From a work perspective the UK has traditionally and often unfairly been labelled as the lazy man of Europe, with strikes, lost work days from sickness and union disputes all impacting negatively upon the image of the UK, and in some cases reducing the level of foreign investment. Since a period of employment rationalization in the early to mid-1980s the UK has become a leaner and more productive economy with daily work patterns and holidays often being dictated by economic demand rather than tradition. A conventional working day will start at 8.00/9.00 a.m. and finish at 5.00 p.m., with lunch around 1.00 p.m. for approximately one hour. Many SMEs also open on a Saturday between

9.00a.m. and 5.00 p.m. and around eight public holidays are available each year within the UK.

Costa Coffee was established in 1971 when Italian brothers Sergio and Bruno Costa started a wholesale operation. This wholesale operation was paramount in supplying roasted coffee to caterers and specialist Italian coffee shops across the UK. Costa's unique roasting style came from their Italian background and primarily Sergio's experience of blending and roasting coffee from his time spent as he grew up in Parma. Where Costa inherited its unique flavour from was down to its individual production process. The coffee beans were slow roasted at reduced temperatures hence producing a fuller, less bitter flavour. With a mixture of Arabica and Robusta coffee beans the unique espresso formula was created. Both the roasting process and their special blend Mocha Italia are mainstays of the Costa business today.

The first Costa coffee store was opened in London in 1978, after the family moved from Lancashire. Growth initially was slow but by the end of the year a further two stores had opened and growth expanded at the rate of two stores per year with the help of their family and friends in the business. In 1988, the production of the coffee beans moved to the more convenient location of Old Paradise Street in Lambeth, London, where the roaster and green beans (those waiting to be roasted) are stored.

Developments in technology, such as the new roaster were crucial to the Costa Coffee family and with these important developments the company witnessed huge growth during the 1990s. The company had increased to 186 stores by 1999, and in 2000 3.7 million cups of coffee were being sold each week.

Costa is now one of the leading UK branded coffee shops, and with over 300 stores and host units in a number of complementary retail outlets, including selected Ottakers and Waterstones bookstores, WHSmith and Homebase stores, Marriott Hotels and Middlesex Hospital it has become a major player on the UK coffee scene. The brothers' innovative and entrepreneurial characteristics have even been evident with their most recent venture, that is, opening coffee bars inside select branches of Abbey National to bring the customer the first coffee shop in a bank. Below are some facts and figures about Costa Coffee:

1. Costa is one of the largest chains of branded coffee shops in the UK with over 300 outlets.
2. Costa coffee has a unique way of making coffee because:
   (a) all Costa coffee beans are slow roasted for 22 minutes to ensure a smoother flavour than quick roasting, which can produce a bitter taste

   (b) Costa has 30 years Italian heritage perfecting the art of coffee-making
   (c) Costa source and buy their own beans from all over the world.
3. Costa coffee is made by hand, rather than by the automated coffee machines used in some other chains.
4. Costa offers customers a Fair-Trade coffee option, which can be requested for any of their coffees. In addition to this, all the traditional and Earl Grey teas are from Tea Direct. This is offered through the partnership with Cafédirect.
5. Examples of alternative locations and Costa concessions include stores at the London Eye, Middlesex Hospital, the BBC at Shepherds Bush and Abbey National.

Fair-Trade

Costa offers its customers a Fair-Trade coffee option on all its coffees. Fair-trade coffee guarantees the growers a better deal through a fair price and better working conditions. This is done in conjunction with Cafédirect who are one of the UK's leading Fair-Trade companies. Costa also helps its growers of coffee beans with investment opportunities to help build the business and communities of their suppliers. This ensures that the coffee growers always get a fair price no matter what the global market price is.

The profit that has been produced from the sales of Costa Coffee has helped fund major community projects. Such community projects include road improvements in Uganda, which allowed farmers and distributors to gain easier and quicker access to the factory. Costa also aided in the funding of a woman's association in Mexico providing courses on midwifery, the production of vitamins from local plants and child-rearing.

In 2003, Costa developed a new brand, Frescato. Frescato was developed as a cool coffee drink to be drunk in the summer season. Frescato was a massive success with over two million cups sold since its launch. In the development of their new product, Costa have decided to expand their range with two new flavours being introduced to the Frescato family. Costa has also developed a food range from light hearty snacks to breakfast accompaniments. The range includes crudités, Fruit Salad pot, Pesto Pasta salad, Chilli Chicken Pasta Salad, Tuna Nicoise Salad with cos lettuce. They keep their sandwich menu constantly updated to offer their customers the best experience possible.

The philosophy that Pizza Express builds itself on is that on which the very first pizza restaurant was based. It is about the atmosphere and ambience that the stylish surroundings offer combined with the high-quality food at value for money prices. The same principles also apply at Pizza

Express's sister company, Café Pasta restaurants – with success built on perfect pasta dishes using the finest and freshest ingredients. Pizza Express promotes its restaurants as a place where everyone is welcome, from the business lunch to a special occasion celebrated in one of their special rooms.

In 1948 Mr Peter Boizot MBE tasted his first pizza in Florence and from this moment the first thoughts of Pizza Express were born. When he returned to the UK in the 1960s he realized that there was no pizza to be offered. He decided that for it to work in the UK, a good pizza was required to be made up of the finest ingredients and to be cooked authentically. But this could not be achieved unless he had a special oven which could reach the high temperatures necessary to deliver his product.

After obtaining the first Pizza Express oven from Rome, and a chef to operate it, Peter set up the company's first restaurant in London's Soho. The business quickly took off and in 1967 he opened his second restaurant, this time in Bloomsbury. The interior of Pizza Express restaurants was evident, with the popular artist Enzo Apicella commissioned to transform the buildings. This unique concept of eating pizza in exquisite surroundings helped create more restaurants year after year and they continued to open to meet the demand from Britons eager to taste authentic Italian pizza.

Pizza Express was floated on the London Stock Exchange, as one of the UK's most successful private restaurant businesses, in February 1993. Three years after selling the franchises, the majority of the restaurants were bought back, ensuring that the business could all go in the same direction, enhancing the brand and making it go from strength to strength. This has led to the total of over 300 restaurants in the UK and Ireland, and the serving of 16 million customers a year.

Top on the Pizza Express agenda is the restoration of old buildings and the links Pizza Express have with Italy go beyond the sites they occupy and the authentic food they serve. Not only do customers enjoy the food that is on offer at Pizza Express, they are also contributing to the work that is being carried out on some of the most historic buildings in the world. Pizza Express has supported the Venice in Peril Fund since 1975. Pizza Express created the Venetian pizza, specially crafted for the purpose of collecting money for the Venice in Peril Fund, by the founder Peter Boizot. Every time the Venetian Pizza is ordered, 25p of the price is donated to the fund and over the past 25 years £1.4 million has been raised.

The Venice in Peril Fund was established to offer financial help to restore Venice following devastating floods in 1966. Given the situation of Venice, it stands to lose some of its greatest monuments, sculpture and buildings. Although the Venice in Peril Fund is constituted to help restore buildings in Venice it has expanded its commitment to include buildings within the UK that are older than 1750.

Pizza Express was one of the first ever pizza restaurants who decided to venture in to the retail market. In January 2001, in partnership with the large retail chain Sainsbury's, they launched their best selling high-quality pizzas and garlic breads, and to the surprise of many they started to sell well. Since their entrance into the retail market they have slowly expanded their range including their inventive dough balls. The range can now be found in over 130 Waitrose stores as well as Sainsbury's, and in Hong Kong from their partners Park 'n' Shop. In conjunction with Geest PLC, who are one of the largest manufacturers of freshly prepared foods, the pizzas are made to the company's exact requirements. The construction of the pizzas is delicately formed, with the bases hand-stretched, and toppings are applied individually by hand. The ingredients are matched as closely as possible to those found in the restaurants. The only differences that may be found on the pizzas is the mozzarella, which on the packaged goods tend to be cubed so that it is easier for home cooking.

Sales reach almost 140 000 per week showing the demand made by the consumer. Although sales are high this has not had an effect on turnover within the restaurants as customers are still returning to the restaurants. Not only are the pizzas available in these retail shops there is also a selection of oils including the Pizza Express House Oil and Balsamic Vinegar. A Pizza Express Bagged Salad is available at Sainsbury's. Each bag contains a specially selected range of salad leaves together with a generous pot of their renowned house salad dressing.

CONCLUSION

As has been detailed in this chapter the Jewish and Italian communities of England, whilst distinctive and unique in origin, share similarities associated with entrepreneurship and business intelligence. Indeed both communities have prospered greatly with little or no financial assistance or formal business training and have paradoxically greatly improved business education for the masses in the bequest of financial gifts and professorial chairs to higher education establishments.

These business characteristics are not exclusive to the Jewish and Italian communities of the North of England, but are themselves shared by a number of ethnic communities native to the urban landscape of the North West. Where the Jewish and Italian entrepreneurs differ from other ethnic entrepreneurs is in their cultural outlook, which manifests itself in business practice and development. This scenario has already been exemplified in the case of Pizza Express and Stylo Barratts, where the need to develop and market products akin to the entrepreneurs' own style and beliefs are key to the successful creation of any business venture. Indeed, not only are these two communities similar in business outlook, they also share similar life ideals in relation to the importance of the family structure and the trust associated with it. In the case of The Costa Coffee Company, the family bond which facilitated the brothers' product knowledge and business interest was key to the formation and eventual success of the business. It can also be argued that such business acumen is developed from an early age, with family members maintaining strong links with their historical and cultural origins and using such experience within the business, as was the case with Sergio and Bruno Costa who had experience of coffee blending from their time spent growing up and working in Parma.

As for the future, the entrepreneurial position taken by the Jewish and Italian communities in the North of England over the last 200 years should be further encouraged and applauded. The long-term success of such business ideals can act as a learning mechanism for other potential business entrepreneurs, resulting in the creation of economic prosperity, full employment and the regeneration of the region. If we are to look at the North of England, a region that at one time employed thousands in heavy industries such as mining, steel works and shipbuilding, it is clear that such employment trends will never be repeated. History has shown that whilst many jobs have been lost in the traditional heavy industries, the service sector and retail industries have often taken the place of traditional employers and have become the new postmodern employment providers. The industrial past of a region can often act as a blueprint for the future, and this itself can guide and facilitate the regions' new entrepreneurs. We can therefore end this chapter where we started by congratulating the Jewish and Italian communities of the North for building and creating an entrepreneurial ecosystem, rich with retail superstructure and a legacy which can be used to further develop the region. Whilst much has been written about the growth of the retail community in the North of England, it is clear that much has still to be done, as opportunities for and channels to financial support and educational development need to be made more widely available. We may yet see additional growth in the retail sector with new and innovative retailers being trained to realize their full potential and continue the good work, which was started by such innovators as the Ziffs, Silver, Morrison, Marks, Spencer, Costa, and Boizot families.

REFERENCES

Chapman, S. (1999), *The Cotton Industry: Its Growth and Impact, 1600–1935*, Bristol: Thoemmes Press.
Elazar, D.J. (1999), *British Jewry*, Jerusalem: Jerusalem Centre for Public Affairs.
Evans, E. (2000), *British History*, Bath: Parragon.
Glazer, N. and D.P. Moynihan (1963), *Beyond the Melting Pot*, Cambridge: MIT Press.
Williams, B. (1987), *History of Liverpool's Jewish Community*, Manchester: Jewish Museum.
www.barratts.co.uk (accessed 22 September 2006).
www.morereasons.co.uk (accessed 22 September 2006).

Index

Titles of publications appear in *italics*.